FOOTPRINTS
ON THE **LAND**

Donita,
I hope you
enjoy the stories!
With Warm Wishes,

Adam
7/03

FOOTPRINTS
ON THE LAND

AMERICAN
STORIES
ABOUT RACE

HELEN H. HELFER

THE BARNSTABLE BOOK COMPANY
OSTERVILLE, MASSACHUSETTS

FIRST EDITION

ISBN 0-9679333-1-5

Library of Congress Control Number: 2002115502

The Barnstable Book Company
Box 234
Osterville, MA 02655

Copyedited by Linda Lotz
Interior design and composition by Jenna Dixon
Proofread by Beth Richards

Printed in the United States of America

1   3   5   7   9   10   8   6   4   2

for my son
Hasani Olushola Issa

and in memory of

Father David Gracie
and
Marian Gray Secundy

CONTENTS

APPRECIATIONS

There are many special people I want to thank who encouraged me to move forward on this venture over the past six years, starting with my son, who wrote the following note to me on March 5, 1996: "Here's the stuff you asked for. I hope it helps. I'm very proud of you. I have no doubt that you will complete this book. You have my full support. Love, Hasani."

Mary Wagner, professor of "The Personal Narrative" course at San Francisco State, also provided powerful support. During one of her many challenging assignments and helpful feedback sessions, she handed out the following piece by James Baldwin, which I've kept close to my computer all these years: "Something that irritates you and won't let you go. That's the anguish of it. Do this book, or die. You have to 'through' that. Talent is insignificant. I know a lot of talented ruins. Beyond talent lie all the usual words: discipline, love, luck, but most of all endurance."

Another quote that got me through difficult days was from my architect friend and neighbor Vince deForest, whose story is in this book: "What you're doing right now, whether you recognize it or not, is all a part of this empowerment because you wouldn't be doing it unless it didn't serve some purpose outside of self. That's your contribution because through the words that you write, your sensitivity, what you bring to the equation, is going to be manifested all over the place. You may not know who it's going to touch, who it's going to reach in a certain way that makes them act a little differently, just like my opening up the book to Frank Lloyd Wright, not reading one word, just getting that picture — a profound impact on me." Thank you, Vince.

I want to raise my glass high to the extraordinary people whose life stories about race are in this book. All gave generously of their time in being interviewed, editing and reediting their stories, and sharing their photographs. One friend rewrote his story by hand, and many others had a difficult time finding old photos in shabby cardboard boxes or forgotten drawers and attics. Thank you all for your participation, your incredible patience, and your unique contributions. Thanks also to those whose stories are not in this volume. Your willingness to be interviewed is greatly appreciated.

The years 1998 and 1999 were the most intense traveling times, gathering many of the narratives across the country. I couldn't have done all the driving and interviewing without the extraordinary help of Cheryl and Lacey Mamak, Barbara Wagner, and Edwina Beier. Thank you all for your companionship and support.

I want to give well-deserved credit to Shelia McCloskey, the best graphic designer at Cape Cod Community College, who gave me my first clear image of what the book could look like with the text and photos in the right places. Her sense of humor during times of angst was also greatly welcomed. Thanks also to Professor Gail Guarino, who introduced me to Sheila.

To my fellow writers in Oregon, the San Francisco Bay Area, and Cape Cod who critiqued my work over the years and provided invaluable suggestions, thank you and best wishes for whatever you're writing today.

I want to thank Dr. Beth Roy, my next-door neighbor in San Francisco, and author of *Bitters in the Honey*, a powerful book on the integration battle at Little Rock's Central High School and its legacy forty years later. Beth generously shared her book proposal with me and provided great moral support.

After receiving many rejection letters from publishers across the country, I finally found one right here on Cape Cod. I want to thank Wallace Exman of The Barnstable Company, for his sensitive, focused, and patient help in editing the manuscript, as well as his ongoing encouragement. Thanks also to his talented colleagues: Jenna Dixon for her clear layout and design, and Linda Lotz for her impeccable copy editing. Grateful thanks also to proofreader Beth Richards and cover designer Laura Augustine.

To all my friends and colleagues, including Margaret Welsh, Judy Goddess, Natalie Lopes, Peggy McGraw, Lynn Scott, Mary Jo Aagerstoun, Pat Mathis, Steve Coyle, Ricardo Millette, Marcie Cohen, Tess Beistel, Nancy King, Dick Keltner, Diane Ross, Paul Boden, Malik Rahim, Laura Ware, Tom Ammiano, Michael Nolan, Father James O'Malley, Paul Sussman, Karen Clopton, Carren and Earl Shagley, Lynn Mannix, Rick Devine, Howard Gong, Jeff Bachman, Barb and Mort Steinau, Betty Burkes, Jackie Loring, Rosemary Reed Miller, Linda Weiner, Virginia Rasmussen, and to the many others who have encouraged me in this project and asked over the years, "How's the book coming?" thank you all. Here it is.

PREFACE

As a white-skinned woman, I don't have to think about race on a daily basis. As the mother of a young, black-skinned man, I do.

I grew up in a white middle class neighborhood in San Francisco in the 1940s and 50s, in an unhappy family with working-class values and biases. My mother's family had immigrated from Italy in 1904 to a small mining town in northern New Mexico called Dawson, where she was born and grew up. My father's family had lived in various towns in Kansas since the Civil War, when his great-grandfather fought for the Union. Like most American families, we didn't cross the color line, nor recognize that there was one. We lived within our safe narrow boundaries and expected "those people" to do the same.

Three major events had a profound effect on my life in terms of race and racism: In 1967 I fell in love with a Black man. In 1972 my father disowned me when I told him. In 1975 my son was born.

I began this book as a memoir, believing that each of us has an important story to tell and that we can learn from one another through our personal narratives. While I continue to believe that truth, I've also had the privilege of knowing many smart, loving, and diverse people in my life. Most of these special individuals and their grown children have addressed the issues of race, racism, and white privilege within their families, their places of work, the broader community, and national political arenas for many years. Their strong stories have greatly enriched this book.

According to my edition of Webster's dictionary, the word *strong* has many meanings, including "not easily affected or upset; morally powerful, having strength of character or will; able to think vigorously and clearly; not easily defeated; and having many resources." The women and men you will meet in this book all share these characteristics, some more quietly, others more politically, but all with the innate inner strength that is encompassed by the definition of the word.

There are also many colored threads that run through these narratives. Some of us have been married to or lived with a person of another race. Eight of the families in the book, including mine, have raised interracial children. Joseph Smooke, who is Jewish, recently married his sweetheart, Sharon Li, who is Chinese. Judy Heumann, who is also Jewish, married Jorge Piñeda, who is from Mexico. Terry and Connie Dellmuth, a white couple with two biological children, Jennifer and Chris, adopted a Black baby boy, Jay, in the early 1970s. Chris is now the father of three interracial children.

Barbara and Lee Wagner's oldest son Jeremy, who is white, pledged a Black fraternity in college. His sister Sarah was often mistaken for a Latina at Columbia University in New York. Shiloh Kaho has also been mistaken as a Latina, particularly when she lived in Southern California's Orange County. Her sister, Gabrielle, could easily pass as white, but identifies strongly as biracial. Their mother Karen is white; their father John is Creole.

During the past five years I have talked with over sixty friends and colleagues from Seattle, Washington, to South Yarmouth, Massachusetts, from Philadelphia, Pennsylvania, to Albuquerque, New Mexico. Because the issue of race in my life ran across the Black-white fault line, both within my family and in my involvement in the antiracist movement, a number of my friends and colleagues reflect that racial divide. Native American, Latino, Chinese, Filipino, Chicano, and Jewish storytellers round out the racially diverse narratives.

Numerous storytellers in this book were active in the antiracist movement of the 1960s, the women's movement of the 1970s and the disability and affordable housing movements of the 1980s and '90s and continue their activism today. Others are involved in their workplaces to make them more open, tolerant, and inclusive.

The storytellers include two Vietnam veterans, a vice president of a bank, a carpenter, a tenant organizer, two junior high school teachers, a foster children's advocate, two professional photographers, an affordable housing director, an Episcopal priest, and seven young adults committed to racial justice in the twenty-first century.

My interest in talking with all these people was to listen carefully to their lives, learn from them the point in time they became conscious of race and racism, and how these two issues impacted them as children and adults. I also wanted to know how they felt about where we are now as a nation on the race issue — and where we are not.

In the last chapter I address four areas of unfinished business in American life that need to be consciously and clearly dealt with if we are to call ourselves a nation of true equality and justice for all. These areas are: teaching American history, white privilege, affirmative action, and reparations. But it is important that the stories come first. So many of us learn about our families, our traditions and values through stories told around the dining room table, a campfire circle, or old scrapbooks and photo albums: stories like those of Alan Parker, a Native American who grew up on a small reservation in northern Montana and faced the hardships of that colonial system; my son's godmother, Baraka Sele, who grew up in rural Michigan and learned at an early age how the color of her skin separated her from her white friends; Bill Sorro, a Filipino who grew up in San Francisco with his immigrant father, white mother, and five siblings and recognized as a little boy his secondary status in the larger white society; and myself, who learned at age thirty-two that the color line is very real.

There is joy as well as anger expressed by many of the storytellers, most directly by the men and women of color as the recipients of our country's ongoing racism, almost invisible to most white people. There is also a growing awareness by the white storytellers that although we can never personally know the horrors of racism—past and present—we clearly need to learn the advantages of being white in a white-dominated society.

Racism continues to be deeply embedded in America's psyche. W. E. B. DuBois wrote in his seminal 1903 book *The Souls of Black Folks,* "The problem of the Twentieth Century is the problem of the color-line." It is the problem of the twenty-first century as well. Thirty-six years after the publication of the Kerner Commission Report following the 1967 race riots, we have not come far in leveling the racial playing field in this country. The 2000 U.S. Census figures on income by race shout that fact. The median income was the highest ever recorded for white households, at $44,366; but for Black households it was only $27,910.

As Frank Joyce of People Against Racism in Detroit wrote many years ago, "The first step in any solution of any problem is its correct definition. To this day, whites have attempted to devise a realistic definition of the race problem. The task has been fundamentally evaded by the belief that the race problem is a Negro problem. In fact, whites do not have a Negro problem: they do have a white problem."

I hope to address this problem through the stories that follow, stories that can become a bridge between those of us who have actively struggled with the issues of race, racism, and white privilege, or may see racial injustices in our society but are uncomfortable speaking out, and those of us for whom these concepts seem strange or irrelevant in our lives.

As we enter the early years of the new millennium, silence on the issue of race by the white majority and selective amnesia about our country's painful racist history are not options. Wounds born in slavery and the Long Walk will continue to fester until we consciously recognize the past pain and begin the healing within our own lives and in the places of political and corporate power in our society.

My story and those of my son, friends, and colleagues are an offering to that process of greater understanding and reconciliation. They are stories of pain, joy, personal and political struggle, discovery, and reflection. They leave their unique footprints on the most profound issue that continues to divide us as a nation.

Finally, a word about the word "Black." When I first began this book, I capitalized both "Black" and "White" when referring to the two racial groupings. However, I became uncomfortable capitalizing "White" because the vast majority of us who are white don't self-identify as such. There are white storytellers in the book, including myself, who are learning to understand the advantages we have as white-skinned people in our country, but we don't, as a rule, use the word "white" to racially identify ourselves. We'll most often identify ethnically, as I do on occasion, saying "I'm half Italian, and very proud of it." In contrast, most Black people self-identify either as African-American or Black. I therefore decided to honor that self-identification and capitalize Black throughout the book.

H.H.H.
March 26, 2003
Cotuit, Massachusetts

PART 1

PHILADELPHIA

1962–1971

JOHN SENNOTT

MARIAN GRAY SECUNDY

BARBARA WAGNER

LEE WAGNER

JEREMY WAGNER

SARAH WAGNER

KEVIN WAGNER

NANCY CHISHOLM

JIM KELCH

VICTOR WILBURN

DIANE BATTLE

DAVID GRACIE

HARVEY FINKLE

CAROL FINKLE

TERRY DELLMUTH

CONNIE DELLMUTH

CHRIS DELLMUTH

JENNY DELLMUTH

JAY DELLMUTH

LUCIA FAITHFULL

JAMES KELLY

STEVE STEVENSON

REY

RON WHITEHORN

left my home state of California on June 20, 1962, carefully packing my one suitcase for the long flight to Philadelphia. The cozy house where I lived with eight other students was full of sunshine that early morning. I didn't know it would be my last day living in California for twenty-three years.

I had just finished a year of graduate studies in social work at Cal Berkeley and was tired of academia. I loved my racially diverse and engaging housemates and getting acquainted again with my hometown of San Francisco. The House on Un-American Activities Committee hearings had just finished in city hall, where protesters had been hosed down the wide marble staircase, and the free-speech movement at Cal Berkeley hadn't yet taken hold. It was still a vibrant place to be. Peter, Paul, and Mary were singing for free. Bob Dylan and Joan Baez were hot, the Hungry I and Jazz Workshop were both going strong in San Francisco, and Gus Hall and the Communist Party had a table in front of Cal Berkeley's Student Union alongside every other conceivable political party or cause.

But I felt the need to leave the classroom and explore new worlds, so on that morning, I carried my heavy suitcase downstairs and had one last breakfast in our large kitchen. My housemate Connie, a brilliant Mexican American from Los Angeles, drove me to the Oakland airport. We passed the campus's Sather Gate, drove past the street where Jimmy Lynn hosted his fabulous parties, and finally glimpsed the panoramic view of San Francisco across the Bay.

I felt a trace of sadness passing these special places but was filled with excitement at what lay ahead. My first real break with the past was under way—leaving behind my father, a difficult man who I knew loved me very much; my mother, whom he did not love; and my brother, six years older than me, who loved my mother very much and was living at home again after four years in the air force.

When Connie and I arrived at the Oakland airport, we hugged hard. I picked up my suitcase and slowly walked to the ticket counter. "The plane's

3

delayed for two hours because of mechanical difficulties," I was curtly told by a sloppily dressed ticket agent.

The World Airlines plane was an old propeller-driven model, a relic from World War II. Four hours later it managed to become airborne. It flew lower than the jets of today, so I could glimpse more of the geography below, beginning with the grandeur of the high Sierras.

My brother Wayne and me with Mom and Dad in San Francisco, circa 1947

I'd never been east of York, Nebraska, where my grandfather had lived and died seven years earlier. As we flew over the farmlands of the Midwest, I thought about the only grandparent I'd ever known and the fractured relationship that had existed for years between him and his only son.

In 1951, when I was eleven years old, I met my grandfather for the first time. Up until then, I never knew that my father's father was alive. Neither of my parents told my brother or me why, in that summer heat, we all got into our new pea-green Pontiac and drove hundreds of miles east to this quaint town in Nebraska where I was greeted by an old and very friendly man and his second wife, Laura, a robust and engaging woman. They lived in a grand, white, three-story corner house with a wrap-around porch and views of two tree-lined streets. A wide stairway led up to the spacious second floor, where rooms were rented to elderly men, who would join us on the porch even during the afternoon thunderstorms. Grandpa and Laura lived on the first floor, where we enjoyed her delicious homemade biscuits and large wholesome meals. I remember letters and Christmas presents for the next seven years from these two special people. In 1955 we returned for a second and last visit. Grandpa died in 1958.

I would learn years later that my father had disowned him for marrying Laura on the day of my grandmother's funeral. By that time, my grandparents had been divorced for many years and living in two separate states. My grandmother died suddenly of a broken neck from a fall, and my father severed relations with Grandpa for over ten years, the same period he would disown me twenty years later.

I planned to work the summer of 1962 at the venerable Germantown Settlement House in one of Philadelphia's most historic and integrated neighborhoods. My Berkeley housemate, Don, had put me in touch with his best friend Bill Moyer, a longtime Quaker activist. Bill kindly referred me to the job and offered me a place to stay in his group home called the Broodercoop (loosely meaning "brotherhood" in German).

When my plane finally landed in New York around midnight, its mechanical problems returned, and we had to be bused to Philadelphia. I arrived at the old, gray-stoned Victorian row house around 2:00 A.M. — twelve hours late. On the window was a large, neatly printed sign that read, "This house has NO bomb shelter. Our only shelter is peace." I opened the front door and placed my suitcase on the floor inside the vestibule, then opened the second door. To my left was a steep, narrow staircase. I proceeded precariously up the stairs. A young white woman with straight blonde hair met me at the top of the first flight, introduced herself as Larcy, and said that I'd be staying in her room because she'd be leaving in a few days. We walked up

Wayne, Grandpa, and Dad in York, Nebraska, 1951

another flight of even narrower stairs. A young, light-skinned Black man asked if I had any luggage. "There's a very heavy suitcase, but I could wait until morning," I said. He replied, "I'd be glad to take it up," and he did. My new room was sparsely furnished and disorganized. Two front windows looked down to the street far below. Larcy's mattress was on the floor, across from the narrow bed that was to be mine. Desperately tired, I took a bath before going to bed to cleanse the travel sweat. It was an oppressively hot and humid night. I knew I wasn't in California anymore.

I awoke to the clip-clopping of a horse, looked out the window to a rainy and overcast day. Below me, an old man sitting on an old but durable grocery cart was being pulled slowly down the street by a horse, a sight that would soon disappear from the neighborhood scene. I dressed and went downstairs, where I met Charlie, a white, pasty-faced Swarthmore student whose bedroom floor, I soon learned, was the repository for countless empty beer cans. He graciously offered to make me breakfast. I gratefully accepted cantaloupe and soft-boiled eggs and was squeezing some orange juice when a slim man in his late twenties wearing a bright smile walked into the kitchen and introduced himself. It was Bill Moyer, the friend of Don's who had found me the job, and my first friend in Philadelphia.

After breakfast Bill drove me downtown to introduce me to the city. We walked several blocks in the rain. He held a large black umbrella, and as we talked about interracial housing and his work trying to stop blockbusting, I became aware that many of the passersby were Black, unlike in San Francisco and my Berkeley neighborhood. I returned to the Broodercoop by bus and wrote eleven postcards, letting friends and family know that I had arrived safely in the "City of Brotherly Love." Later that afternoon I discovered the piano and tried awkwardly to play. A stout, dark-skinned Black woman walked into the front room, then left. I followed her into the kitchen, where she was preparing our dinner. "You must be Helen." Her name was Ora Williams, and I could hear opera music floating down from her second-floor room. Swamy, a third-floor resident from India, came in and asked, "What time did you get in?"

"Around 2:00 A.M.," I replied.

There were six of us eating together around the dining room table that evening. I learned that we were each responsible for preparing one dinner meal a week, except for Sundays. When it was his turn, Swamy always made the same delicious curried chicken.

My summer job was in the Germantown Settlement House's early childhood day-care program, mostly Black youngsters from the surrounding neighborhood. When it ended in late August, there was a boisterous party in the playground. My coworker, a talented Black woman author, gave me a one-word poem: "Be."

I decided not to return to California quite yet. There was still much to explore and absorb in this old, strong, diverse, crumbling city. A job was posted at the Reed Street Settlement House in South Philadelphia, an amalgam of traditional Italian, Irish, Polish, and Black subcultures, mostly modest- to low-income families in brick row houses with well-scrubbed marble stair stoops. I didn't know it then, but for the next two years I would be a community organizer for $5,000 a year.

Before I began my first full-time job, Ora Williams and I traveled back to California to gather up my belongings. She looked forward to her first trip west. We took a Greyhound bus to Long Beach, where my folks had then lived for seven years. I told them that I was traveling with a Black friend, knowing that they'd be civil when we briefly stayed with them. My brother Wayne had brought home a Black air force buddy from his days in Amarillo, Texas, and the visit had gone smoothly enough. But remembering my days growing up in a white San Francisco neighborhood, I instinctively knew that my parents' civility should not be mistaken for acceptance.

During my childhood, my family lived on a steep curving street called San Felipe Way on the foggy west side of the city. Our old Spanish-style home had a long brick staircase leading up to the front door. From the top landing on clear days you could see the Pacific Ocean and the seal-laden Farallon Islands. "We live just two blocks from St. Francis Woods!" my mother would exclaim to anyone within earshot.

St. Francis Woods was—and is—a very exclusive, cleanly landscaped mansion-studded neighborhood. As with our area, only white families lived there back then. We all inhabited racially segregated homes, and still do in most neighborhoods today.

My mother and I would often go window shopping downtown, wearing hats that she had carefully made. We'd eat lunch in the aromatic Italian neighborhood of North Beach, slowly walk through Chinatown to buy candied ginger, or pass on to the fresh shrimp salads at Fisherman's Wharf. The Chinese community had not yet migrated to the flatlands of the Richmond District, nor had the thousands of Russians and Vietnamese arrived who live there today. Blacks lived in the Fillmore or Bayview–Hunters Point, and Latinos in the Mission District. I never questioned the way it was, nobody in my family talked about it, nor was I aware that it should be any different.

My dad and me in our San Francisco backyard, circa 1948

The "color line" was invisible to most white families when I was growing up, and still is today. The line was clear, however, to those who had to abide by it. Whenever we'd chance to drive through the Fillmore district, which was primarily Black, my father would make disparaging remarks about "those lazy drunken people," an interesting observation coming from a closet alcoholic. In the early 1950s Willie Mays tried to buy a house not far from us and created an uproar. My mother and her best friend Marion were among those outraged. "How can he even think of living here?" I heard them complain during one of their daily marathon phone calls. *Doesn't he know his place?*

I was very fond of our old house, and when my father was promoted to general manager of the Radio Marine Corporation of America's office in San Pedro, I wept when I learned that we had to leave both the house and the city I loved. My favorite room was the two-story basement. The upper level was spacious enough for our Camp Fire group that met every Friday

Dad and Mom, seated at far right, at a Radio Marine Corporation dinner in the 1950s

after school for seven years. There was room for a Ping Pong table, which served as our arts and crafts center, and several stacks of orange-crate shelves where we kept our treasures. Beyond our space was a small red-lit room where my brother Wayne developed his rolls of black-and-white film. Our black 1940 Oldsmobile with running boards and my dad's company jeep were parked on the lower level. There was still space left for Wayne and his high school buddies to work on their Harleys, and room every election day to be our neighborhood's polling place.

My mother was the leader of our group. Aside from her sewing projects, hat making, leather tooling, and jewelry making, this cluster of fourteen Camp Fire Girls was her life. My parents' marriage was a disaster. Father handled it through work, alcohol, and a submerged rage. Mother handled it by trying to live much of her life through me.

We had one Jewish girl, Reva, among us WASPs, and Mother was very proud of that fact, extending her racial and cultural line that far, but no further. My best friend Maureen Casey (whom I nicknamed "Mo") was a proud Irish American and the biggest talker in the group. Her father worked at the Tanforan race track and, like mine, was a closet alcoholic. Mo and I loved to play duets on our upright piano in the living room. "Smoke Gets in Your Eyes" was one of our favorites. Linda Hull, the same tall height as me and much brighter, and Judy McCook, the red-headed, tough tomboy I tried to emulate, were my next best friends.

On October 30, 1950, at ten years of age, I wrote in my Camp Fire book:

Me, on the left, with Mo and Reva on a Camp Fire Girls trip to Yosemite, winter of 1954

Our group had a Halloween party on Monday. We decorated with orange and black crepe paper. My mother said that we have done a very good job. When the girls came to the party they put on their costumes. Leslie was a sad sack, Louise was a ghost, Maureen was an old fashion girl, Judy B was a Russian girl, Judy Mc was a tramp, Snooky was a majorette, Ruthie was a gypsy, Linda was a baby, and I was an old fashion girl too. Everybody brought refreshments. I brought six apples. We pulled taffy and played games. I think we had a very good group activity.

Those were the innocent days. It is hard to imagine from today's perspective how much my life and the lives of my family and the friends I loved have changed. In 1962 both Linda Hull and Judy McCook would be dead—Judy, with her mother-in-law, in a plane crash when a suicidal passenger stormed the cockpit and shot the pilots, and Linda on a winding road in the Alps when she was a Fulbright scholar in Italy. Years later, Mo Casey contracted multiple sclerosis. I don't know today if she's alive or dead.

When we moved to Long Beach in 1955, I attended Woodrow Wilson High, a predominantly white school with elitist sororities and fraternities on campus. I clearly felt the class line there, punctuated by the fact that I was very tall and socially awkward in a strange new environment. Neither my best friend, Margaret Welsh, nor I have ever attended any of the many class reunions since we graduated in 1957.

When I started at Long Beach State College, the campus was new, with great expanses of grass and trees where buildings now grow. A large, stark VA hospital stood next door. Many men there were veterans of the Korean War and attended the college, far too many in wheelchairs. A friend of mine, Dick Johnston, had white hair at age twenty-six. He had survived Pork Chop Hill, one of the most vicious battles of the war.

It was at State where my racial consciousness began to awaken. Sally, my first mentor and friend from the neighborhood Presbyterian church, inspired me to follow her footsteps and become a probation officer. Dr. David Dressler, a short, bustling Jewish man, was head of the Social Work Department and former chief of New York State's parole system. The correctional field created productive rehabilitation programs for prisoners and parolees back then, believing that there was hope for their futures outside the prison walls. Those days are long gone.

Dr. Dressler became my second mentor and friend until his death fifteen years later. My favorite class story of his was about another professor and good friend, also Jewish: "Dr. Korber lives in a nice middle-class neighborhood near campus," he'd tell us. "Now you know what he looks like—tall, lean, wavy gray hair. One day he was watering his lawn and a car slowed down with a family of four inside. The driver rolled down his window and began talking with him. 'We've been looking at the house for sale down the street. Could you tell us something about the neighborhood?' 'Yes, of course,' he replied with great zeal. 'It's a great place to live, lots of kids and good schools. It's close to the college, too.' The driver hesitated, then asked in a low tone: 'Are there any niggers living around here?' Dr. Korber pulled himself up and replied, 'As far as I know, I'm the only one!'"

Patricia was my first Black college friend, although we rarely socialized outside of school, except for class social gatherings. She was also studying to be a probation officer, and we'd often eat lunch together in the campus cafeteria. One day she told me of her growing up in Louisiana. Because the schools were still segregated when Patricia was young, she had to ride the bus past the large white school to her smaller and much less endowed Black school — every day, morning and afternoon, for twelve years, not able to get off the bus because her skin was the wrong color. Even though she loved her Black teachers and the education she received, she was reminded daily of her inferior status. Her simple story, told in a soft, even voice, was an epiphany for me. The year was 1959.

I disengaged emotionally from my family that year as well. My parents' relationship, always a disaster, was deteriorating rapidly. Mother tried to leave Dad during my sophomore year. With her suitcase in hand, she stayed with an old friend for the night but went back the next day. Dad refused to go to counseling, and Mom was too afraid to leave again. At age fifty-two, and not having worked since World War II, she was scared, so she stayed and suffered for it.

Ora Williams and I arrived at my parents' home on an early August evening. They lived on a modest tree-lined street two blocks off a major thoroughfare. A fig tree and a lemon tree grew tall and strong in the large backyard, as did my father's rose garden. My parents would live in that house for thirty-three years.

One would not call Ora an attractive woman. She was dark, large boned, her nose broad, her lips thick. And she was brilliant, a survivor in a society that did not respect her as a human being. She knew that and didn't give a damn, which was one of the reasons I liked her.

During our visit, my mother quietly told me that "she smells bad." I didn't respond, nor did I say anything about my yet unformed future plans. My parents thought I'd eventually come back home. They didn't have a clue about the relief I'd felt to escape their dysfunctional relationship by moving to the other side of the country.

My brother Wayne was then working as a welder for Procter & Gamble in San Pedro and living at home. For the trip back to Philadelphia, he sold me his 1953 Oldsmobile with the stick shift on the steering wheel. I waved good-bye to him and Mom as Ora and I pulled away from the curb, pointing the car east. It would not be smooth sailing. We took the highway that is now Route 80, and although we didn't encounter any problems racially along the way, we did face challenges with the car. The first was a flat tire in the middle of the hot Nevada desert, thankfully in the cool of night. Between the two of us struggling with the jack, we changed the tire and kept going. In Rawlins, Wyoming, the crankshaft broke. On the Pennsylvania Turnpike, the clutch faltered, but we limped into Philadelphia late one night, greatly relieved to have arrived safely.

I wanted to be closer to my new job, so I moved from the Broodercoop to an old, small "Father Son and Holy Ghost" house in Queen Village, then a working-class neighborhood just north of the settlement house. There was one room on each of the three floors, with a narrow, winding stair connecting them—thus the triple name.

My elderly Italian neighbor who lived behind me had an outhouse in her backyard. My bathroom was on the second floor of my small row house. Its window looked over my neighbor's yard and beyond to the Delaware River. She never closed the door of the outhouse, so as she sat on the toilet we'd wave at each other as I brushed my teeth every morning.

There were no Blacks living on my narrow cobblestoned street. The brick row houses were crammed together, and everyone knew who was coming and going. I had a multicolored group of friends. The Polish woman across the street, tight-lipped and unfriendly, would give me a mean stare whenever we'd chance to meet. The huge annual New Year's Day Mummers Parade always began on second and Catherine, around the corner from my home. In the early 1960s, blackface was still allowed in the parade.

At the settlement house I was the key staff person for the South Philadelphia Expressway Committee, a coalition of Italian, Polish, Irish, and Black families and small businesses. My job was to secure relocation monies owed to families and businesses being displaced because of the construction of the Delaware Expressway—Route 95, which now links Maine to Florida. The committee was successful in getting funds (but not enough) for the 420 families and businesses whose properties would be demolished and in moving the expressway two blocks over from its original planned location, thus saving over 1,200 homes and businesses.

A smaller but equally important project was the Manton Street Neighbors, a group of Black families that was formed to acquire an empty city-owned lot nestled in the middle of their block. The lot was turned into a playground, and at the dedication ceremony, they presented me with a simple certificate of appreciation I still treasure.

My favorite settlement house job was unpaid—playing the piano for the talented Italian teenagers who put on an annual sold-out show in the cavernous gym. We'd end each evening with a rousing rendition of "Everything's Coming Up Roses." I hoped for all of them that that was so.

It was at Reed Street Settlement House where I met my friend and mentor John Sennott. He was a constant support and the respected and sometimes outspoken community organizer for United Neighbors Inc., a large settlement house in the neighborhood north of Reed Street, and just as ethnically mixed. John is the oldest storyteller in the book. He's now eighty-five years young. His nickname for years was "Tiny," a playful reference to this large and powerfully built man. I particularly wanted his story told because he grew up in a time of extraordinary racial strife—Jim Crow, separate and unequal schools, and the like—yet he is one of the most accepting people I've ever met. Much is owed to John's grandfather and mother, who instilled in him an enduring sense of empathy and fairness. John and his activist wife Liz live in a charming Victorian home in Media, Pennsylvania. Even though he's almost blind, John still travels and loves to talk about the old days and the many unique people he knew and whose lives he touched.

JOHN SENNOTT

'm a Maine Yankee. I was born in South Eliot, Maine, just over the bridge from New Hampshire, in 1919, on the twenty-first of March, which is the first day of spring even in Maine. The first thing I remember was when I was about three years old, living on a hill farm in Vermont which my grandfather had given my mother and father as a wedding gift. My grandfather had a profound effect on my life. Even though he was in his nineties, he would hold me on his knee and talk with me about why he had a big sign on his big red barn that read, "Workers of the World Unite at the Ballot Box." He taught me the alphabet by using some of those letters. Of course, that was the slogan of the Socialist Party, and you can imagine how few Socialists there are in the state of Vermont! He always used to tell me about how he traveled around after the Civil War in the Midwest working with the cooperative movement. By the time I was in high school, seeing him on vacations, I had quite an exciting way to live—to help people do things together. It was so different from my school friends.

John Sennott, on the right, with his sister in Maine, circa 1924

In New England you had a different kind of racism. The Polish, Lithuanians, and Italians were just beginning to come in when I was going to first grade. I had a teacher who had them sit by themselves, but one day when my mother came to get me, she saw that and straightened them out quick.

My family moved to Orange, Massachusetts, when I began high school because my father opened a small business there. I lucked out because I had a principal who had *Time* and *Life* magazines and *Scribners* in the library. High schools up in that area didn't have nice books and magazines like that. He had become a minister of the Unitarian Universalist Church and a pacifist, and I really didn't know what that was. I knew it wasn't right to go and kill people with guns. This was in the mid-1930s, just prior to the war. We wrote letters to people who were locked up in jail in Europe. We would send money because we felt for these people, and sometimes we'd get letters back. Little did I know that fifty years later they would call it Amnesty International. I got a chance to meet two people from Europe when I was still in high school. They got out of Europe and moved here. I couldn't believe that anyone would want to kill those nice people.

I attended the teachers college in Keene, New Hampshire, in 1938. At that time there was only one Black student and 400 white students. I really didn't understand about Black or white or otherwise. The Black student's name was Smith, and my name was Sennott, so I would march with her sometimes in activities. She was a very nice girl. There were also two Black businessmen in town. One ran the hostelry in the Cheshire House Hotel. He took the bags in and out. He was a bachelor from Washington, D.C. Years later I found out that he had bought a fancy hotel in Washington. The other man's name was Sloan. He and his wife had a tailoring business, and the only time you saw them was in church. There was just one church of any substance in town, and they went to it. When there were church suppers everybody went; they did too.

I went to Hudson, New York, in 1945. (I didn't graduate from college. For two years I went blind, but I always did some kind of work.) In Hudson the Blacks all lived on two streets. There were about fourteen Black families, not many. They had a church, and I was invited two or three times a year to worship with them. I was working at a little community center that some United Church women had put together. All they had was athletics and Ping Pong. They didn't do anything with the community. I was there for four years. I had a great drama workshop because a woman who lived in a hotel nearby had been on the stage with Tallulah Bankhead. She was an old lady, about seventy-eight, but she could teach and sing any damn song that had ever been on Broadway. She loved these kids and took them on tours to other towns all over the county.

I was only making $3,600 a year at that time, and the board said they couldn't pay me any more. I was offered a job by a program director in the county government. He was really head of a reform school, but they didn't bill it that way. It was in the beautiful Berkshires, but after I got there I saw how staff beat the children. It took me back to killing people in Germany or Italy because you don't like them. They had some people there like that, and I didn't know what to do. I told my wife Nancy that I couldn't stay. I didn't have any supportive teammates there either. There was one social worker, but she was so chicken she would always say, "But Tiny, I didn't see them *do* anything."

So here I am, and my children Stevie and Johnnie are one and two years old, and Nancy is taking care of them as well as being a house-mother. We had fourteen kids living with us, and I wasn't a trained child worker. I went to the chief and he said, "I'm changing things as fast as I can, John. Just give me a couple of months." I said, "I can't take it. That fellow Riley stood there beating a kid and I went over and stopped him. He turned around and he told me, 'Get out of here or I'll take you too.' I told him, 'Riley, if you move one step, they'll have to get the wagon to get you out, because I will pull you down,' and he threw the bat he was holding as far as he could in the bushes and walked away."

I was scared. I went down to Great Barrington, the nearest big town, and called this woman from the National Federation of Settlement Houses. I said, "Is that job in South Philadelphia still open?" "Oh, yes," she said, "are you interested, Tiny?" She asked, "Where are you?" and I said, "I'm at a pay phone." She said, "Stay there by the phone and I'll call you back." And she called back and said, "Miss McCullough, the executive director at St. Martha's House, wants to know if you could be there Monday morning for an interview." It was a new job—a community worker's job.

I hitchhiked down for the interview. I had a few bucks, but I wasn't going to spend all my money. I got three rides from Albany to Philly. I went in the Y near city hall, stayed overnight, got shaved, dressed up, and walked down to 8th and Snyder—not that I couldn't take the trolley for twelve cents, but I wanted to see the territory. There were no trees, no grass, nothing but telephone poles, and I thought, "Where am I? Am I in hell or what?" I stopped at a candy store—there was a thermometer and it was eighty-four degrees at 8:15 A.M.

I was hired as the first community worker in the settlement houses in Philadelphia—September 1948. I was paid $2,600 a year with a free apartment.

I was there for four years. St. Martha's Settlement House was right on the line—west to Broad Street was solid Italian. There were Irish and Polish people around 2nd Street and pockets of Black people who had been there a long time. They had come up from the South, worked in the navy yard and all around the city.

I took an interracial group of children—ten to twelve years old—to a free public swimming pool, and the local neighborhood men, all Italians, came in, and one of them tried to beat me but couldn't because I stayed in the water. Then I saw they were going to hurt the little kids, so I went over to him. He had a night-stick, and I took it away from him. He was so mad he jumped in the water, and I jumped in the water too. I'm like Shamu, and I rolled him over once and he thought he was going to drown. His own buddies weren't coming in after him because none of them knew how to swim anyway. It wasn't pleasant, but I didn't want those kids to get hurt.

I left St. Martha's House because I had to have more money. I was making about $3,000 a year to feed two children and a wife, and we had to move out because they wanted to use the apartment for a program. I went to United Neighbors Settlement House in South Philly and stayed there for the next twenty-nine years.

I think there's been a lot of progress on the issue of race because I see people walking and working with each other. I see labor unions where Black people are officers. In the old days you could have a Black person in charge of something in elementary school, always a figurehead. Not today. But there are still a tremendous number of subtle bigots out there.

Morris Dees from the Southern Poverty Law Center is a very close personal friend of ours, and they are doing it the way it has to be done with some people. That's to simply say, "Obey the law. This is the law in America, and you

John Sennott in his settlement house office in South Philadelphia in the 1980s

can't go around burning down people's houses and churches, and we're not going to let you. There's enough people in America who can put up enough money to put you out of business. There's enough people that will elect judges who can't be bought off," and I believe that. Look at what Morris's group did. They decided they couldn't get to first base in education, so they hired the best people in the game to make films on teaching tolerance. They gave the films free to 60,000 schools in North America. So when the law center asks me for money, I say, "Amen." ■■■

When John retired seventeen years ago, the local Philadelphia paper read:

> John Sennott has proven that a person can make a difference. After thirty-five years as a community organizer in South Philadelphia, Sennott's name will live on when the Ridgeway Recreation Center, located at Broad and Christian Streets, will bear his name. As one of the first paid community organizers in the United States, Sennott came to Philadelphia in 1948. "Back then, Philadelphia was a Republican town with a corrupt political machine. To get something, you had to be Republican. The sons of immigrants realized they didn't have to take it when they returned from service after the war. Together we worked to change the city's political character by changing the city charter," Sennott said. At a recent tribute to Sennott in Washington, D.C. during a meeting of the United Neighborhood Centers of America, a friend remarked: "Like FDR, he makes people like him and want to help him. This quality is what makes the difference between a good community organizer and a great one."

John Sennott and his wife Liz in their Media, Pennsylvania, home, 1999

Marian Gray was my second Black friend, a smart, attractive woman in her late twenties whom I met through Bill Moyer at the Broodercoop. Marian and Bill were classmates at the Bryn Mawr School of Social Work and are still good friends almost forty years later.

I spent my first Christmas Eve in Philadelphia with Marian and her family in their large, attractive brownstone home in North Philadelphia, the heart of the Black community. Her father was the proactive pastor of Bright Hope Baptist Church, one of the largest and most influential Black churches in the city. In the hallway of their home were photos of Reverend Gray with President Kennedy and Attorney General Robert Kennedy, as well as local dignitaries. Marian's brother Bill was home for the holidays from Drew Seminary. Later he would become a U.S. Congressman and executive director of the National Negro College Fund.

After our holiday dinner, Reverend Gray insisted that I call my parents in Long Beach, which I did. I knew enough not to mention that I was calling from the home of a prominent Black minister.

For the past twenty-five years, Marian has worked with the Office of Ethics in Medicine at Howard University in Washington, D.C. She is now at Tuskegee University in Tennessee consulting with a similar office there.

The racial incident Marian described during our conversation came as a complete shock to me. We had known each other for years, and this was the first time I had heard the story about her father, who in the late 1940s had been forced out of the state of Florida by the KKK. It would be too easy to say, "white America doesn't do things like that anymore." I would argue that blatant and more subtle incidents continue to occur at a rate far greater than we would like to admit, and are just as damaging.

Marian died of a heart attack in December 2002. She was 64 years old.

MARIAN GRAY SECUNDY

I was born in Baton Rouge, Louisiana, in 1938, the oldest child of my parents. My mother is from Louisiana, and she and my father met at Southern University in Baton Rouge. My father was teaching in the Demonstration School when she met him. They married right after she graduated from college. He was working on his Ph.D. at the University of Pennsylvania in Philadelphia, where they returned after they married to pursue their graduate degrees. She got a master's degree at Temple University in home economics. They then went back to Louisiana, where he continued to teach at Southern University and she got a job teaching at Grambling College.

When I was three, we moved to St. Augustine, Florida. My father was given the presidency of a school in 1941 called Florida Normal. It was a small Black Baptist college. In 1945 he assumed the presidency of Florida A&M College, which is now Florida A&M University, and we moved to Tallahassee. He was president there for five years and left in 1949.

As a small child, one of the racial experiences I had was in Tallahassee. I had gotten on the bus with a woman who was our caretaker and sat on a seat in the front of the bus. A white woman on the bus sitting next to me took a magazine,

Marian Secundy and her brother Bill in Florida in the mid-1940s put it under me, and dumped me on the floor, because you weren't supposed to sit in the front of the bus. I was about six years old when that happened. I can also remember shopping with my grandmother when we were in Louisiana. The rule was that we could never ask to go to the bathroom, and we could never ask for water because she wasn't going to use segregated facilities. It was always very traumatic to go downtown shopping because we, as small children, couldn't do anything. You were taught that you couldn't do certain things because of your race. Beyond that, we were very shielded and protected. We lived in a Black community there. The only encounters we had with white people were shopkeepers and people who would come to campus, usually white liberals from the North. Those were the only contacts I had with whites until we moved to Philadelphia.

The reason my father left Florida was the major story about race in our family. But first, you need to know that I come from a very privileged background. My grandparents on my mother's side are both college graduates. My grandfather was a Greek and Latin scholar who was educated in schools in Louisiana founded by the abolitionists. He was also a math teacher and taught at junior colleges in Louisiana and the local Black high school. My grandmother was an elementary school principal and a graduate of Bishop College in Texas. They had three children. My mother was the oldest of those children. All of them had college educations. My uncle was a physician. He came to Howard University and graduated with an M.D. in 1948. He was also one of the Tuskegee Airmen during World War II.

As I mentioned earlier, my father was president of Florida A&M from 1945 to 1949. At that time, all the states in the South had a "separate but equal" Black university or college. A&M was hoping for an insider to become president, so there was some internal tension when my father became president. He was thirty-five years old, a young, frisky, and very good-looking man. He also became very active in recruiting northern Black faculty with Ph.D.s, which was unusual for Black colleges then. There was a significant number of Black people on the campus and in the community who were not welcoming of outsiders from the North. During the years he was president, he made many significant changes in terms of buildings, faculty, and upgrading the entire institution.

It was at the beginning of the McCarthy era, and in reviewing papers some years after he died, I discovered a good bit of correspondence between him and the House Un-American Activities Committee. One of its directives asked college presidents to have their faculty sign loyalty oaths. My father refused to have the faculty sign. That's where his troubles initially began with the white establishment, although there were a number of people on the campus who were not happy with his presidency.

In the spring of 1949 several definitive things happened. One of them concerned Juanita Kidd Stout, who had come to the faculty from the North and later became a judge in Philadelphia. Like all southern cities, Tallahassee was very segregated. You could not try on clothing in the stores if you were Black. You could buy, but things needed to be purchased and taken out. Juanita Kidd Stout had apparently ordered some clothing and went down to pick it up and got into an altercation with the salesperson in the store, who called her by her first name. That was the last straw, and Juanita came back to the campus and organized what was one of the first boycotts of that store. It turns out that the store clerk was the cousin of a very significant person in the state legislature. That incident blew up into a major challenge to my father about what kind of people he had working for him, and people not following the acceptable system.

At that time my father's father, who was a Baptist minister in Philadelphia, died. My father left to go to the funeral, and a number of explosive things happened on the campus while he was gone—student protests and their reaction to racism in Tallahassee. When my father returned he was confronted with a number of charges regarding his conduct and challenges from the state legislature and the governor relative to the conduct of the college. He was called in by the state government and asked explicitly did he believe in segregation. Nobody had ever asked him that question directly before, and he said, "No." After that answer, and all the charges accompanying that, they asked him to resign.

At the same time this occurred, the Ku Klux Klan was beginning to get active. The KKK, when we were away for my grandfather's funeral, had burned crosses on the lawn in front of our house, and there was a great deal of intimidation. Students were hysterical, and my father was given forty-eight hours to get out of the state; basically, he was told that he would not be provided with any protection after forty-eight hours.

I was eleven years old, and my brother Bill was nine. My memories of what happened are very different than the other members of the family. (My mother says I have a very dramatic imagination!) All of us were traumatized, so it's difficult to know what really occurred. What factually occurred was that my father was saying he was not going to leave. He was finally convinced by friends and my mother to get out of the state. She was left there to pack up the house and get us out as quickly as possible. There was no immediate threat to her, but he had to leave. So he left with my foster brother Charles, who had come to live with us when we were at Florida Normal. We weren't able to pack up everything, so friends took furniture and things and promised to send them. Most of it we've never seen again. We were driven to my grandmother's in Louisiana and remained there for a year. My mother was given a job at Southern University as the dean of students.

My father was looking for work in Philadelphia. There were many letters from all kinds of people answering his request for employment, and they made it clear they just couldn't take the chance of giving him a job. We didn't see him for a year. During that time he came close to a massive nervous breakdown. He'd always been a bit of a drinker, and I also think he became an alcoholic during that time—a very young man whose career was completely shattered. Emotionally distraught, unable to get work, he was finally offered a job by the Murphy family, who were editors of the Afro-American newspapers. There were two major Black newspapers at that time, the *Pittsburgh Courier* and this one, which is still in operation today. My father became the editor of the *Afro-American Newspaper* in Philadelphia. At the same time he was offered the opportunity to be pastor of the church where his father had pastored, and that's when he became the minister at Bright Hope Baptist. We were then reunited and began our Philadelphia existence. The trauma of all that had a strong effect on him and his career, and I'm sure on my parents' marriage.

In Philadelphia, we lived at 16th and Jefferson in an all-Black neighborhood. When we moved there in 1950 the neighborhood was working-class. It was long before Blacks were moving into white neighborhoods. The block where I lived was very unique. There were these fabulous brownstones occupied by prominent Black people. Across the street from our house was Hobson Reynolds. He was an undertaker and a very prominent Republican. Next door to us was an AME (African Methodist Episcopal) bishop in a fabulous mansion. Our house had been owned by a white physician before my father bought it. Another house across the street was still owned by whites, who remained there for many years. Next door was a couple who had turned their house into apartments, and he had a pool hall and barbershop on Columbia Avenue. On the other side of him was an architect whose name was Lasayya, a West Indian man married to a Haitian. Their daughter currently is a judge in Philadelphia, and one of their sons is a relatively famous filmmaker. A block away were Raymond and Sadie Alexander. Across the street from them was Dr. Turner, the first Black administrator in the school system of Philadelphia.

My father's church was four blocks away at 12th and Oxford. It was a church of working-class, lower-working-class Blacks, relatively few professionals. It was always between 500 and 1,000 members. It now has on the rolls 2,500 members. My father was pastor for twenty-two years, and my grandfather had been there almost that long before he died. My brother Bill became a minister and has been there almost twenty-five years. He will be the last of the line. None of our children has chosen to go into the ministry, but you never can tell. My grandfather begged my father to come back to the church long before he did.

My father always had a great commitment to educating people and encouraging them. There are some interesting people whose lives he touched—Althea Gibson, the tennis player; Joe Frazier, the boxer who was a member of our church; Lasalle Lufall, a major cancer surgeon at Howard, now president of the American College of Surgeons; Jessie Clark, a member of the City Council in Philadelphia—all of these are people he helped. He also saw that all the young people in our church who had any potential got to college. He sent them all over the country to historically Black colleges. He got people to take them for no money, he got free scholarships, and he would take money out of his own pocket.

In our whole family, everyone was into education. I never intended to go into education as a field. I chose social work because the message passed down from my family was that we were privileged, and therefore we had an obligation to serve others, particularly Black people. There was no emphasis on self, it was that you always paid attention to what other people needed. The road to doing that was to educate yourself. The negative part of growing up in a situation like that was that whatever you did wasn't enough. I remember if I brought Bs home, the question was: "Why weren't they As?" It was much more from my father than my mother.

When I went to Girls High School, there were no Black teachers at all. I was very grounded by Black teachers in elementary school with all kinds of confidence building. I don't remember having any problems with any of the teachers in high school or college, except there were very difficult courses in high school. I don't feel at any time that I was being imposed upon racially in terms of my academic work.

There were two racial incidents in high school that I can recall. One was instigated by the music teacher, Miss Gore. We had chorus after lunchtime. Miss Gore stopped the class and said, "I don't know why all the colored girls are always asleep after lunch." It was very embarrassing, and I went home and told my father. He came up to the school and raised pure hell, and the Black students threatened to quit the choir.

The other incident was when I started applying to college. I applied to all the Ivy Leagues and all the Seven Sisters. The vice principal called me in and wanted to know why I thought I could possibly get into any of those schools. She didn't say anything about race, but she was very discouraging. I went home and told my father, and he came back to the school and laid them out. There were over 100 of us graduating in our class. Only three of us went to Seven Sisters schools. One girl went to Smith, one to Barnard, and I went to Vassar.

When I entered Vassar in 1956 there were only four Black students there, and there were never more than six while I was there. I got into all kinds of discussions at Vassar about race. Many people had never been exposed to Blacks at all, so we were curiosities. During those years the message from my parents was to go and integrate, don't create problems, try and blend. It was long before Black consciousness or Black Power, and as I was leaving Vassar, the civil rights movement was just starting.

In 1960 I organized a picket line at Woolworth's in Poughkeepsie, New York, with several other Vassar students. There had been no active student protests at Vassar since the 1930s until we picketed Woolworth's. It was a big deal, but before we did it we went to visit the dean of women (we called her the warden). Her name was Elizabeth Drewea. To show you how compliant and appropriate we were in those days, we made an appointment to ask her if we could picket Woolworth's! She looked at us (she had been active in the 1930s—Vassar had always had active, social change kind of women), swallowed, and said, "You know, young ladies, in my day no one would ever have asked that question." That was all she would say. We left not knowing if that was a yes or a no. We decided that she meant that in 1930 nobody dared go ask permission to do something they thought was morally correct—they would have just gone and done it.

The Vassar picket line in Poughkeepsie, New York, in the early 1960s

So we went downtown and picketed Woolworth's and created all kinds of stir all over the East Coast. Dean Drewea and the president drove around watching us during the whole time. We found out later they were very proud of us. We were written up in *Time*. *Life* magazine contacted the college, took lots of pictures, and wanted to do a story. It was never published in *Life*, and I'm sure it was because the college thought it might hurt its fund-raising if the conservative Vassar ladies disapproved. But the *New York Times* wrote up a big article. It was the beginning of Vassar becoming somewhat more activist. By 1965 Vassar had begun to take more Blacks and also went coed.

I took a course in the administration of justice my junior year and got sent to the New York Women's Prison, Bedford Hills, to observe. The warden was interested in having young women as role models for the inmates. She offered several of us summer jobs, which was great pay. I went to work for Bedford Hills for three summers. In the course of that time I decided to do social work.

After graduation my father wanted me back home for graduate school. He bribed me with a car, a pale green Ford Falcon, for my Vassar graduation if I went to Bryn Mawr School of Social Work rather than Smith, my first choice. I lived at home until I married Bob in 1965.

A major racial story in my life was my relationship with Dick Taylor. He was the first white guy I really dated. Some-time after the first year at Bryn Mawr, Dick started making overtures to me, and I was floored because he was gor-geous. It became this hot and heavy romance, and I was in love in love in love. My parents were OK with it; they had some comments but they didn't try

Marian Secundy, on the right, with her mother, father, and brother in North Philadelphia, mid-1960s

to do anything to stop it. Dick was involved in the American Friends Service Committee and good causes, and I was following him around like a little puppy. The relationship didn't last more than six months, but during that time I had convinced myself we were going to get mar-ried. Looking at it from Dick's standpoint, I think it was primarily sexu-al regarding his interest in me. This was before the pill, so we never did anything other than very heavy petting, but the passion was definitely there.

Dick was brought up by his father and stepmother. He also had a grandmother who was the real matriarch of the family. He was very dependent upon her approval, and I never met her. That was a big issue. He took me home to meet his father and stepmother. He had a little brother about nine years old. It was a big issue for them to agree that he bring me to dinner. It was like *Guess Who's Coming to Dinner?* His little brother brought a Confederate flag to the table and set it up.

Nobody said a word about it. Everybody was very nice, but neither the mother nor father told the boy to take the flag off the table. These were Quakers too, and Dick never said anything either.

Things started getting tense between us after that. He began to withdraw emotionally. The big reason he used for why our relationship wouldn't work was that I was so grounded in middle-class bourgeois values and he wanted to go live in Harlem and work with the poor. We ended up with him saying we couldn't do this. But the other thing was that he couldn't tell his grandmother. He couldn't get over her disapproval. Shortly after that we broke up, and I had months of sheer agony and grief at Bryn Mawr because our classes were small and he'd be in the room. He eventually married a Jewish woman, so he was able to go that far. That was my awakening experience about interracial dating. Dick just couldn't face up to the fact that with all his ideals and principles, he couldn't cross the line.

The other thing that affected me profoundly was John Kennedy's death. Somehow that was my absolute fall from innocence. That period —King, Bobby, and Kennedy's death—broke my heart. I felt that after that whatever idealism or hope I had just got grounded in reality. I don't think I grieved any more actively for anything than when Kennedy died. I've tried to understand that in the context of what he represented. And it is all that Camelot stuff. We grew up knowing that King was going to die, and he was a very close family friend. We knew it was just a matter of time. I grieved more for John Kennedy than I did for my father's death. It wasn't just a grieving for John Kennedy, but for something that I lost.

When my father died, the one statement I found in his handwriting which I pasted on a book is, "Education is the greatest legacy a man can leave for his family." That was the whole theme of my family. I raised my children, I hope, with the same commitment—but not as strong— about service to others and certainly about education. I didn't discourage them from making money, or from taking care of themselves financially. When I was growing up, making money was a bad thing to do. Bad white people made money. Good Black people don't worry about money. That was implicit in my family. I think it's implicit in whole generations of Black people up until our children. Entrepreneurial activities are also a way of serving, and we weren't taught that at all.

What I see myself doing now, in the last third of my life, is continuing to try and make a difference in educating students around the specifics of certain issues: the dignity of people in health care situations; the importance of adequately communicating with patients; public policy and political involvement; and particularly social change that's related to health care. To me, South Africa represents a great hopefulness, but even there I found I'm much more conservative than I ever thought, more accepting of the gradualism in change in terms of the economic conditions. I found myself talking with some people and thinking I was sounding like Jesse Helms! That's also maybe age.

I try not to be too cynical, I'm still hopeful. I worry about the future for our children in terms of race. The most dramatically horrible significant bifurcation of the Black and the colored populations is economic bifurcation, not racial in the ways that it was. There's always the glass ceiling. The real dividing issues are economic—the haves versus the have-nots that are never going to have. Leon Dash is a Pulitzer Prize–winning author at the *Washington Post.* He wrote a book called *Rosalie: Five Generations of a Black Family*—drug addicts and alcoholics—five generations. I feel very hopeless about that. I can't go out in the street and do anything about these people, nor do I have a desire or ability to play a role in changing that, except at the public policy level. It's a real tragedy.

Despite racial discrimination and racial differences, our children have places to go and things to do that are remarkable. It's up to them whether they do it or not. I tell my children: "Always remember, be vigilant, and learn how to speak up and stand up." ■■■

After spending two years at the Reed Street Settlement House, I decided to complete my master's degree at the Bryn Mawr School of Social Work in community organizing. My first postgraduate job was with the Philadelphia Anti-poverty Action Committee (PAAC), a national program that began during Lyndon Johnson's presidency. PAAC divided the city into twelve geographic service areas. I was responsible for four of them. In a chapter I wrote in *The Field of Social Work,* a textbook used widely in colleges around the country at that time, I said:

> I would encourage an even wider participation of social workers in government programs, for there seems to be an ambivalence in the social work field to "get involved" in programs that operate in the "political arena." Social work, historically, has been heavily concerned with individualized services at some period more than a concern for society—or social consciousness. Today more of the early "community action" aspects are again coming to the forefront. We are not, as a profession, perceptive of the political world in which we

must operate. If social workers are to be relevant, we have to learn the commonalities and differences between social work and political democracy — even if, upon occasion, we might get our fingers burned.

As I reread this statement, it is just as relevant today as it was almost forty years ago.

It was during my first summer at PAAC that I met Barbara Wagner. I can still remember the brightly colored scarf she wore, which matched her bright smile and engaging manner. She had just completed a year of graduate studies in social work in the Midwest and had come home to Philadelphia because her father was dying of cancer.

Her story movingly describes the intense discord between her mother, a strong practicing Catholic, and her father, a strong practicing Jew. Barbara innocently was caught in the middle. It's a story of triumph in what she painfully learned growing up, which was to know your roots and accept others regardless of skin color or what God they chose to worship.

BARBARA WAGNER

I f it's true that a person's values take root in early childhood, I'll need to take you to the home of the Jewish half of my family, where I spent my first eleven years. My parents and I shared space in my father's parents' home, along with two bachelor uncles, assorted animals, and a rather diverse and constant group of day visitors. The home was a large three-story attic row house built in the late 1800s in the Northern Liberties section of Philadelphia—a neighborhood where many eastern European immigrants, primarily from Russia and the Ukraine, had settled during the late 1800s and early 1900s.

My grandmother Sarah was a dominant force in this household, especially for me, being the youngest grandchild and the only girl. Her busy kitchen and tight hugs were a refuge for me whenever I needed to get away from my parents' arguments or my mother's rigid discipline. What an incredible survivor and "earth mother" my grandmother was, although by particular adults whom she considered competitors, such as her brother's or sons' wives, she was considered a tyrant who demanded attention and family loyalty. She had given birth to six sons. Before immigrating to America, her family had been farmers and operated a small inn for travelers, including the czar's military. Among the items they carried with them from Russia was their precious samovar. Aside from its intrinsic beauty, this object represents my heritage, and I cherish it.

My love of gardening comes from watching this "peasant" woman grow anything and everything in her little backyard. Her garden was surrounded by an old wooden fence, which separated it from a trash-filled rear alley. Peach trees and flowers made it a lush oasis and haven for me. My grandfather was a professionally trained singer and musician in Russia and continued to sing and teach here in Philadelphia. Although my grandparents were both Russian Jews, their "cultures of origin" were very different. She was illiterate, and he had been educated. Their marriage was "arranged," as was the custom within the immigrant population.

By the time I was born in 1942, the neighborhood included African Americans and a few Latinos and was a typical working-class community of modest businesses and homes with pockets of dire poverty. The entire area was bulldozed in the late 1950s through the mid-1960s to provide space for light industrial development. My grandparents' home was the very last building to be razed. My parents and I finally moved into our own home. I began to conquer my shyness and even had a best friend who taught me how to ride a bike and play jacks. Unfortunately, my parents' marriage continued to deteriorate, even though they now had the privacy they had been denied for so long.

It's difficult to remember the defining moment when I became aware of racial differences. In second grade I desperately wanted to be included in the jump-rope games that the Black girls played, but my extreme shyness hindered most of my childhood socialization with any children my age— Black or white. I don't remember feeling a sense of

Barbara Wagner and her mother in North Philadelphia, 1944

racial differences. My father and uncles were lawyers, and their clientele included all kinds of people, rich and poor, Black and white. It was not unusual for Black people to be in our house, and I don't remember that the topic of race was discussed in those early years in any derogatory context.

As I entered high school something happened that made me aware of racial differences for the first time. Although I didn't have any close Black friends; I loved R&B and soul music, and collected lots of these records. My white friends didn't share this interest and considered me somewhat strange. Comments were made that questioned my values about race. Until then, I hadn't separated music into "white" or "Black."

It was in college where my consciousness-raising really began. While in the process of changing my major three times, I stumbled into the undergraduate social work program in my junior year. As I realized through psychotherapy in later years, this career choice wasn't so impulsive or arbitrary. Down deep, I felt a responsibility to solve the world's problems.

From my early life experiences as a shy, unhappy, and lonely kid, I always felt an intense sensitivity toward people who were sad, lonely, scared, and poor. So naturally, my first job out of college was as a caseworker with the County Board of Assistance! The scope of poverty I encountered each day was overwhelming, but I was convinced I should continue to help people. After a year I entered Case Western University's social work program to sharpen the skills I needed if I wanted to stay in the profession. This was in 1965.

I had never lived away from home before. It was frightening and liberating. I had two roommates. Liz, who was white, had an electrifying personality and political views that were revolutionary for most of us at that time. She was from New York City, the daughter of a federal judge serving a term in prison. From Liz I learned about the plight and exploitation of migrant farm workers, the immorality of the Vietnam War, the passion of country and gospel music, and how to smoke unfiltered Camel cigarettes. My other roommate was Natalie, who was Black. She came from a fairly traditional middle-class background in Indiana. I honestly and naively didn't think there was anything unusual in our apartment composition. We were just three graduate students living together. We were served an eviction notice three weeks after we moved in because Natalie was Black. It blew my mind and brought me face-to-face with racism. We became the first test case for the new Ohio Fair Housing Law, which we won, and we continued to live in that apartment for the entire year. That confrontation introduced me to advocacy and how it relates to social change. It wasn't enough to feel bad about social conditions. There were corrective actions that could be utilized—policies and laws to be challenged and difficult personal decisions to be made.

My father was ill with colon cancer, so I returned to Philadelphia to complete my second year of graduate school at Bryn Mawr College. Participation in civil rights and antiwar activities was definitely a significant part of my life, but I continued to feel on the periphery. The merits of the need to protest were justified, but I think many of us also participated because it was the "thing to do" and the "place to be seen."

My first job after receiving my master's of social service was with the Philadelphia Urban League. At that time I met Lee, who was the director of their Housing Information Service. I was totally mesmerized by his commitment to social change through fair housing activities and his participation in civil rights activities in the South. He was also an anomaly for me—he had graduated from the Baptist seminary (after getting a college degree in business) and was divorced with a child. In combination, these "negative" characteristics were reason enough for my mother to disapprove of the relationship. My uncles supported my mother's position, especially after their private investigator reported that Lee was a professional "blockbuster" and worked with Blacks. My determination to continue the relationship and our subsequent marriage widened the gap I already felt existed between me and my immediate family.

My religious heritage is Jewish-Catholic. Instead of being encouraged to acknowledge and celebrate this diversity as positive, it became a heavy burden and source of great divisiveness between my parents, and between me and my parents. It sadly lasted until my father's death shortly after I graduated from Bryn Mawr and my mother's death thirteen years later. They never understood the devastating effects of their individual brands of self-righteousness—what a waste of precious time in the name of religion. But it taught me how powerful is the awful feeling of being different, of being rejected, even within your own family, simply because of ethnic, religious, or racial origin. I promised myself that my children would never have to experience that kind of oppression.

Lee and I have three children—two sons and a daughter, ages twenty-seven, eighteen, and twenty-four. It's been hard at times for lots of reasons. As a family we have triumphed over two marital separations, financial problems, addiction issues, illness, and Lee's and my legacy of anger, dysfunction, and depression. But legacies, like people, are complex, and I recognize that the legacy I inherited also

The Wagner family today

contains compassion for people in need, a deep commitment to social justice and knowledge, and a tenacious grip on those things which affirm the joy and beauty of cultural and racial diversity.

I know that Jeremy, Sarah, and Kevin are ready to carry on this legacy with their own children. The culture each is shaping reflects real racial diversity and pride in their own mixed ethnic and religious heritage. When white friends ask me if I am concerned that my kids date Black people, I say no, because it seems a perfectly natural thing for them to do. I think a more important message is what I have struggled with for so many years: "Who am I?" I want them to know their roots, to have respect for who they are because this self-acceptance must precede the capacity to respect other people.

One of the real tragedies today, especially in our urban areas—whether you're Black or white or "other"—is that so many kids don't have knowledge of or feel much of a connection to their family's heritage. There's no past, and the future is too abstract. It's only the present moment with which they can identify. The struggles of our ancestors are really so similar, only the names and faces change.

Do I feel optimistic about the future? On a personal level, I feel hopeful because the human spirit can triumph over most adversities. But on a collective level, I'm not so sure. For thirty-three years I've been working with inner-city residents in Philadelphia as a social worker. I've worked in the fields of housing, job training, juvenile justice, developmental disabilities, community gardening, education, and children's health (lead paint poisoning), and most of the time we've had to confront the devastating effect and legacy of poverty. This society has never liked or trusted poor people. They are "dirty, they smell, and they don't want to work." They remind us of everything negative in ourselves and this society. But instead of removing obvious barriers to self-sufficiency, the country—government and corporate powers—continues to go out of its way to ensure the marginalization of poor people, including the working poor, through a ridiculously low federal minimum wage, unrealistic and short-sighted housing and job-training policies, inadequate and disproportionate funding for public education, and a health system for poor people which actually makes them sicker.

For sure, racism is alive and remains a topic that doesn't make for easy, dispassionate dialogue within any audience. But I believe the pervasiveness of poverty and its insidious ramifications must be confronted. ■■■

Lee Wagner was an "army brat" and lived in many different places in the South and North as a young boy and teenager. Out of this fulcrum he traveled his own unique path, first to a seminary near Boston, then on to the South and the civil rights struggles of the 1960s. In more recent years, he has built and rehabilitated low-income housing in some of Philadelphia's most neglected neighborhoods. He is a quiet, proud man and has grown a deep commitment to his very special family.

LEE WAGNER

I was born in 1940 in Binghamton, New York, and when I was about four years old my father joined the army. He was first stationed in Anniston, Alabama, where the family joined him just before I finished the first grade. We moved to Tupelo, Mississippi, where I started the second grade. I don't remember any African Americans in either place. We then moved to Starkville, Mississippi, a small university town.

My father was a recruiter at the local army headquarters office. The schools were all segregated, so I saw very few Black people. During our first year there, my mother got very sick. The first Negro I knew (as we called Black people back then) was the maid of a white woman who lived across the street. She was sent over to take care of my mother. This woman was very kind and helpful to my mother's recovery. I was very young and not very cognizant about race at the time.

We then moved back to Binghamton, New York, in 1950 during the Korean War. We lived in an old barracks, then moved to an old trailer located at the entrance to a dump, and finally to a new public housing

Lee Wagner, bottom right, and his family in the mid-1940s

project. This was all in the fifth grade—three different schools! My father was in Korea, and due to major surgery that I needed, he was sent home. Then we moved to Henderson, Kentucky, where my father became the company commander of H Company in Fort Breckenridge.

I used to have to walk through a Black community there in order to get to school. I remember the people lived in shacks—wood frame houses on platforms with a cinder block foundation at the four corners. People would sit out on the porch, and whenever I'd go and come from school, they would wave at me and say "Hi," and I'd wave and say "Hi" back. I didn't think twice about it.

My brother and I were considered Yankees when we were going to all these different schools in the South, and people didn't like us. We were in a sense discriminated against. They couldn't stop us from going to the schools because we were white. When we moved to Kentucky and people asked me where I was from, I'd say, "I'm from Kentucky." At that point I didn't want to tell people I was from the North. I always thought that had something to do with my outlook later on and my values.

When we came back to Binghamton in 1953 my father went to Germany. I was in junior high and high school. I played football, and the schools there were integrated. We had Black kids on the team as well as classmates. I don't recall any racial incidents. We had one group of Black friends that used to sing together. They would sing, and we would join in—"the whities"—but we had a lot of fun. Race at that time wasn't a big thing on my mind, and I don't remember a lot of talk about it during my teen years.

I went to college at Syracuse, and when I graduated I went into seminary at Andover Newton outside of Boston. This was 1962. Our ethics professor was Harvey Cox, who was well known at that time. He had just written a book called *The Secular City* and was very involved in the Southern Christian Leadership Conference movement. Several of us students joined with others and went to Selma, Alabama, and participated in marches there. Another professor of ours went with a group just before us. His name was Jim Reeb, and he was murdered in Selma. He was clubbed to death by southern whites.

It was during that experience in seminary when I got involved in social change and racial issues. In 1965 there was a new program in Philadelphia called Metropolitan Associates of Philadelphia (MAP). It was an ecumenical movement that trained theological and lay people to get involved in secular issues. The program was trying to get the church related to society in a new social activist way. The first job I got was with a white real estate broker in West Oak Lane, which at that time was just beginning to undergo racial change. This broker was talking the right talk on the outside, but what he was doing on the inside was soliciting listings—it was a scare tactic kind of thing. White people were fleeing, and most of the sales were to Black families. I exposed this guy in the *Philadelphia Bulletin* by writing a letter to the editor, and he fired me.

I then went to Germantown and started working with a Black real estate broker. He eventually became the first Black representative on the Pennsylvania Real Estate Commission. He also got caught later on using escrow funds in Atlantic City and blew it all! He taught me a lot about the real estate business. Back then it was difficult for Black brokers to get listings, even in Germantown, which was integrated. While I was working with him, the Delaware Valley Fair Housing Council started a new project called the Housing Information Service. They asked if I would be its director. I took the job, and that's when I met Barbara.

The basic purpose of the program was to assist Black families get fair treatment under the fair housing laws so they could buy homes in white neighborhoods, particularly suburban neighborhoods. As time went on, there were fewer people interested in the program in terms of finding housing in white suburban areas. They wanted help with their rental problems, so I was getting more involved with tenants' rights.

Then I was offered a position with the Maple Corporation, one of the first nonprofit development corporations set up outside of a church. We developed housing in some of the poorest Black neighborhoods in Philadelphia: Mantua, Strawberry Mansion, and a new construction project right off the Boulevard at Broad Street. I left there in 1970, and Barbara and I got married. We had a great wedding with lots of people there!

In 1975 the director of the Kensington Development Office asked me if I would come and help him there. I had always wanted to work in a low-income white community, which is what Kensington is. During that time a lot of the affordable housing program funds were directed toward minority communities, where I had mostly worked, and there were considerable populations of poor whites in the city. Now I know why I wouldn't do it again.

There's a great deal of racism in Kensington, and there always has been. We had people threaten us if we sold to Blacks or Hispanics. Even people who worked in the office were racist. People on the board were racist. There was an Asian person on the board who was afraid of having Section 8 clients living next to her, be they Black or white, whatever; she wasn't going to let this happen. Here's an agency that's concerned about affordable housing for everybody. Strange.

I remember my father saying once that "Blacks were going to take over the world." It shows you where he was coming from. We never had any deep conversations about what I did. When it appeared in the newspapers that I was in Selma, Alabama, my mother didn't know whether to be proud or hide in the closet. She was ambivalent about the whole thing, but she probably leaned a little more on the proud side. My parents didn't guide me toward hate. When I look at young white kids in Kensington, there's so much hate of anybody who's different than them.

As a child and young adult, I could never understand why God would like one group and not another group, how the Baptists could be right and the Methodists wrong. I never could accept the concept that just one group was right. I didn't even want to be a Democrat, but in order to vote in primaries, you have to register as something. I don't like to be labeled or be a member of cliques or groups.

I never had any difficult experiences within the Black community, or any minority community. I'm not saying that everybody liked me, but I would walk through houses and down streets and was never harmed. It's not that I don't have any prejudices. If I am angered by something, it doesn't matter if it's a white person or anyone else. Because I'm a self-conscious person, I'm much more reticent to get pissed at a Black person openly, and more likely to repress it than I would with a white person. I'm not a confrontational person either. I know there are a lot of poor whites in Kensington and throughout society who are good people.

When my son Jeremy joined a Black fraternity, I was a little worried. Why was I worried? Because I tended to think that a lot of Blacks also hold prejudice and bias and that what he did was very uncommon. Jeremy was a person who, up until a certain point in his life, didn't even want to play with Black kids. Then in about the sixth grade he made a change and all his friends became Black. I think this bothered Barbara and me, the fact that he went from one extreme to the other. We were living in a racially integrated community and believed in integrated life, and Jeremy was detaching himself, but I don't think it was a racial thing. I think it had a lot to do with his feelings about the quality of my parenting of him. He separated himself a lot from the family, and rightfully so. Our relationship today is much healthier, and I think we have a lot better understanding of one another. All three children date and socialize intimately with racially integrated peer groups.

Thirty years. I can imagine if I were Black: 200 years. Thirty years we've been trying to work to change things, and there are some changes. I still feel that on the whole, this is basically a racist country. I do. There have been some gains, but it's nowhere near where a lot of us dreamed it would be. I haven't given up, but I feel I've done my thing, and now it's up to others to keep pushing. I am disenchanted that the country still seems to be—in the communities, in Congress, in the corporations and businesses—so racist.

Philadelphia is as segregated today as it was thirty years ago, by choice, not by law, as it was in the South. The schools are either predominantly white or Black or Hispanic, and you can't help wondering: how is this really going to change? I don't have any answers anymore.

The best we can do is create the doorways for people to go through. They still have to push. Laws are necessary, but laws don't change people's minds.

When I first went to Selma I was working in a church as an assistant minister in a low-income community. This was around 1964. The minister of the church said to me that change comes very slowly. "You can't just change people overnight." To me that was a cop-out. Today, I look back and say, "Yes, change certainly comes slowly." But I don't regret a moment of my life. It's been very interesting, and I'm proud of it. I didn't make any big marks, but at least I've been a part of something—of history. I don't have to have my name up there. ■■■

Jeremy Wagner, now in his late twenties, is the eldest child of Barbara and Lee. Most, if not all, of Jeremy's friends are people of color. He pledged and was accepted into a Black fraternity in college, a rare experience for a young white man in today's segregated society. His musings and questions about that decision, as well as his difficult but rewarding work as a teacher at Roberto Clemente Middle School, offer a unique opportunity to ponder and better understand the complexities and importance of relating to one another across the color line.

JEREMY WAGNER

Race has played a major part in my life and trying to find myself, who I am. When I was one year old my family moved to Germantown, and we were one of the few white families on the block, let alone the neighborhood. Early on, race wasn't much of an issue for me, because my friends had been supplied to me through school or activities my mother had gotten me involved in. As I got older—as early as seven—I started to hang out with the kids in the neighborhood and on the street.

I was the only white kid, and it wasn't an easy thing. I felt I was definitely the outsider, and in order to fit in I had to figure out who that outsider

Jeremy Wagner as a little boy in Germantown

was. To my friends and their families, a white person was not a good thing. People had had very bad experiences with white people. Early on, I understood slavery and bits and pieces of racism enough to realize I was on the wrong side. Much of the oppression in this country was due to the white man at the time. Even though I had two loving parents who had many friends who didn't seem to fit the "white" image my Black friends and their families were talking about, I felt part of that bad image. It was difficult for me, the guilt of that, and not even understanding a fraction of what that really meant.

As I got into high school there was lots of fighting, lots of male territory, lots of social groups—and because I was white, it was difficult for me. I thought I was a target. It was easy for people to gain their status by finding people that were weaker than them. The color of my skin automatically made people assume I was weak. Getting involved with Black women, which I was, made Black men angry. I'd be at parties and get punched for nothing. I had some very good friends in the eleventh and twelfth grades. I was the only white guy in certain Black circles. Once people realized that I wasn't phony, was just a cool guy and had cool friends, they were willing to accept me.

I went away to college in 1991 at the University of Maryland—a huge school with about 35,000 students, predominantly white, and about 6 percent Black. I have no idea why I chose this school. I didn't know a soul and had to start over with making new friends. When you have a lot of insecurities, which I had, it's hard to start over, so I drifted toward the people I had the most in common with, city Black kids, male and female. I can make surface-level friendships with anybody, but I didn't feel I had anything in common with many of the white students. One was the lack of urban experience—they weren't from a city and the other was that I wasn't white like them. When I would go to places with my parents, like bar mitzvahs or bat mitzvahs, I wasn't white like those people were white. I didn't talk the same, listen to the same music, or talk about the same type of issues. Their lives seemed so much easier than mine and my friends'. I don't say that white people don't suffer because I know they do. I knew my friends had struggles inside of them, and their character was built upon that. As I've grown older I realize that people of all colors have their struggles.

The funny thing is that I look white, but many people assume that I'm other than white. I've been in many conversations where someone will say, "Those white people said, and you know how white people are." Conversations I'm not supposed to be allowed to be in, and people would say to me when they realized I was not Black, "Well, you're not white." Something about my character and personality puts a lot of people at ease from the instant they meet me and they assume that I'm not white. My talk has a lot of slang, and the way I carry myself may throw some people off. If I was lily white "from the door," I would never reach that level of intimacy with people. It's not like spying, but allowing people to let their guard down.

So when I went to college I was looking for new friends and thinking fraternities. I looked into some of the white fraternities and didn't want to click with the guys enough to join, and I had friends back in Philly pledging Black fraternities. I looked into them, and it was what I wanted to do at the time. The main reason I pledged Kappa was to gain acceptance. You had to go through so much physically and mentally, and they were going to accept me. They didn't even know at first that I was white. I went through months of pre-pledging, meeting with them and doing crazy things. When they found out I was white, they called back to Philadelphia to people they knew, and they said, "Oh, Jeremy's cool. He's not trying to be Black, this is just him."

Jeremy Wagner, second from right, with his fraternity brothers at the University of Maryland

So they let me in, but said, "We want you to say that you're Black while other brothers come to visit while you're pledging because we don't want you to get hurt." And I refused to do that. Once I was accepted into the fraternity, I questioned whether I went too far. Had I crossed a racial boundary?

I began questioning what I did and whether I had a right to join a Black fraternity. This and other Black fraternities were started for the sole reason of assisting people who had a lot of disadvantages and who were kept out of not just social groups but any opportunity in college. It was hard to survive financially and mentally, and that's why these organizations were started. At the same time, they were supposed to reach out to the community and give back. The community work I did was my saving grace—you don't have to be a certain color to help, and that's OK.

I made a lot of friendships in the fraternity and learned a lot about myself, especially in terms of race. And I think they learned a lot from me. I went on TV—a cable show—on BET (Black Entertainment Television) about joining fraternities of another race. As I look back on it, I can really see the point. There was one guy who was a member of a different Black fraternity who was really opposed to me. I can understand his argument that these fraternities were formed because Black people couldn't get into anything else. And why should you want to get into this? Why should we let you?

I returned to Philadelphia after college and began teaching at Roberto Clemente Middle School, which is about 85 percent Hispanic and 15 percent African American in a very poor neighborhood. I was told my race would be an issue—a white man in front of a class of all Black and Hispanic students. For me it wasn't an issue, because the kids made me what they wanted me to be. A month or two went by before they figured out that I was white. By this time, race was not as much an issue as my experiences in life were.

For many of the kids, they've had no experiences with white people. I see that at their age how race has separated them totally from America. There's two different worlds going on. The news the kids hear, like the president speaking on different things or the mayor—that's not even real to them. Their news is what's happening in the street. They don't feel deprived of anything because they don't know any better, and I don't know when it's going to change. My kids can't read, and this is junior high. It's quite obvious that slavery was barely a hundred years ago, and if you were looking at a book back then, you were killed. Reading isn't important in the homes of my children. One is that their parents can't read. I'm not saying these kids want to be dumb, but they've learned to survive without reading, and their world is not one in which they have to read. They don't know how many opportunities are being closed to them. The government must play a much bigger role in teaching people how to read. It's the key to finding freedom or not. To be heard you need to have the skills to read and write.

I worked in a school that was predominantly white, and the kids were very very prejudiced. I'd see a kid in September, and by June he's calling a kid "nigger this and faggot that," and he'd say, "My dad taught me that," and I'd tell him, "You're wrong and your dad's wrong." He'd look at me as if to say, "Who are you to say that something my father told me is wrong?" That school was in Kensington–Port Richmond, and now I teach in the Puerto Rican part of the neighborhood. They're right next to each other, but worlds apart. Both are very poor, but there's a difference in how they look at their poverty. The white people seem to be saying, "We're poor, but we're not supposed to be poor. Something happened here. We got in the wrong line and were jerked off." And the Black and Puerto Rican people accept they're poor because they're Black and Puerto Rican. As proud as they are individually, these social mecha-

Jeremy Wagner, standing third from right, with his junior high school
students on a field trip

nisms have been instilled in their minds that they accept the life they
are living. The everyday survival of getting up and taking care of your
kids is so hard that on some issues they have to back down and accept
their place in these neighborhoods—and that's terrible. No one is coming in to save them, and every day they're being more and more
ignored.

Physically, from living in these neighborhoods, my kids have asthma, lead poisoning, chronic illnesses where they're out four days a
week, or a family member so sick they have to stay home and take care
of them. I've got one girl whose entire extended family—sixty-nine
people—were indicted when she was about seven years old. It was the
first million-dollar crack corner here in Philadelphia, and they arrested
the whole family except for one seventeen-year-old aunt and little
Marilyn. Now Marilyn has to take care of her at the same time dealing
with her mom and everybody being in jail. Her mom was supposed to
get out last Christmas and was given twenty-five years more for stab-
bing somebody. Sitting right next to Marilyn is Aguardo, who is thirteen
and has to do everything for his father because he was shot and para-
lyzed from the waist down.

One of the reasons I know so much about my kids is because I've
made friends with them and have gone into their lives. It's incredibly
painful for me, but because of that I see their struggles. Many people

don't understand what it's like to be African American or Hispanic in Philadelphia and live in these poverty-stricken neighborhoods—and they're poverty stricken based on race.

My race has afforded me many privileges—I'm talking about all the things that have happened since birth: my mom putting a book in front of me, my family not being in and out of jails and not having severe illnesses. My mom fought to get me into the best public schools in the city, and that's what saved me.

Philadelphia is very segregated. It's either all Black or all white. When I go out now that I'm older, all of my close friends are Black, because these are the people I've grown close to over the years. But they're not secure enough in themselves and worry about what people are going to think about being with a white guy, or what my family will think about me bringing home a Black woman.

When I went to school, kids were graduating from high school. My kids get tuxedos and limousines to their eighth-grade graduation because that's likely their last graduation. Most of my kids don't go past tenth grade. You're allowed to drop out when you're sixteen, and the schools would never tell you this, but I think they encourage it.

The entire educational structure of this country needs to be changed. The way schools and districts are structured now goes back to the industrial revolution. They were set up by factories, and that's what the kids are. They're a product and are turned out. The teachers are the assembly-line workers, the principal is the supervisor, and the superintendent the CEO. That's fine as long as you want to make robots, and as long as those robots do their jobs. The problem is that in the 1990s these robots you're turning out are not equipped, even the white ones. They are not prepared to use their advantages to help people who are disadvantaged.

The pain that people of color feel about themselves—being ashamed about not being part of white America. I don't want to be part of white America, and neither do they, but the fact that they're kept out of it hurts.

I think the everyday person's mind is becoming more open to the acceptance of different races, but until major things happen, like equal education for everybody, nothing will change. I've personally enjoyed the diversity of the different races I've known and wouldn't have it any other way. It's made me a stronger person and so much more in touch with myself. It's still an issue with me. ■■■

Jeremy's teaching experiences prompted me to think back on my early years as a student in three San Francisco public schools — light years away in time, race, and class, but uncomfortably close in terms of our racial isolation and what we were taught and not taught.

At Commodore Sloat Grammar School, Aptos Junor High, and Lincoln High School, there were no teachers or students of color in any of my classes. I don't recall any lessons or discussions about race in school. I was thrilled with my fourth-grade teacher, Miss Smith, a large, plain woman who always wore black dresses down to her ankles and sturdy black shoes. She would read us adventurous stories of pioneers (read "white pioneers") moving west to California and Oregon, and I longed to be in one of their wagons. No one ever explained why the Indians were outraged at these intruders on their ancient and, in many places, sacred lands. In high school I received an A+ on a major paper about Hitler and the Holocaust, feeling the pain of that era in my bones. But I learned nothing about Native Americans, slavery, or what the Civil War was really about. I loved Lincoln in a naive way because he "freed" the slaves. I learned nothing about Reconstruction, the thousands of lynchings into the twentieth century, Jim Crow in the South, and segregation in the North. I was taught "white" history, draped in unspoken superiority, no questions asked or pondered. Through self-education, friends, and life experiences, I continue to learn a more balanced and honest history. I've learned, for example, what the Civil War was really about — and how it's still not over.

Jeremy's students are mainly Hispanic or Black, all very low income, all living in one of Philadelphia's poorest and most neglected communities. All the members of my extended family are middle class and white, including my brother's wife and children and my eight cousins and their children. Like 98 percent of white American families, we grew up in white neighborhoods; most of us attended primarily white schools and, except for me, did not marry outside our racial boundaries.

I didn't think about race when I was growing up, or about the privilege of wearing white skin. The idea of having to think about who I was "racially" was simply not part of my consciousness. It has only been in recent years that I've begun to better understand the meaning of the term "white privilege." As a result of that growing comprehension, I have a responsibility — without guilt — to address that privilege and what it means to people of color who do not have that privilege.

I was delighted, after returning to San Francisco in 1985, to attend an Aptos Junior High School reunion organized by one of the students in my class of 1954. There were only a small handful of us there from that old era, all white, as were the other alumni in the auditorium that day. I played in the orchestra from 1951 to 1954, a very shaky second violinist. Almost forty years later, on the same old auditorium stage, there was a much larger and multicultural orchestra—Black, Caucasian, Latino, Filipino, Asian—an extraordinary and hopeful change.

Sarah Wagner is the second oldest child of Barbara and Lee, and their only daughter. She is one of the most creative young women I've ever met. When she was at Columbia University in New York City, she was often thought to be Latina. She did her senior thesis on how Americans with mixed heritage self-identify. Her story addresses several key issues: Why do we need to label ourselves at all? Why is everyone so interested in who we are racially? Does it really matter?

Sarah continues to live in New York and is pursuing a career in dance and theater.

SARAH WAGNER

One of the biggest frustrations I've experienced in my twenty-four years has been trying to live by my own beliefs, that a person's race should not matter in a society that is totally consumed by the issue of race. My personal experiences with race began at an early age. My brothers and I grew up in Germantown, which is a predominantly African American neighborhood. Being one of two white families on the street, I could not help but be conscious of my race. I remember walking one day with one of my best friends from the street, when I heard two men walking behind me. One guy commented to the other how unusual it was to see something like us—a young white girl and a young Black girl, obviously friends, hanging out together. That was one of the first incidents that brought the larger issue of race home to me. I was aware that my friend and I were different races, but I hadn't realized how other people noted the difference—and that maybe it was unusual.

I also became aware of the difference between my school friends and my home friends and who I was in each environment. I went to a public grade school and had a fairly diverse group of friends. It was when some of these friends (mostly white) commented about the way

I acted that I realized something was different about the way I was growing up. My school friends said I had a tough-girl image they didn't really understand. I felt at times like I had to be two different people in order to fit in everywhere. There was the "Street Sarah," who hung out with her friends in the neighborhood, and there was "School Sarah" with these other friends. Looking back, I see that part of my toughness was growing up with two brothers, but also having to show that I could hold my own on a block where I was one of only a few white people.

Sarah Wagner as a little girl in Germantown

The older I got, the more race became an issue. As a child you can be somewhat oblivious. By the time I got to high school, race, racism, racial divides were all smack in my face, whether I wanted it to be or not. Although my high school was racially and ethnically diverse, groups tended to segregate themselves to a certain extent. I really tried to weave throughout different crowds and was fortunate to have a lot of friends from different backgrounds. Maintaining these friendships was not always easy. For example, with the Black community at school there were times I felt self-conscious because I was white, but not the idea of what a "white" person was. Growing up in Germantown had a huge influence on my interests, my style, everything. In terms of music, dress, etc., my older brother and I leaned more toward "Black" culture. The Black community at school was one in which I had to show I could fit in. Since my brother was referred to as "the Blackest white guy at Central High," people had some idea of what I might be like also.

It's difficult to talk about these things, because I don't want to overgeneralize. It was not an ongoing situation where I was hyperaware of my race or where I really made a concerted effort to fit in. What was most important to me was that people knew me as an open, easygoing person with lots of different interests who can get along with, and understand, all different kinds of people. I didn't want people to think of me in terms of my race because I didn't think of them in terms of theirs.

Up until that point, it was a very Black-white issue. Then when I got to college, a funny thing happened. All of a sudden, everybody thought I was Latina. I've been mistaken for just about everything. A taxi driver once asked me if I was Japanese, but I think he needed glasses! There is such a large Hispanic community in New York, especially up around Columbia where I was a student, people just assumed that was where I was from. Unless someone asked me and found out I wasn't Latina, the assumption was that I was.

It was at this point I really began to be aware of myself and my identity. When you first get to college, everybody is trying to meet everybody and find a crowd to fit into and find people like them. Everybody was asking me, "What are you and where are you from?" It caught me off guard, because before then I hadn't really ever been questioned about my ethnicity or race. Because I had grown up weaving among these different crowds and feeling like a part of every crowd, as far as I was concerned, I was from Philly, and that's all there was to it.

But as far as most others were concerned, that definitely was not all there was to it. The term *multicultural* was everywhere and on everyone's mind. At least once a day, every day, someone would ask me, "Where are you from? Are you Puerto Rican? Are you Mexican? Cuban, right?" I'd say, "I'm from Philly." "No, you know what I mean." Of course I knew what they meant, but it bothered me that it was so important to them to know—that before they knew anything else about me, they had to categorize me according to my ethnic or racial ancestry. At first I wanted to play a game with them and say, "What do you mean?" to which they'd respond, "Come on, you know what I mean." Nobody wanted to come out and say, "Are you Black? Are you white? Are you Hispanic?" because they knew it sounded tacky and inappropriate. But if it's so important for you to know this information, you should come right out and ask your question. If you don't want to say what you mean because it seems inappropriate, perhaps it is and you shouldn't be asking in the first place.

Don't get me wrong. I don't have a problem with people asking me about my background, and I am happy to share what I know about it. If I felt that someone was truly interested, then I would go into detail. Otherwise, I'd just say, "I'm a little bit of everything." For those who really pursued it, I'd say, "Well, what I know of for sure is Russian, Polish, English, French, German, Native American," and they'd say, "Wow, no Puerto Rican? No Spanish? You're sure?" I even had people who thought I was just denying it, that the Latino ancestry was there and I didn't want to accept that part of myself. To them I could only say, "Who knows, maybe you're right, I probably am a little bit of everything." But in my head I thought, "Can this line of questioning get any more ridiculous?" And then it did. After the "denial" of my Latina heritage, the next thing people would latch onto was the Native American in my blood. As if it were a fad to be a certain minority. When I'd rattle off my ethnic list, they'd say, "Oh, you're Native American." That is the smallest part of my background, and people would want to know, "What side of the family? What tribe?"

I was able to see how people view race by the questions they were asking. I felt they were looking for a way to make me acceptable. That made me wonder, "If it wasn't for the Native American part, would you walk away from me? Are you questioning whether you should be associated with a white person?" It became this absurd exercise in pigeon-holing—all these labels that don't explain or describe anything. All they do is keep us separate from each other.

Groups at college tended to segregate themselves into their own communities more than in high school. I seemed to fit in with everybody because they couldn't quite figure out who or what I was. My immediate group of friends was very mixed. We would throw parties and invite everybody from all different circles, and we prided ourselves in bringing these different groups together. People who ordinarily would never hang out in the same place were having fun together, and it was great.

It was at this time at school that my experiences with race really took a turn. Because so many people thought I was Latina, and because I spoke Spanish, I automatically fit into that crowd. That meant I was also accepted by the Black community, and all the minority crowds. That was fine with me, because in terms of interests, those were the crowds that I had the most in common with and wanted to hang out with. At the same time, it was a head trip because I knew that if some of these people knew that I was of European extraction, things would be a lot different. I tried not to take it and myself too seriously in all of this, because it would make me crazy. I certainly did not want to develop a complex about race. But it was strange, and I found myself playing up to the part to a certain extent—not to do anything out of the ordinary to appear to be Hispanic, but not downplaying anything, either. As far as I was concerned, if you're going to assume something about me without bothering to find out the truth, then that's on you. It was like reverse "passing."

Sarah Wagner, on the left, with two Columbia University friends

One of my classmates at school was half Cuban, and she liked the fact that I was often mistaken as a Latina. She started to encourage me to play it up. I didn't like that it had gotten to that point and began questioning myself and my own identity. "What does race mean to me, and do I not want to be white? Do I like that people mistake me for somebody else?" All this started coming to me, and it was really heavy. One day I heard a woman speaking on a radio show about her experiences with race. She was a very light-skinned Black woman who had fit into the white community for a long time on the same "don't ask and I won't tell" premise. She had just written a book admitting she was Black and pretending to be white. This really hit home, because I wasn't exactly pretending to be Latina, but I wasn't not pretending either. It bothered me that I found myself connecting more with a people I don't have in my background, and wasn't connecting with my Russian or Polish ancestry. I now feel a responsibility to find out more about my own heritage.

It was these personal experiences that led me to the topic for my senior thesis, which was how college-age Americans of mixed heritage self-identify. I quickly found out that I was not alone in my frustration and annoyance with a society that insists on labeling its members. All the students in my paper expressed that they didn't want to be Black or white or Latino—they just wanted to *be*. They wanted to be accepted and understood for who they were as individuals, not just for what race they were. But this society pressures, if not forces, us to identify ourselves according to our race and ethnicity, as if saying that you are white or Black actually says something about who you are on the inside. Writing this thesis and talking with people who turned out to have similar views as me has helped me feel a little better about the whole situation. I now know I was not totally ridiculous or idealistic to want to be known for who I was as an individual.

I would like to be optimistic about race, but I'm not. In terms of my own identity and resolving my feelings about it, I feel optimistic. I will continue to grow and learn about myself and my heritage, as well as continue to have all kinds of friends, and work with people from all different backgrounds. But on a broader level, I feel the situation has gotten completely out of control. The racial paradigm operates on such a subconscious level that people are hardly aware of all its repercussions. People do not realize that words like *race* and *ethnicity* are used to represent concepts that our society has constructed. They are the creation of a culture that felt the need to label and separate to justify other actions, such as slavery.

If you look at historical sources, race has never been an objective scientific classification of human group variation. It is a sociocultural phenomenon that is separate in concept from biophysical variation. Words like *race, ethnicity,* or *nationality* don't have a solid, scientific definition, yet we continue to use these categories to separate and judge one another. The prevalence of this belief system, the adherence to these categories, leads me to be pessimistic about the future of race in our society. I want to think that things can improve, but if we haven't been able to learn from history by now, will we ever? Do people really want to? I don't believe society is ready to commit to changing things. If you see society as a human body, racism and all the issues involving race are so in the gut. They flow through the whole bloodstream of this body. It is an extremely self-destructive system. ▪▪▪

Kevin Wagner is the youngest child of Barbara and Lee and was a drama student at Syracuse University when we talked. Like his sister, he is also pursuing a career in the theater. As a sensitive young white man, he continues to struggle with racism and what to do about it.

KEVIN WAGNER

The first thing I remember as a young kid growing up in Germantown is that I had three very close friends, two were African American and one was biracial. I went to an elementary school that was predominantly Black. As a young child, I couldn't recognize the fact that most of my friends were Black. They were just my friends, and we connected on the same vibe.

When I was in the fifth grade, we moved from Germantown into another predominantly Black neighborhood. I was the only white kid in the class, which was very tough at times. It was hard for them to deal with me as the only white kid. It was also difficult because we were connecting on the same level and had the same experiences in many ways.

The next year I moved to a junior

Kevin Wagner, second from left, and friends in a Germantown park

high school that was mixed but predominantly white. Kids came from all over the city to that school. There were kids from low-income families, white kids coming with their issues, and African Americans with theirs—and sometimes these things clashed. Despite the fact that this school was much more diverse, the majority of my closest friends were still African Americans, because I felt more comfortable being around Blacks. In seventh grade my friends became more mixed, more diverse. That was hard, because a lot of my African American friends accused me of "selling them out." Eventually that ceased, and we all became friends. It came to a point where I had to have a diverse group of friends, but there was still that bridge that was hard to cross. A lot of my white friends' parents were raised in certain ways, and that teaching fell upon their kids.

When I was around thirteen years old I had a white friend who lived in Port Richmond in North Philadelphia. Feelings of racism and hate toward other people run deep over there. Most of the white kids in my junior high school were from that area, and their stereotypes carried over into the classroom. One night I decided to sleep over at my friend's house. During the late evening I hung out with him and one of his friends from the neighborhood. We sat outside on the train tracks across from his house and shared a forty-ounce beer that his friend had stolen from his dad. During the next hour I had to listen to this kid vomit out derogatory comments about anyone who wasn't white. I remember feeling very ashamed of myself and not able to look him in the eye. I felt ashamed because I was too scared to say anything. Then he made a comment about Jewish people, and my friend broke out into laughter and told his friend I was Jewish. He actually apologized, although it wasn't very heartfelt. Then he said, "But you don't act like a Jew." After that, I didn't visit my friend that much. I'm still very hesitant to go to Port Richmond because I fear I might actually say something back next time.

I went to Abraham Lincoln High School in Northeast Philadelphia, which is a predominantly white neighborhood, but they brought kids in from all over the city. In high school the white kids sat at their table, the Latino kids sat at their table; everybody stayed with their own groups, which was sad because that wasn't the type of environment I wanted to be in. Most of my friends were white. (Now my closest friend here in the neighborhood is African American.) I did have other friends in high school who were African American, but because of the low level of trust, we couldn't make the full connection. I would see this and want to take a step forward but couldn't. Sometimes you can't step over those boundaries.

Now I'm at Syracuse University. Syracuse is predominantly white and very upper class. That's difficult to deal with also, because my family never had a lot of money. We were always a little above most of my friends, which was tough, because I always felt a bit guilty. Now the tables are turned at school, and I'm the one who's broke all the time or out there with a job. I'm on my own—half and half. (I'm living by myself, and my parents are still paying for it!)

I'm in the Drama Department, which is almost all white. In my freshman class there were three students of color out of about fifty of us. What I've been exposed to now is dealing with homosexuality, because there's a lot of gays in the department. That was new for me, having to deal with my own homophobia because I was never exposed to that. Just like race, you have to look beyond the issue and accept them as persons. I still find myself at times more comfortable around African Americans, but I don't try to limit myself. I try to seek out as many friends as possible of different nationalities. I have a Lebanese friend at school for the first time.

Times are changing for the better, but I think racial groups need to make things stronger in their own communities first to bring out awareness for themselves. After that's done, maybe we can all come together as a whole. We can't forget the past—it's there—but we need to move on.

I have one white friend who lives in a predominantly Hispanic neighborhood. He feels a lot like I do. There's no need to judge people. We all bleed the same color. I have Black friends who were so comfortable with me they forgot that I was white. They'd say something about white people, and I'd say, "Now wait a minute, man," and they'd say, "Kev, you're a Black guy trapped in a white guy's body." We try to make a joke about it, but I think sometimes that's pushing it behind. We're not really dealing with it. People need to talk.

Race is always going to be an issue. We can't forget it, but at the same time we have to become equal. We have to learn from each other, or nothing is going to change. ■■■

I met Nancy Chisholm in 1965 when she and I lived in Powelton Village, near the University of Pennsylvania in West Philadelphia. Through her later position at the Department of Housing and Urban Development (HUD) in Washington, D.C., where I also worked, she created the Section 8 housing program that secured safe and affordable housing throughout our country, a pivotal program for thousands of limited-income families.

Terry, her first husband, died many years ago. Visually, he and Nancy were definitely an interracial couple. However, they held very similar values, even though their families' economic and social histories were worlds apart. Nancy and her second husband, Ed, whom she met at HUD, now live active lives in the New York Adirondacks.

NANCY CHISHOLM

My parents had the ultimate mixed marriage, because the ultimate mixed marriage is a profound cultural difference. My mother was from a family that came to this country in 1640. She had ancestors who fought in the American Revolution, ancestors who founded the small town that we lived in, Greenville, Pennsylvania. It was about midway between Pittsburgh and Erie and seven miles from the Ohio border. Her father was president of the bank and president of the country club. She was an only child. Her mother was a social butterfly. You couldn't be more "crème de la crème" in a little town of 9,000 people. She went to a finishing school, then on to Thiel College, which was the local college.

My father was the assistant football coach. He was first-generation American who spoke only German until he was fourteen years old. He went to Springfield College, which was the YMCA college, on a football

Nancy Chisholm, on her mother's lap, with her family in the early 1940s

scholarship, then went to work at Thiel. He was coming from the bottom end of American society, if you will, and she was from the top end. The feeling we children got from that marriage is that those things didn't matter. What mattered was your individual integrity and your individual choices. There was no one right way to live your life, but you had to be true to yourself.

Our town was very white. There was one Black family that I knew when I was growing up, and another family I knew later. Race wasn't an issue because there were so few Black families. There were a few Jewish families. My mother was close to one of the Jewish families, and I was close to another as I grew up.

I got my graduate degree from the University of Pennsylvania with a scholarship from the Lutheran Church. My notion was that I'd teach in Lutheran colleges. When I graduated from Penn, I realized that all the Lutheran colleges were in the boonies. I came to Philadelphia for the first time when I was twenty-one years old and liked it. I did volunteer work with kids at a church and visited the ghetto, which was right next to where I lived. Not wanting to move to the boonies, I asked the Lutheran Church, "What else could I do to pay off my debt to you?" I became a Christian education worker in a church in Philadelphia—in fact, two churches. I worked half-time in a church in Mantua, which was a very-low-income Black community, and half-time in a church in West Philadelphia, where most of the older people were white but all of the young families were Black. I worked mainly with the teenagers there— six days a week, long ten-hour days, with Black folks. I learned a lot from them. They were wonderful people with incredible courage, particularly the folks in the ghetto. What it took to survive in Mantua was a lot. Of course, I was wet behind the ears, didn't know a goddamned thing, but I could admire them and try to be a support for them.

I did that work for about a year. I then spent three months in Europe volunteering in children's camps in southern Germany and Belgium. When I was in Belgium I went to a museum in Brussels, where I saw a Reubens painting of Black faces and began to cry because, to me, home was Black faces. My life was with Black people, and I was homesick. What that tells you is that you can identify across the races just like that! There's nothing to it. They're people. We're all people.

When I came back from Europe, I went to the Bryn Mawr School of Social Work. I realized you had to have a master's degree to get a decent job in social work, right? I ended up at the Commission on Human Relations for my second-year internship. I worked on fair housing issues, which was a tremendous challenge. After my degree I stayed on, and a year later I was the fair housing director. We did wonderful, successful stuff—not just that we were good-hearted, but we accomplished a lot. We made a major impact on the level of discrimination in the rental market in Philadelphia—a major impact.

At that time I fell in love with Terry, who was my boss. I respected him a great deal. He was a bright man. He was also, for me, a rock. He came from a family who knew who they were. They had a dignity, a self-respect that was so impressive. I loved him almost instantly. Really, literally. It had to do with his way of approaching problems and his intellect—and his height! I remember talking with a secretary who was sitting at her desk. I was looking down at her, and there was this voice beside my right shoulder, and I turned around and stared directly into somebody's chest. I said, "God, he's tall." And that was it. I fell in love with him instantly. I didn't think, "Oh my God, he's Black." I just thought, he's so tall, and that wonderful voice. I got to know him over the months, and I loved him. It just wasn't a big deal that he was Black.

I called up my father to say, "I'm about to marry a Black man," and my father, who had no experience with race, asked, "How Black is he?" How do I answer his question? Of all the stupid things, I said to him, "Well, he's darker in the summer than he is in the winter." Isn't that stupid? What should I have said? He's coffee with two creams? Or one cream? My father didn't know how to react to my answer either, but he wasn't particularly negative about it.

When I told my sister, with whom I'm very close, she said, "They smell, don't they?" You got the picture. My family had no understanding whatsoever, so I said, "Well, not if they take showers." My sister was always very gracious when we visited her home, and she was fine.

Nancy and Terry Chisholm on their wedding day, 1969

When my son Brad was born, there was no problem either. My older brother, who is kind of the odd man out in our family, said, "What about the children?" I understood what he was saying, and I said, "What about them?" In those days—I was married in 1969—people said things like that.

Terry's first wife thought she was too goddamned upper middle class to have anything to do with Terry's family in Georgia. From the time they were married (which was many years before) he had had no contact with his family. None, which to me was awful. So before we were even married, we got an invitation to his sister Ann's graduation from Howard. Terry's father was married three times, and his third wife was Terry's age. His sister was his father's daughter by his third wife. So I said to Terry, "We gotta go. You don't just ignore invitations like this." D.C. isn't very far from Philadelphia, so we went. Ann was blown away. She didn't know that I was white, but we were there. Her brother was there, too. There was a huge age difference between Ann and Terry. She's now forty and Terry would be about eighty.

When Brad was born, I said to Terry, "This kid's got to have grandparents. They're important in a kid's life, and I want Brad to have connections with his Black side and the South." Terry had nothing to do with his father or stepmother in all this time. I said, "We're going down to visit them." So we went and had a fabulous time. They lived in Quitman, Georgia, a tiny town outside of Valdosta, and we drove down and stayed with his father and stepmother.

The stepmother's son lived across the street, and they threw a big party for their generation. Here I was with all these Black folks. I was close to thirty then, with long blonde hair below my shoulders, and this adorable little baby that was sort of light. Everybody had to come stare at me and stare at this baby. They were very friendly and very nice—but they did look very hard! I brought Terry back to his family, so I think I came with three-star credentials because of that.

Terry's sister-in-law was great, and I liked her a lot. I had to go to the drugstore and pick up something for her, and her family ran a tab there. "You just tell them you're picking up something for the Chisholms," and I said, "Laura, you've got to be joking—they'll take one look at me." "No, no, it's all right," she said. "Everybody in town knows. It's all right." It was true, because I walked into the drugstore and said, "I want to pick up something for Laura Chisholm." "Oh yes, we have it." The color barrier was nothing. Everybody in town knew that this crazy-assed northerner Terry had married this white chick, by God. But the sister-in-law's prescription—that's just fine.

The people there were great, but they did tell me there was a Black teenager who was dating a white girl and they were murdered, burnt up in their car not very long before we were there. They said, "It's all right. You're from away. You're going away." We weren't invading the local mores. The year was 1971. I had mental images of that scene the whole time I was there.

On our way home we stopped for take-out food at a restaurant. The people looked at me and looked at Terry, and here was this adorable little kid running around. I swear they thought we were weird. These people had a very different set of values. They were saying, "Holy shit, how do I relate to this? These people are well behaved, well spoken, their kid's adorable, but they're breaking everything I ever believed in my whole life." You could see that in their eyes.

When we moved to Washington, D.C. in the early 1970s, Terry and I both worked for HUD, which then had about 3,000 employees. He became the area manager in Washington and had a swearing-in ceremony. There I was with Brad as an infant, and a lot of people in HUD's central office had no idea I had any relationship with Terry. There was a lot of "Oh, we didn't know you two were married," but it wasn't hostile.

I've talked with Brad a few times about him being biracial. He sort of doesn't identify with either race. Race for him has not ever been a big issue. He's been raised in a biracial society because he went to Capitol Hill Day School, where there were Black kids as well as white kids, and tolerance is obviously a value. In high school he went through some dif-

ficult things, but none of them had anything to do with race. Then he went to Antioch, which is an incredibly liberal college, and race wasn't really an issue there. When I ask him what race he really identifies with, he says, "Either one, it really doesn't matter." He's into his own stuff, which is fantasy and role-playing, and that's another world of its own. The woman he married is white, and her mother is southern and doesn't seem to know that Brad is half Black. I wasn't about to tell her. That's for them to say. It's certainly none of my business.

Nancy and Terry Chisholm at HUD in Washington, D.C., in the early 1980s

When Brad was little, I wanted to teach him that he was a Black child, to understand that he has that history—that it's important. His grandfather was the first Black person to run for public office in Brook County, Georgia. He lost, but he did run. He was also a deacon in his church and a very important person in the Black society at that time—important in terms of aspirations and dignity—an elegant person. I told Brad all of this, and when he was a baby, in the middle of the night when you're rocking a baby and you want him to go to sleep and you sing to him, I used to sing the Black national anthem to that baby! Over and over and over again.

Terry and I came from very similar backgrounds—law-abiding middle-class church folks when it came down to it. We both had master's degrees from Ivy League colleges. My parents had a much larger cultural difference than Terry and I did. My father came from Germany and didn't speak English until he was fourteen. He grew up in a German ghetto in Reading, Pennsylvania—culturally very different from my mother.

A long time ago Terry and I tried to figure out who Brad looked like. We stood in front of a mirror and I said, "Well, our noses aren't very different, and our mouths are similar—yours might be a little bit fuller than mine, but mine's full, too. Our eyes look pretty much the same. The color is different, but otherwise we do look pretty much the same."

I do believe Terry and I were something special—special in the sense of making a declaration of what the world should be like. What we were saying is that race is not a barrier in human relationships, and that people who were important to us, people we respected and admired and loved, could be our special friends regardless of what else was going on. We were able to relate to the individual and care about the individual, and they cared about us—and that's what was important.

Race was an intellectual fascination in the 1960s—Black folks weren't, but the context was. I think we need to pay more attention to the 1960s, what people were willing to be open to. We're not as open to that stuff now as we used to be. People look down on the 1960s as an aberration of American history. While that's true, on the other hand, what happened then is so important in American history because we were open in an egalitarian way that hasn't happened since then or before then, either. Lord knows we need it again.

We have a worldwide problem with intolerance. People are not raised with the kind of self-confidence and independence and security that they need to have, which has nothing to do with ethnic identity, but with their own skills and abilities as individuals to be able to function in this world. It's happening all over the world that people have to look down on somebody, have to hate somebody, have to think that somebody is not as good as they are in order to feel valuable.

In this country, there really are two Black communities—the middle-class community and the poor community. The middle-class Black community is very much like the middle-class white community, but poor Blacks are different—different from other Blacks, too. It's not a color difference, it's a cultural difference that has to do with poverty, welfare, education, everything. I just don't see middle-class Blacks as being different.

Children should be raised understanding how valuable they are as people, and for me, the Black/white in America is a really big deal. But you also have this thing in Bosnia, where they all look exactly alike and where we couldn't possibly tell them apart—Muslim and Christian—and lots of people are being killed. There's hardly any cultural difference at all from our perspective, and there's hardly any cultural difference between Black and white, either. It's that we're not raising our children with a sense of personal security, that they are who they are and are valuable. ▪▪▪

I met Jim Kelch and his wife Bev in 1965, when Jim and I were graduate students at the Bryn Mawr School of Social Work. We've been friends ever since. After a six-year struggle with failing health, Bev died in 1997. Jim continues to mourn her, as evidenced in the following poem he gave me:

"Death will not come as an unexpected visitor, nor shall his attentions be seen as unwelcome release. For to live after you my love (My Bev) is but to die. May 14th, 1999."

Bev was definitely the organizing principle in Jim's life. She was the dramatic and talented extrovert, and Jim the pipe-smoking, thoughtful professor, a good and lasting match. How Jim met and courted Bev is the heart of his story, confirming that there is magic in how some people can connect and make that connection bloom through the years. Bev left behind Jim, their three beautiful children, and a grandchild — now two grandchildren.

Jim clearly connects the twin issues of racism and classism and veers from being hopeful to very disheartened about these critical issues facing our country today.

JIM KELCH

I was born in Philadelphia on June 9, 1938. My earliest recollections are as a young kid during the Second World War. I remember strange things like the ration tickets to get food and how you had to get the little pills to make the margarine yellow. I went to schools in Philadelphia. I started Central High School in 1952 and graduated in 1956. That period at Central shaped me intellectually in terms of what my goals and ambitions were. I lived in a working-class neighborhood in Germantown, right off Germantown Avenue. It was an integrated neighborhood—predominantly Black but there were white families in the neighborhood. There was not a whole lot of interaction between the families, but as I recall, civil, friendly. I remember Mrs. Casey—she and her husband lived across the street from us, and she was an elevator operator at Central and very proud of me going there.

I went to Emlen Elementary School at Chew and Upsall. It was roughly 70 percent white and 30 percent Black. At Central High School the racial disparity was pretty acute. In my class of about 260 guys, there were fewer than 10 Blacks. There were subtle racial dynamics going on. I don't remember being personally victimized by any blatant act of racism. My father had said to me, "You're probably going to have to work twice as hard as the white boys," and I said, "Well, that doesn't seem right to me, but if that's what it takes!" So it wasn't that I was questioning the injustice of that. Blacks knew that the cards were stacked that way, and if you were going to succeed academically, you would have to resign yourself to the fact that you would have to work harder. You couldn't wallow in self-pity and talk about "isn't it terrible, and it's not fair." That's why at times I get so disheartened and frustrated with young Black people today when they talk about "it's not fair!" and I say, "Who the hell said it was fair?"

My dad and mom never had the benefit of a higher education. They both grew up in South Carolina, and in their time, education for Blacks went up to the eighth grade, if that far, and that was it. Before I was born my father owned a bakery, and he was functioning as an entrepreneur. When I came along he had gotten a job with Widener School for Crippled Children. He had worked for the Widener family as a cook in the 1930s, then as a bus driver for the school district, and that was a pretty good position for a Black man then.

The entire faculty at Central were white males. Other than the librarians, there were no female teachers. There was one Black substitute teacher, and that was all. As someone said, "Did you have any role models?" No, not in that sense. The Philadelphia school system, at least in terms of teacher appointments, was a very segregated operation. Up until the late 1950s they had two lists—one for white teachers and one for Black teachers—from which they made assignments. Black teachers were only assigned to predominantly Black schools.

When I went to Howard University I won a Student Welfare Council Scholarship. It was started by Black schoolteachers to provide funding for promising Black students going to college. The leader then was Marie Chase, who was the principal of Martha Washington School in West Philadelphia. The opportunities for college were very narrow—I knew that. Clearly, as a high school student I knew the ceiling was still there.

I had my mind set on going to Princeton, and Princeton accepted me. I knew I would need financial aid. (If you tell people what the tuition was then, they would laugh at you, but it was a lot of money for my family in 1956!) Princeton was willing to provide me with partial scholarship funding. But I took an exam at Howard University and won a national competitive scholarship. That was ultimately the reason why I went to Howard. I wish I could tell you it was for strong ideological reasons, but it was not at the time.

Having said that, going to Howard was probably one of the most beneficial decisions I ever made, because it opened my eyes to Black intellectual excellence. I used to say to my wife Beverly, "I would have probably become one of those obnoxious Black snobs had I gone to Princeton—so full of myself with this Ivy League education!"

Not only was I intellectually stimulated at Howard, but in all other respects—my social awareness, my political consciousness, all of that. It was hard as a college student from 1956 to 1960 not to really be challenged by what was going on.

When I went to Howard, and given the development of the civil rights movement, I was encountering Black professors—E. Franklin Frazier was a professor of mine. I took philosophy courses with Dr. Eugene Holmes and Dr. William Banner, and I ran into Sterling Brown, who I'm indebted to for shaping not only my appreciation of poetry but also my appreciation of life.

And at age twenty—and since Beverly died last year, my kids and I have been talking about this—at age twenty for some reason I am chosen by fate to fall in love with the person who becomes the organizing principle of my life.

I started out at Howard in 1956 with a high school sweetheart whom I thought I was deeply attached to, and she was deeply attached to me. Well, it was about Valentine's Day and she sent me a "Dear Jim" letter! In April of that year my mother died. I was just eighteen years of age, and I thought my life had just fallen apart. Less than two weeks after my mother died, my friends were trying to cheer me up at Howard, and I went to a dance on campus. While there I was talking and dancing with a girl I knew from Philadelphia. This person, Beverly Gail Barnes, happened by and saw me dancing. In those days, Philadelphians danced in a very distinctive way—it was called the Philly Bop. Much of Beverly's family lived in Philly, but Bev lived in Hampton, Virginia. She was trying to learn this dance and was fascinated by it. She wrote later that "he's kind of cute, and he's dancing the Philly Bop and I'll have to meet him."

She was a sophomore and had just pledged a sorority and was very socially active and popular on campus. I had been relatively low profile, but I informed her in June—a month after we had met—that I was going to work at a camp in Virginia and would like to come see her. She said, "Well, why don't you write me, and we'll see." So I did, and she never wrote me back. Later she told me she had a boyfriend, and there were some other things happening and she just didn't want to encourage me. I took that as a rejection, so when we went back to school I would see her and was very friendly, but I wasn't going to put my head on the chopping block again I don't think!

When she came back to school in 1958 she told me her dad had died and she and her mother had moved to Philadelphia, where most of her father's family lived. With uncharacteristic bravado I said, "Beverly, I'm taking you out Thanksgiving." So she went out with me. After her death I found a journal going back to 1958. I apologized to her for reading her innermost thoughts and personal business, but I read about all these guys who were interested in her. I got intensely jealous. "How the hell could she go with this jerk? Didn't she know I was standing there waiting?" Anyhow, she writes in her journal that she did go out with me on Thanksgiving night 1958, and we went to see Ahmad Jamal and Dakota Staton at the old Broadwood Hotel at Broad and Vine. She wrote that I was "nice." At least she said "nice" and I wasn't a complete jerk!

I took her out the following night and said that I really would like to see more of her. She doesn't say anything more about me until December of 1958. However, the journal of 1959 starts off with "Had New Year's dinner at the Kelch household. The care is growing." (I've shared all this with the kids.) I was scared as hell because I knew I had fallen in love with her. Here I am, aged twenty, naive, unsophisticated, no worldly experiences, but I just knew this person had a special appeal for me that I had never felt before.

So I went back to Howard and from there on we see each other every day. By the middle of January she wrote in her diary, "I made a joke about marriage," and she said, "much truth said in jest." I think I told her I was head over heels in love with her. She was a little more cautious about it.

Then there was the Immaculate Reception. There's a football game where Franco Harris catches this ball as it rebounds off someone's helmet, and they called that such a miraculous play. In our lives, Beverly and I had what she claimed always to have been Divine Providence: She had a dream on January 25. It wakes her up, and she has a compelling urge to call me and to tell me for the first time that she loves me—and she does at 4:15 in the morning. In those days, there was one phone per dormitory hall. Guess who answered the phone at 4:15 that morning. Me. Now I was not stalking the halls to answer the phone. I don't know how that happened, so Beverly always said it was Providence. She knew then that we had to get married. And that's what happened. By February we were talking about marriage. I gave her an engagement ring on her birthday, April 22. We were married on July 14.

I had taken a job at the State Youth Development facility at 2nd and Luzerne. It was a detention center for adjudicated juveniles. I was a counselor and worked there for a year and a half. The director of the facility asked me if I'd be interested in a career in social work. I hadn't thought about it, but by the spring of 1965 he said the schools in the Philadelphia area sometimes offered fellowships, and that's when I found out that Bryn Mawr did, and I applied and was awarded a fellowship. They had the Community Organization sequence, which is what I wanted.

Jim Kelch's tribute to his wife Bev at her funeral in 1997

In the meantime, Beverly wanted a family and I was dragging my feet, so in 1964 she announced to me that she was having a baby and said, "I hope you participate!" So our first child, Kuaye Noel, was born the week before I started Bryn Mawr—September 20, 1965.

Four years later, I heard Temple was starting a new School of Social Administration, and reading Beverly's diaries I found this: "Jim was interviewed for a position of this new school on August 14, 1969. The following week they offered him the appointment. Jim officially started as an assistant professor September 1."

In my almost thirty years here I've approached the issue of race on a more scholarly and systematic standpoint. One of my areas quickly became the history of social welfare, and in doing that it brought me in contact with the historical record of race relations in this country, which has played such a dominant role. That became one of my special areas of interest and concern. I had already developed heroes. I met, when I was a student at Howard, William Edward Burghardt DuBois. He was just about to go to Ghana in February of 1958. Dr. Eugene Holmes brought DuBois as part of Black History Week (it wasn't a month back then), and Dr. DuBois gave a lecture. Those of us in the Philosophy Club had the rare honor of spending an hour or two with him after his public lecture just questioning him. That was an incredible, fascinating experience for me. He was almost ninety years old then, and he talked about his controversies with Booker T. Washington as if they happened yesterday.

After listening to him I went out and bought *Black Reconstruction* and some of his other work, so my interest in race relations probably was shaped and formed at Howard. I had gone through the sensitizing and radicalizing of the 1960s, but once I became a faculty member at Temple, it became a serious area of study, contemplation, and thought. I always try to make that an integral part of the history of social welfare. I don't think you can understand anything about American society unless you're able to conceptualize the racial dynamics that have existed from the beginning of the settlements here in North America and have been a major dynamic in shaping the political and social posture of the country internally and in the world.

I never thought of teaching at a university as such. I thought of social work as being too connected to the establishment, that it had to establish much more of a connection to its reform tradition, advocacy for the powerless. I was a founding member of the Philadelphia Alliance of Black Social Workers, which predated the national organization. It was the model for the national organization. There was a conference here at

Temple recently where they celebrated the thirtieth anniversary of the founding of the Philadelphia organization.

In 1965 things were breaking all over. The civil rights movement, the Black Power movement was gaining ascendancy, Malcolm X had just been assassinated. It was such ferment. And it was a time when social work, as a profession, was trying to get a sense of its appropriate role. Among Black social workers, people talk about the colonialization of Black America. Social workers turned out to be some of the primary gatekeepers, so many of us were asking: How could we alter our sensibilities and work for the empowerment of poor people?

I get so frustrated because you cannot convey to young people now what the atmosphere was like in the 1960s. It was what you breathed. It was everywhere. The idealism of the period—in the sense that we could make this a true democracy, that we could eliminate racial injustice and economic inequality—all of that was such a part of that mix. To be alive then, you couldn't help but be affected by it.

The hope that we could make a difference was so great. I guess it was part naivete and part the invincibility of youth. It just seemed that we could change America, and there was such a spirit of racial amity. What we would call "whites of goodwill" were working in all kinds of capacities; not only were they going south and putting their lives on the line, but there was a sense of a partnership across the races.

Things have become so polarized. I become extremely disheartened when I see the level of polarization. I see it in classes at Temple University. Race is such an obstacle to dialogue. Obviously I was hoping for the best when President Clinton talked about initiating the new dialogue on race, but it's so difficult to talk about it now, much more so than in the 1960s. Maybe that's because things were blatant then. You saw the horrors of racial inequality, and maybe it's more subtle now, but it seemed to me there was a greater readiness to talk about it then. The blight of race in American society is going to forever inhibit the achievement of full democracy as long as we don't confront it. Now I find students tend to be very polarized around the racial question. They can't talk to each other honestly without attacking each other. There's a stridency now that I just think inhibits frank and open discussion where you acknowledge that people are struggling to come to terms with all kinds of issues. We've retrogressed in terms of the potential for dialogue.

It's more difficult to maintain an idealistic posture now. Everyone wants to get on with ensuring their futures in terms of economic livelihood. It's almost quaint now to talk about student radicals who were committed to changing society, rather than advancing their economic interest. No one wants to talk about the causes in society. Also, from an economic standpoint, it's much more competitive now. A college degree doesn't guarantee the good life anymore. In some respects there's been some resegregation of neighborhoods and schools, and I think that people don't experience each other like they used to. You can run into kids that have never been out of their neighborhood. They're parochial in their experiences and in their thoughts. So difference is threatening.

Regarding the interaction between race and class, there's some strange patterning that has gone on in the last thirty years—certainly since the 1960s. You had a tremendous increase in the Black middle-class, and at the same time you had a crystallization and consolidation of a Black underclass—the desperately deprived (I don't like that whole "underclass" terminology), which have extremely limited hope or belief that they can alter their situation. It's almost as if nothing matters anymore because nothing's going to change. In the 1960s, one of the major propelling factors in the civil rights struggle was a coherence of racial identity. That racial identity has been fractured to a large extent by class dynamics now. So you have this growing middle class, which really identifies more in terms of class than race, and many of them don't have a tremendous amount of sympathy for that Black group at the bottom which is hopelessly stuck. I think the racial dynamics are much more unclear, more muddy.

This whole class phenomenon—Gates and his colleagues up at Harvard have talked about this, as have Cornell West and others. You have this schism among Blacks, and it's class driven, such that you have Black middle-class students at Penn who have no concept of the Black masses and don't want to have any concept of them! They tend to see their lives as being above that. The intersection of race and class is such that increasingly I think that pure race is becoming less of a defining factor, that it is being interacted with class dynamics, which causes different patterns to emerge. I think kids growing up today are probably more affected by their class status than by their racial status. I'm not saying that racism has disappeared, but if you are born poor, that alone can be the determining factor in your life. Obviously if you're Black or Latino it has even more of an effect.

Temple is now moving away from its historic mission of really being an institution for the sons and daughters of the working-class. Our strategy now is to capture the middle-class. We've gone after the white and Black suburban population, which is growing. The incidence of Blacks in suburbia has exploded. Those who can, leave the inner cities and are sending their kids to schools that are in keeping with their middle-class status. I don't understand why we don't have more Latino students. We've been averaging between 18 and 20 percent African American students. Latino students have only been 5 percent or less, with a Latino population of well over 100,000 and growing in Philadelphia. It looks like we're moving in the opposite direction. We're now giving preference, whatever their racial identification, to kids from the suburbs.

A lot of it is driven by economic factors. We've become much more narcissistic as a society. I think the 1980s were a disaster for the spirit and soul of the country, that we really thought we didn't have to have compassion, you didn't have to think about those at the bottom, those who suffered all kinds of social disabilities. That's extended into the 1990s. I looked at the *Inquirer* the other day—a piece on executive compensation, and it's obscene. People should be able to make what they think they need to live on, but they make 200 times what the average production worker is making, and it's crazy. No one is worth that, not really.

There are economic dynamics going on, but I just don't see us organizing ourselves for the twenty-first century in terms of a just society. There are some hopeful signs. I don't think social reform is dead. Angela Davis said she gets the sense there still is quite a bit of idealism and desire on the part of students to make for a better world. The forces counteracting that are so powerful—you've got to be concerned about getting a job and making a living, and once those things take over your life, it's hard.

We best beware lest we lose our soul and hope we haven't lost it already. I vary from optimistic to very disheartened. I'm not a cynic yet, but I do become very saddened by what I think is the gulf which is growing between white and Black, the haves and the have-nots. In some sense that's more ominous, because it hardens the white-Black divide and deflects people's attention from the fact that there is still significant racial discrimination and institutional racism that must be rooted out. To the extent that people think they're OK and are insulated from it, they won't work to change it. I still think race is a salient issue and an unfinished struggle, but I see that struggle being complicated by all of this other stuff which is going on, and I don't know where it's taking us. ■■■

n October 1966 I wrote the following letter to my parents:

Dear Mom and Dad,

I'm enclosing an article from the *Philadelphia Inquirer* explaining my new job. I can only add that I'm thoroughly enjoying this adventure. I've gotten many responses from the article, including the enclosed letter from Edith Helfer who lives in Canandaigua, New York. I've never heard of the place, but thought you'd enjoy reading her letter. Do any of the names she mentioned sound familiar to you? If they do, you might like to answer her letter and fill her in on our side of the family.

With love, Sis

What I didn't tell my parents was that Victor Wilburn and I had met and fallen in love when I was the Ludlow community organizer in North Philadelphia and he the architect hired to rehabilitate a block of abandoned row houses. The project was a collaborative effort between my group, primarily Black and Latino, and a wealthy, suburban, white Main Line church. At that time, the city had over 30,000 abandoned homes, 600 of which were in our small neighborhood called Ludlow. On many of the blocks in that low-income community, more than half the homes were boarded up. Over thirty years later, there has been little change.

When I met Victor, he was the father of five children from his first marriage, Kimberly, Diane, Susan, Leslie, and Victor, Jr. Victor grew up in segregated Omaha, Nebraska, in a poor but strong Christian home. As you

Helen Helfer is now a full-time social worker for the Ludlow Community Association.

Run-Down Area Hires 'Lobbyist' to Press Its Case at City Hall

By ROSE DeWOLF
Of The Inquirer Staff

The Ludlow Community Association, a group of 200 residents from a small, rundown but hopeful section of Philadelphia, lays claim to being the only community group with its own full-time social worker.

The social worker is Bryn Mawr College graduate ('65), Helen Helfer, of 3701 Powelton ave. Her job, she says, will be to badger city officials to make good on their promises to the embattled citizens of Ludlow and to help the citizens help themselves.

EMPTY HOUSES

"The unique thing about this job," says the tall brunette, who formerly worked for the Philadelphia Anti-poverty Action Committee, "is that I'm not responsible to a politician or to a government agency or to a social agency. I'm responsible only to the people of the community."

Ludlow is the area lying roughly between 8th st. and Germantown ave., Montgomery ave. and Girard. It is characterized by battered and empty houses, littered streets, unemployment and poverty.

Earlier this year, the residents of Ludlow, headed by association president Marvin Louis, complained loudly and effectively that Philadelphia officialdom is ignoring the area.

TWO GRANTS

The resultant publicity reactivated the lagging Community Association and brought some outside help to the area, not the least of which is the money that is paying Miss Helfer.

The United Presbytery of Philadelphia gave a $15,000 grant over a period of three years and the Feis Foundation matched it.

The Central YMCA donated Miss Helfer's office furniture. The Temple Presbyterian Church donated the office. And the youngsters of Joseph House cleaned it and painted it.

In addition, the Central Baptist Church of Wayne, Delaware county, financed a study of Ludlow's problems and possible solutions this summer, and the Board of Education made the local Ludlow School a "community center" open until 10:15 P. M.

That much has been concrete help.

SOME PROMISES

The promises are worth noting, too. Several groups have pledged to help alleviate the poor housing conditions. The Department of Recreation has promised a play area within two years.

On Friday, the members of Ludlow's bootstrap-pulling Association will meet with officials from six city departments and agencies to get something more than promises.

"We haven't done anything to change the neighborhood yet," said Louis. "But we've made a start. And Helen will be on the job to see that everybody concerned remembers us."

The *Philadelphia Inquirer* article in my letter to Mom and Dad, 1966 will see, his father was not only a Pullman porter but often held three jobs at a time to keep his family fed, housed, and clothed.

Victor has endured much racism in his personal and professional life, both overt and subtle. He has passed on his survival skills, work ethic, and love to all his children, including our son. His perception of where our country is now regarding racism can be summed up in one word: chaos.

VICTOR WILBURN

I was born in 1931 and grew up in Omaha, Nebraska. I always thought of Omaha as a great place to be from. I never missed it, and I don't look back at it. It worked well because everybody stayed in their place—whites stayed in their part of the city, we stayed in our part of the city where we had our churches and the stores run by Jewish merchants. You just ignored how Jewish merchants would pat Black women on their hind ends and have all this kind of "come on" talk with them. You waited your time in line, paid for your milk, and left. It was sort of a ritual, and you got used to it.

In terms of Omaha, if you have a Black community, you don't have to worry about whether the schools are segregated or not. You just build

them in the right place, and they automatically segregate themselves. That's the way the schools in Omaha worked for me. The high school was in sort of a neutral place, and so it had white and Black kids. The school was very proud of its college prep. At that point my parents indoctrinated me that "you go on to college, no matter what." And I did.

I vividly remember when my dad and mom took me to Iowa State College in Ames on a Sunday for my first year. I was riding in the back seat of the car, and Mother and Dad were sitting up front and the radio was on. It was about 4:00 in the afternoon, and I remember think-ing, "Where am I going and why am I doing this?" When we arrived, Dad took me to my room at the YMCA and said, "Now son, you do your best. We're counting on

Victor Wilburn as a teenager in Omaha, Nebraska

you," and he drove off. That was the loneliest feeling I can remember in my life. Dad didn't go to college and didn't quite have an idea of what he was telling me to do the "best" about. That's not a criticism, it's admiration. I hope I can do the same for my children and say, "Do your best," and not have a clue to what it's going to mean.

Ames was a white school, and I was the only Black in the freshman engineering class. I was in architectural engineering, but the school was mainly an agricultural college. Because of the race thing, I wasn't on campus in a dorm. They found a room for me in the local YMCA. It was all strange to me. I could have just as soon been in China. That wasn't an occasion for offense, that was an occasion for "how am I going to get through this?" I had limited money and had to work, so I found a job in the women's dormitory cleaning dishes. I had to get up at 5:00 in the morning to set up the tables and clean dishes. I got a free breakfast, and did the same for lunch and dinner, so I could eat all I wanted.

When I later transferred to the University of Chicago, I worked in a packing house one summer. The people who did the dirty work there were Black, and I saw that loud and clear. It was hard work—and dangerous work too, as I look back on it, because there were about a hundred ways to be hurt. Thankfully, none of them happened. I can't say that I can tie my work there to any kind of unpleasant encounter. I remember the men were rough and rowdy guys, and they had a reputation for fighting all the time. One thing I'm grateful for from that experience is that I did value money. I spent it with a sense of wanting the best I could get for those dollars because I earned them. They were very hard to earn.

When I attended Harvard Graduate School of Architecture I found an appetite for things I would probably never have. It was the place where I heard language used like I never heard it used before. I liked to listen to the lecturers and watch the finely crafted reasoning of how they came to a conclusion. I was mesmerized by the wide variety of accents I had never heard before. The readings were astonishing. For example, I

Victor Wilburn with his daughters Kimberly, left, and Diane in Cambridge, Massachusetts

was dumbfounded when I read the Hamilton papers, or the founding of the First National Bank and some of the debates that went on with the constitutional framers who were frightened of the masses. They were saying, "Let's be sure that property rights are sacrosanct, that if we risk this business with the masses, that our property and our money stay in the hands of the right people." Our banking system started out doing that, and it does that to this day. That was stunning. I had no idea just how the well-off and privileged had hedged their bets. I had always thought it was just a great old experiment in democracy, and it wasn't at all, because our founding fathers could have bailed out at any point and gone back to being the moneyed, privileged, landed gentry at any time—and to some extent have already done. Now that's classism. And that's the thing I don't expect will ever go away.

My dad was a Pullman porter, and he used to tell the story of John D. Rockefeller. He'd always ask Dad to wait on him because Dad knew how Rockefeller liked his toast and bacon done—practically burned. Dad would boast that John D. Rockefeller always tipped him with a silver dollar. My dad accepted the phenomenon of a Rockefeller. He had no knowledge of how Rockefeller was a sinister man in the sense that he was greed and power driven and that he wiped out endless people to build Standard Oil and then double-dealed to build Pennsylvania Railroad. Dad had no knowledge of that, let alone an opinion about it. He just knew that John D. Rockefeller was synonymous with everything you could dream of. For him to single out Dad and say, "You can bring me my burnt toast," was a high mark for him.

Victor Wilburn with his sisters Betty and Katherine and their parents at Independence Hall, Philadelphia, circa 1971

If I were to put myself in my dad's place just for a moment—first of all, I'd have to reckon with the fact that I'd have to be a waiter. Dad had no trouble with it because he had no choice. He had a family to support. He'd walk the streets looking for any kind of work until he had holes in his shoes, and we used to pack newspapers in the holes so he could stay reasonably dry. What I learned from him was that you gotta do what you gotta do. You put one foot in front of the other and do it.

I don't want to serve anybody or cater to their whims. But my dad was a proud Pullman porter, and as I look back on it, I think we need something to be proud of, and if that's what it was for my father, that's great. Hang on to it.

When I was much younger, racism was all I knew, so I never really understood what was wrong about it. Now it's a power struggle. Sometimes I think it is innate and ingrained in human nature to want to have someone "below you." I look, for example, to the ethnic struggles in Europe and think, "What's the racial component of that? It's for sure slaughter. It's as hateful as it could possibly be." The potential of it in this country is significant, but certainly less so than it was at one time, or at least it seems to me.

But there's all this subtle indoctrination. The fact that all the 10:00 P.M. news on violence is Black faces, and that when a Black man rapes a white woman you see his photograph, you see all his features. When a white man rapes a Black woman you don't see anything to speak of, and so all of that is like indoctrination. That's what I see here in Washington anyway.

When did I become aware of racism? The 1960s played a role in that. There was the expectation that it could be better and that it just took a giant push to get it better. We're coming to the table for our slice of the pie, and this is going to be a better world because we're going to make it a better world. All of those thoughts for me were strong. When you try to act on them and get into urban renewal, for example, I was embarrassed that I didn't immediately see that urban renewal was Black removal. It took me years before I picked that up. I was thinking about that the other day when I was sorting through old drawings of Ludlow in North Philadelphia. All those dreams . . . all you have to do is drive down any of those streets now and they look indistinguishable from the way they looked in the 1960s.

I don't see any pattern to my life's experience with racism. No question about the presence of it, and I guess I'd say to you that I think it'll be around for a good long time because it has so many forms. It's like a chameleon. It pops up in a hundred different ways. I don't think of it as something you can stamp out. I see it as something you coexist with. Sometimes I sense racism as a gut feeling like a breeze blowing across me—I feel it in my bones, and sometimes it comes as an aftersound. I don't even appreciate it until I think about it.

You learn to adjust some of your values and try to set your course on "well, here's what I want in my life, no matter who thinks of me as Black, green, or blue, and I like to think I'm clever enough to know how to get it." I've always felt that in our society the more difficult and chaotic it gets, the greater the opportunities. I grew up in the status quo where if you're an architect you have to be a member of the country club and circulate in the right circles. That was never available to me, so it never happened. But when a recession comes and everyone's scrambling to build or get the Metro system done, they're somewhat less fussy about whether you're a member of the country club, and more concerned about whether you can do the job cheaper. In some sort of strange way, opportunity comes in hard times, and we try to take advantage of it.

I don't want to demean making an issue out of sitting in the front or back of the bus, but if you say, for example, we've come a long way from the 1960s, speaking of Black folk now, have we made any headway in the economic arena—beyond owning a Mercedes and having millionaire Blacks? I don't doubt that that's an accomplishment, certainly for a few, but in terms of getting at the way we really function in this society and where the real seats of power are, we're no nearer to it than we've ever been. I sometimes catch myself thinking when we take our version of democracy, with its hidden devices of racism, and export it to other countries like Russia or Japan or wherever, I think, "Wow, I hope these folks realize we're bringing them a plague of greed and market economies and profits."

So do I want recognition that I'm Black and OK? Or do I want to be treated the same as the powerful insider? (I'd be crazy to expect that, and I'm not really sure that I want that.)

A very good example of my confusion is our relationship. When I found out about your father's negative reaction to me, I have to say it was the first focus I ever had about you and me about race. When I met you, you weren't a white woman, you were a dedicated person. When we had a relationship and raised a child, you weren't a white woman, we had a dedicated relationship. You became a white woman briefly only when I found out about your father's reaction, because I then focused on being a Black man, so that's how it pops in and out of my consciousness.

Of course I knew I was a Black man—what I meant was that I had to pay attention to it, I had to bring into focus and reckon with it. In Omaha I didn't have to reckon with it. I could lose myself in the Black crowd. I had an understanding of who and where I was. I "knew my place," I hate to say it. But your father's reaction reminded me of my place in a way that startled me.

When it comes to racism, I want my children to be like the fox. I'm told that before the fox goes into the chicken house to kill a chicken, he circles around the house several times just to be sure the dog or some other foe isn't there. The fox will have no trouble killing a chicken, but he's quite cautious before he does it. I would say that our society is a place to be quite cautious. Don't assume that anything is going to come your way, and don't lose sight of the fact that some mean, vicious things can happen to you.

Racism is becoming a little obsolete in the sense that hostility is around us from drugs, ethnic and economic woes, rampant militarism, guns, terrorism—those are so "here and now." The inability to get into the country club or being called a Black so-and-so seems like so much old trivia. Today there's a churning world going in strange directions. Racism still plays a role, but it seems like the picture is getting bigger. I don't have any sense of resolution. I have a sense of chaos. ■■■

M y life has been enriched by being a "stepmother" to Victor's five children from his first marriage. Diane Battle is his second oldest daughter, and like all children of color in our society, she had to face the issue of racism early and painfully in her life. It did not stop her from growing into a strong professional woman, loving wife, and mother — but the unwanted baggage is still there, still clearly remembered and carried.

Diane has been in the banking business all her adult life. She is now vice president of a large bank in Columbia, Maryland, and the mother of three dynamic and beautiful daughters, Leah, Alicia, and Chrissey.

DIANE BATTLE

I was born in Cambridge, Massachusetts, which didn't mean anything to me at the time, but later going to school, particularly Black children told me that I spoke funny, that I spoke good English, and I could never quite figure out what that meant.

As a child I remember thinking my skin was such a pretty brown, and I loved the color. I remember looking at my arms in particular and being so pleased to be such a pretty color and being struck at how African Americans are so many wonderful colors. I wondered why white people seemed to be one pale shade, except in the summer, when I thought they looked a whole lot better! I'm a very visual person, and colors actually stimulate my senses.

I grew up in what must have been a very progressive, predominantly white neighborhood called Powelton Village in West Philadelphia. There was one other completely Black family that was frankly so bourgeois and we were riffraff, so they didn't deal with us. I have a close friend whose mother is Japanese and father is Black. There were other interracial couples, but the rest of the neighborhood was white. All of my early childhood friends were white children. Our community was fringed by a poor Black neighborhood, so the Black children I went to school with were at the outer edge of the neighborhood. I had a turf of three blocks, and they lived way beyond that perimeter.

I knew that I was a Negro, that's what we were known as then, but that didn't have a meaning to me. I didn't have a sense of racism. I didn't get any inklings of it until the end of elementary school. Suddenly children who I had played with forever stopped inviting me to sleepovers. I over-heard a couple of fights between my friends who wanted me over and their mothers who didn't. I really think it was about race, but it was never spoken about.

Young Diane (Wilburn) Battle, far right, with her sisters, brother, and grandparents in Philadelphia

It became more apparent when I went to middle school. One of my dearest friends was Joan Hewitt. Her father was an Episcopal priest. We were starting to think and talk about dating boys. But to have his white daughter hear me talk about Black boys—or potentially want to be with one of the Black boys I was with—was a problem. Her parents made it clear that she was not allowed to associate with me anymore. I remember her being embarrassed and hurt, and me being shocked because we had been friends since the first grade. They had bandaged my knees, and I'd eaten more sandwiches and spent more nights over there—it was my other home.

My mother talked a lot about people being equal and not to judge people by the color of their skin. We didn't talk about racism or bigotry. I knew who Martin Luther King was. I knew what he was doing was important, but there was never any discussion of Black Power or discrimination or rights. I knew my father went to Washington for the 1963 March, and he felt it was important, but it was a misty thing out there that he was doing for Black people. I'm not sure I understood that it was really about me.

By the time elementary school was over, you came into my life. I was more struck by the fact that you were tall rather than white. You were the tallest woman I had ever seen in my life! You were taller than my father, and you were very blonde. I guess because my world was a white world and my school was a third Black and all my playmates were white or mixed races, I hadn't connected all of that together.

When I was in middle school, a magnet school called Masterman, there were a lot more Blacks. The whites stuck together and the Blacks stuck together. I tried to find a group of Blacks to stick with, because the one or two white friends from my elementary school fled to other white people. It was clearer to me that I had this line to stay on, but more difficult because I was still hearing about my good hair and proper speech, and not really fitting in.

As kids, when my parents were home we listened to classical music and jazz. I didn't dance, and my Black friends thought I was really weird. I knew none of the top-ten hits. I knew nothing about the Temps, the whole Motown sound thing. The discovery of Black music was a wonderful thing for me. I did go to a Black church, but it was a very bourgeois Presbyterian church. We were out in fifty-nine minutes. My mother once took us to an AME church up the street from us. It was physically a beautiful church, and to hear a pipe organ jump to gospel music was quite an experience. We didn't go back because we were actually frightened by it. In Black churches, people get the spirit and get happy. We thought they were having epileptic fits. My mother was laughing hysterically, and we were trying to get her to help all these twitching people in church. My sister Susan was having a mild asthma attack, so we ended up leaving. My brother Victor kept saying, "Mom, help the people! They're sick, Mom, help them!" Church was the only place I never saw whites. To me, churches were highly segregated, and still are.

When I was at Masterman I became quite a reader and started reading Black history. That was in the late 1960s and we're really into the Black Power movement. I was startled to read *Before the Mayflower* and really get an idea of what slavery was about, other than the five minutes they'd spend on it in elementary school when they told us Abraham Lincoln freed the slaves. Then they'd look at us like, "yeah, y'all were slaves and that's all you ever did," and you felt embarrassed. That's what Black history was to me. We were all down singing on the plantations someplace and we ought to have a tremendous loyalty to Abraham Lincoln. I used to always choke up on his birthday because he had freed the slaves and somehow that was a good thing, and I don't mean to laugh, because I still appreciate Lincoln for freeing the slaves, but it's a little more complicated than that!

I was reading and discovering what a wonderful culture had come out of Africa and how much history and science and language and math and the written word came out of Africa. I had something to be proud of. It wasn't Old Black Joe on the plantation that was the end of my heritage.

I remember I was wearing panty hose and there was one color—Golden Penny—which was coppery brown, so you either wore Golden Penny or, if you were dark, Jet Black. That was it. So now you're trying to wear a little lipstick, but there really isn't any. There're fifteen shades of pink, and there isn't any eye makeup because there's fifteen shades of blue or white or beige. There's no foundation, and so reading *Seventeen* magazine about great makeup for thirteen-year-olds is a very frustrating experience because I would ride downtown and walk all over and couldn't find a thing that would look good on me.

I am of that generation that you had to get the kink out of your hair, and the Afro coming of age didn't help me. I didn't know at the time that my grandfather's mother was white. We have whites and Native Americans in the family, so our hair doesn't have a lot of kinkiness in it. Good hair was important when I was a child—whatever that is. It was important not to be too dark either, and as a brown person people would tell you, "You're OK. Your nose isn't too wide. Your hair's good. Your English is good, and you're good."

Around that time I visited my friend Carla's mother, who is Japanese, telling her about World War II and the atrocities the Japanese committed and how unbelievable that was, not connecting that she was Japanese. She said, "Yes, that's all true, but there's another side of it." She gave me a book about the Japanese concentration camps. Her family had gone to Manzanar in California, and I was stunned—it's Jews, it's Japanese, its Blacks. I'm still not connecting how this thing works, but thinking, "Who would take Carla's mother and grandmother, this wonderful woman who spoke no English, who'd say, 'you want cookie little girl?' and that was it." Years later I found out that she, as a young married woman with a young family, owned 500 acres of land which is now prime real estate in California, and they were snatched off of it. After she got out of Manzanar she stopped speaking English. She just decided she was not going to speak the language that ruined her life and shoved her family into a poverty that they never recovered from.

It seemed that with you being in my father's life I had to begin to reconcile the issue of this anger and resentment that I felt against whites, knowing that the whites I know now are descendants—or not—of dead white people who did all of this stuff. And some of the whites I know probably ran the Underground Railroad and were abolitionists. You can't point out the evil white people in a group, or the descendants of those people, so how can you be angry at all white people who weren't there, just like you weren't?

My personal experience with the Black Panthers was an excellent one. They had started a breakfast program for children. They walked seniors to get their checks and took them grocery shopping and collected money for the homeless. They were great philanthropists in a poor neighborhood that nobody cared about. Half the Black Panthers were older brothers and sisters of my playmates. They were not violent, so I never understood all this stuff in the national news about this violent, horrible group of people. They were the good guys as far as I was concerned, and I supported them.

I began to realize what disinformation was, and I saw what our Chief of Police Frank Rizzo was prepared to do—disinformation about my neighbors as far as I was concerned. You're very naive about those things when you're entering high school. My eyes still well up when I say the Pledge of Allegiance. I stand up. I am proud and happy to be an American. So there's a level of disinformation that is telling us that these are un-American people, except they are doing things that are highly American and highly Christian in my mind.

I went to Girls High School, and culturally, as a young Black woman, that was a wonderful place. I was sewing my African garb and wore it once a week. I was a member of the Black Student Union, and we used to talk about starting the revolution. We were going to stick dynamite in the school's water fountains that never worked. We were blowing up the damn water fountains because the water was rusty—to hell with the revolution!

Gil Scott Heron was a musical poet, the precursor to rap music. When you think about rap, there's a musical poetry that's been around a very long time in the Black community. He talked a lot about the revolution coming, so of course we thought it was going to be one of these weekends when we were in high school. I remember thinking about the plan for our family when the revolution started—how we should all congregate to be safe, and how I was going to hide you out because, you know, we were going to kill honkies but we weren't going to kill Helen! I struggled saying the word *honkie*. When you're in high school you try to be cool, so I was willing to use more derogatories than you would under other circumstances. But *honkie* was particularly offensive to me because of our relationship—the only white person I was getting to know personally where I didn't feel you were going away like my childhood friends or my neighborhood mothers. You were a part of my life, and this was a good thing. So I stage the revolution and kill off honkies, but Helen is not one—and nobody better call her one, either!

I went to a small white college called Chatham in Pittsburgh because they gave me a large amount of money. That was another quantum leap forward, because the main flagship building was the home of Andrew Mellon. There were a lot of people who came from money, and then there were the working people's sons and daughters. To be with people who had never seen any Blacks except on television, that's a deep thing to try to talk with someone who has never laid eyes on a Black person.

Diane (Wilburn) Battle at Chatham College, Pittsburgh, Pennsylvania

Chatham had about 500 students, and they claim there were 50 Blacks, but I only knew 38. We figured they counted the maintenance people! What I found tiring was whenever there'd be a question about—supposedly every Black woman was on welfare—all of the negative stereotypes, somehow we were expected know what it's like to be a welfare mother in the projects. Well hell, I've barely been in the projects myself! I found that level of ignorance annoying, and I'd try to say to them, "Let's talk about whites in Appalachia. All that inbreeding. All that toothlessness. What can you tell me about that?" They seemed indignant that I thought they would know about "those kinds of people."

I decided I was not going to be a symbol. I have to be who I am. I got a devilish pleasure telling them my father went to Harvard, that my parents were both professionals, my sister went to college, my cousin was in the Air Force Academy. It was nice to learn to talk about that without a chip on your shoulder. You become combative when you're always having to explain everything. People want to know what "chitterlings" are. Well, I don't eat them, and they're "chittlins."

I got out of college knowing there was racism, coping with it, but also learning not to deal with it—professors who were racist I would just drop the class. I was working way too hard to deal with some problem you have that I can't fix—and I'm paying you money to do this? I don't think so.

As an economics major I had more professors who were interested in the love of learning. They wanted to teach anybody who wanted to learn, so once I got to my upper-level classes, I had people who wanted to mentor me. There was a level of it that was very lonely because there were no other African Americans majoring in economics. I'm back in this white world again, and there were a lot of great people, but sometimes you're lonely to see brown or hear someone say, "Girl, I'm hungry for some greens."

By choosing to go into banking, I perceive banking to be one of the last bastions of WASP men. This was especially true in the late 1970s. They're pretty darn threatened by all of us running around trying to take over their space. It's an incident if you're a Black woman, because they've got to compete. There're also a lot of uppity white women who are a pain in the ass and don't want to go home and have all those babies. Men have that competitive thing, and the fact that they have to compete with men of color undoes them in a way that is scary.

As I started working, some of the unspoken words of racism were "you don't go to the city—that's where all those Black people are, poor Black in particular." A number of Jews I knew took vacation days for Rosh Hashanah or Yom Kippur. The whites had to test them when they came back to work and asked, "Were you in synagogue?" And they'd tell them these stories, "Oh, we were golfing!" because they couldn't say they were in synagogue worshipping their God because it was going to be a career problem to be understood they were a Jew and a person of faith. Being Catholic seemed to be crude because if you had a really refined white face you gotta be a Protestant—an Episcopalian preferably! And I thought, "Wow, what a pecking order."

Feminism in some respects has troubled me because the feminism of my college years was about destroying relationships with men—the man is your enemy. And the Black tradition is about Black women trying to support Black men who were being emasculated by society. There was a lot of the feminist agenda that probably didn't include that angriness, but some of it was angry women who had to work out their issues. But there is tremendous sexism in the workplace, and there are many men whose true relationships with women are about subservience.

I've been in the banking world my whole adult life. It played out very painfully because Leah's father and I divorced, so then I was a single mother, and they had a rule that you didn't leave until 6:00 P.M. If you had any loyalty or decency, you stayed until then, so I was there until 6:01 and ran screaming out of the building, but it hurt my career—being a mother and being a young mother. I was the first of my group to get married and have a child. Women started putting off having children until twenty-seven to thirty to get to a certain point. Here I am twenty-three years old. I'm in a trainee position. I can't stay late because I have to get to a baby-sitter. This is all a shock to the system, and I'm insisting that I'm leaving because I want to be home with my child.

When I was at Nationsbank, a bell went off for Hugh McCall, the president, because his daughters were hitting a glass ceiling, and he needed to look at cultural and gender diversity at Nations. It finally hit him that all his senior management were white men. He has daughters in their thirties and now all of a sudden he's interested in how this is working or not. He hired an outside consultant, and I got this memo to come to a meeting of vice presidents and above. I got the worst headache, because years ago I stopped talking about my issues with race and sex. I just act them out, and with certain people I act like a prima donna and a bitch because I want them to understand that they gotta stay up late at night to f*** me—excuse my French. When they see that you are combative, they think twice about messing with you.

I get in the meeting and the consultant said, "I have to admit this region is remarkable because there are 40,000 employees in this three-state area. There are 3,500 officers and 20 African Americans—male and female—at vice president level and above, and statistically that sucks. When I look at other parts of the franchise, they're doing better. I have to tell you I was stunned when I looked at the numbers when you consider we're looking at Maryland, Virginia, and Washington, D.C., so it's not like we're in Arkansas where there isn't the density or education level. This is the 1990s! So all of this should have been done, and I've told Hugh that it sucks here. You've got a lot of work to do with these kind of numbers."

Diane Battle with her daughter Leah in Columbia, Maryland, 1999

This woman knew what she was doing. To listen to a woman who was African American in the investment trust area who managed a billion-dollar portfolio. She outperformed everybody by 20 to 30 percent in terms of the investment strategies she employed for her clients. It was at the point where large clients wouldn't deal with anybody but her, because she was just making too much money. It reminded me about how far we've come, but also how far we still have to go.

Where are we going with race and class? I think on one level we are deteriorating. The underclass is growing tremendously. There are fewer opportunities for poor Blacks to get out of where they are. We are moving toward a class society—the haves and have-nots. College has become so expensive it's a luxury. That scares me, because I don't know what I'm going to do for my daughters, except that I will have no money to retire on.

Our society is really about the top 5 percent controlling the masses, and there's a great deal of disinformation to keep people at the status quo. So the issue of racism is just another tool for the 5 percent to control the 95 percent. We have to continue to change that and remember that if you become the 5 percent, don't get so wrapped up in your financial security that you forget your obligation to the poor and disenfranchised.

Problems are fixed one person at a time. I know a lot of people doing things one person at a time, and that groundswell is a quiet, unnoticed movement. Everyone I know is doing volunteer work, is mentoring. I couldn't have said that ten years ago. One of my models is a minority businessman. He operates the largest Black business in Maryland. He employs 450 primarily African Americans around the city. He's also established several joint ventures with other African Americans who have just begun their business endeavors. In this way he is helping others actualize their dreams while earning a fair return on his investment. When I think about my friend, I am encouraged. ■■■

M y father wrote many letters to me during my nine years in Philadelphia. He always addressed me as "Sis." Here's a typical one that began with an apology for a long gap in communication.

December 10, 1968
2850 Eucalyptus Ave.
Long Beach, CA 90806

Dearest Sis,
I don't know whether you can stand the shock of this or whether I can stand the shock of writing it as it has been a long time since you've heard and a very long time since I've sat down to a typewriter. Let's both hope we can survive the ordeal.

Your mother is at her usual rush, rush, rush of baking this and that and getting her packages on their way. Yours went forward yesterday so it should get there in time.

Sister Babcock is all up in the air—literally—over her forthcoming trip to see her chubby daughter. Understand she is leaving a week from tomorrow and will probably be back soon after the first of the year. The old gal is as jumpy as ever and still all on the negative side. [Mrs. Babcock was the mother of one of my best high school friends, Phyllis. Four years later, their visit to see Victor and me would play a pivotal role in my finally telling my parents about him.]

Don't see much of your illustrious brother and his family as they have their problems what with three kids and all the rest. The young one is walking quite well and is as fat as a butterball. They will be here with us Xmas, as well as Bev's father and mother. Personally, will be just as glad when it is all over as the season has become so commercialized that it no longer serves the purpose that it was originally planned for.

Well, Sis [after two single-spaced pages], I've just about run dry so had best not bore you any longer. Please excuse this messy typing. It's been a long time since I've pounded this thing and the old fingers are rather stiff. Wish for you all good things in the coming season and hope that one of these days you will once again pay us a visit. God knows if we will ever pry ourselves loose from here and make a trip east, but things may shape up a little better in the coming year — hope so.

Best love from us both and keep your chin up. Know you must have a very trying job. Dad

While I was working in Philadelphia, I became aware of a small antiracist group that called itself People for Human Rights (PHR). It was begun by a group of white men who addressed a fundamental issue in American society: institutional racism. My community organizing work in South and North Philadelphia, hearing Fannie Lou Hamer speak in a crowded church in Germantown, living through the assassinations of John F. Kennedy, Malcolm X, and Martin Luther King, reading the Kerner Commission report after the riots of 1967 — all this and more moved me to join this burgeoning group. I knew that our society did not value Black people, nor did we as white people recognize the problem of racism as ours, not theirs.

The image of my Black college friend Patricia growing up in Louisiana, passing by the white school every day, not being able to get off the bus because of the color of her skin, was never far from my mind. As a white woman, I needed to be involved in an effort that consciously grappled with this divisive issue — one that continues to divide us in the twenty-first century.

I hadn't yet joined People for Human Rights when the demonstration at St. Ladislaus Church occurred. The following article that appeared in the *Philadelphia Tribune* in February 1968 prompted me to do so:

People for Human Rights organization is a group of white people concerned with racism in Philadelphia and surrounding communities. They view the racial turmoil besetting the nation as a "white problem" not a Negro problem. As such, they see their role as one in which they have to work in the white communities to bring to their attention Negro history and the various facets of racism throughout our society.

"Whose side are you on? The Blacks or the whites?" shouted an angry white man to a group of white pickets as they marched in front of the St. Ladislaus Church, 17th and Huntington Park Ave., two weeks ago. The pickets, members of the People for Human Rights organization, didn't answer. If they had, they would have probably answered "neither white nor Black, just the side of justice." It's because of their concern with justice that this white organization has developed in Philadelphia in an attempt to do something about what they term the "white problem."

"Those who support our ideas feel a responsibility to humanize white people in conjunction with support for Black power," said Peter Countryman, 25, one of the founders of PHR, as he talked in the Tribune editorial offices.

"There is definitely a role for a white group to concern itself with more than just civil rights," he continued. "Some of us feel we also have to address ourselves to the racist attitudes of the white community and white power leadership," said Countryman who is a graduate student in political science at Princeton University.

An Episcopal priest named David Gracie was the key founder of People for Human Rights. David was a tall, brilliant, striking-looking man, and deeply spiritual. His experience with Ethel Watkins, a Black woman in Detroit who moved into a white neighborhood, became his epiphany and his reason for becoming a priest and fighting racism for the rest of his life. He took Jesus's words to heart when He said: "What you do to the least of these, you do to me." David was always acting his faith in his church, on the streets, in city hall, and in his community for "the least of these."

I talked with him in an old colonial parish hall in suburban Elkins Park, just outside of Philadelphia, where he was, at age sixty-six, an interim pastor. I hadn't seen David in twenty-six years, and he looked just as strong and vigorous as I remembered him. Two years later, he'd be dead from a rare blood disease. He told me when we talked that at his funeral, not yet foreseen, he wanted Ron Whitehorn to play the guitar. That wasn't to be, but when I was in Philadelphia in the fall of 2001, I gathered up ten friends, all of whose stories are in this book. We dined at an old, dimly lit South Philadelphia Italian restaurant. There were only a handful of other guests, so after we ate, Ron took out his guitar and we sang some of the old movement songs for David. I'd like to think he was listening.

DAVID GRACIE

I grew up in Detroit, and my parents were immigrants from Scotland, working-class folk who came there to find work. My dad worked for the Ford factory on the assembly line for thirty-five years, and when we got older, my mother worked at Sanders Bakery. I was born in 1932.

The first thing I knew about city government as a child was when neighbors came to the door in our working-class neighborhood, where there were immigrants from different parts of the world, but nobody Black. They were trying to get signatures to take to the city council to get racially restrictive zoning. I don't know if my parents signed the petition. They were not racist in any overt or bitter kinds of ways, but they went with the flow. They were trapped, as were other working-class people in that neighborhood, because having a nice family home with a garage and rose garden out back made such a tremendous difference in their lives, coming as immigrants. They knew that if the neighborhood changed, as others had changed, they were going to get the wrong end of the deal because they would sell like everyone else, and the real estate guys would take advantage of them. That whole ugly business was the story of growing up in Detroit. That was the constant threat—the color line was down at Joy Road and would it get any closer.

Young David Gracie, on the right, with his parents in Detroit, Michigan

Given all that, I went to a grade school in the neighborhood where we had some remarkable teachers, one of whom read Richard Wright stories to us in the literature class; another played Paul Robeson records for us in the auditorium—"Ballad for Americans." That same teacher, Eula Leonard, organized a visit for sixth graders, a little delegation to visit an all-Black grade school. I was chosen to be on the delegation. (In those days, I was chosen to be on everything.) We felt like little ambassadors. We were going to the Black neighborhood, and we were greeted at the school as if we were ambassadors. It was the day of their Christmas pageant (in the days when you could still do that in school). Cut to many years later at a high school reunion, and I'm with Josephine Briggs, who was with me that day. She's now living in Grand Rapids, Michigan, and she said to me, "David, that visit changed everything for me. I was a very pious little Catholic girl, and we're in that auditorium, the first time we're with Black people. My brothers had taunted me when I left the house, 'You're going to that nigger school.' But I still felt important because I was chosen to be part of this group. Coming down the aisle was little Joseph and Mary, and I loved Mary, and here was a girl my age and my size and she was Mary and she was Black. Something turned around in me, and I've never been able to have a racist thought since." It was an epiphany for her. For me, it opened the door. It was my first step across the line.

When I was eleven years old in 1943 there was the Detroit race riot. I remember listening to the radio in my room about the troops in the city and the tanks. I have a memory of a Black man badly beaten up, staggering down the street.

Everything in our culture was teaching us that you had to stay separate to survive. I remember during one of Roosevelt's elections, picking up flyers in the playground that someone had scattered there. "If you vote for (the presidential candidate or the mayoral candidate) you'll have Blacks living next door to you." That was the great fear we grew up with.

When I was a teenager I used to listen with great fascination to a Black radio station. You got the gospel choirs, and that music was so attractive to me. I heard them announce there was going to be a gospel quartet concert at the Masonic Hall in the Black community of Detroit. I got on the streetcar and crossed the line again, and it was a packed hall. I think I was the only white person there, and I was taking it all in.

Then came college at Wayne University in Detroit and the chance to really meet and become friends with some Black people and also get acquainted with some Jews, which hadn't been possible up to that point. I had a summer job with Awrey's Bakery, which was on Tireman near the Black center of the city. The bakery was Jim Crow, and this was 1952. They had separate locker rooms, separate areas of the dining room, separate toilets. I figured if I had to pee I was going to the closest toilet, and that made a lot of friends for me. I got to know Black people for the first time in my life. I'd sit with them in their part of the lunchroom. It wasn't ostentatious—I just thought, "This is stupid, and here's a chance to meet some people I never met before." The white workers just looked at me and thought, "Hell, he's a college kid. He doesn't know any better."

I went into the army in 1954. Truman's order to desegregate was fairly recent. Our basic training company was racially mixed, so by and large, that was a good experience. I remember the frustrations by some of the Black kids who were still routinely being assigned to the truck-driving units. We were down at Camp Chafee in Arkansas. We had one

Black lieutenant in basic training, and that was certainly novel. I was then shipped to Germany and worked in an intelligence unit for the rest of my time.

I came out of the army and didn't know what I wanted to do. I had married Shirley, who I met in Germany. She's from England, and we were young and foolish. She was pregnant by the time we came back. I needed to make some money, and civil service had an opening in the Detroit Commission on Community Relations. (It really was their race relations commission, but they were too coy to say "race relations.") I got a job as an investigator. I got to work with Joe Coles, who was a marvelous "old school" Black human relations worker with a lot of political connections. He saw to it that I got introduced to the Black community in Detroit, and few other white people had such an opportunity. We'd go to lunch at the Lucy Thurmond Y which was the Black Y, and there would be the editor of the *Michigan Chronicle*, the up-and-coming politicians, and wonderful discussions and arguments and joking about politics.

In those days, if a Black family moved into a formerly white neighborhood, that sometimes led to arson. My job was to investigate reports, see if the police were responding properly, be in touch with the community organizations, and try to make something positive come out of some very tense situations, one of which—if I needed another epiphany at that point, that's what it became. It was also a very important experience for my wife, because she also came to know the woman in the house.

A woman named Ethel Watkins moved into a house on Cherrylawn Avenue. The closest Black home owners were several blocks away. It was a white working-class neighborhood that was pretty tense, because they figured they were next for the turnover, but by golly, they were going to protect themselves. It was *Raisin in the Sun*, that's what it was. Jimmy Delrio, a Black realtist (Blacks weren't allowed to call themselves "realtors" back then), sells Ethel this house. Ethel was a seamstress and did beautiful things with a needle. She lived alone. When she moved in, the shit hit the fan. The neighbors started by turning their porch lights on at night to send her a message, then they gathered on her lawn, and it began to take the shape of a mob presence night after night. Threats were telephoned in and false fire alarms were sent in. The police were on the side of the neighbors and were going to do as little as possible to protect Ethel. Our work was cut out for us, so Joe and I were on the case, getting to know Ethel, talking with the head of the NAACP, and sitting with police brass, telling them they had to provide protection for this woman.

One Sunday morning I went to visit Ethel, and we had breakfast together, looking out of her picture window to the front lawn. As we're eating, the mob starts to form again, and it's Catholic neighbors coming back from Mass. That was the special moment for me, sitting with Ethel and looking out at the mob. We got rid of the mob finally, and this is a story I like to tell in sermons sometimes, because it shows what just a couple of people can do: Close friends of ours lived not too far away. He had been a Wobbly in his day, and they didn't want anything to do with racial discrimination. I went to visit them, and they asked, "What can we do?" I told them, "The simplest thing you can do is go visit her." So they did. By this time we had jacked up the police, so their presence was stronger out front. My two friends went to visit Ethel at dinnertime, so the mob's not there. But by the time they leave, there's the mob and the cops. The two of them are spotted on the front porch, and Rose Petransky, who was the ringleader of the mob, said, "They're white! Let's go get 'em!" So my dear friends had to get from the porch to their car, which is down the street, and Rose and some others started to chase them. The police had to act, and they arrested Rose on the spot. My friends got away safely, then Rose Petransky went on trial for disturbing the peace. She was found guilty and fined. There was no more mob after that.

One of the reasons I went to seminary was because of Ethel Watkins, thinking that racism is demonic and it's the kind of demon that maybe needs a spiritual cure. Not long after I got out of seminary in 1958, I was asked to join the Episcopal Society for Cultural and Racial Unity. John Morris, a priest from Atlanta, was the organizer, and he asked a number of white priests from around the country to go to Medgar Evers's funeral in Jackson, Mississippi, to be honorary pallbearers. That was an experience I will never forget.

On the way back from the funeral I was interviewed in Detroit by the Vestry of St. Joseph's Church, which was a racially integrated congregation. The bishop wanted someone to go there who could sustain that kind of congregation. He offered me the job, and I said yes.

When I was at St. Joseph's Church, I had a lot of latitude to move on racial issues. The "biggie" there was in 1963: Northern High School was down the street, and the student body was all Black. The students walked out, demanding quality education. They were fed up. A number of their parents were backing them, and a number of them were members of St. Joseph's Church, so I just walked down to the picket line and chatted with the parishioners. I said, "You don't want to be out in the street all this time. We have this big church, so come on down and use it." The church became the Freedom School for a couple of thousand Black high school students, and it also became the lightning rod for the whole city. Folks were angry as hell with me and the church for "mixing in" this way and encouraging students to stay out of school and civil disobedience and blah blah blah. But we brought that off because the congregation was behind it, and those who weren't kept it to themselves. The bishop was behind it because "better they're inside this church than out in the street rioting."

My last summer in Detroit was the time of the racial uprising of 1967. It all kicked off not far from St. Joseph's Church, and we went to sleep at night in the rectory coughing from the smoke of a burning city.

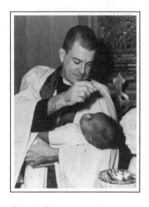

David Gracie performing a baptism at his Detroit church

It was a shattering experience for all of us, including our little children, who saw some of the violence up close. For me, the Kerner Commission report made some sense out of the uprisings, and that report became my text in educational programs in Philadelphia: "two nations, one Black, one white" described what we had become.

The war in Vietnam was harder for that congregation because it was more complicated. My approach was, I'm joining Clergy and Laity Concerned About Vietnam, I'm going to Washington for their first demonstration, and here's why. I explained it to the congregation and did not imply that everybody had to agree with me. Gradually enough support developed that we were able to establish a draft counseling center in the church, one of the first in the country to do that. Then I ran into my bishop. He was a hawk, and I calculated, "Well, my bishop is not only a hawk, he has a column in the *Detroit News* preaching this war and if I continue here, I'll be in open conflict with him. My congregation is aided by the Bishop, and at some point, it's going to hurt my congregation unless they are willing to be involved in this kind of a fight on this issue." I tested the waters and came to the conclusion they were not, so that's when I left Detroit. I called Bishop Robert Dewitt in Philadelphia, whose urban missioner had just left the diocese, and he hired me to fill the spot.

Bishop DeWitt was an opponent of war. I carried that opposition to the streets of Philadelphia and called the war racist. I was branded in the *Philadelphia Inquirer* as the "priest who encouraged the burning of draft cards," which I hadn't done. I was encouraging people whose conscience moved them to turn their damn draft cards in, and I and other clergy would take them. As part of the resistance movement, I spent a few nights in jail in Philadelphia and Washington, D.C.

In Detroit we had formed People Against Racism, which was an organization of white people trying to counter racism in their own communities. It was inspired by the Northern Student Movement, which decided they didn't have to go south for the civil rights movement, there was plenty of work to be done at home. PAR supported the student walkout at Northern High School. When I came to Philly I wanted to see something like that develop here and talked up the idea with Steve Gold, Peter Countryman, and other folks, and People for Human Rights came into being here. PHR did antiracist education, demonstrated against police brutality, and cooperated with the Black Economic Development Conference in its demands for reparations. PHR was a very lively group for a number of years.

After working with the bishop as his urban missioner and getting involved in antiracist and antiwar organizing efforts, I decided I wanted to get into parish ministry again. I went to Kensington, feeling the call we in PHR were giving ourselves to go into the white working-class community and try to do something about racism. The part of Kensington where I first served in a church was very white and blue collar. The racial lines were the main streets—one side of Front Street was white, and the other side was Black. South of another street was Hispanic. I got on well with my congregation and found them willing to work to improve race relations.

An opening occurred at St. Barnabas Church in West Kensington, which is Black and at that time was becoming increasingly Hispanic. I served there for four years. I was teasing Father Paul Washington about that the other day because Paul can be terribly outspoken. I said, "You may remember, Paul, when I was installed at St. Barnabas Church at 3rd and Dauphin? I asked you to be the preacher and you came and very impolitely said that you were troubled by the fact that the bishop was quite able and willing to appoint a white priest to be in charge of a Black congregation, but you never see the Bishop appointing a Black priest to be in charge of a white congregation. Paul, that was absolutely true, but damned impolite!"

The congregation at St. Barnabas gave strong support to the Kensington Joint Action Council, which was organized around nonracist principles. It was a group that included at every point whites, Blacks, and Hispanics in that part of Kensington, and our church was an important part of that. I used to tell people, "We are the community organization at prayer every Sunday morning." When Jesse Jackson would call a demonstration in Washington, folks at St. Barnabas wanted to go, and we did.

I left there because of family reasons. Being a priest in the inner city puts strains on one's family because it's a trip they're not necessarily ready to take with you. That's true whether your congregation is Black, white, Hispanic, whatever. I asked myself, "How can I continue to do my ministry, including antiracist work?"

David Gracie in one of the many demonstrations he participated in during his life

At that time the Protestant chaplain's position at Temple University opened up, so I went there and became more involved with the Church of the Advocate, which was up the street. I started to collaborate with Father Washington on his life story, which Temple University Press published in 1994—*Other Sheep I Have: The Autobiography of Father Paul Washington.* Paul's story is the story of the Black freedom movement in Philadelphia, as well as the story of the movement for women's ordination in the Episcopal Church. The first women priests were ordained in the Church of the Advocate on July 29, 1984. I was proud to have a part in that wonderful, rebellious act.

As chaplain, I tried to get students at Temple to understand their community and get involved with it. I did that for ten years in partnership with the Reverend Joan Martin, now on the faculty of the Episcopal Divinity School in Cambridge, Massachusetts.

The Quakers then hired me, and I was with them for seven years as their national peace education director, operating out of their headquarters at 15th and Cherry. There I had the experience of working with a truly multicultural workforce in an organization that was committed to affirmative action. I had the experience there of some of the struggle and pain that comes at the point of, "We're all working together and we all share the same values, but we have to learn how to *be* together and really respect one another."

I retired from American Friends Service Committee when I was sixty-five, made myself available to the bishop, and he asked me to come to St. Paul's here in Elkins Park. I came here and discovered this wonderfully diverse congregation. Come to Sunday service here, and you'll find families from different parts of the Caribbean, two African families, African American families from Cheltenham, some from the immediate neighborhood, white folks, a Christian married to a Jew, a

Protestant married to a Catholic—it's just great! My task here was to be interim rector and help them keep this wonderful thing they have.

As interim rector I should not be imposing my politics on folks. But when I see an opening, I take it. There was a statewide demonstration against the death penalty in Harrisburg a week ago. I announced a couple of weeks before that this was happening, and the position of the church is very clear. "I'm going to Harrisburg and take part in this, and if any parishioners would like to come with me, I'd be very happy." Five folks came with me, including three youngsters who had never experienced a demonstration before. One was back the next Sunday telling his Sunday school teachers that this country is just too racist to have a death penalty.

I much prefer to persuade people and move with people and not get out on the ramparts unless it's necessary. It's a slow deal, and unfortunately I look around me and don't see coming up through the ranks too many people who are even engaged in that effort. There is more and more pietism. People want what's good for their soul's salvation. But you can have both. That's what St. Barnabas Church did. They loved Jesus and sang hymns and laid hands on one another for healing, then they'd go to the community organization march.

But the church is almost as segregated as ever. That's really troubling. In our Montgomery County deanery, St. Paul's is practically the only church in the whole county that brings Black delegates to the meetings.

I must say that having grown up in the Jim Crow era, it's delightful to see some of the great changes that have been made in my lifetime. Some people are learning to think in affirmative action terms and act on that basis in their workplaces.

As a country, we're learning to be imperialist in a big way. We're picking up where the Brits left off, and if the natives don't fall in line, you bomb them. It's very ugly and very evil, and we have such morally mediocre leadership that it makes you tremble. You look around for other leadership and you see Bill Bradley coming along, who is a person of integrity who actually knows what racism is, and has within himself the potential to teach others and do something about it. Then you look at the rest of his program and you say, "Gosh, more of the same."

The class issue must be joined if there is going to be racial equality in our country. ■■■

In the spring of 1968, with riots exploding in other large cities in the aftermath of Martin Luther King's murder, Mayor James Tate slapped a decree on the citizens of Philadelphia that prevented any group of more than eleven people from gathering in public. People for Human Rights had already planned a demonstration in front of Representative William Barrett's home on a busy South Philadelphia street to urge him to support antipoverty legislation Dr. King had initiated. We decided to go ahead with the demonstration despite the mayor's decree.

Ten of our members, closely watched by the police, held up picket signs and handed flyers to passersby. My friend and Department of Social Services coworker Harvey Finkle and I were watching from across the street. After much deliberation, we decided to be protesters number eleven and twelve, one over the limit. When the police failed to disperse us as we stood in front of Barrett's home, we were carted off in a paddy wagon, the first time I had ever been arrested. The case went all the way to the Supreme Court, where it was finally thrown out. Here's how the episode was reported by the *Philadelphia Inquirer*, April 14, 1968:

Twelve persons protesting Mayor James Tate's emergency proclamation banning large gatherings were arrested Sunday while others from the same organization escaped arrest at another demonstration when Democratic City Chairman William J. Green Jr. invited them into his home.

Episcopal urban minister Father David Gracie, who demonstrated at Green's home, said the protesting group, People for Human Rights, had planned the demonstrations before the mayor issued his proclamation last Friday night.

Father Gracie said the demonstrations were not originally planned to test the proclamation. "They have become a test of the proclamation," he said, "but they were not framed as such."

The clergyman said the group was meeting last Friday night when it learned of the proclamation. "That was our moment of decision," he said. "We decided we would go ahead with this demonstration because we felt is was important to show white support."

The arrests were made outside Barrett's South Philadelphia home as the demonstrators distributed handbills. The seven men and five women were placed in waiting police vans after they refused to disperse. Barrett, a Democrat, was not at home.

The demonstrators demanded that Congress "draft legislation to meet adequately the demands of America's poor."

After being fingerprinted, photographed, jailed, then released eight hours later, Harvey and I were not sure what our boss Steve Brody might do to us the following week. At our Monday morning staff meeting, he called us his "jailbirds" with a twinkle in his eye. Harvey and I were both pleased at the honor.

Harvey grew up in Northeast Philadelphia, now a primarily Jewish neighborhood. In the 1930s and 1940s it was mostly gentile. His racial awareness began in the 1950s, when he was a teenager playing basketball with Black youths and hanging out at a famous live music bar that allowed interracial couples in its cramped booths. He is the father of two extraordinary adults, Josh and Abby, both of whom were born deaf.

Harvey left social work in the 1970s to pursue a career in photography. It was a good choice. He is a nationally known photographer, capturing the humanity of homeless families in North Philadelphia, El Salvadoran refugees in Nicaragua, and other extraordinary people around the world.

HARVEY FINKLE

I grew up in a working middle-class Jewish family in Oxford Circle, Philadelphia, the beginning of Northeast Philadelphia. Most of the people who lived there were white and Christian. Eventually it developed into one of the larger neighborhoods in the city which is predominantly Jewish. Back then the Jews were the minority, and we paid some dues in school and the neighborhood. People let us know, and there'd be fights—"dirty Jew" and stuff like that. In some ways it helped me have some connection with what it's like to be discriminated against.

When we moved there, housing was cheap—it was just before World War II started in the United States. Our family came through the depression. My father and his brothers had an auto graveyard. They used to buy wrecks, take them apart, and sell the pieces. He worked seven days a week, left at 7:00 in the morning and came back at 7:00 at night and was exhausted. My mother ran the house. They were Roosevelt Democrats, as all Jews were (and any kind of group that had come through any sort of discrimination or oppression). A coalescing of all minorities—white, Black, ethnics, united with the New Deal.

I remember family dinners where our grandparents and young people would come together and have discussions. One of my uncles used to be arguing with my father and the other ones, and I found out later that he was a Communist. There was an egalitarian toleration, and at least from afar everybody was created equal.

The first relationship I had with somebody who was Black was a maid who was with us for a long time. She'd come a couple times a week and was part of the family. Then my mother would complain if things weren't perfect. But my parents would help out her family with clothing and furniture. When she had trouble with her kids, I remember going down to 22nd and Catherine, my first incursion into a Black neighborhood. I was about eight years old.

My own development was the stuff I read when I was young that impressed me. I remember reading *Freedom Road* by Howard Fast, which dealt with slavery and post-slavery, then citizen Tom Paine, who was a revolutionary, and people came to despise him. *Common Sense* was the pamphlet that inspired the revolution, but in the end, when everybody got nice and comfortable, they turned on him because he continued to profess that people were still being persecuted. Then, *The Jungle*. Those were three books that dealt with working-class ethnics, so I think they instilled feelings of the underdog.

The two things that led to relationships with Black people were sports and music. We used to have a neighborhood basketball team, and we'd travel all over the city, like to 25th and Diamond—Raymond Rosen homes, which was public housing. We also used to play at 18th and Lombard—that was all Black, too. We'd take the trolley to go there. The first game they'd win, and the second game we'd win—then we'd have to run out! It was their neighborhood, so we'd call a cab and escape, then we'd come back for a third game. The games were good. Intermingling and appreciating people with talent was great.

When I was about sixteen years old my father used to drive a group of us halfway to school, then we took the bus from there. We used to listen to this offbeat station, and once I heard this great piano player. It was Erroll Garner, and I said, "This is really great music," and it was the beginning of getting into jazz, which was predominantly Black. We started to sneak into the local jazz clubs in the city. It was alive and authentic and captivating—and the people were, too.

At the end of high school and the beginning of college we used to go to the Blue Note in Philly and also saw some nasty stuff that went down. The Blue Note was this little club which had all the great performers— Billie Holiday, Charlie Parker, Dizzy Gillespie, Thelonious Monk, Miles Davis—every great musician played there. There were also some mixed couples sometimes. We're talking 1951–52. We were just teenagers at that time, but we'd give a dollar at the door and they'd let us in. It was just exciting the way everybody got into it. I remember being in the Blue Note, and Rizzo* was running the 12th and Pine Police District. One day the doors blew open, and the leather coats and rifle guys came in and walked around. We were sitting at this rectangular bar, and there was a row of seats around the bar, and that was the extent of the club. Rizzo knew there were mixed couples there. There weren't many places where they could go back then. It was a show of force, nobody was arrested, they'd just storm around and then leave. It all had to do with race.

I went into the army in 1953 and was stationed for a year and a half in France. I don't think the army was more than several years integrated. I was in a company at an air base in France that was one-third southern white, one-third Black, and one-third Italian, mostly from north Jersey and New York. I don't recall there was any relationship between the southern whites and the Blacks. The major city around our air base was Nance, and that's where Blacks and most of the northern whites went. There was another little town where the southern whites went. Nobody Black better go into that town. It was almost like redux South. I was mostly with the Italian guys. They were like the Jews from the Lower East Side. They were lukewarm when it came to relating to Black people, and for myself, I worked with the Blacks and we had fun together. I got to know them personally, and we played ball together and with other companies on the air base who were also mixed. In the sport thing, the Blacks and whites mix much easier. There were more personal relationships and more understanding of how deeply ingrained racism was. The army broke down all the stereotypes—you began to meet some smart Black guys with good heads who were smarter than the white ones back home who were complaining about how dumb they were. The big term back then was "nigger lover." Any white guy who had a relationship with Black people was called a nigger lover.

I came back from the army and went to Temple University. When I returned, the school was more integrated. I remember one guy named Paul Reed, a middle-class Black guy. When he graduated, everybody was looking for jobs, and he said, "I made it. I'm in corporate America!" It was like a really big number. He said it as a joke, but it was true.

I graduated in 1958 in accounting and went to work with the County Board of Assistance as a caseworker for about a year. The caseload I had was 60 percent white and 40 percent Black. If you made a generalization

---

*Frank Rizzo became chief of police in the 1960s, when PHR was at the height of its demonstrations. He then went on to become mayor, serving two terms.

about each group on public assistance, it seemed to me that the Black people had much more resourcefulness. The white population wasn't as smart and had fewer resources. In other words, Black people were there for a different reason than white people—neither one being deserving or undeserving. The issue was race. It was more difficult for Black people who were sharper to get out of their situation because of their race, so they were stuck in it. They might have more goods personally going for them, but there were fewer opportunities out there for them to climb into.

After a year I went to the Penn School of Social Work. I didn't know anything about schools of social work, but I liked what I was doing, and if I was going to stay in the field I needed to find out how to do it. I graduated in 1961. I met a guy who approached me in school that I became friendly with. I was married at the time, my first marriage. He was a Black guy. His name was Wynn Adams, and he asked me if we'd like to come over and have dinner with him and his wife. So we went over, and he was married to the daughter of the district attorney in Pittsburgh. She was white, and they left Pittsburgh. The four of us really became good friends. I'd like to think the reason he approached me was because he felt I was somebody he could approach. I remember one night we were walking past the Academy of Music at Broad and Locust when the concert was breaking, and the discomfort you could see that he felt, and people would stare.

I think People for Human Rights was a natural for me. It was like an outlet—to be part of something more radical, more progressive. My involvement was when you and I were having breakfast at your place and someone said they needed more people in front of Barrett's house. We went down to be observers, and they said, "We need two more people." We helped everybody get arrested, including ourselves! But my formative stuff was more from the 1950s, not from the 1960s. PHR was really people from the 1960s. They were much more able to come together collectively, I think. Most of us were isolated beatniks from the 1950s.

More fulfilling for me was the People's Fund that was working to put something together and stick with it. Looking at it thirty-plus years later, it's still there. You remember the early discussions about whether we should be a lefty common cause educational operation or a fundraising organization for those groups out there on the cutting edge. It was concrete, what we were doing (maybe it's my accounting background). We could quantify it, even if it wasn't much. About four years after we founded the People's Fund it became Bread and Roses. Other people came in and saw that our tactic not to be tax deductible had run its course. I think we were the original—the other one was Haymarket in Boston, and Vanguard came shortly thereafter in San Francisco.

I left social work during this time. There was a coalescing of things: I learned that I couldn't work a bureaucracy. Also I learned that my son Josh was deaf. It was 1970. I took a year off to do some photography, then I struggled to make some bucks in the field. It was long years of drought, but I liked what I was doing, and eventually it paid off personally and professionally.

In Philly I became known as the "movement photographer." People would let me know what was happening politically, so I would go to these places and photograph them. In the meantime, I would get freelance jobs through hospitals and different social agencies, and it just grew that way so I could subsist on doing photography and still do

Harvey Finkle learning sign language with his children Josh and Abby in the late 1970s

stuff I wasn't paid for. I hooked up with a group in New York called Impact Visuals that was started by a writer for the *Guardian*. One of the things he did was supply photos to Left publications, like *Progressive, In These Times, Z Magazine,* which couldn't afford to pay the going rate from photo agencies.

I once did a thing on Jewish survivors of the Holocaust through an agency that served refugee groups. Then I did a thing on the resettle-ment of the Indochinese. I got a grant in the early 1980s to do a documentation of the four different groups that came from Indochina and settled in the area. I did a thing with the burnt churches, where I was able to go south to document some communities where the churches were burned. The National Council of Churches knew I'd done this, so they invested more money to send me back there. We had an exhibit, and eventually it was

URBAN NOMADS
PHOTOGRAPHS BY HARVEY FINKLE

Harvey Finkle's cover photograph for the Kensington Welfare Rights Union shown in a beautiful annual report they did and used fifteen to twenty of my photographs.

I worked with an organization to document the single people who've been cut off of welfare in the state of Pennsylvania, the general assistance category. We showed the exhibit at the public library for three months. We also showed it at the state capitol in Harrisburg, and later we showed another piece on the Kensington Welfare Rights Union. A receptionist in the rotunda there said to me, "I know that woman. She was arrested here." She points to one of the photographs and says, "These are really wonderful people."

In regard to where we are now on the issue of race, I think we're entering the dark ages. At some level, when you look at the general picture, race has driven what occurs in this country. Politics has thrived off

Harvey Finkle, the movement photographer, and his ever-present camera

of using the racial card to gain power. From Reconstruction right through the southern strategy with Nixon to the Willie Horton photograph—it's race, and white people go for it all the time. A great line from Lyndon Johnson was, "You can pick the pocket of the poorest white person as long as you make him feel he's better than any Black person." And that's the way it's run. It's constantly used, and in a sense, I'm not optimistic. I think the legacy of Clinton will be that he ruled over the time when the greatest disparity of income among Americans occurred. I think that goes for white and Black, and he hasn't done very much about it. The middle-class is shrinking, and more people are going to suffer the consequences—everyone in the lower classes—white, Black, whatever. It's class that suffers, but it's race that's the instigation.

What keeps me going? It's what I do. Despair will come even when things are great at times. It won't stop me from what I'm doing. ■■■

I met Carol Finkle over thirty years ago through her husband, Harvey. She is the mother of Josh and Abby and, because of their deafness, has been tenaciously active in the deaf culture ever since their births. Ten years ago she founded and continues to skillfully lead Creative Access, a unique nonprofit agency that serves thousands of deaf people by providing interpreters in major movie and stage theaters in Philadelphia. She also brings in deaf entertainers from around the country who perform using American Sign Language.

The deaf culture, which Carol calls "the last oppressed minority," is bonding and uniting, while also mirroring the larger hearing world when it comes to the issues of race, racism, and class.

CAROL FINKLE

I grew up in Philadelphia, in Mt. Airy, and had a typical middle-class lifestyle. I have one older brother and a half brother. I grew up virtually without a mother, except for the years when my father remarried. That relationship was not a nurturing one during my teen years, and the fact that I had no mother bond throughout that critical time of my life still impacts me. At fifty-five years of age I still would love to have a mother figure around for comfort, even though I consider myself a strong woman.

Race came into my life at a very young age. Because of my mother's early death at age thirty, my father worked six days a week and remarried so he would have someone to raise my brother and me. Part of his aspirations of being middle class was to have a maid. Lola worked for us sometimes five days a week, and other times one or two days, depending on the affluence of my father's business.

Lola was my first memory of a person of color. I loved her. She was my protector and confidante. She would take me home to her house in some poverty-stricken neighborhood. One of my favorite early memories is that she took me to bingo at the church the nights we spent together. I remember I won once. Then the next morning she would get up at 5:00 and cook fried chicken and pigs' feet. We would have that for breakfast before getting on the trolley to come to our house, where she'd clean and cook for us all day. She was a great asset in my psyche.

The negative memory I have is saying something I was very ashamed of for years. I must have been around twelve. My stepmother was nagging me to pick up my clothes, and I said, "I don't have to, that's why we have a maid." I disassociated my love for Lola to this perception of her as a slave-type person. I always remember that jolting me even as I said it and being very ashamed, but it's really symbolic of how insidious the whole relationship was in terms of how I perceived her. It's because she was Black, not just because she was the "maid." Had she been white, I don't know if I'd have felt quite the same.

My high school was Germantown, half Jewish and half Black. I had

Black and white friends, and I don't remember any conscious racism or problems or feelings on the subject during my teenage years. I was very shy and didn't go out a lot. But when my father was away on one of his rare vacations, I had a party my senior year in our house with some girlfriends. I was feeling very sexual at sixteen, risk taking, smoking cigarettes. I didn't drink, but everybody else did. We snuck out the Manischewitz wine and they all got sick. There was one young woman there named Diane, and she was to me the epitome of sexual awareness and maturity. She told us about things, and we'd say, "They did what? They put their lips where?" We were freaking out, giggling and squealing. She was gorgeous, she was Black, she was a dancer. I was completely in awe of her. I think she led to my ability to leave home two years later. Here was a young Black woman who had things about her that were far more admirable than any of my Jewish friends. She also made an impact on me that I didn't have to get married to leave home.

A young Carol Finkle enjoying a boat ride

I didn't go to college. I couldn't pass the college exams and had no support at home to help me with it. I thought the only two schools in the universe were Penn State and Temple, and they both rejected me. So I moved out of my parents' house, got a job and an apartment when I was nineteen. It was 1962. Two years later, after having met and been with Harvey, he encouraged me to go back to school. I went to summer school and got all As, started school at age twenty-three, and it was wonderful. I had a great four years. Then I was nine months' pregnant and ready to deliver Josh, with six courses to go. It took me another eight years to finish!

Josh was born deaf, as was his sister Abby. It was traumatic. It impacted our lives forever—on our consciousness and our needs for parenting that were already beyond the pale for most people. It was a quantum leap because of the impact of deafness on our children and our family in every conceivable way. That journey has been extraordinary for us. It also led us to witness the whole issue of racism in a community that was already an oppressed minority with a generic umbrella of deafness.

American deaf culture reflects racism and homophobia and other biases on how we're able to relate to groups of people in general—then you factor in another minority identity on top of that. I call the deaf the last oppressed minority because they're so completely invisible historically. That's only started to change in the last decade or so, but even with the passage of the ADA (Americans with Disabilities Act) in 1990, the quality of life of deaf people still remains precarious in terms of how much they are included. We still can't go to a damn American movie as the "mixed" deaf-hearing family we are because Hollywood got themselves exempted from the very law that was supposed to assure equal access to every part of life for Americans with disabilities. Movie producers still are not required to provide captioned movies for us or the 28 million people with hearing loss living in this country.

Another example was when Abby got onto an airplane and the hostess wanted to know if she spoke in braille, because the plane had braille magazines. Can you imagine? It just leaves you slackjawed, but it's typical, even in 1998.

Josh and Abby both have very good friends of color—Latino, Black, and other ethnic backgrounds—because the umbrella of deaf culture is more bonding and uniting. American Sign Language bonds culturally deaf people before anything else. In one way, where people might be more prone to be racist, it has the reverse effect because of the commonality of language—a visual sign language in this case. In another way it's schizophrenic, because a group that's been very oppressed often takes on the values of the dominant culture in a stronger way so they can fit in. In our society, a major way of fitting in is to be racist—like it's OK to have Black friends when you're young, but you don't marry them; it's OK to be liberal and have gay friends to a point. Josh's best friend is Black, gay, and deaf. He jokes, "I need a T-shirt that says "I'm Black, Gay, Deaf, and Available!" Every nuance of humanity is found under the deaf culture umbrella.

Carol Finkle with her children Josh and Abby at Josh's graduation from Gallaudet College, Washington, D.C.

As youngsters, I heard many of my kids' friends say things about Blacks that reflect society's racist perceptions, like "these people don't work hard," or "I hate to say this but they're lazy." Even I sometimes find myself clicking my car doors if I see two Black boys walking down the street. They could be my best friend's sons, but because I don't know them, an automatic buzzer goes off in my head that says "there's danger." It's totally irrational and implanted in my psychological makeup. It's so much bigger than anything I can consciously wash away, and I consider myself—on the continuum of racism—far on the lesser end, but I'm still very aware it's there.

I don't know if it's more class than race sometimes. Abby's roommate and one of her best friends in the world is a middle-class deaf Black girl. But in the deaf community they have an expression: they use a sign for hearing near their head, which means their heads are "hearing." Their psyches are hearing even though they're deaf, which means they don't participate in the deaf culture, their sign language skills are nonexistent, their heads are "hearing." Same with Black/white. As I think about it, Abby's friend is Black, but she's white, she's middle-class. Her class appears to have more of an impact than her color, although I'm sure when she goes out into the work world the glass ceiling for a Black woman is even thicker than for a white woman. There are so many nuances to the layers of how it plays itself out.

In the deaf American society you can't just have a National Association of the Deaf. You have Black deaf advocates springing up with chapters all over the country. You have Latino deaf organizations, Jewish deaf organizations. Why? Because the deaf world is made up of every single minority that exists in the hearing world. You also have the elite deaf community, which means your family has been culturally deaf (meaning the preferred means of communication is American Sign Language) through many generations. It's the most prestigious community in the deaf world. They have very strong feelings about hearing families adopting deaf children, deaf parents with hearing children, how they raise them, and deaf-hearing marriages. The first major commercial film on this subject just came out, *Beyond Silence*. This is 1998!

Carol Finkle, back center, with some of her CRAccess theatergoers in Philadelphia

Can you imagine if it had only been this year that the first major film about the Black experience or the Latino world came out? That's what I mean by how invisible deaf people and all the issues still are.

The interpreter community is a major factor in the deaf culture, and racism raises its face there too. Interpreters are the link between the deaf and hearing worlds, so there are interpreter organizations in cities across the country. No surprise, but Black interpreters had to create organizations separate from the white mainstream ones. Why? Because racism exists within that community just like it does everywhere, so they need a strong group to lobby for equal pay and rally against job discrimination.

The need for role models is so important. My children are incredible role models in the deaf world, but they're white and middle-class. As great as my children are, they only supply one aspect of the need. We need more Black deaf role models for *all* deaf children to look up to.

One thing my organization Creative Access does in Philadelphia is showcase performers from the deaf culture who present in American Sign Language. It was important to make the world of hearing arts accessible to deaf people, but it was equally important to create opportunities for professional deaf artists to shine in the mainstream, for all audiences. We provide voice interpreters for the hearing audience, so it's a reverse communication access issue. We bring great Black deaf performers from around the country to be here—dancers, actors, poets. We had a Latino comedian here last year who told stories about deaf culture from the subcontext of Hispanic culture. It's part of what I do to help leave society a little more conscious than it was when I started out twenty-five years ago.

Having said that—Black, white, or otherwise—the mind-set of hearing parents hasn't changed much since Harvey and I had our kids. They're still afraid of deafness, they're still afraid of sign language, they're still filled with foolish and harmful notions and stereotypes about what it means to be deaf and how sign language will impact their children's development. The very choices they need to be making, most still don't make. It's the old story that love is not enough. With all that I've learned from our family's journey, I thank all the gods every day—the Christian God, Buddha, the Mayan gods—that Harvey and I were able to come to understand what our children needed based on who they were, and not on what our society needed them to be. ■■■

Terry Dellmuth grew up in various lily-white suburbs around Philadelphia and was an original founder of People for Human Rights. As with Harvey and me, he was arrested outside of Representative Barrett's home the weekend Martin Luther King was assassinated, several days before Terry's planned wedding. He has held major jobs in Pennsylvania's state government for many years, where he witnessed rural institutional racism firsthand. Terry is the proud father of three exceptional grown children, Chris, Jenny, and Jay.

TERRY DELLMUTH

I was a product of parents who on one side were German and the other, English. Both cultures and both families never really dealt openly with the issue of race. If they did, it was sort of negative. My father's mother lived in Camden, New Jersey, and that was "way downhill." She was a widow, and all around her were Black families. She didn't want to move. It was the family homestead. Interestingly enough, she evidenced her racism because of the way she would talk about "the coloreds," but she was very friendly with the neighbors she knew.

I grew up on a farm and then in various suburbs, lily-white communities, except for a few Black families who were domestics or labor workers. The Blacks I grew up with I played sports with. My family didn't socialize with Blacks. We took a year off when I was eleven and went to Australia and around the world, where I saw an awful lot of poverty and people of all races. The trip raised my race consciousness considerably.

Terry Dellmuth, lower right, in his suburban church boys choir

In high school I had summer jobs where I did a lot of construction work with Black workers and had a good relationship with them. I earned respect by being able to pull my load physically. My whole perception of Blacks and other races was a very skewed one.

After college, where I met a scattering of middle-class minorities, I moved to New York City. I started working in the Boys' Club with a Puerto Rican former gang, then moved into the Boys' Club. In exchange for my room and board I worked four nights a week in the game room. I was dating a girl who was in social work, and it got me interested in the profession. I then went to the Bryn Mawr School of Social Work, where I really honed my own sense of social justice.

All of this was against my parental upbringing. I grew up with views that I had to counter with direct experience. I was then really separated from my parents and had a real falling-out with my folks for a while. A lot of our different opinions were not around specific issues, although what I did for a living, which was moving toward social work, was just unheard of to them. They had higher expectations. The people I worked with—people in gangs or who were in trouble or needed help—were the "losers." "You deserved what you got," is what they would think. My grandfather was a minister, but I can't remember any kind of lessons about race by him or anyone in the family. We were taught to respect people and treat them as equal, but there was this whole other unspoken, less overt racism.

After graduate school, I was working with the state of Pennsylvania in a preschool program, and I was sent to Chester, a predominantly Black low-income town two miles from Swarthmore. It was and still is at the bottom of all the state statistics, and has been for years. Even today it has remnants of being run like a plantation in a politically controlled county. In 1964–65 there were nationally focused race riots in Chester that Stanley Branch led, with state police joining local police and lots of heads being beaten. I was helping to set up programs in Chester for the state. One of my assignments as executive director of the newly formed Police Commission was looking into police brutality charges. That was an eye-opener: the racist attitudes of especially the local officials, the pent-up feelings of the residents of Chester, and the rage seen on videotape of the local police as they waded into demonstrations swinging nightsticks.

Around 1967 a handful of us organized People for Human Rights in Philadelphia. A lot of us had worked in poor Black communities, helping in any way we could. The thought struck a number of us that so much of what we were dealing with was an institutionalized white racism that permeated public policies and had to be dealt with. A lot of times, we as white liberals were also meeting our own needs. We were struggling with how we could be more effective, while also not taking on paternal roles in the Black community. There was a growing sentiment in the Black community to be wary of good intentions by whites.

People for Human Rights was very much a direct action group, putting demonstrations together, confrontations, having our heads on the line a few times. Martin Luther King's death really galvanized us. Many of us were arrested together. We formed reading and study groups in the suburbs about white racism, and part of that was trying to reach folks who might never get involved, but would only hear stories. Some of our frustrations were the "keep our hands clean" attitudes of many of these suburban people. Many were part of church organizations, too.

Connie and I were married in 1968. We had two children of our own. Before our children were born, we began to talk about adoption, so we knew that was an option for us. Then Chris and Jenny came along, and we were very heavily involved in our life with them. There were so many children in the world—there was a large group, especially Black kids, who were in foster care or institutions and had been abandoned. The system wasn't dealing with that situation well—in fact, it hadn't dealt with it for years. So the more we talked about it, the more we realized we didn't have an issue with the race, background, or culture of the child. As we started looking at it more seriously, we decided not to have other children ourselves. The adoption agency put us through a lot. In group discussions about race they raised questions concerning what shade of child you'd be comfortable with (and the group was all white). Some said they didn't want Black children, only white.

As parents of a Black child, it's been an opportunity to confront our own attitudes about race. I'd like to think that we've given Jay a good family life while keeping him in touch with his African American heritage. It's helped Chris and Jenny to be really grounded in their appreciation of diversity, while helping the whole family have a fuller life.

Pennsylvania is one of the hardest states to deal with public racial policies. I worked in state government for thirty years and to this day there's this dominant rural, suburban, antiurban (especially Philadelphia) attitude. It's still difficult for many state officials to give Philadelphia its fair share of programs because of the perception that it will be wasted by all the poor people, the big unions, inefficient government and schools. But many times it's just a code screen of racial attitudes.

Connie and Terry Dellmuth with their children Chris, Jenny, and Jay in Harrisburg, Pennsylvania, in the mid-1970s

The public acceptability for what you do is stated differently now than thirty years ago. It's just a more subtle form of racism. When you get up into the hinterlands, however, it's not very covert. In this current administration in Harrisburg we've had people at the highest deputy levels in the departments make statements that we've had to take to the governor's office and threaten to go public with what they said. Such things as, "Putting money into Philadelphia is like putting it in a black hole." Some of these folks don't even know how to hide their racism.

There's been a lot of advancements on the issue of race. In some ways we're getting to the harder and more subtle areas now. Many middle-class Blacks also have walked away from the lower-class problems, not unlike many of the white ethnic groups before them. The economic gulf is getting bigger and bigger. Some of the same analysis we had thirty years ago is true now—there's an underclass and the majority of it is racial minorities. There's a greater percentage of folks with lots more money now than there was thirty years ago and they don't want to give it up. You can see it with resistance to tax reform and providing equitable resources to public education.

When the stock market crashes, there's going to be a lot of fallout. The states aren't going to be able to provide welfare to all those who need it. I don't feel optimistic about the outcome, because I believe we're riding a crest of arrogance and denial as a society toward our underlying problems, especially as it regards race.

I still believe that our democracy and the institutional structure in this country are basically sound. But we have about 60 percent of kids in urban areas that aren't finishing high school, and most are minorities. As long as that's happening, we're sending most of them to prison. We can't deal, as a society, with minorities as we have in the past. We need a reform strategy that deals with economic and social disparities, and the underlying racism.

A lot of this is economics. The suburban schools around Philadelphia can afford to spend $2,000 per student more each year than we can in the city. That buys a lot of things, like smaller class size, computers, and better facilities. It's one of the challenges and opportunities, as the millennium approaches, that has to be dealt with before the costs —social and economic—become too great. ■■■

Connie Dellmuth grew up in a Christian family of "haves," but tragically she lost her minister father to a heart attack when she was in high school. Given her privileged background, she clearly understands the advantages she has as a white person and what she and Terry could and could not give to their adopted son Jay. She is also keenly aware of how people view her multiracial family and how they view Jay, as an African American male, particularly when he is alone.

CONNIE DELLMUTH

I was the oldest of four children. My father was a charismatic Episcopal minister, beginning with an inner-city parish in Baltimore, where I was born in 1944. It was there my upper-middle-class mother began her own journey—the feisty, independent, college-graduate jazz piano-playing sailing instructor becoming the minister's wife, backbone of parish life, and mother of four children in rapid succession.

Connie Dellmuth, as a baby, with her parents in Vermont

After parishes in Montpelier and Burlington, Vermont, my father was recruited to join the headquarters of the National Episcopal Church in Greenwich, Connecticut, where we lived in a carriage house on the grounds of the church estate. Our five years in Greenwich exposed the four Midworth children to a very different way of life: wonderful in many ways, but not real. My father traveled the world on church business, and my mother felt the brunt of keeping us centered in what was important while combating her own isolation.

At age forty-one, my beloved father had a near-fatal heart attack, in the days before bypass surgery. After his slow recovery, we moved to San Francisco, where he became the minister of a large urban, multicultural church. We plunged from the rarefied schools of Greenwich into the huge and diverse public schools in the heart of the city. After two exciting years there, which included my exuberant father making parish calls all over San Francisco in his clerical clothing and matching black and white Austin-Healy sports car, he died suddenly of another heart attack, at the age of forty-three. My mother, transformed of necessity from a minister's wife to a single parent, moved us back to Burlington, Vermont, where she bought our first house, got her first paying job, and finished raising her children.

My childhood was spent primarily among people who were the "haves," not the "have-nots." But somehow I understood that many people were being excluded from a life of comfort and privilege, primarily because of their skin color. I always knew I wanted to be a social worker—that seemed the venue for helping people and promoting social justice. As a newly arrived senior at Burlington High School, I pushed the parish church to participate in the grape boycott which had been organized by Cesar Chavez in California. I didn't analyze the boycott as an economic or political tool, but I understood that migrant workers were being treated inhumanely and that no one should be standing by and just watching—even people in far-away Vermont.

During my sophomore year at Colby College in Maine, where the world didn't intrude much and most Colby students were dreaming of a junior year abroad, I went as an exchange student to all-Black Fisk University in Nashville, Tennessee. This was in 1963, at the height of the civil rights turmoil. I felt compelled to try to walk in others' shoes and learn firsthand about racism and oppression. I became part of a student movement in a series of demonstrations there and actually spent some scary time in the Nashville jail. It was an eye-opener to live with Black men and women, to understand more about their issues and life experiences.

I became friends with Enoch Jones, a young man from Mississippi. Enoch intended to follow his father and become a Baptist preacher. He had never really known a white person before, and I learned from him about fear and racism. He was very uncomfortable being seen with me. I understood more about that later.

Two weeks after I graduated from Colby I started my master's program at Smith College School of Social Work in western Massachusetts. I picked Smith because it was organized around two nine-month field placements, and I was ready for the real world. My last field placement was in North Philadelphia—definitely the real world. There I met Terry, an activist social worker who had been hired by Smith to teach their social work students. Our first date was on a picket line when Spiro Agnew came to town, and our social life revolved around People for Human Rights, an antiracist grassroots organization that tangled regularly with then Police Commissioner Frank Rizzo. Terry and I were married in six months, almost by proxy, because he was arrested days before the wedding, protesting a police ban on groups gathering to observe and protest the murder of Martin Luther King, Jr.

Connie Dellmuth's wedding announcement, 1968

In 1970 Terry and I, with baby Christopher, packed a U-Haul and moved to a coal-heated farm outside Harrisburg so that bearded, hippyish Terry could work as coordinator of human services in Governor Shapp's new administration. Jenny arrived shortly, and we were so enjoying parenthood that we began thinking about adopting more children. We didn't feel we needed any more genetic Dellmuths. There were lots of kids in the world who needed families. We worked with an adoption agency that dealt with "hard to place" children, which at the time meant older children, children of color, children with disabilities, or sibling groups.

The issue of adopting a Black child was a very natural progression. There were lots of Black children available for adoption. As soon as we met Jay—he was nineteen months old and in a white foster home, weighing seventeen pounds and wanting to be hugged—that was it. This was the little guy we wanted to bring home. We did talk about the issue of race when we realized we would probably adopt a Black child. We tried to think about what kinds of adjustments and accommodations we would want and need to make for him. I think we were very idealistic. We lived on a small farm out in a very rural area of central Pennsylvania. We knew that at some point we would need to find a more diverse neighborhood for us all to live in. We wanted that for our other two children as well.

We also thought about how we would introduce Jay to what we could understand about Black culture and traditions and Black friends. We thought we could just kind of do it and it wouldn't be an issue. We'd just have to figure out how we could make up for that part of his life. I think the overriding issue was that each child is unique, and this child was unique. What Jay needed most was a family, which was in part rationalization, although it seemed clear he didn't have a choice between us or a Black family. This was a child who was going to stay in foster care if we didn't adopt him. I think we felt we were, among all the white people who would adopt a Black child, among the better equipped. Again, I think we were fairly naive with what that all meant.

We moved to a mixed neighborhood in Harrisburg when Jay was two and Chris was ready to start school. It was a pretty middle-class area, where the families of color were primarily racially mixed couples or prominent Black families who sent their kids to private schools, and a few families like ours. The public schools were 90 percent people of color, mostly Black with some Asian and Latino populations. We felt this would work because it would help Chris and Jenny understand what it was like for Jay to be the only Black person in our family. They were going out to a culture where they were very much in the minority.

I have been thinking about the decisions we made along the way. We are committed to public schools and to urban public education. I sometimes wished we didn't have that baggage of commitment because it would have been much easier to send all three kids to a Friends school or a nearby suburban school, which was becoming more diverse. The Harrisburg school district is a poor urban district, with all the attendant problems and insufficient resources for students who needed a lot of support.

For Jay, school was a hard experience. He has always been shy and introspective, especially outside the family. He had a minor learning disability, which didn't seem serious enough to have him identified as a special-education student. Helping him develop a strong and positive sense of himself was our biggest concern and challenge. He once wrote a story about himself which he called "The Harrisburg Dummy." He was and is a gifted athlete, excellent in track, wrestling, and soccer. But in the classroom, he was just another Black boy sitting in the back of the classroom. He was never able to feel valued or successful in school.

Chris has his own story. He has always been "burdened" by being a short, smart white kid with glasses in a tough Black school setting. He developed a very strong identification with the urban Black culture, so if you saw him walking or heard him talking on the phone you might well think he was Black. His approach was to assimilate himself into the middle of the Black culture. When he was ready to go to college, his first choice was Howard University in Washington, D.C., but we told him he had to go somewhere where he could learn to be bicultural! Jenny, as a resourceful middle child, managed to find a diverse group of girls who supported each other and did very well socially and academically. They created their own multiracial community.

Jay always found a friend. He had one white friend in the neighborhood, very bright and intellectual. His parents were both attorneys. Jay would teach Giles how to ride a bike and how to throw a ball—all the active stuff, and Giles would teach Jay how to play games and learn about computers. They had a very nice relationship, although Giles went to private school. Jay had one friend in school named Leander whose skin tone was very dark. I think Leander's mother was a little taken aback, because we would take Leander on vacations with us. It was hard for her to cross the color line once she understood who Jay's family was.

I've seen a lot of people's reactions to Jay and to us. We have gone to the New Jersey shore with two other families every summer since Jay came into our family. The other families included two children who are deaf, which has added another dimension of diversity for all of us. There have always been very few people of color at the beach. We've seen lots of people who see Jay and look around to see where his "family" is, and of course they can't tell by his skin color. When I see Black kids here, I wonder if they're adopted or where their parents are. How has this made Jay feel, deep inside?

We had some overt experiences over the years of Jay's growing up, which remind us that racism is very much a part of our culture. At the beach, the township police would often stop Jay when he was out walking by himself at night or with other kids. There's an implicit assumption of malign intent when mainstream folks see a Black adolescent, especially when there are few people of color. In Harrisburg, when Jay was nine years old he came home from school having forgotten his house key. He walked around the house trying to figure out which window to climb in. Our neighbors, who had lived beside us since we moved there years before, called the police. Three police cars came up to our house where Jay was sitting on the front steps. Finally the neighbor came over and said, "Oh, I recognize him. He does belong here."

Some things have turned out differently than I thought when we welcomed Jay into our family many years ago. I think it has been hard for Jay not to have a clear foundation of his biological family, roots, and racial identity. We have loved and supported him, and he us. We are a family, and we are fiercely proud of him. But we couldn't give him an extended family that looked like him or that shared some of the same experiences of growing up Black in this country. We weren't able to replace, or create, or supplement that foundation as easily as we thought. Although we have worked at it and think of ourselves as very open to diversity, Terry and I found it harder than we thought to meet and become close to Black families. Part of it is where we've lived, the work we have chosen, and the career paths we have pursued. Our communities are not yet integrated, in the real sense of the word. Terry and I climbed the organizational ladder in state government, he in education and me in mental health, and most of the people we knew and worked with looked like us. There is still not a level playing field for people of color, no matter how talented.

In the two years I spent with a family center in North Philadelphia, I had the opportunity to work with and learn from many families for whom poverty and racism were a condition of life. It helped me to see the strength and resilience of children, families, and communities, not just the despair and pathology. People cope with and transcend enormous odds in terms of poverty and racism that those of us who are born with white skin and resources don't comprehend. I came to understand the concept of white privilege as what we are born to, not what we earn. I look at how the world responds to my Black son Jay and the way he looks, and then how the world responds to me and how I look. All the assumptions people make about me because of my class and my color have nothing to do with my values, or who I am as a person, or what I have to contribute—nor, of course, about Jay as a person.

I now work in Washington, D.C., with programs all across the country which are implementing services for children with mental health problems. These programs serve many children and families of color, but the leadership does not reflect the diversity of the communities being served. Until that changes and people of color have an equal opportunity to participate fully in all this country has to offer, racism will touch all our lives, not just Jay's. In 1975 when we adopted him, we thought we would see the end of racism before he grew up. We all have to work harder. ∎∎∎

At twenty-eight, Chris is the oldest biological child of Connie and Terry. He has strong beliefs about race and racism and is the proud and supporting father of three young biracial children. He's also very observant about other biracial couples and how racial patterns have changed over the years. Chris recently graduated from Temple University's School of Law and now lives and works in Harrisburg, Pennsylvania.

Chris, Connie, Terry, Jenny, and Jay Dellmuth at Long Beach Island, New Jersey, 1999

CHRIS DELLMUTH

I don't know how much of my childhood I remember, or a special time of being aware of differences, like some people are colors other than white, or the differences placed upon those differences.

I went to public schools in Harrisburg, which was a very city-type experience, very urban, very poor—probably 85 percent Black. Most of my friends were Black growing up, except my best friend, Chris, who was a year older than me and a lot taller. In my class with my friends I was called "White Chris," and when I was with Chris I was "Little Chris." That's just the way things were—how people would keep us straight when they were talking about us.

The summer after ninth grade I went to an academic camp at a university for three weeks. It was for academically talented youth and was predominantly white, mostly kids with a lot of money. I got to be close to people who were very different from me. The main difference was class more than race, although they seemed very tied together.

One of my best friends from camp lives in Rye, New York. He came and visited me and I went to visit him, and it was worlds apart. They were very upper class and lived in the low area of his neighborhood. It seemed that all these people had money and they were all white. All of my friends' families were broke and mostly Black.

Before I went to Penn State I spent six months in North Carolina, and it was total culture shock. It was the South, and you hear about how it was then, and it was total shock to realize that it is still like that. The division was very clear and very explicit. It was "them" and it was "us." And it's all of them against the Yankees, white or Black.

When I got to Penn State, it seemed the white kids were worried about where to park their Porsches and BMWs and going to parties. It didn't matter what they did in school. They'd graduate and their dad would get them a job in some nice banking firm or something, so school was really a time for them to cut loose. In my high school class, going to college was a privilege, and you had to work for it. It was expected of me because of my family, but for most of my friends it was not a reality unless you were lucky or worked very very hard. For the white kids at Penn State it wasn't a struggle. They didn't know what people were facing to try and get to where they were, and that stood out.

When I was at Penn State, which is supposed to be a big liberal school, we had a huge race riot. It was after the Michigan football game, and the whole campus was drunk. It was me and my friends against a bunch of white kids. They drove by and some words were exchanged and we started fighting them, and pretty soon about 150 people in the street were fighting. When it started out it was a race issue, and when the battle lines were drawn and everybody else was joining in, it was a very clear line—except for me. I had some concerns that people on my side, who were supposed to recognize me, might not!

It was weird afterwards because this type of thing happens in a lot in schools. They'd have panels and everybody gets together and has race relations discussions. At Penn State nothing was done and nothing was said about it. It was as if it never happened.

I was in a class on international agriculture. The professor had been to Africa the semester before and done a project in villages where the women were in charge of running the agriculture. They were breeding chickens and pigs and helping the women in the village breed them for better characteristics so they could get more meat. He showed a picture of some of the village women with a new pig they had raised. The kid next to me whispers to his girl, "Some of them nigger bitches like to lay with pigs." Right next to me in the middle of class! I got up and hit him. He grabbed his face and said, "Why did you do that for?" and the whole class was in an uproar. It was terrible, but I didn't make a big issue of it. I hit him and told him, "You know what you said, and don't give me any bullshit like that," and I sat back down. The professor was oblivious. I don't think he wanted to get involved, then it was over.

I imagine my three children are going to face some problems. People notice and are pointing out that they're not exactly of one race or another. I hope it's not soon and I can prepare them for that. The Black lady I work with, her daughter is probably ten years old and very dark skinned. She goes to school in New Jersey, a 90 percent white school. Her parents are middle class and worked hard to get there and have a sense of their Blackness. The daughter came into work one day because she was suspended. I asked her, "Why did you get suspended?" She said, "Well, I got into a fight." I said, "That happens, but it's not really the way to solve your problems and it's not what you should be doing, so why were you fighting?" And she said, "This boy called me a 'nigger,' so I hit him." I told her, "He probably deserved it. Did he get suspended?" She said, "No." I remember a situation with Jay when he was at Westtown Friends school. He was playing soccer and something like that happened. I don't think he got into a fight; he wasn't very confrontational, but he was pretty heated.

I've got a lot of concerns about where race relations are in our country today. It seems to be really tied to the economy. When the economy is going well and we're prospering, it's much easier for people to get along. But if the economy is on the down side and people are struggling, we like to point to somebody else for what our problems are. People need to group together and have a common foe, be that religion or race or class. I don't think there's been a tremendous amount of progress in the past ten to fifteen years. There still seems to be a lot of division, and in some ways is becoming more so.

You'd think that with more mixed-race couples and more minorities joining the middle and upper classes, people would have more in common, so that the differences would be less important, but that doesn't seem to be the rule. Interracial couples are becoming more accepted, but it doesn't seem to be bringing the cultures together outside of each individual couple.

When I was younger, most mixed-race couples were a Black man and a white woman, but now—for the past three or four years—I've been noticing more white men with Black women. Most of my relationships have been with Black women, and it's funny when you see a white dude with a Black girl on the street. They stand out, even to me, who's been in that relationship. You wonder, "How did that happen?" But it's good, it's encouraging. You hope it's not just because of the novelty or a little rebellion, but because two people found themselves and are being happy together. ■■■

enny Dellmuth is the biological daughter of Connie and Terry, a smart and athletic young woman. She's not afraid to confront racism and wants to consciously contribute to undoing people's often false assumptions about one another based on the color of their skin. Jenny graduated from the University of Minnesota's School of Law and continues to live and work in Minneapolis.

JENNY DELLMUTH

One of my earliest memories involving race was going to the playground with my brother Jay. I was about seven and he was six. We were swinging on the swings and a little girl in the playground started, "I see a girlfriend and a boyfriend," and I got really mad. "It's not my boyfriend, it's my brother, so shut up!" We got that a lot, and I had fun with it sometimes. People would ask me how Jay could be my brother. My favorite story was when I was in eighth grade I told a guy

Jay, Jenny, and Chris Dellmuth
in Harrisburg, Pennsylvania

I had a crush on that Jay was my brother. He said, "How could he be your brother?" and I said, "Recessive genes." And he said, "No! They can do that?" I always liked having a Black brother. It made me feel special. I like to shock people and get rid of their assumptions and generalizations. My family was really good at that.

It was funny that my parents didn't know how to do Jay's hair. They didn't know how to do my hair, either, but they really didn't know how to do his. Chris and I used to get bowl haircuts from my grandfather. He'd put a bowl on our head and cut around it, and that was our haircut. We tried it with Jay and it didn't work, so he was a real Buckwheat for a long time. He learned to do his own hair, his saving grace.

When I was in high school we all played soccer on the same team. There were very few Black or white people on the team—it was mostly Vietnamese. I was the only girl, and I had fun with that. I liked being different, and that wasn't an issue with me. But I remember the football team was all Black. To me, it was really a form of racism—the Blacks against the Vietnamese. I always had a problem with that because these were my friends they were talking about. It also disappointed me because a lot of Blacks complain about being stereotyped and discriminated against because of their race, then I saw them doing the same thing to the Vietnamese. I didn't ever think I could talk about it fairly because I didn't want to put down the Blacks. But so often I've seen minorities making fun of other minorities. I guess it's a way of shoring up their own self-worth, but it bothered me.

I never felt that I didn't belong. I was lucky, because it was really easy for me. Looking back, I'm sure Mom and Dad had a really hard decision to make in sending us to an inner-city public school. They both had good jobs, and we could have gone to a private school. I think it was a really important choice because we did get a sense of all walks of life, and to value people for who they are and not what they look like.

When Jay went to our high school I can understand why he had a lot of problems. Chris is very "ghetto-y" sometimes. He can talk like it and walk like it. For me, I can go back and forth, depending on who I'm with. But with Jay, Black people can accept a white person who is culturally Black, but they have a very difficult time accepting a Black person who in large part is culturally white. I could see him struggling with that.

There was one mixed girl in my group of friends. When we went to college, she went to Penn and became a Black militant and denounced all of her white heritage, all of her white friends. She wanted nothing to do with us. She had found her culture, and that's what she was embracing. We were mad and hurt because we were such close friends. Part of it was my own disappointment when I went to Princeton in not making more of an effort to be among the Blacks. The new culture for me was the white culture, so that's maybe why I didn't make an effort to be with Blacks because that's what I always had.

I've always liked to help people out. When I graduated from Princeton I became a case manager at a homeless shelter—a job that was supposed to last two months, and I was there for three and a half years.

I think my background enabled me to take the focus off of race. I had experiences that helped me fit in wherever, and because of that, race was a nonissue with me, just as economic class was. I feel I'm able to help the down-and-out who are usually Blacks and Latinos, because I'm not a crusader from the outside. I've really been there.

I did see a lot of covert racism at the shelter, particularly when we had visitors. My first week on the job, I'm twenty-three years old and have no clue what I'm doing. I'm standing in the hallway and talking with one of my Black coworkers who'd been there for fifteen years and was training me. A Black couple came in, and they were asking questions about giving donations. They addressed all of their questions to me, and they just assumed that I was the worker and my coworker was the client. After they left, both of us laughed about that, but whites and Blacks coming in would turn to me more readily.

I know and understand that I don't have a full sense of racism because you can't really understand it unless it's directed against you. I can empathize and sympathize, but I don't know what it's like. Even when I was a minority, I was a minority in a subculture, but a majority in the greater culture.

I'm very interested in native, minority, and aboriginal cultures. When I was in Australia earlier this year, there was a bunch of young people traveling there—from Europe, America, all over the world—mostly white and middle-class. (The upper class stayed in hotels, we stayed in hostels!) There was one aboriginal cultural park near Cairns in northern Australia. It was one of the most fantastic things I did there. I got a sense of what native Australian culture was like, but nobody else from the youth hostel really seemed to care. The Aborigines, just like the Native Americans, have been stripped of their dignity and heritage, forced to be assimilated in a culture which is against all their beliefs. They have the same problems of alcoholism and lack of employment as you find here.

In this country I think we've come a long way regarding race, but I think people think we're farther than we are. A lot of people assume, "Well, civil rights was ages ago," especially in my generation. To me, that's not true. The way people deal with racism is they're not classifying it as racism. It's society against people of color who then rage against society, but it's not a productive rage. When I went away to Princeton, I'd call my brother Chris and ask him, "What's the scoop on our friends?" and he'd say, "This person's in jail, this person got shot, this person's dead," and that's what we dealt with. It was really sad to see.

Mom and Dad were especially good at learning how to value differences. I love differences now, and change, and new things. That's something I'm really glad they brought to us. A lot of people just don't have it. My own personal crusade is that it doesn't matter if you're female, white, Black or whatever, it's just you. I was a female playing on a male soccer team, and that was OK. In college I played boys' club soccer, and it didn't matter. To me, it's not a big deal. When it comes down to it between you and the ball, gender and race don't matter. That's how it should be in all of life. ▪■▪

J ay Dellmuth is the adopted Black son of Connie and Terry. His is a very different story from those of his siblings, one that continues to unfold as he searches for his roots and his own sense of identity in a world that tests Black men in ways difficult for white people to understand. Jay lives in Philadelphia and works in a downtown architectural office.

JAY DELLMUTH

I was adopted at nineteen months from an agency in York, Pennsylvania. I was living with my two grandmothers in York. My mother had given me up from conception, so I was adopted and moved in with the Dellmuths.

I don't really remember when race was a big thing. Sometimes when I was coming down to our summer house at the shore, a predominantly white area, realizing I was Black but not seeing myself as any different from anyone else. I was still too young to understand the whole thing. I did see a lot of Black families, and they were very open and nice—that always felt good. Some of the white families were standoffish and didn't want to talk with our family. That was always sort of sensitive.

Going through elementary school was quite an experience, because the kids start to see differences. I felt like I fit in well and had some friends. Even then there were definite divisions of race. There was first hall, second hall, and third hall. First hall was the academically solid students, second hall was a step down, and third hall was the special-education students. In terms of race, practically all of the whites were in first hall, second hall was predominantly Black, and third hall was all Black. One time I had a lunch detention for doing something I wasn't supposed to do. It was my first time going down to third hall and visiting that whole area. I was viewed as an outsider, and they asked me, "Why are you here? You're a good kid."

Middle school was a whole other experience. When I went there it was an old warehouse-type building and there were no walls in a lot of the classrooms. There were divisions between them, but your main classroom was looking out into other classrooms. This school was also predominantly Black. There were a lot of racial fights and a lot more tension. People went off into their little cliques. I think that's where I first saw it, in sixth grade. My sister was still there (she was in eighth grade), so she had her group of friends and I kind of fit in with them. I had my group of friends, not that racially mixed. They were a lot more accepting of me and didn't see me as anyone different.

The middle school classes were also divided by academic group. It really didn't dawn on me that it was really a dividing of races and a conscious decision by the school in doing it. In high school there was a lot of the same dividing, but there were even less white students. It was more going out for sports—a lot of the students weren't into the education they were getting. I was not accepted because I played soccer— that was a "white boys' sport," so I sat with the soccer team at lunch. There were a few white students, but most of the players were Vietnamese or Cambodian. We all hung out together and got picked on together. The football team was constantly kicking our soccer balls way out—the football coaches didn't say anything. The soccer coach tried, but got no response. It's sad the school allowed that to happen.

I attended a Friends' boarding school the last two years of high school. It was an excellent decision on my parents' part and my part to get out of my old school. I was just living for the moment, not planning to go to college because I was so unhappy and getting abused verbally. When I went to Westtown my junior year, in 1991, it was a whole new experience. People were very nice and open and focused on their studies. We'd talk about books we were reading and our opinions about history and English. It was a whole interactive environment. I had a Jewish roommate, and we were really good friends. He was the opposite of me —I was athletic, and he was very smart and very unathletic! In terms of race at Westtown there were a few Blacks there, maybe 15 out of 600 students. Even there they kind of stuck together, but it was a different sort of thing, more like a family structure. They were very accepting of me. I didn't see myself as a part of it, and didn't want to be part of the white group either. I was friends with almost everyone, but I was off on my own, stayed in my room. Many times I was star of the soccer game and everybody would pat me on the back and congratulate me. It was so hard to accept. I would just go into a shell and say, "You're just joking," and push it aside. In hindsight I wish I could have given back to them. I was so shy, thinking I was different from them. I was the most valuable athlete my senior year, and that was a really nice feeling.

I decided to go on to college and picked Syracuse with 14,000 students. Instantly when I got there people were upset as to how the school did the housing for freshmen. It was high-rise dorms, maybe about fifteen stories, and predominantly Black, Hispanic, and Asian students. Then there was "Mt. Olympus," where all the white students were. It had to be a conscious decision by the university. You can't place 7,000 students in a dorm and say it was random. It was really upsetting to me to see that. Because of my parents and the amount of money they made—and because I didn't check the box as to what race I was—I was placed in an all-white dorm, a "quiet lifestyles" dorm. There were quiet hours every night. There was another Black student there, an upperclassman.

I met a lot of people and fit in very well. At that time the problem for me wasn't fitting in with whites, it was fitting in with Blacks. They thought there was something wrong with me and openly said so, like there's something mentally wrong with me that I want to be the way that I am—white, which was the way they perceived me. That was really disturbing to me and depressed me that I was considered not Black.

I see myself as Black, and even white students were saying, "Wow, you're more white than me." I grew up in the city, gotta have that to be Black, you gotta go through all kinds of hardships, you gotta be bitter about slavery. You have to have all of these things to be Black. That was the most difficult part of Syracuse for me. Having a white girlfriend and receiving looks, saying things or laughing at us. I did have some Black friends who were OK with who I was, but when I was with my girlfriend or my roommate Jay, we were instantly pushed aside.

When I was on my own it was a different thing. People would say, "Hi, who are you?" So I'm the mystery Black person at Syracuse out of 14,000 people—it amazed me that I would be this project for them. There were a lot of Blacks who'd say, "Just hang out with us, and you'll pick up something and be all right." In a way it was comforting, but they were trying to change me to fit their mold of the person they thought I should be. It wasn't the person I was, and it just didn't work for me. Some people saw it as me neglecting my heritage, my race, and lying to myself about who I am. I've always known that I'm Black in every situation that I've gone into. I wasn't going to change myself, my personality, for something society wanted me to be or other people wanted me to be. It never seemed right. I still get very emotional about it.

I think—on the larger issue of race—the issue of Hispanics outnumbering Blacks in the twenty-first century will raise tensions between Blacks and Hispanics because we haven't reached that point—we've been surpassed. A lot of Blacks now struggle in our communities and are not really progressing that fast. All the crime and drugs and shooting are pulling us back. We're being passed economically and socially by a race that we would say was below us ten or fifteen years ago.

I don't think relations between Black and white are going to get any better either—maybe even worse. There should naturally be more Blacks, Hispanics, and Asians in our government, especially high up. I don't think we're going to see it, and it's going to be a problem. It's the same in the corporate world, where I want to work. Corporations are like government structures—branching out into different countries, exploiting the workforces in those countries. We have so many minorities from different countries that we are suppressing and bombing. It just makes more enemies of people within our own society. ■■■

Lucia Faithfull was a very active member of People for Human Rights. Although she grew up in a wealthy suburb of New York, her story shows how she grew from that background to become acutely conscious of the racial and class divides in our society. Her growing awareness led to an active life with her first husband, Ronald Stevenson, in the Communist Party. After his death over a decade ago, she moved to Seattle, where she now works for a large and diverse job-training program. She and her second husband, Kelly, live in a country-like setting with a generous vegetable garden worked and enjoyed by friends and neighbors.

LUCIA FAITHFULL

I grew up surrounded by woods outside the town of Bedford, New York (Westchester County), forty miles from New York City. My father was a lawyer who commuted to the city. My mother took care of the family and the household. My two sisters, Sidney and Gail, were nine and six year older than I was. My early schooling took place in a one-room schoolhouse, "the little school," walking distance from home. All of my social interactions were with white people except for one Black maid who took care of me when I was a baby and the weekly visits of the garbage collectors.

My isolation from any real-life contact or exposure to the social or political currents of the time created a blank page in my consciousness. My parents raised me with values based on a belief in equality and democracy. This was reinforced at the "little school," where cooperation in all of our activities was the rule.

Throughout all of my years of formal schooling until I attended college this picture did not change. But there were things that began to bother me. I remember taking the train to New York City. As it would pass through Harlem, I observed the cramped and decrepit apartment buildings close to the tracks. I developed this strong sense that there was something wrong. Why was there such poverty? This was in stark contrast to my life. It was not until the early 1960s that I became conscious of injustice and racism in particular.

My first acquaintance with an African American person occurred in the summer of my sophomore year in college. I was introduced to Father Lorentho Wooden, an Episcopal minister of a large parish on the Upper West Side of Manhattan. He encouraged me to go to the March on Washington that very summer. That was the first thing I ever did of a political nature, and it was a turning point in my life. A year later he influenced my decision to pursue community organization in graduate school. He helped to create the inspiration for working for change by organizing people to change their circumstances. This seemed like it could be a path to saving the world.

Going on the March on Washington was a powerful experience. As our buses rolled in and out of D.C., Black people from the neighborhoods lined the streets, waving and cheering and encouraging us. In all my years of going to numerous demonstrations in the Capitol I have never seen the like of it since.

The sight of the sea of humanity from the steps of the Lincoln Memorial was awesome. The combination of the heat, humidity, and crush of the crowd to hear and see the speakers on the podium caused me to retreat to the cool shade of the trees lining the reflecting pool. To my enormous regret, I dozed off just at the time Dr. King presented his "I have a dream" speech. The power and energy of the day still rolled over me and provided the momentum and vision for future actions and struggle.

While I was attending graduate school at the School of Social Work in Philadelphia, I was impelled to work and organize around issues of racism by a local event. African American high school students organized and demonstrated to get African American history in the curriculum. When the chief of police, Frank Rizzo, busted heads after giving his word the police would maintain peace and order, that was it. That's what really got me started on a road of ongoing political involvement.

Progressive-minded whites such as Terry Delmuth, Father Dave Gracie, and others began organizing People for Human Rights (PHR) to confront white racism. I became an active member, a student of racism and the fight against its many forms.

Not long after, Dr. King was assassinated. It was a searing and troubling event that impacted the whole nation. At that time, I had difficulty understanding the rebellions that took place in city after city. But what was most significant for me were the connections King was making between the civil rights struggle, the rights of workers, and the injustice of the imperialist war in Vietnam.

By the late 1960s, after working on PHR's antiracist consciousness-raising education activities, several of us joined forces with some activists in Resistance and other antiwar groups to form a political collective. We moved together into a house in a poor, white, working-class section of the city called Kensington. There we hoped to plant our progressive antiwar, antiracist ideas. With a few exceptions, the folks in the neighborhood were not receptive to our presence. Over the course of twelve months, they resisted our efforts to the point that it became an untenable living situation, and our collective split up.

In the spring of 1970 I went to Cuba on the Venceremos Brigade. The magnetism of the Cuban socialist revolution was irresistible. The dramatic changes taking place in that nation were mind-boggling. Cuba, under U.S. imperialist control, was a blatantly racist society. Under socialism, elimination of inequities among the races was consciously promoted in all major policies. The Cuban government focused on building Cuban society for Cubans. Their efforts were aimed at achieving equity in all areas—cultural, educational, economic, social, and political.

Now that's a hard proposition to contemplate. How could the years of inhumanity, exploitation, lynchings, and the residue of slavery and Jim Crow be erased when our economic system perpetuates and promotes racism? The Cuban system was making great strides in this arena and developing models that we could—and still can—learn from.

The experience of being in Cuba and learning more about socialist goals and ideas prompted me to join the Communist Party in 1972. The comprehensive programs and goal of bringing Black liberation to the fore of all activities tied the different currents of my experience together.

In the early 1970s I worked along with Angela Davis and Charlene

Mitchell in the founding of the National Alliance Against Racist and Political Repression (NAARPR) and staffing the national office in its first five years. The struggle against the legal system's racism in its multiple forms was our daily work. We counted some successes in the freeing of the Charlotte Three and the Wilmington Ten. But other cases and the reinstatement of the death penalty were more stubborn.

During these years I married my comrade, Ronald Stevenson, an African American man born in 1921 in Council Bluffs, Iowa. We had to demonstrate to my family that a mixed marriage could work and needed to be respected on its own merits. In time, we were successful, but Ronnie was never comfortable visiting my home in the segregated white suburbs. He could never relieve himself of the fear that the Klan might appear, so we accommodated with short visits.

In our fourteen years of marriage we shared many experiences. I gained a very intimate view of the pressures of racism on our (his) family and other African American friends. My understanding of the difficulties of Black men and women growing up and living in the U.S. was enriched through this relationship. I also considered myself privileged to have shared in the warm acceptance of his parents and other family members of his generation. This amazed me, given the history of racism in our country. Ronnie's grown children developed a cautious approach and, in time, loving support.

We shared a common endeavor in his work to build the antiapartheid campaign in the United States. Several South African freedom fighters graced our home and inspired our work. We strove to make the connections within the trade union movements in the U.S. by building support for sanctions against South Africa.

The most challenging part of our relationship was learning that unconscious racism is or can be a constant companion. I learned that I needed to continually strive to become aware of its many forms and that it could manifest itself in daily interactions with people who are close and strangers alike. This could occur by commission or omission. By failing to take on a racist comment or act, I was complicit. This is— and will be—an ongoing process until I die.

Now I have the good fortune to share married life with James Kelly, an African American man who was born in the segregated South in the mid 1940s. Many of his early experiences with segregation, racism, and poverty were not so different from the previous generation. My family had progressed in its appreciation and acceptance of my second mixed marriage and of our relationship. Various family members have broadened their relationships outside white society and have been enriched by them.

Where we live in the metropolitan Seattle area, institutional racism still exists in many forms, but the subtle manifestations of racism in everyday interactions are just that, subtle. For Kelly, this is minimized in great part by his good common sense, his engaging personality, and his bright mind. In our numerous road trips on the West Coast and on

Lucia Faithfull, on the right next to the scarecrow, with friends in her large vegetable garden

his recent photography trip through northern New York State and New England, we have never encountered a sign of hostility, and we have been able to share wonderful experiences with strangers along the way.

Regarding the status of the racial situation in this country, in some ways, a lot of things have changed. Certainly segregation as it was practiced up until the civil rights era has changed in form. Antimiscegenation laws are off the books; the Voting Rights Act has been passed. The numbers of African Americans and other minorities elected to public office are on the increase. African Americans are reaching higher levels of the corporate structure in increasing numbers.

However, the statistics still reveal disproportionately high numbers of African American children with lower academic achievement (not aptitude), higher health risks, higher dropout rates, and higher incarceration rates. As far as I know, poverty levels have not greatly diminished in the African American population as a whole. This is occurring at a time when the disparity between the super-rich and the poor has become glaring. Too many statistics tell a story that reveals we have a long, long way to go.

The organizations that are involved in the struggle to make America a more democratic and equitable society are going through a lot of changes. I am hopeful that the NAACP under the current leadership will become more of a focal point for continuing this struggle. There are many efforts going on at the grassroots level, such as Break the Cycle, a project my stepson Ronnie Stevenson and his family have been working on since the 1980s. This has promise for improving the educational achievement levels in the elementary and secondary school grades.

The so-called welfare reform has some potential for moving poor women into productive work environments. The danger is they may end up being worse off economically. Employers may use this low-skilled workforce to reduce the wage and work standards, using new forms of racism as their wedge. As the five-year clock winds down for women to get off welfare, we could have an explosive situation, especially if we experience an economic downturn.

There have been numerous disturbing trends exemplified by groups and individuals with mind-sets and actions typified by the white supremacists such as the Aryan Nation. In Jasper, Texas, a Black man was dragged to his death, the 1990s version of a lynching. The forces behind the anti–affirmative action proposition in California are active in Washington State right now, and that will be an area of focused struggle for all democratic-minded antiracist people in our state as we approach the 1998 election. (The electorate followed California's lead eliminating affirmative action provisions in the state arena.)

To provide a level playing field and to bring about true equity and humanness in our social relations among the races, all democratic-minded people will have to adhere to Frederick Douglass's saying, "Freedom is a constant struggle." ■■■

I met Lucia's husband, James Kelly, in 1990. His story reflects how, as a young Black boy growing up in the South in the 1940s and 1950s, he learned from his strong grandmother how to survive and thrive during that dangerous time. In the army he realized, without rancor, how his life could have unfolded if he were white. Kelly is a very talented photographer and manages a gallery in the foothills of Mt. Rainier.

JAMES KELLY

I was born in 1945 in South Carolina, and unfortunately I lost my mother at an early age, eighteen months old. My sister was two weeks old, and my grandmother took on the chore of raising me, my sister, and my older sister. She lived in Auburn, Alabama, a small university town about twenty miles east of Tuskegee. I grew up in a one-parent household. My early years of positive discipline are because of my grandmother, and my early exposures to everything that I've done and why I'm the kind of person I am today is a credit to her because of the way she brought me up. Very strictly.

I had occasional visits with my father in South Carolina but was always coming back home and doing my school time with my grandmother. I wasn't allowed to participate in a lot of sports and stuff because I had to make a contribution to the household, so I worked.

I realized that being a Black boy was different through the guidance of my grandmother. We weren't allowed to do certain things—you don't go there. It was our geographic location in the city, the borders. I was at the beginning of the Black border. There was a fence in front of my yard, which separated us from the elementary school that I could not attend. My sister and I had to walk about three miles to school every morning, and we bypassed this school yard that was fifty feet from our door. But still I didn't see the wrong in it, I didn't understand it, and I didn't question it because if you're comfortable with where you're going, you're OK with it.

There was an early incident when I was about nine years old when my grandmother made sure we all got in the house one evening because there was a convoy of Ku Klux Klan coming through our neighborhood. They were going to burn a cross in front of this man's house and give him the opportunity to move out of the community because he had allegedly looked at a white woman. My grandmother had us turn the lights out (which were kerosene lamps at that time), and that's when the questioning began. Why is this? That's when I first started getting educated.

At the same time I was also getting positive education, because my two best friends were white kids who lived in the last house on the border of the white community where the pavement ended. My house was the first house in the Black section, which was a dirt-topped road. The school that was at the border of our property had a tennis court, and at night my sister and myself and those two kids, Carl and SueCarol Huntley, would all go and play tennis on this tennis court. In exchange for our teaching them how to roller skate, they would come over to our house and play. Our grandmother was always cautious about how we played and that we stayed in the open. I was getting signals that it was kind of all right, but be careful. Carl and SueCarol's dad was a military person who himself interacted daily with Blacks and whites. That was very helpful. The police came one night when we were playing tennis and they tried to shoo us away, said that we shouldn't be there, but their dad came out and said, "These kids play together all the time, so leave them alone." The police left, and there never was another incident.

I had more positive experiences than negative ones. I didn't have any negative experiences that were so bad and out of line that turned me off to anybody.

The first real sense of what it felt like to be Black was when I went into the military. One of my friends from this little town, Carl, went to a school that offered trigonometry—a white city school—and I went to a county school, and that course wasn't offered there. He and I went into the military together, but when we took the officer's candidate test, he was qualified to go to the artillery and I was not. I was only qualified to become an infantry officer, and the reason was that he had subjects in his high school that I was not offered. That was the first time I felt the difference—that day when we got our results back. I felt that if I had been allowed to go to the same school, we would have had equal opportunities. This is something the city and county did to me. The hope to attend Auburn University was denied because they didn't accept Blacks at that time. But you just go on, and I went on. I didn't hold it or throw bricks at somebody's house.

I ended up going to the artillery. I spent my time in Vietnam in an artillery unit, but I was a noncommissioned officer and Carl was a commissioned officer. We did see each other in Vietnam and later in Germany, but he was a major and I was a staff sergeant. You see, that all began back in high school. It just carried on. I don't hold it against him. We were still the best of friends.

I was in the military for ten years, from 1963 to 1973, and I don't think I was slowed down at all because of race. My rank came fast. I couldn't see it if it was there. It didn't affect me. I don't think I was in denial. It was just that in the military we were all green, wearing green uniforms. That's what I sensed. When I was in Vietnam for a year it was survival, taking care of each other. It wasn't taking care of somebody because he's Black or white. We were all given the same amount of ammunition, we were all given the same equipment to survive, the same food.

After leaving the service I went back to Georgia to find work and see how it was. I found out it was a lot different than the past ten years in the military. Things were not much changed. I went to a job interview, and the person who interviewed me told me that my qualifications were good, but "I want to be honest with you, I think it's going to be difficult for some of these older white men to take orders from you. It's also going to be difficult for some of these older Black men to take orders from you because you're only twenty-eight years old." I understood that and thanked him for telling me. So I decided to come to the Northwest and try to get a ride on the Alaska pipeline and get work up there. You had to apply to the union, and I didn't think I had a chance, so I applied for a job at the VA hospital in Tacoma, and I worked there for thirteen years.

During that time I was pursuing my photography as a hobby, and it had become a second occupation during my off-duty times. I was accumulating equipment and darkroom gear, and I finally came to a point in 1996 when I decided therapeutically my photography was where I wanted to be. It was my connection to people—without verbalizing with them I was communicating with them through my work and my love for nature. Luckily, with my wife, we've survived these past two years. I know if I work on my marketing more, it's going to get better. I have the gift, but I'm not a very good businessperson. I would rather give a picture away than sell one. You can't survive like that!

In terms of race, I think this area is a very fruitful place, partially because of all the military bases and our connection to Asia. If you compare it to New York City or Los Angeles, we probably don't have as many Blacks as some of those cities, but a mixed couple rarely gets a second look here that I notice. I have gotten some looks when Lucia and I have gone out together—it may be from another Black woman who may give you that look, "Why couldn't you find your own kind?" I've gotten some verbalization, too, early in our relationship. It was young, immature people, and I understood that and I ignored that. There are so many mixed couples. It seems just as harmonious as our relationship, so it's not unusual. I've known Black men married to Asian women, I've known Black men married to Caucasian women, and I've known a few Black women married to Caucasian men. In fact I just had an opportunity to do a show for this Black lady who is head of our county media relations and is married to a white man. I didn't look at her differently. I think people are coming to the point where they're not looking at their partner as being Black or white, but as being a partner, a person that you love, that you care for, a person you want to spend the rest of your life with.

James Kelly, Hasani, me, and Lucia Faithfull at their home near Seattle, 1990

In the past, I think people tried to do something that was culturally safe, culturally accepted because the spouse has to expose the other spouse to potential abuse from either side of the family. By Lucia taking me, it was a setup for abuse if her family wasn't accepting, and vice versa. I could be doing the same thing to her. One of the first things we did early in our marriage was take a plane and fly to Alabama. We went to my uncle's nightclub, and she was the only white person in there, but she was safe because my family was there. The first thing she did to me was fly me to Bedford, New York. You could count the Blacks that were there, but I felt safe and accepted. My family adores Lucia. She's not a color, she's just a person.

I'm very comfortable about being where I am tonight, but then you see or read about what happened in Texas—the Black man dragged to his death. So you know that things still happen. I got in my RV last September, and 5,000 miles and ten states later I had traveled by myself and went through a lot of little towns and I associated with a lot of people along the road—day and night—and I never felt unsafe once. I was on trails doing my photography and never felt threatened. And then when you hear something like what happened down in Texas it still reminds you that everybody has not accepted that we are all human.

I think that things have changed. The incidents that we hear about now are small. They're not big incidents like people getting hung. If we were to go back to when my grandmother was eleven years old, there were public hangings, so we are progressing as a society. I don't know if it's fear of being sued or some of it is genuine acceptance. I would like to think there is more acceptance of each other as another human being. ▪▪▪

I met Steve Stevenson when I was a community organizer in the North Philadelphia neighborhood of Ludlow and he was working with the suburban church that hired Victor to rehabilitate several abandoned row houses. Steve was involved in several key social change groups in the 1960s and actively participated in some of People for Human Rights' major demonstrations and strategy sessions.

From his rural roots in Wisconsin to his Peace Corps work in Africa, where he met his future wife, to his return to Wisconsin with his son, Steve has made great contributions to the diverse fields of antiracism and agriculture. Over the years he has held several key positions at the University of Wisconsin in Madison, where he continues his good work today.

STEVE STEVENSON

I was born and grew up in a small rural community of about 2,000 people in southwestern Wisconsin. My family was a farming family, but by the time I arrived, my folks were living in town. So I was a town kid. The distinction when I grew up was whether you were a town kid or a country kid. We had a farm—in fact, a fifth-generation farm that was homesteaded by my great-great-grandfather from Kentucky

Steve Stevenson with animal friends on his family's farm in Wisconsin

in the 1830s. The farm is one of the ten oldest in the state of Wisconsin that have been in the same family since white people's settlement. I'd spend summers and weekends out at the farm. Both my parents were teachers—my father was a history teacher and an athletic coach, and my mom was a home economics teacher.

I grew up in a really healthy environment. Small towns have upsides and downsides, and the upsides are that you really could be involved in a whole range of activities. I tended to be a pretty good student and athlete, sang in the choir, played in the band, was in the high school plays. In terms of the racial stuff, this was Wisconsin and farm country. There were no Black students, no nonwhite students at all in my high school. Tribal folks got pushed into reservations in Wisconsin, but none in southwestern Wisconsin.

Back in high school I sensed two things that played out later, and continue to play out in my life. For some reason, ethical questions were important for me and were more defined than I think would have been the case normally. Growing up in the 1950s in a rural community, there weren't many institutional mechanisms to live out those values. The church was the primary institution that engaged in any kind of overt way, and I became very religious in junior high school and high school. In fact, I wanted to be a Baptist minister. I also developed a streak of contrarianism with that stuff too. In high school the major ethnic splits and divisions were along religious lines—they were Catholic-Protestant or Catholic school–public school as they played out in the school systems. In junior high and high school I dated a Catholic girl, which really was crossing some lines.

Looking back, there was this super-good religious kid and this other style which was rebelling against that. In college I dated a Jewish woman. You can begin to see the escalation here, OK? I ended up marrying a Black woman. I think that, frankly, that decision was part of that oppositional kind of stuff. It was lots of other things too, but I think that played into it. There was also a certain fascination with things different.

After high school I went to the University of Wisconsin at Madison, which was the place where better students in the state's high schools went. I was a very good student and all that stuff, then went to graduate school at Johns Hopkins in history. But I got tired of academia. I love academia, but when I take it in large chunks it gets real wordy and ungrounded. So I left, and at the same time I was leaving the church.

The next major step to engage race was when I went into the Peace Corps in West Africa. The Peace Corps was really a secular missionary trip. Young people who grew up in the 1960s had secular mediums to express their values and particularly their oppositional values, whether that was the civil rights movement or the antiwar movement. Those of us who came out of small towns in the 1950s didn't have that stuff. It wasn't there. The Peace Corps for me was a major transition out of the church. It made some sense to me.

It was in Africa that I first really engaged race—what it meant to be a white person and a minority person. I was also fascinated by a great deal of African culture. That's when I began to date Black women— Black Peace Corps volunteers. That's where I met Fay. She was in West Africa on a Ford Foundation program. She was beautiful, bright, vivacious, and had a whole bunch of wonderful qualities that were independent of race. So we met and fell in love. I came back a year early, in 1965, and went to graduate school in sociology at the University of Michigan. She came back and we were married in 1967 and then moved to Philadelphia.

My mother was very threatened when she realized I was serious about Fay. I'll never forget the time we came back for Christmas break. It was the first time I took Fay home, and Mom did this super hostess number, even sacrificial. She moved out of her bedroom and insisted we sleep in her bed, etc. But then we were driving back to Madison to catch a bus to Ann Arbor, where we lived. When we went to get in the car, my mother made it very clear she was going to sit in the front seat. I was driving the car, and when we got to the bus station in Madison, she turned around and told Fay to get out of the car because she wanted to talk with her son. She turned to me (Fay was then standing outside on the sidewalk) and said, "I sent my son to Africa and he never came back." She got out and turned to Fay and, as Fay later told me, said, "You can have anything in this world you want except my son." What I remember is Fay crying and running into the bus station. I got out and dove in there, and I've never been as angry, as livid, since.

We decided to go ahead and get married. On this side of that reality,

Mom was pulling with everything she had. Once the decision to marry was made, Mom came around and was a very strong supporter of Fay. In fact to this day she and Fay converse, exchange Christmas cards, birthday cards, the whole nine yards.

Steve and Fay Stevenson's wedding day, with his parents

I've seen that happen in other situations where people have their perceptions about what's real. As long as it's on this side of fait accompli, they pull and do everything they can to maintain the status quo. However, once the deal is done and they've got to make some choices about affirming or not affirming people that they love, the old strategies won't work anymore. People then often come around. It's very interesting stuff.

My father was much quieter about that whole thing. I can't help but think he was part of a modulating influence on mother, because he liked Fay a lot. Actually, they were big buddies. Fay and I probably should have stayed friends and not married. Part of it was the whole cultural stuff in the 1960s in which it was kind of hip to be an interracial couple.

I left graduate school with a master's degree in 1967. I had spent some time in Philadelphia during the summer between my two years at the University of Michigan. That's when I met Victor. Dick Broholm's church, a liberal church on the Main Line, wanted to get involved somehow with the Black community in North Philadelphia but didn't know how. They were smart enough to know they just didn't come in and do the paternalistic liberal number, so they hired me that summer to help negotiate and analyze what might be good opportunities. The best idea seemed to be a collaborative housing rehabilitation effort in which Black community leaders identified the houses that made the most sense to rehab. The resources the suburban folks brought to the collaboration were a set of business and financial skills and connections. Victor was hired as the architect for the project. It was a pretty good model, but it was part of that pre–Black Power paradigm in which liberal, suburban white folks came in and hooked up with Black communities.

White folks would be afraid to come into North Philadelphia, but on the other hand, I remember driving Marvin Louis, president of the Ludlow Neighborhood Association, out to the suburbs for meetings in the evenings, and he was afraid out there. It was so dark and there were so many trees, and people could be hiding back there. It was a wonderful learning experience for me, having folks from Bryn Mawr being afraid to be in North Philly and folks from North Philly being afraid to be in Bryn Mawr!

That kind of work and an interracial marriage fit together at that time. Then the Black Power stuff hit. Both that kind of work and interracial marriages were challenged. That's when I stopped organizing in Black communities and began the Suburban Action Center. The word coming out of the Black Power movement was, "White folks, go back into your communities." I didn't quite know what the hell that meant. There were some SDS folks who had a Marxist analysis who said, "That meant working in poor white or working-class neighborhoods." I had enough of a sense that for those of us coming out of middle-class white backgrounds, it was as much an invasion working in those communities as in the Black communities.

That's when the Suburban Action Center began, and I spent three years there working on issues that later got picked up by the Johnson administration, like the War on Poverty and affirmative action legislation. We were, for instance, trying to get low-income housing in Abington, Jenkintown, those kinds of suburbs. Those folks didn't want low-income housing. Later on, there were attempts to force those communities through some government programs and subsidies to do that. We were also trying to get companies to hire Black folks. We didn't have a prayer in hell, but the motives and notions were good ones.

Steve, Fay, and their son Sean Stevenson, late 1970s

That was when our marriage was getting in trouble. Some of the most painful stuff for me is remembering what it meant to be a white man in an interracial marriage at that time. (Most interracial marriages involved Black men and white women.) Going to a primarily Black party was often particularly painful. During the earlier integrated period, you were kind of held up to a certain degree as an example. When the Black Power stuff hit, man, it flipped fast and viciously, frankly. Fay was a very attractive woman, and there was a great deal of "hit on the white dude's wife" kind of thing. It took me a long time to heal. In fact, I can still feel it in my stomach as I talk about it now: the invasions, the challenges, and not being able to do anything about it.

Add to that Fay's own sense of being not quite sure who she was because her father was white. All kinds of very powerful sexual, psychological, and identity issues were at play, and the relationship was very troubled. Actually, our son Sean was conceived as a way to give us something that we had in common, a way to save that relationship. It never happened, but that was part of the motivation.

We separated when Sean was two years old and we had to make the decision of where Sean was going to go. I think if Sean had looked Black and been a female, he would have stayed with Fay. But Sean was a male and he looked white. When he was a little kid, he really had blonde hair. The contrast between him and his mom was incredible. He looked like a Scandinavian kid. If the pixels and genes had gone some other ways, it might have cut different, though I'm not sure Fay was in any position to be a primary parent at that point either. Whether I was or not I'm not sure either, but he went with me to Philadelphia. That first year, which combined single parenthood and beginning teaching, was one of the two toughest years I've ever spent in my life. Sean and I survived, however.

Since then, Sean and Fay have renegotiated a strong relationship, and she and I maintain a friendship and mutual commitment to parenting. ▪▪▪

L ike Steve, Rey (he requested that I not use his last name) grew up in Wisconsin, also in a white community where one was either Protestant or Catholic. His spiritual path took him to seminary and a racial epiphany in Roxbury, Boston's largest Black community. His work with the Freedom Rides of the early 1960s caused a fracture in his family.

Rey left behind the church and his early Marxist thinking, creating his own unique spiritual and political life. He continues his journey in Eugene, Oregon, where, among other talents, he is a master carpenter and craftsman.

Rey, as a baby, taking a bath on his farmhouse porch in Wisconsin

REY

I grew up on a 320-acre dairy farm in northern Wisconsin. The closest city was over 100 miles away. I had one sister and four brothers. My mother was a homemaker and farmer. My father was a farmer and truck driver. We raised crops of corn, oats, and hay for the dairy herd.

Our community was mostly Scandinavian, with some Germans and a smattering of other ancestries. It was all white and mostly Protestant. There were a few families that were Catholic and some who were not church attenders. My family attended a small Free Methodist Church with a dozen other farm families. The church was located on an acre of land in the middle of our rural community. Other families in the area attended churches, mostly Lutheran, in the local town, which had a population of about 1,000 people.

Rey and his younger brother on his family's farm

My primary school included grades one through eight. It was a one-room school in the country, with one teacher for all eight grades. The experience was pretty much the three R's. Educational resources were quite limited and related very little to the wider world.

High school included other farm communities and the local small town. The divisions among the students were religious. There were Protestants and Catholics. These were not spoken divisions generally, and did not affect friendships or dating. It was, however, understood that Protestants should not marry Catholics, and vice versa. Marriage across religious lines did happen without much fanfare, but mostly people coupled in their same religious groups. These religious attitudes, along with the rampant anticommunism of the public education in the 1950s, had the effect of setting up thought processes for categorizing people as "us" and "them."

Rey as a teenager, circa 1956

My part of the country was pretty much all white. There were two Black men who lived in the area, in two different places. I never met either of them and was not aware of their existence until my later high school years. There were also Native American communities within fifty miles from my home, but I was not aware of them until high school, either. I do not recall any discussions of Black–white or Native American–white issues in my high school education.

The first racially related incident I remember happened when I was at college. My roommate—who was also from my high school—and I had gone to a state high school championship basketball game. One team was primarily Black players, and the other was all white players. The team of Black players won, and on the way home, my roommate said he really hated to see the Black team win. I became indignant that he would make such a statement based on race. I don't remember the basis of his or my argument. I also don't know why I viewed this differently than my roommate, as I do not think racism or racial stuff was ever talked about in my family.

During my last year of college, some people made a film showing racism involved in housing rentals for students at the university. This was the first year or two of the 1960s. The House Un-American Activities Committee (HUAC, the antidemocratic House of Representatives committee made popular by Senator Joe McCarthy) wanted the film and had a subpoena issued for it. They considered it to be subversive and made by subversives. They did not consider the racism it showed to be "un-American." I was asked to join in a demonstration against HUAC. Even though I agreed with the film showing racism, I was very opposed to demonstrating. Public displays like that seemed very distasteful and rude to me at this stage of my life.

I graduated from college in the early 1960s. I left college not knowing poverty still existed in the U.S. If people were poor, it was mostly a result of their being too lazy to work. That was the principal teaching I had received on poverty. I was also beginning to discover—outside the classroom—that the Civil War had not ended racism.

After graduation I moved to the Boston area to attend theology school. A fellow student persuaded me to do my fieldwork at a Christian social center in Roxbury, the largest Black community in Boston. The center had been started two years earlier by a Black student from the theology school. I began by supervising teenage basketball gym time and eventually served as director of teenage programs. The center soon became the Massachusetts headquarters for the Southern Christian Leadership Conference, which was led by Martin Luther King, Jr.

My experience in Roxbury was the most dramatic in my life to that point—and perhaps since that time as well. I thought I was going into Roxbury to help people in need—and maybe I did to some degree. Mostly, however, I learned the nature of the world I lived in, which was very different than what I had learned in the classroom. This was my first time to encounter racism and poverty in a direct way. Roxbury provided me with a lot of cynicism about the education and knowledge I had experienced up to that time.

One "getting reeducated" experience happened as I was out in the Roxbury community trying to register people to vote for an upcoming election. A young Black couple answered my knock on their door. They, quite angrily, told me to go vote, that the candidates were mine and the system was mine. Later, back at the center, I told folks about this young couple who must have been "Black Muslims." When asked how I knew that, I told them how they had responded to me. The staff explained to me that a person did not have to be a Black Muslim to feel disenfranchised and angry with the system, with me symbolizing the system, and as a white man telling them what they should do. Once explained, I could easily understand this. But until then I had felt I was doing "good" work and no one could possibly be angry with me. I began, at this point, to realize how deeply entrenched racism was in my mind and in U.S. culture and that the anger of those oppressed by it could be very powerful.

Another experience that opened me to my own racism involved a boy about ten years old. He was having some minor difficulties, and I went over to talk to his parents. They led me into their lovely house and openly talked with me about their son and his needs, what they were doing, and how I could help. It turns out the son was actually a foster child, and they had a couple more foster children and a couple of their own. As I walked back from their home, I realized how much I had approached that house with stereotypes of poor families, of Black families, of dysfunctional families. My overwhelming feeling was that those folks are doing just fine, and all I am doing is being taught what it's all about.

The systemic nature of racism had become a practical reality for me through the work I was doing. My sense had started out with a kind of missionary approach: "These folks don't know they are victims of racism unless I help them." I am not sure if that attitude is more laughable or more embarrassing, but it was one I had to come to terms with to work for a just world. Reading *The Autobiography of Malcolm X* during this time helped me open a lot of doors to my own identity as a white man. Also, H. Rap Brown and others were saying that Black people needed to do the work in the Black community. White people needed to go back and work in their communities—that is where the racism is, and that is where change is needed. I was at a point in my own awareness that I knew this was true for me, even though I had no real desire to be in that part of society that was, and wished to remain, racist.

The issue of race became the source of a fracture with my family. The event that most typified the break had to do with the Freedom Marches in Selma, Alabama. I was coordinating the bus rides from Roxbury to Selma. Some fellow students at the theology school said they would provide me with the money necessary to go to Selma if I wished to do that. In the end I decided to continue doing the bus coordinating work because we were shorthanded.

I wrote my parents about this incident and how grateful I was that these folks thought enough of me and the work for justice that they would make that monetary sacrifice. My mother wrote back a rather indignant, angry letter saying that my friends should keep their money and that I did not demonstrate and do public displays like that. I wrote back explaining my position and mailed my mother's letter back, saying, "I don't accept hate mail." We never talked about that again, though my mother tried several times to open the subject. I do not know how such a conversation would have ended. I just know I was not willing to because I would get too angry. I see my action now as a missed chance to do work in the white community and help growth and healing to take place there.

These experiences during my years in theology school had a dramatic effect on my life. The racism and sexism in the religious institutions made them places I did not wish to work in. "Go work in the racist white communities" was a powerful idea to me, yet not strong enough to get me there. However, during this time of uncertainty, my sense of creation, of spirituality, changed. My belief in a set of beliefs that were true for everyone came to an end. I was made aware that the spiritual path was one of discovering the "God" within myself, within each person, within all of creation. This awareness opened a door for me. I could define my own spiritual path. Just because I didn't believe in an institutional religious belief system did not mean I was rejecting a spiritual understanding of the cosmos. In fact, becoming aware of the Divine in all of creation meant embracing the equality of all that is life. This actually strengthened my resolve to seek justice in my world.

Evolving out of my experiences was a clearer picture of the world's socioeconomic order. I could see that capitalism is not the greatest economic system. It simply controls the information sources, and they keep repeating over and over that capitalism is the greatest—and it starts to sound like the truth. Capitalism was based on systematic destruction of the materials of creation in order to increase the great wealth of the very few at the top. The divisive, destabilizing effect of racism was good for capitalism by keeping the have-nots at odds with each other rather than at odds with the haves. Racism was little changed except for some well-publicized window dressings.

Vietnam was a continuation of this global conquest for the world's resources. Vietnam provided much information about U.S. racism, and racism provided much understanding about the invasion of Vietnam, as well as the racial and class makeup of the invading soldiers. For a while my understanding of these issues was very Marxist influenced.

Then I realized that I used Marx as I had previously used Jesus. With a particular belief system I was trying to force the happening world into that framework. For me, I could not do work or reach understanding within this framework. I needed to do whatever I might outside of it—as much as that is possible. Justice, fairness, and creativity mostly happen outside the frames of control, stability, and entrenchment of the powers that are, and hope to continue, in power.

I don't have an overarching idea or plan for continuing my living in a way that addresses equality and racial justice. On a personal level I try to allow no "buts" in my understanding of racial issues, as in: "I believe all people are equal, but," or "I believe in justice for all, but." On the political level I try to be in the way when the forces of racism try to move back into control, whether through the guise of being for states rights or through something that gets called conservatism or through saying that affirmative action laws are just reverse discrimination.

Now, thirty-five years after the beginning of my awakening, I feel that not much has changed in the political, economic, or social fields regarding racial equality—and other varieties of injustice. I do feel that I personally live a much fuller and freer life because of my much wider embrace of the truth of creation, and from being free of defending the untruths of racism, sexism, and classism.

The economic divisions between races and classes are worsening. The access to information, to truth, is more and more limited as it becomes controlled by a few white-owned or -controlled corporations. There is less and less investigative journalism. Education seems to be more a learning of white cultural values and language rather than learning the values of community, sharing, unity, and healthy self-awareness. Affirmative action is attacked through a Klan-inspired misinformation campaign to make it seem to be reverse discrimination. We are all encouraged to take up a revisionist history that says no one is responsible for past racism—and present racism is really something else. Some declare us a racist-free society, and therefore there is no need to worry about anyone being abused, misused, or cheated because of racism. Reactionary forces like these are cause for vigilant concern and action.

We need to continue to develop caring communities outside the consumer-blinded world. It is in these social processes of creating, caring, and sharing that the seeds of sustainable, healthy life will continue to sprout and flourish. The process of justice is in its greatest danger during these days of the "global economy" and will continue to require our nurturing through struggle and creativity. ■■■

The most potent People for Human Rights demonstration I participated in occurred at the Bryn Mawr Presbyterian church the week before Christmas 1968 to support Cesar Chavez and the grape boycott. About fifty of us gathered at my home in West Philadelphia, dressed neatly and warmly. We left in a caravan of cars driving slowly from the modest-income brick row houses of my neighborhood to Bryn Mawr and the wealthy mansions of the Main Line. The church was a stunning Gothic structure, set far back from the street and surrounded by a large lawn and trees. Many of Philadelphia's movers and shakers attended this church. The minister drove a Porsche.

We stood quietly in a single line on the sidewalk, holding copies of the most recent *Presbyterian Life* magazine, which had a photograph of Cesar Chavez on the cover. There were several police cars parked on the street, but they kept their distance. One of our portly members had dressed as Santa Claus, and he handed out grape lollipops and copies of the following handout to parishioners as they entered the church. I have read and reread this statement over the past thirty years, and its message speaks to me as clearly and powerfully today as it did when it was first written:

Why We're Here

The Bryn Mawr Presbyterian Church has supported many programs seeking to alleviate the plight of the poor and powerless.

Like many of you, we have been moved by the desperate needs of our society. We have given money to causes, we have gone into the city to minister to the needy through work camps, tutorials, inner city missions and the like.

And like many of you, we are distressed when, in the face of the problems, these efforts are almost totally ineffective. We have begun to realize that such efforts are treating symptoms rather than causes. This rich country does not meet the basic needs of many of its members. We believe this is a result of their exclusion from participating in decisions which directly affect their lives.

We come today because members of this church occupy decision-making positions in powerful institutions. One of these members is Mr. Paul Cupp, who you suggested would respond reasonably to a request to support the farm workers' struggle by removing California grapes from his Acme Markets. We met with Mr. Cupp two days later;

his answer was an uncategorical refusal to honor the boycott. He felt responsible only to his board, stockholders, and customers, who he said gave no evidence of not wanting grapes.

We feel these are not good reasons for this decision which adversely affects the lives of over 200,000 farm workers, and which if reversed, would have no serious effects on Acme. Many consumers have shown concern about the grapes, and chain stores in other cities have honored the boycott.

Renaissance and Removal

You, as well as powerless agricultural workers, have little control over the decisions which affect the fabric of our society. A series of articles in the *Bulletin* in 1965, entitled "Philadelphia's Movers and Shakers," delivers this theme. One editorial describes the small group of business and professional men who comprise Philadelphia's civic elite as a "second level of government which lacks a democratic foundation. None of the 'movers and shakers' are popularly elected." These men are given much credit for "pressing forward with the physical, intellectual, cultural, and economic renaissance which has already made Philadelphia an example for urban America."

Of course, this "pressing forward" of the renaissance pushed large numbers of Black families out of the way of progress and into overcrowded ghettoes.

Mockery of Democracy

We do not wish to pillory Paul Cupp as an individual. Our main point is that his actions HAVE THE EFFECT OF GOVERNMENT, but he and his institution are not accountable for this effect. AMERICA ACCEPTS AND VALUES THIS LACK OF RESPONSIBILITY. Behind our public facade of democracy, we have built an authoritarian structure in which we treat the will of powerful men and institutions as the will of God.

People for Human Rights feels that the root of many of our society's present problems is that the decisions made by powerful institutions and their leaders are not subject to review by the hundreds of thousands injured by those decisions. Furthermore, neither you nor we have any conventional way to influence decisions made by this elite. We are here today to ask you to challenge this mockery of democracy; we ask you to join us in placing responsibility on those who make decisions.

Bryn Mawr Presbyterian Church and Repression

The unaccountable power we have described affects not only the poor and powerless. A number of your members have told us we should be grateful for the help of powerful men (e.g. those powerful members of your church who have "helped the colored"). This advice implies that we should also remember what such powerful persons could do if they did not want to help. We feel you should know that a number of people associated with your church put pressure on a college President to censure one of our group, a college professor, after his visit here. We would like you to consider why he should have merited such a response.

Change not Charity

All of us could help meet some of this country's desperate needs if we find ways to make the major institutions more accountable to all the people. One such way is to move institutions in which people do have a voice — such as your church — to confront those institutions in which the exercise of power is responsible only to the interests of the powerful. We believe that your church is in a unique position to take effective action in the grape boycott and other instances of authoritarian exploitation. Such action for change would be of far greater help to the powerless than the traditional charitable endeavors your church has been supporting. *As a first step, we ask you to help see that the grape boycott is honored in Acme and all stores in Philadelphia.*

Ron Whitehorn was one of People for Human Rights' key ideologues and organizers, its best guitar player, and the main author of the Bryn Mawr handout. In the weeks after our demonstration there, he and several other PHR members successfully negotiated with key church leaders, including Paul Cupp, to take grapes off the shelves of Acme Markets.

After I left the group in 1970 to help start the People's Fund (now Bread and Roses), I lost track of Ron. I knew that, like Lucia Faithfull, he also joined the Communist Party in the early 1970s. In 1998 I heard his voice on a National Public Radio program. He was a teacher, and his class of low-income Black and Puerto Rican junior high students were cleaning up an old, trash-strewn Quaker cemetery in North Philadelphia.

Ron now lives with his wife Patty, a nurse, and their two teenage children in an attractive semidetached brick home in Philadelphia. He continues his creative activism through his work as a teacher and role model.

RON WHITEHORN

I was born in 1942 in Queens, New York. My dad was a traveling sales-man, and my mom worked a variety of part-time jobs to help out. While conservative politically, my parents stressed values like fair-ness and respect for others that helped shape my politics. They were always supportive of the choices I made in my life, even if they didn't agree wholly with them. Later, like so many who were prodded by the events of our time, they changed politically and came to take a certain pride in my radicalism.

When I was eleven years old, we moved from suburban Long Island to Vermont. My first strong sense of the existence of poverty and class comes from this period. It wasn't like the Vermont of today—more like Appalachia. Many families lived in tar-paper shacks, kids without shoes and warm clothing, farm families struggling to survive. My family had modest means, but compared to most people in the town, we were privileged. I went to a two-room schoolhouse without toilets and other amenities. Our town, Halifax, was referred to in more prosperous, neighboring villages as "Hell of a Fix." At the regional high school, other kids made fun of kids from Halifax. It was my introduction to the two sides of the tracks.

After college, I began to teach at an elite boarding school. In this setting I was pretty well insulated from the growing political turmoil in the country. But I was changing politically. Based on the unfolding events in Vietnam and my own reading, I abandoned the cold-war liberalism that had passed for my politics and

Ron Whitehorn as a high school student in Vermont

embraced the New Left. Faced with the prospect of getting drafted, and aware that a ruling-class utopian school was probably not the best place to work for the transformation of U.S. society, I left my teaching job and joined VISTA.

I was sent to Baltimore to be trained. That was the first real engage-ment I had with Black people. Up to that point, my understanding of the civil rights struggle was very abstract. This was the period when the antipoverty program still had some liberal content and before it was completely destroyed and bureaucratized. Among the group of us in training were some people involved with SDS (Students for a Democratic Society), which for me was a real provocative kind of exposure. Here we were at the University of Maryland School of Social Work—that's where they housed and trained us—which was located in what was then a white Appalachian community. So when we went out to get a hoagie or go to a bar after the sessions, we were in a white community.

There were some Black people in our group, and we'd go to these bars, and they wouldn't serve us. We were really outraged, like what was this all about? Consistent with our training, we organized and started a boycott at this one bar near the university. We leafleted about the segregation of the bar, and the people in the VISTA program were appalled. This is not what they meant. "Go do this when you're out of here, but don't do this in our backyard." I ended up being one of the spokespersons for the group. They told us, "You can't do this, it's not that we don't agree, but . . . ." We would have none of that. We went to the media, and first the staff tried to bag us from the program, but all the other VISTAs to a person said, "If they go, we go." We didn't succeed in desegregating the bar, but they didn't succeed in sacking us. What they did do was to send me to Philadelphia, which was the last place I wanted to go!

This was the period when the whole Black Power movement was emerging, and I got involved with Friends of SNCC in Washington, D.C. I basically understood their critique and identified with it. I felt that what Stokely Carmichael and Rap Brown were saying was where it was at. Meanwhile, I was in VISTA. I was placed in the Crime Prevention Association, which still exists. They ran four boys' and girls' clubs in West, North, and South Philadelphia and the city's gang-control program. They were a classic white-dominated, colonial kind of social work agency. All the administrative positions were held by whites. Their board was overwhelmingly white, with some token Blacks. The field staff was all African American, but they were being supervised by middle-aged Jewish guys who lived in the far northeast or the suburbs.

I was sent there with a guy who was a Catholic priest who had joined VISTA because he was frustrated by the church hierarchy. The agency didn't know what to do with us. So they had us tutor and work in the boys' club. We were supposed to work with the gang kids to get them jobs. Half the day we'd look for places they could get jobs, and the second half we'd hang out and play basketball with them. The whole thing was a sham. We got to know the gang workers, who were pretty hip guys, and some of the gang kids. That was good, but in terms of the aims of the program, the jobs that were available, like dishwashers, were deadend jobs, and the employers were really hostile to these kids. And who are we—a couple of white college kids telling them to go get a job at Lyntons? I could see this agency was a rip-off. It wasn't doing anything to change the fundamental conditions of life in the community. In fact, it was reinforcing the power relationships.

Myself and a couple other VISTAs got involved in doing some tenant organizing and worked with welfare rights and some positive stuff, and eventually I got bagged. They fired me because I refused to stop doing this work, which was off the clock. They felt really threatened. At first they said, "Oh, you shouldn't get involved with these people. They're Black nationalists and antiwhite." When that didn't work, they just said, "You can't do these things, and if you do them, you're out." So they fired me. I didn't care, because by that time I saw working in that community as a political contradiction, even though I was learning a lot. It was clear to me that as a white radical—which is how I saw myself—this wasn't what I should be doing.

It was during that time that I met Rosemary, who is Black, and we got involved. She worked at the girls' club in Mantua. I ended up moving in with her. During that period I wasn't really being an activist. What jarred me out of my apathy was the assassination of Dr. King. That's what propelled me to People for Human Rights. I remember that Rosemary and I, after we heard the news, went to this church around the corner on Spring Garden Street. We went in, and people were just sitting there quietly. We sat there for a long time. Then this Black man went up to the piano and played "We Shall Overcome," the most moving version of it. It was a clarion call for me to action. I left that church determined I was going to get off my ass and make a difference. Like many people, I was appalled by what was going on.

That's when I got involved in PHR. At that time I had gotten a job with the Department of Welfare. I was very enthusiastic about PHR and really identified with its perspective, the notion that it was important for white people to be taking up the question of racism with other whites. I liked the people I met, and threw myself into it in a major way.

The initial project I got involved with was the Liberation Schools that we started. I was on the committee—that's how I got to know Terry Dellmuth. I was a teacher in a couple of the schools out on the Main Line. The model came from the civil rights movement. The Freedom Schools had been set up in the South to teach Black people their real history, to liberate them from the racist version of who they were and where they had been, and to give them the kind of foundation to wage a struggle for freedom. Our notion was that whites also had to relearn that history in order to understand who we really were and where we were at, and to understand the current situation in the country and, by extension, the world. We developed a whole lot of materials that were critiquing the traditional white supremacist version of our history as a country.

I got fired from my job at the Welfare Department after we had a demonstration when Hubert Humphrey opened his presidential campaign in Philadelphia and Mayor Tate rolled out all the red carpets. The antiwar movement had a big demonstration, which we participated in. Part of what we were going to do was to burn our voter registration cards because our choices that year were Nixon, Humphrey, and Wallace. The theme was, "There's no choice, so burn your voter registration card." I dutifully trotted out there and went to burn my voter registration card, and these four big burly guys jumped all over me and kicked my ass! They charged me with assaulting them, so I was arrested. It was a serious case. If I had been convicted, I could have gotten twenty years. They charged me with all this nonsense, which was a bunch of lies. I did resist them—I didn't know who they were—they didn't have their uniforms on. They were the civil disobedience guys. Some of my coworkers were there and testified to this in court. The head of the Welfare Department felt really bad, but the mayor personally ordered that I be fired. I was a good caseworker and they liked me.

After that I went to work full-time for PHR. I was the education director, but basically what I was paid to do was to organize high school kids. Out of the Liberation Schools we organized the Philadelphia High School Student Union and rented a place up at Broad and Olney. I then became the de facto executive director. The honesty of the people to work through what it meant to be a white radical in that period, and deal with work and family and develop some coherent analysis of American society—I remember those meetings and discussions, and whereas there were some frustrations, it was an important and very informative experience.

I remember the week-long occupation of Cookman Church and the demonstration at Bryn Mawr Presbyterian church. We had subsequent meetings with some of the businessmen there who, based on our whole confrontation, wanted to have a dialogue, and that was interesting. These guys were big-time corporate types, and Paul Cupp, CEO of Acme Markets, complied and took the grapes off the shelf.

I later left PHR amicably, which was disintegrating at that point, and became drawn to workplace organizing. A group of us eventually formed the Philadelphia Workers Organizing Committee, which started out as a Marxist study group to discuss common practice in organizing in shops. It later evolved into a local Communist organization.

Initially I worked in a warehouse that was unorganized, no union or anything, and it was mainly young white guys and some older African Americans. I made some efforts to organize a group to win some demands from the company, which I thought down the line could be the basis for a union organizing drive. There was an experience I had that was very instructive in terms of the role that racism plays in the workplace. My expectation was based on my past involvement in organizing, which was that the Black workers would play a more advanced role, be more prepared to be involved than the white workers would be. In fact, I found that the Black workers were very reticent to get involved. The young white guys (Italian kids from South Philly) were all ready to go. They were resenting the inaction of the Black workers. I had some rapport with the Black workers, so I was trying to get a handle on it. They were reticent to open up about it and put me off.

Then I analyzed the situation and noticed that one of the practices that was really offensive about the boss was he called the Black workers "boys." These were guys in their thirties and forties. His racism was more paternalistic, except for the assignment of tasks. He always had the Black workers take the trash out. For him, I don't think it was a conscious thing, just, "Boys, you can take the trash out." And they solemnly went along with it. What were they going to do? It occurred to me that this was a real barrier to the unity of the workers, because the white workers had unity with the boss about this. They didn't see anything wrong, because it coincided with their view of what the Black workers' role should be. They would grumble about how the Black guys don't stand up, and I said, "Well, you know, you don't stand up when he calls them 'boys,' and tells them to take out the trash. How come he never asks you to take out the trash?" That led to a whole struggle and discussion among the white workers.

About a week later, the boss comes back and says, "Yo, Leroy. You and the boys get the trash out," and this guy John DeMizio from South Philly leaps up and yells, "I'm takin' the trash out. Why don't you ever ask *me* to take the trash out? Leave these guys alone. You're always picking on them." All the Black workers' jaws fell down, and that just created a whole different dynamic. To me, it was a good, concrete lesson in how you build unity, and the burden of building that unity is on the white workers.

The committee started as a handful of people, and over ten years grew into a sizable organization. We had a paper with a national circulation of 3,000 to 4,000, and groups we were loosely affiliated with all around the country. We were a distinct trend within the new Communist movement. We were of the view that the biggest problem with these new groups was dogmatism, the kind of slavish imitation of Mao, Stalin, Lenin, and the substitution of recipes and formulas for real analysis and concrete thinking. We argued that the real test of theory is that it's a guide to action. So aside from being involved in the "Stop Rizzo" movement and the women's movement and the Black liberation movement, we made some definite inroads in the unions here in the city. We were also a national voice. It was a completely consuming existence.

The group disintegrated in 1981, and it was over the issue of racism. The group began as an all-white group, coming out of the student movement and so forth. But we had a perspective from the beginning that we wanted to build a multiracial, multinational organization for basically the orthodox Marxist reasons. The way we saw doing that was through developing an advanced theory and practice around the issue of racism. We saw that as the critical task in terms of how you build a multiracial organization. In terms of our abstract understanding of the question, it was pretty good. The literature that we wrote—and I was one of the theoreticians—I had no issues with it.

We did slowly recruit African American intellectuals and workers and political activists to the group, but not at a fast pace. So we asked the question: "If the Black workers are more advanced and we're the vanguard, have the right analysis and the way forward, how come they're not in this group?" In an attempt to answer that question, we made an effort to critically analyze our practice and our ideological weaknesses. That developed into the Campaign Against White Chauvinism within the group. There were a lot of problems with the way it was carried out—a lot of self-righteousness and moralizing, some of it very divisive and destructive. I think the core intent was good, because what we had to look at was the ways in which our own racism was impacting on our work and our relationships with Black people and other oppressed nationalities. That was not something people were very willing to do.

A lot of the minority members of our organization were involved in interracial relationships. Rosemary was a case in point. She became a member of the group and a leader. Almost all the African Americans were involved in interracial relationships, and we really started analyzing the content—not just of those relationships, but relationships generally. What we often found was that in our organizing we tended to concentrate on those minorities who were most accommodationist—

the ones who thought we were cool! The people who didn't think we were so cool were summed up as having nationalist tendencies—we didn't listen to them. The people who thought we were "right on," they were "right on." But they weren't necessarily the people who had the influence and the standing with the masses of the workers. Often they were people who were somewhat compromised because of their rather dependent relationships with whites. There was a two-sided dynamic going on—on the one hand there was our racism; on the other hand there was the capitulation to that racism on the part of the minority comrades who in many ways mirrored our attitudes.

In my case, I had clearly used Rosemary, who had been a leader in the Black Panther Party and had many relationships in the local Black liberation movement, as a political credential to bolster a perception that I was a politically advanced antiracist white person. Simultaneously I had tried to isolate her from independent-minded Black people who were likely to be critical of me and my so-called leadership.

Another lesson for me from this process of self-examination was that we middle-class white leftists have a class bias that working-class whites are more backward than middle-class people when it comes to racism, even if our abstract politics promote the working-class as the vanguard. My experience during the Jesse Jackson campaign really underlined this.

In the late 1970s I met and married Patty Eakin, a registered nurse who was heavily involved in organizing nurses. Patty and I moved to Kensington, then a predominantly white, blue-collar, ethnic neighborhood, in the early 1980s. We got active in community struggles around housing, education, and other issues and in independent politics as well. Like most progressive whites, we rallied to Jackson's call for a Rainbow Coalition and worked in both his presidential campaigns.

But when it came to aggressively taking his campaign to the neighborhood, we held back, finding all kinds of excuses to defer this work. We were afraid we would be isolated or worse if we came out strongly for Jackson in the community groups and with our neighbors. After some struggle, we finally did just that, going door to door with a flyer we developed and bringing the campaign to our community organization, with positive results. We were surprised by the openness and support we encountered, support that was evident on election day, when Jackson got a substantially larger vote in those divisions in which we had campaigned.

In terms of my own activity, my political life today plays itself out mainly in my professional life, in my work as a teacher. I'm the cochair of a union community outreach committee that tries to build links between the community and the union. Concretely, that means primarily with the Black community, given the student body of the school system, which is upwards of 80 percent minority.

Ron Whitehorn, sitting center left, with his junior high school students in North Philadelphia

In the last year I've consciously shifted my focus to my classroom and my school. I felt that I was involved in this global stuff and I wasn't really devoting the time and attention to the work I was doing from 8:00 to 3:00 every day. The same analysis is very pertinent there in what's making a difference in the lives of the children I'm trying to teach. The school is in a very poor Puerto Rican and Black drug-infected area. I don't look at my students as victims, even though they are victimized. What's most striking to me is their vitality and their energy and their intelligence. That's in spite of their conditions of life.

I spoke to this group of teachers yesterday on how we're supposed to be talking about our small learning community and organizing that better. I shared with them some letters my students had written to Lucretia Mott,* whose father had been lost at sea for several years. When my students read about this experience, I asked them to write to Lucretia as if she were alive today and write about how you think she's feeling, not knowing where her dad is, and share any experiences you've had, where you've had some of those anxieties or feelings of loss. It was a real revealing event because, first of all, I loved that they identified with Lucretia Mott, who is a culturally alien figure, but they really liked her because of her passion for justice and equality. So they wrote her these letters, and they talked about how their fathers are dead, or their dads are in jail, or they've never seen their dad—and wrote about it in this good, spirited, matter-of-fact way. But it was very poignant and really telling in terms of what their lives were like.

Our school is very old and is practically falling down around us. The students are clear that these conditions mean their education is not

*Lucretia Mott (1793–1880) was an abolitionist and feminist. In 1833 she and her husband helped organize the American Antislavery Society, and in 1840 they were delegates to an international antislavery convention in London. Because of her sex, Mott was excluded from the proceedings, and she subsequently devoted most of her time and energy to securing equal rights for women.

valued. I took a group to city council hearings on the school budget and a march demanding equal funding with suburban schools. The students were enthusiastic participants. In the council chambers, some kids left to use the bathroom and the sergeant at arms wouldn't let them back in. In the old days, I was always getting thrown out of city council for one thing or another, and now I almost got thrown out again, making a big scene and demanding they let the students back in. The sergeant at arms said I was setting a bad example for my students to which I replied, "I'm setting the best possible example." The kids loved it, and we won.

I think race remains the single most central social and political question in our society for some very important historical reasons. I really see it as the key to whether the progressive movements move forward. When you look at what fuels the growth of the Right, even though it's not always overt, you don't have to scratch the surface very hard to see that racism is the primary ideological appeal of the Right today. To the extent the Left can't counter that, it's disarmed ideologically. If you look historically, whenever progressive movements have gone forward, it's been when they've been able to have some element of correct orientation on the question of race. Like the gains of the 1930s—the CIO—it was accompanied by a rudimentary understanding that the question of fighting segregation was bound up with the forward progress of

Ron Whitehorn with a petition and a neighbor in Kensington, North Philadelphia

labor and the working-class. The civil rights agenda was seen as part of the core of the progressive movement. To the extent that's been the case, we've moved forward. ▪▪▪

The most moving and lengthy demonstration I participated in was when People for Human Rights marched outside a small Methodist church in the heart of a large, very low-income Black neighborhood in North Philadelphia. Cookman had only twelve commuting white parishioners when the week-long takeover began. A beautiful gym, kitchen, and meeting rooms had never been made available to the community. We closely coordinated our support actions with the Black Economic Development Conference and an active group of young Black teenagers, who initiated the takeover of the church. Once the teens gained access, someone called the police. The civil disobedience squad, led by Lieutenant George Fencel, came immediately and kept a daily watch on our activities, but never interfered. Fencel was one of the best cops I've ever known. The following press release was issued early in the afternoon of July 3, 1969:

> The Philadelphia Black Economic Development Conference (PBEDC) announced today its full endorsement and support of the Black youth in the Hartranft section of this city in their claiming of the Cookman Methodist Church, 12th and Lehigh Avenue as being the rightful property of their community. The youth and PBEDC in this reparational action, described their stand as one which reestablishes the original purposes for which the church and its facilities were intended.
>
> The Church, a well constructed and maintained building, has numerous classrooms, a gymnasium and other facilities which are vitally needed in the nearly all-Black community. The young people who occupied the building today indicated that leaflets are being distributed throughout the community announcing that study and recreational programs are immediately open to them. They said it was immoral to have such fine facilities closed to the community all week and to have non-residents come in once a week and open the church just for their selfish worship purposes. The group made it clear, however, that they will in no way interfere with those worship services, and the parishioners can feel as free to come in on Sunday as they ever have. They said they would hope the church members could even have a more meaningful worship knowing that their building is being used for such constructive purposes — indeed, serving the work of God.

It was 11:00 A.M. on July 3 when People for Human Rights went to Cookman Methodist Church and began support action of the Black occupation there. Although the church itself was open to the community, PHR threw up a picket line outside to support the youth and lessen the likelihood of any interference with the programs inside. PHR publicly avowed that its presence would continue until the Black leadership (PBEDC) discontinued the demonstration. Every day during the occupation, over 300 children came to roller-skate, play ball, do artwork, and discuss Black history. Many of us from PHR and our friends and spouses stayed overnight at the church to further support the efforts of the youth.

Sunday culminated the first phase of the occupation. In the morning, the church's interim pastor held a forum-style service with a few of the Methodists attending with us. (Later it was learned that the pastor had called his twelve parishioners to say that he could not guarantee there would not be trouble if they came on Sunday.) The afternoon's "Black worship experience" saw over 100 people representative of all those involved in the Cookman struggle: community children and adults, Methodist parishioners, and lots of us.

A new reality set in on Thursday, July 10 with the eviction and arrest of the eight Black ministers who had occupied Cookman along with the Black youth from the community. The next day, twenty members from PHR entered Methodist headquarters, 1701 Arch Street, to protest the evictions. The bishop's office was locked, and we proceeded to occupy the bishop's antechamber the next floor down. The bishop was in a meeting elsewhere in the building. Ron Whitehorn and I sought to extract him, which we did, as well as the others in his meeting. On learning of our occupation of his office, he said, "Oh no, have them come upstairs." This was done, and the sit-in proceeded. Despite some confusion as to whether we were there on our own initiative or whether "the Blacks had sent us," it became obvious to the Methodists that they were indeed being sat-in on, and we had no immediate intentions of vacating their air-conditioned headquarters. Their lawyer reiterated his belief that we were manipulating the Blacks. The action settled down to an all-day affair, with pleasantries exchanged between PHR and George Fencel's civil disobedience squad, and occasional outbursts from the Methodists. In the afternoon we released the following press release:

> Members of People for Human Rights, a white antiracist organization, have entered Methodist Headquarters to protest the eviction of eight Black ministers from Cookman Methodist Church. We believe, as do these ministers, that churches should be responsive to the needs of the people of the community. Cookman Church, in the midst of a Black community, has been closed to this community. Its recreation facilities have not been in use since the city funds were cut off. During the community action, the church came alive—educational and recreational programs were immediately set up and involved hundreds of people. This action by the Black community was not a "take-over" or an attempt to invade another's property, but rather a community's attempt to reawaken the church by making it responsive to the needs of the people.
>
> We plan to remain until the demands of the Hartranft community and the Philadelphia Black Economic Development Conference are met or until they request our withdrawal.
>
> Repeatedly Methodist officials have stated they will not discuss the disposition of Cookman with community representatives until

that church building is vacated. This emphasis on the primacy of property rights over human rights was the basis of church support for slavery in the past, it is the basis for exploitative investments in the present, and may be the basis of church support for fascism in the future.

We are opposed to racism and therefore support Black demands for reparations from white religious institutions.

While we do not intend to prevent anyone from entering or leaving Methodist offices, we recognize that our presence will in some measure be disruptive. By its very nature, opposition to the deeply ingrained racism of our society is disruptive.

Just before 5:00 P.M. the injunction arrived, and there were many deliberations coming down close to the line. A last-minute telephone call from one of our leaders and the Black representatives allowed us to leave before violating the order.

When visiting friends in Philadelphia almost thirty-five years later, I happened upon an article by an African American woman working with families transitioning from welfare to work. She was the minister of Cookman Methodist Church.

PART 2

WASHINGTON, D.C.

1971–1985

LORETTA NEUMANN

VINCE DEFOREST

CAROLINE DEFOREST

HASANI ISSA

BETTY KING

VALERIE JOAN

MARY ZEPERNICK

SHARON PARKER

ALAN PARKER

I wrote my first letter to my father in the summer of 1950 when I was ten years old. I was away from home for the first time, a whole week at a newly constructed Camp Fire Girls camp in the High Sierra. I remember sitting on the bus, passing deep, tree-filled gorges as we climbed higher to our mysterious destination.

I wrote to my father because even at that early age I knew he enjoyed writing letters, unlike Mom, who found writing difficult. She was the talker of the family; he was the writer. He never spoke much. Our dinner conversations were never about ideas or our lives, but how badly the food was cooked. At breakfast, Dad would hold his newspaper high in one hand, a Camel cigarette in the other, and drink his black coffee in silence.

Silence was a large part of my relationship with Father. I remember a story he'd tell when his work buddies came to our house for dinner. During World War II he worked at the Port Reyes Radiomarine Station on Tomales Bay, north of San Francisco. One night his radar picked up a Japanese submarine in the bay — silently moving beneath the surface, in and out of range, then disappearing as quietly as it came. In later life I came to realize that was a perfect picture of his relationship with me — submerged and hidden, silently moving, then leaving.

His strong black steel Underwood sat on his desk at home, and he'd frequently type letters to his old work buddies, our few family members, then to me when I left home in 1961. They were newsy notes, with an undertone of grumbling, like the one he wrote to me at Christmastime in 1968. In his later years he'd include a smattering of complaints about his deteriorating health. His neat signature would always appear at the bottom of the last page.

So I wrote to "Mr. Wayne H. Helfer, 30 San Felipe Way, San Francisco" that summer fifty-one years ago:

Dear Dad,
    It's beautiful up here in the Sierria. The camp is beautiful too. The camp isn't finished yet, but next year it will be. Every morning we have

to cook our own breakfast. This morning we didn't have to cook. We just had to eat. We had cold cereal. We eat dinner at 12:30 and we have our rest at 1:30 and supper at 6:00. Before we go to supper we have Flag lowering. We go to bed at 9:30 and get up at 8:00. I don't like to get up but I have to. A few days ago it rained and yesterday it thunderd.

Love & kisses, Helen

During the first ten years I was away from home, Dad wrote to me on a regular basis, and I would write back to him. But all this came to an abrupt and painful stop in May of 1972 when the time finally came for me to write my parents about Victor.

The previous year, Victor and I had moved to the Washington suburb of Silver Spring, Maryland, where he opened his second architectural office on Georgia Avenue, on the D.C. side of the line. During the next two years, we'd spend half our time in Philadelphia and the other half in D.C. Living a split life was difficult for me, particularly since I'd grown to love Philadelphia and the people I was privileged to know there.

I spent my first year in the nation's capital helping Victor set up his new office. I also worked with a small group of activists to establish a new

Victor and me in Washington, D.C., 1972

People's Fund in the city, based on the successful Philadelphia model Victor and I had helped create. We held a large sock-hop fund-raising dance in Georgetown with Carl Bernstein, who appeared as our "Elvis Presley" DJ. Two years later, Bernstein would become nationally known for his book *All the President's Men*. We raised $10,000 that night, distributed the money to ten groups, then went out of business.

Not long afterward, my Long Beach high school friend Phyllis Babcock told me her mother was flying to New York to visit her. Over the years, Mrs. Babcock had become a good friend of my parents as well. Phyllis and her mother wanted to tour the national monuments in D.C., and Victor and I welcomed them to stay with us. "Sister" Babcock (as my father called her) was a strong and tolerant woman from Montana. I was not worried about her accepting Victor, but I didn't want her to return to Long Beach having to lie about his existence to my parents. So on May 31, 1972, I wrote:

Dear Mom and Dad,

I can't believe Phyllis and Mrs. Babcock will be here next week. It will be good to see both of them again — haven't caught up with Phyllis in over a year, and I wasn't able to see Mrs. B when she came east four years ago.

I have some good news — but I know it may not be good news to you. We never talked about what really mattered to us. It was always easier to keep important things below the surface. But I want to tell you about someone who has been a special part of my life for some time.

His name is Victor. I met him when I worked as a community organizer in North Philadelphia (remember the article I sent you when I got the job?). He's the architect we hired to rehabilitate some abandoned houses across the street from my office. He's a graduate from Harvard and now has two offices, one here in D.C. and his old office back in Philadelphia. We've been spending time in both places, although my job at HUD will begin soon and my commuting days will thankfully end.

For a long time I've looked for someone with whom I could share my life, and I'm very happy to have met Victor. He is bright, extraordinarily hard working with a good sense of humor, and has overcome many obstacles as a Black man. His father was a proud Pullman porter and all of his three children went to college.

After much house hunting, Victor and I found a charming three bedroom home in a beautiful integrated D.C. neighborhood where we will be moving soon. We'd both welcome a visit from you anytime you care to come east.

Love, Helen

Dad wrote back on June 2, 1972:

Helen:

Your letter of 5/31 came as no great surprise, but I have prayed for years — ever since I realized the extent of some of your screwball ideas — that, despite what we both did in trying to give you the best upbringing we could afford, and the excellent education you have received that you would eventually bring us disgrace and shame. This you have effectually accomplished and, as far as I am concerned, the relationship is ended as of now. Nothing you can say or do in this matter will make the slightest difference as the decision is absolutely final.

It is unfortunate that your poor judgment went so far as to bring

Mrs. Babcock into the sordid affair, but I imagine we can live this down as well as have to live down the overall disgrace and shame for what few remaining years we have on this earth.

Under no circumstances are you to plan on paying us a visit for you, in your present status, ARE NOT WELCOME. I am not speaking for your mother, your brother and his family, or anyone else, but the least you can do in view of what you have already done, is to STAY AWAY and DO NOT COMMUNICATE.

W.H. Helfer

I held his letter in my hand for a long time. I finally knew who he was. "You stupid, stupid man!" I shouted to no one. "You're throwing away your only daughter? Why? I could have married a white asshole, and you wouldn't have cared. But a successful and highly educated Black man was taboo. How stupid is that?"

My Hermes typewriter sat on my desk for six weeks, untouched. I knew to reveal my outrage would be fruitless. I also knew that Mother would be of little help in dealing with Dad, for she had absorbed his racism and was too weak to confront the issue. I also knew she would never disown me as he did. I finally wrote back on July 16:

Dear Dad,

I've been putting off responding to your letter not knowing how to start. What shocked me most was your inability to see me as a separate human being, capable of my own joys and sorrows, achievements and failures. My happiness meant nothing to you. As long as I remained inside your narrow scope of "values" I was "acceptable," but as soon as I stepped outside, I was automatically "unacceptable." How simple and sad for you, throwing away a 32 year old relationship, and for what? You seem to enjoy dis-owning family members, and you are the one who suffers most.

If you allowed yourself to take away, just for a moment, the racism that blinds you, you will find in Victor a fine person. At least you could judge for yourself what kind of person he is — and not pre-judge him just because he has a different skin color. I thought you were smarter than that. I was wrong.

There is too much joy in my life to hate you. I don't want to hate you, although there is much about you I don't understand. Please know the line of communication will always be open on this end.

Love, Helen

He never wrote back, and until Mom died ten years later, he never spoke to me. My son, who was born three years after his letter arrived, never knew his grandfather—never received a birthday card from him, or a gift at Christmas, never was able to share his stories with him as he grew into a beautiful young boy. He was almost thirteen years old when Dad died.

The neighborhood where Victor and I bought our old "Main Street" American home was called Takoma, just across the line from Takoma Park, Maryland. The streets were tree lined, and almost every house had a front porch and large backyard. There was a healthy mix of Black, white, and interracial families, mostly modest to middle income. At that time, Washington was 80 percent Black and 20 percent white. Takoma was racially unique largely because of the exceptional work of Neighbors, Inc., and people like Loretta Neumann.

I met Loretta and her eclectic housemates shortly after Victor and I moved into the neighborhood. They were refurbishing a glorious corner Victorian house with great care and talent. Although she has focused her professional life on critical environmental issues on Capitol Hill, Loretta is the past president of Neighbors, Inc. and was a board member of National Neighbors. She and her late husband Tedd McCann gave the most enjoyable and racially diverse parties in our neighborhood, especially on New Year's Eve.

LORETTA NEUMANN

I grew up in Oklahoma City, but I was born in El Reno, Oklahoma, in 1943 near our family farm. My great-grandfather on my mother's side, B. J. Menz, got it in the run of Oklahoma in 1889. Our family still owns a hundred acres of it.

In all of my childhood, the only Black person who comes to mind was a man we knew as "Shorty." (His real first name was Lee.) He worked for my grandfather, Henry Neumann, who, in his later years, had a wholesale produce company which he operated out of his home. Shorty had been with him for years and years. They would get on an old wooden-sided pickup truck with the open back end and haul boxes of tomatoes

Loretta Neumann as a child in Oklahoma City

and lettuce and other vegetables to the restaurants in Oklahoma City. That's how both of them made their living. Shorty also did other kinds of odd jobs—mowing lawns and making repairs around the house. He also helped my bedridden grandmother care for her prize-winning iris garden.

Henry Neumann was my grandfather on my father's side of the family. He was born in the 1870s in Hermann, Missouri, at a time when it was nearly all first- and second-generation Germans. Educated by Germans and raised in a German family, he spoke with a German accent. You can imagine what it was like for him during World War I and World War II, a German-sounding man, even though he was born in the United States. The KKK even burned a cross on his front lawn. At some point he moved to Guthrie, Oklahoma, where he met and married my Irish grandmother, Anastasia Cecelia Morrison. They were quite a feisty pair!

Granddad Neumann was a very big-hearted man. Big chested, too. He looked like what he was, a German merchant. He became wealthy. He was so wealthy that my father had private tutors. But his wealth didn't last. Indeed, he built up and lost two fortunes. One time he lost everything he had in a flood, and the second time to a fire. This was a time when few people had insurance. But no matter what the adversity, he would always come out and go on to his next enterprise. He always seemed so cheerful. I like to think that he lived a happy life and died a happy man.

Shorty, who was his sidekick all these years, watched my grandfather and, like him, saved and invested his money. Shorty was not poor himself. But he was also clearly different. I remember once when I was seven or eight years old, Shorty was over mowing our backyard, and my mother (Bernadine Schwab Neumann) had taken a drink of water out to him. She had a pot on the stove with boiling water, and when she returned to the kitchen, she put the glass in the boiling water. I said, "Why are you doing that?" She never boiled a glass that I'd ever seen. She said, "Well, Shorty drank out of the glass." I remember at the time wondering why it mattered with Shorty, when she didn't do it after me or anybody else. I don't even understand now why I noticed, or why the image is still with me. To this day, it's as if it happened yesterday. My mother died when I was nine years old and I'm now fifty-five, so that was a long time ago.

My father was a lawyer, and he looked out for Shorty after my granddad died. When Shorty died, my daddy made sure that his wife got all the money that Shorty had saved, because she was virtually illiterate. Not only that, when she was bedridden, he bought her groceries and personally delivered them to her. I only know this because one time I went with him and I asked, "What are you doing, Daddy?" He pretended it was nothing, he was just taking her a few things. Later I found out that he had done this every week for several years. He also helped her with her bank account and paid her bills for her, even after she died.

Another thing influencing my feelings on race is my experience of Catholicism in Oklahoma. My sisters and I went to Catholic schools at a time when the rest of the South was segregated. The Catholic schools were integrated, so I had Black friends in high school. There weren't a lot of them, but if you were Catholic, you went there. My dad said, "If you ever date a Negro, I'll go out and shoot him." Well, I was

Loretta Neumann's family in the mid-1940s

really scared. I didn't want him to shoot any of my friends. Later, I found out that there were at least two young Black men whose tuition my father had paid because they couldn't afford it.

What I see from living in the East, Catholicism is different here from what I experienced in Oklahoma. There, we were taught very early that you are what you do, not just what you say. You can't just say that you believe in God, you have to do something to help your neighbor, help the needy. I think some of that ethic explains why my father was putting groceries in a bag to take to Shorty's wife or paying for young Black men's schooling.

My father would, however, sometimes get angry at the Catholic Church. A lot of the priests were going off to South America to convert poor people. My father would say, "We've got all these poor people in Oklahoma City, why don't the priests help them instead of going to South America?"

In Oklahoma at the time, Catholics were a minority religion; only about 2 percent were Catholic, so we were the ones looked down on. My sister Marilyn had a boyfriend who dropped her because of her religion. I had a sense of empathy for anybody else who was looked down on, be they Jewish or Black.

While I was in college I got to know several Africans. I attended Oklahoma State University, which had an affiliate in Kenya, and there were a number of African students. We would have coffee together, and it was at a time when the restaurants were not integrated. I remember being with this one young man, a wonderful African whose father was a chief in his country. But he came to the United States and wasn't allowed to eat in a restaurant! So a group of us said, "Well, if we can eat at a restaurant, so should you." We went together to our favorite restaurant and sat with this young man, our friend, the son of a chief. We were told to leave, but we wouldn't. Fortunately, unlike other places in the South where restaurant owners fought integration, this restaurant didn't, and they served us. After that, we went back many times with our friend and brought others, too. It was very peaceful. And it taught me a lesson.

In 1965 I got married, and the following year moved with my new husband to Norfolk, Virginia. He was a member of the U.S. Coast and Geodetic Survey, a uniformed but nonarmed commissioned corps.

I found a job teaching the sixth grade with the Norfolk school system. It was the first year the elementary classes in Virginia were fully integrated, and we had a number of Black students. Many of the teachers were very upset about it, as they themselves had never attended an integrated school. I was surprised at their attitudes.

I recall one Black girl who was fourteen years old in the sixth-grade class I taught. (Most of the other students were only twelve.) She wasn't fat, but stocky and already full breasted. According to her files, she had a child. She was very tough and picked on one especially pretty blonde girl. She was smart, however, and I rather liked her independence. One day, after she had hit another girl while playing baseball, I pulled her outside in the hall and gave her a lecture. I told her I thought she was very intelligent and had lots of potential. "You have the choice to make," I said. "Either you will grow up to be a very fine person or you will become nobody." I asked which she wanted. She had tears in her eyes. "I want to be somebody," she mumbled. I hugged her. At least as long as I was the teacher there, she never hit any of the other girls again.

After Norfolk, my husband and I moved to Washington, D.C. He finished his military duty and decided he wanted to go back to Oklahoma. I wanted to stay in Washington, so we were divorced. A few years later, in 1974, I end up in Takoma, this wonderfully integrated D.C. neighborhood. With my father's help, I bought a house on 5th Street. It was a group house. Later, we moved a few blocks to our home on Piney Branch Road, which several of us bought together.

It was in Takoma that I discovered Neighbors, Inc., an organization that had been created specifically to foster and maintain integrated neighborhoods. It clearly taught me that the rest of the world wasn't socially integrated. While I had lived a life where I had many Black friends and didn't think anything of it, to live here and have real social integration was quite novel.

Neighbors, Inc., was formed in the late 1950s by people who lived in the Takoma and Manor Park neighborhoods of Washington, D.C. It was a coming together of Blacks and whites, Jews and Christians. It was created during the time of blockbusting, when real estate agents used race to scare whites into moving out of the city. They'd buy cheap from the whites and then flip the houses and sell them at high prices to Blacks.

Several residents in the neighborhood got together and said, "Now wait a minute. The only people making out on this are the real estate speculators." White and Black people agreed that they didn't mind living together, that it would, in fact, be nice to have an integrated neighborhood. This was a collective group of people. That's what made Neighbors, Inc., unique—Blacks and whites working on it together.

I got involved in Neighbors, Inc., in the mid-1970s and several years later became president. I also became a board member of National Neighbors, an organization made up of groups like Neighbors, Inc. In almost every major city, there was an organization like Neighbors, Inc., whose purpose was to foster and maintain integrated neighborhoods. On the one hand, I was happy that in every city there was such an organization, but I was sad that out of a whole city there would be only one neighborhood that was really integrated—not just a few Blacks in a white neighborhood or a few whites in a Black neighborhood, but truly socially integrated communities where they held functions together and partied together and their kids went to school together and they liked each other. That's what real integration is all about.

Out of all this, and the accumulation of my childhood and young adult experiences, I have become a definite proponent of the principle that you have to work at integration. The only way you can assure that is to do it. For example, I made a pledge that I simply would not have a party in my community that wasn't integrated. The point is that if you don't take an affirmative stand to try, then it just won't happen. When I go to other parts of Washington, D.C., and to other parts of the United States (I travel a lot), I'm shocked in this day and age that people don't socialize in an integrated way. Something is wrong if our society is still so closed, so segregated.

Loretta Neumann, on the right, with the new president of Neighbors, Inc., in the 1990s

I was so pleased when President Clinton started his race discussion, and I was very saddened that people did not pick up and understand it.

They didn't really discuss integration. It got lost somewhere. That's unfortunate. Now, of course, the Bush administration doesn't even address the issue.

As far as integration goes, my attitude is that it's just like boys' schools and girls' schools. I always went to coed schools, and I'm glad I did, because I was a tomboy. I toughed it out, and no boy was better than me. But there were an awful lot of girls who were raised not to feel that way. So when they go into a coed situation, the boys take over and the girls never get to exert their power and influence.

It's the same to me with the issue of integration. When everything is segregated, each may have its own power, but ultimately they need to interact. Within the integrated scheme, unless there's equality, one side will dominate the other, just like there was no equality in the boy-girl scheme in coed schools where the boys dominated the girls. If in the integrated scheme the whites continue to dominate the Blacks, you have not achieved anything.

So there are, to me, perfectly understandable reasons why people want to keep a certain element of Blackness—they feel the whites can take care of themselves. So they seek to achieve their own goals and their own leadership qualities first.

I'm in a quandary about it. I don't have an answer. I do feel strongly, however, that we need to work together. We cannot have real integration unless all parties feel equal. ▪■■

Around the corner from Victor's and my home on 5th Street lived Vince and Caroline deForest and their three young, active children. Vince is Black and Caroline is white. He grew up in Cleveland at almost the same time as my white friend Betty King, but in its urban core and living a very different kind of childhood.

Through his work at the National Park Service, Vince is now devoting his life to educating Americans about what he passionately describes as "the most profound multiracial humanitarian movement in our nation's history," the Underground Railroad. I talked with him and Caroline separately in their stunning home in St. Louis, Missouri, which was designed in the 1930s by Caroline's father, a noted architect.

VINCE DEFOREST

My mother died right after I was born, and my father was never around. He was an interior decorator and never lived at our house, but there was a lady and her husband who he hired to take care of my two sisters, brother, and myself.

Kindergarten was the first time someone outside of family acknowledged I had talent in art. We were asked to draw something, and the P-52 fighter plane was something that was very real to me. It was World War II, and I had seen many pictures of it. I drew this plane in three dimensions and found out later that this was very unusual. The teacher was so stunned she took me to all the classes to show the drawing. I was very shy and wasn't prepared for all that attention. But that incident left a mark on me. The fact that art became something very real to me is probably the most important happening in my young life.

My Cleveland neighborhood was predominantly Black, but there was one family, the Yacabuchis, who owned a restaurant and were close friends of my father. I didn't know we were on welfare and were wards of the city. But I knew I was poor because of where we lived. I lived in an alley that was called Hollingsworth Court, and at the end of the alley was a high brick wall. Everybody who lived on the other side of that wall was white. There was antagonism back and forth between the people who lived in the alley and the people who lived on the other side. There were rock throwings, but you never saw a face. It was just something coming over this wall.

I never knew what was going on over there, only what was happening on the court. It was—I don't want to say Catfish Row—but everything was happening there. We had gambling, alcohol, and murder. I remember vividly the murder that happened right across the street. It was gruesome, and I could see the blood everywhere.

I knew the people who were caring for us really did care for us. The only connection I remember with my biological family is that my father might come by once a week. I remember the priest came every Saturday to our house to give us catechism. I learned later it was my mother's wish that we be brought up in the Catholic Church, and my father was Catholic too. I don't ever remember going to church or to mass at that early age. I learned all my Hail Marys from the Saturday visits.

The lady who took care of us was moving. There were four of us—my brother, my two sisters, and myself—who were involved in this configuration, so we had to move. For some reason, this family could no longer take care of us. So we moved to another part of the city, and we were split up again. My sisters went one place, and we never knew where they went until later. My brother and I stayed together, and we moved to an area near 105th Street, the Gold Coast. We lived with a lady who was in her fifties and her husband who was in his sixties. During that move we were introduced to another kid who we connected with and who later became our "foster" brother. We adopted each other, and we stayed together for so long I knew him better than my biological sisters.

We used to make money on Saturdays carrying people's groceries home with our wagons. Because we had ventured out from the neighborhood in our work, we began to sense, in a real way, the stain of racism in terms of name-calling in areas of the city we delivered groceries. We were old enough to go on public transportation, so the realization that we were being looked down upon by certain elements of society became very real to me.

During that period, a social worker would come in periodically. She gave me some appreciation for my mother, because until then, no one had actually talked with me about my mother in terms of who she was, where she was from, anything. Then our foster mother, Mrs. Ivory, got sick and died. By that time I was about eleven years old and had started a new school that was very integrated.

When Mrs. Ivory died, we knew we were on the move again. We didn't know where we were going, but for our own protection, we never developed a strong relationship with anybody. We recognized that to attach yourself to anything you had no control whatsoever about could be a very hurting thing. So we came up with methods of trying to mold a certain independence because we knew we were not in charge. For example, we never called anyone "mother" or "father," no matter who they were. They became an "aunt" or "uncle." The constant concern of a kid growing up and not knowing who you are, then trying to interact with people who are in charge of you, became a game of gymnastics, trial and error.

The last foster home where we lived was the challenge, partly because we were teenagers. This family never had any kids, and we came to understand they could not have any kids, which was the reason they wanted foster kids. It was a critical point in our lives where we needed the most guidance, the most positive direction, the most love and understanding—and we didn't get it. It's not so much that the people could not give it, they didn't know how to give it. The impact on us was horrendous, because every action or nonaction seemed to warrant physical outbursts. Each of us responded differently. My brother Robert is very headstrong, defiant. Our foster brother Tommy was more like myself, kind of laid-back and unassuming. I didn't say a lot, but I thought a lot. In this atmosphere, not only were the outside forces of segregation becoming so real in our everyday lives, but because Tommy was half German, we would begin to hear negative remarks from these people about his family. We were in constant emotional turmoil. It became evident that prejudice has no color. It cut deep.

We had to deal with the mental as well as the physical part. I don't know which one was worse. We knew if we did something wrong we would know the ramifications of it by the lady of the house, who would let us know that as soon as her husband got home he would be told. We knew exactly what would happen. It was like clockwork, and it was like torture, because you knew you'd be allowed to eat dinner, and you knew you'd be allowed to clean up the kitchen afterward, but as soon as the kitchen was cleaned up, there was that key word: "march." We'd have to march down to "hell's pit" (the basement), and we'd get one of the worst beatings, I mean unbelievable. Generally, my brother Robert wanted to be first, and I used to hate that, because my thing was to get in and get out as quickly as I could, and Robert's thing was to be defiant. He wouldn't say anything in words, but he wouldn't cry. Because Robert didn't cry, we felt we were really in for it, because if he expressed himself a little or faked it, we might be able to get off light, but that would make Kofu Jimmy angrier, and he was strong.

We stayed in that house the longest, and what evolved was a love-hate relationship. By that time, we had accumulated a lot of friends, and one of the key ways of dealing with trauma is to extend it out as far as you can reach in terms of people who you can rely on. I developed a real sense of looking outside of self for relief. My relief would be religion, art, sports, people. I would adopt anybody's father or uncle as my uncle. There was this need to identify or relate to something outside of where I was.

This experience gave me a basis of understanding life in a survival mode. It gave me determination, but it left a lot of scars, too. In this situation, you try to be as inconspicuous as possible. If I were to go up the stairs, I knew which one of those stairs made noise, and I would go up those stairs in a way I wouldn't make any noise at all. Years later when I got into my own place, I was doing the same thing. You develop these behavioral patterns—some of them are still with me today.

During that same period, I was doing pretty good in high school, honor roll all the time, but I still pursued the school I wanted to attend to study architecture. We had one school on the East Side and one on the

West Side that offered architecture. The East Side school was predominantly white; the West Side school was all white. Cleveland is divided east and west, and there were no Blacks that lived on the West Side. I just knew when I saw Frank Lloyd Wright's Falling Waters in a *Time* magazine article, I wanted to be able to do that. It never occurred to me that I didn't know any Black architects. It never occurred to me that there was anything called architecture. I just knew that I loved to draw, and that building reached me at a center point, and I needed to go to East Tech. I passed the entrance exam and got in and started specializing in architecture. On most days I didn't have the money to go to school on the bus, and I would actually run the almost fifteen miles to school. I was late a lot of the time, but I was still an A–B student.

Then it happened. The white students and teachers in the school learned that it was going to be merged with a Black school, an academic school that was right in the same area, and this was a Black area of town. The white students and teachers said, "No way, we're leaving." So they packed up their bags and left for West Tech. There were only eight of us left in the class, and after three months, they decided they couldn't continue the class. I was destroyed. So I went to the board of education, because I knew the only other school that offered that program was West Tech. I asked to see a counselor and I told him that I only had half a year to go and I wanted to finish up. Then he started a litany of questions that I soon learned had no relevance at all to what I was asking him for. He asked me if I knew any Black architects. He asked me, "Why don't you take something like woodwork or masonry?" But that wasn't the question I was asking, and after going around in a circle, I knew what he was saying. It really hit me. That was a defining moment. I was so mad I got up from my chair, walked out of the building, and down the street to the Marine Corps recruiting station. I put my age up and asked them when was the next train out of Cleveland. I signed up, didn't tell anybody, and got on that train.

The next thing I knew, I ended up in Parris Island. I had never been down South in my life, but I'd heard about the racism. It didn't occur to me, this compulsion to get away, that I was jumping right into the fire. This was 1954, and the South was the South. Washington, D.C. was the South, even Philadelphia in many ways was the South.

We got on a troop train, and there were about twenty Blacks in the two cars that were connected. By the time we got to Philadelphia, the guy who comes through the cars selling candies came by us. It's not that I never heard the word *nigger* before, but it was so adamant the way he said it directly to our face—no fear, nothing. I was going further south, and this was already happening to me on the train. Fortunately, there were some Italian guys from Cleveland. We locked this guy in the baggage car, took all his candies and distributed them free.

Before we get to Parris Island we stop for breakfast in a little town called Beaufort. As soon as we get off the train, they divide us based on race. I thought all of that was over. I was in the Marine Corps. It's early in the morning, and there's no place to go—I don't know anyone. All the whites moved into the restaurant. All the Blacks they marched around to the rear, and we ate outside. I said, "What did I get myself into?" Even in the Marine Corps racism continued to exist.

I almost got court-martialed because I had reached the point where I just couldn't take it. There was a certain part of me that wouldn't let me go any further. It was when I was in second infantry training—I just broke one day, right in ranks. I was put up for office hours (a procedure that's the step before the court-martial). The Marine Corps didn't have Black officers in those days. The only thing that saved me was a lieutenant who heard about the office hours, and I just laid it out to him. "I'm not used to this kind of prejudice and I'm not going to take it," I told him. He was sensitive to that, and I don't know what he wrote or did, but I got a punishment and not a court-martial—I didn't even like that. I was ready to go to hell rather than allow this thing to roll over me.

The South was very difficult for me. I almost got lynched going from Cherry Point to Jacksonville, North Carolina. It was a cold winter night near Christmas on a Trailways bus. It stopped at every cow pasture along the way, so I get on the bus, and it's almost full. There's only two seats on the bus, so I took one of them near the front, definitely the white section of the bus. The driver looked at me but didn't say anything. The next passenger to get on was a Black elderly gentleman. As he came down the aisle I put out my hand and said, "Here's a seat right next to me," and this guy threw down my hand and stood up all the way to Jacksonville, a long ride. By this time, everybody was aware of what was happening. I was breaking the code. The bus terminal in Jacksonville was very close to the Black side of town. You could tell because the pavement stopped at the railroad tracks, and the dirt road continued on the Black side of town. I got off that bus and ran down the dirt road. I knew those people were just waiting to do something.

I'm sure that my being in the South was the reason I got involved in the civil rights movement and what I'm doing today with the Underground Railroad. A lot of people think it's just a "project," that I can let it go and do something else. I don't have anything else to do, and I know that deeply. Even my kids don't understand it, and if there's been any shortfall in regard to my relationship with them or my wife, it's because of this overriding compassion and need I have to really find who I am.

In growing up I never had a true understanding of our ancestors making it possible for where we are today. I later realized that individuals had done all these things I was not taught in school. There are now programs designed to commemorate these persons, places, and events that are important to American history—and the establishment is not telling it in American history. There are individuals who have sacrificed their whole lives to bring this knowledge to the forefront, like Carter G. Woodson, considered to be the father of African American history. He was trained at Harvard in history in the 1930s and came out of that experience with a Ph.D. in history, but he recognized that he hadn't learned anything and was aware enough to say, "I've been miseducated." He wrote the book *The Mis-education of the Negro*. He started an organization to be sure that we knew our history. When you start learning your history and the sacrifices that people made to bring us where we are today, it can't stop there. Somebody has to take it and give it form. We had a program in the federal government that would enable us to give this history physical form in the identification of historic structures and buildings. We need these physical reminders of the legacy that reflects that American story. They weren't there.

When the 1976 Bicentennial celebration came up, we looked at the commission's position on what it had, and it didn't speak to Blacks at all. It was almost as if we didn't exist. When you looked at the history of 1776, where were Blacks in 1776? They were still enslaved. Why would we be celebrating an event when we were still enslaved? Are we going to talk about that? They weren't going to talk about that, so we felt that we needed to talk about that. That's why we formed the African American Bicentennial Corporation, so we could create some relevancy of this event that was going to happen anyway. Maybe, just maybe, we could use it as a generator for making some important statement. We began to look at what federal agency is responsible for giving visibility and interpreting American history in this country—and that's the National Park Service, through its program of monuments, landmarks, etc.

We looked at their programs to see what they had that reflected the history of the country. Out of 1,500 sites, supposedly representing the history and development of this country through designated certified historic landmarks, only three related to Blacks: Booker T. Washington, George Washington Carver, and Frederick Douglass—three people who are supposed to be reflective of our contribution to this country. No way, so we convened in Washington some of the leading Black historians and social scientists to ask the questions, How should we react to this? What can we do? We put together the program that was later funded and recognized, and now we have over ninety sites that are officially recognized. I was able to get the first Black woman recognized; now we have two. The first was Maggie Walker from Richmond, Virginia, and the second was Mary McLeod Bethune.*

This effort demonstrated for us the whole concept of empowerment, that there are effective ways to get together and determine for ourselves what is important. When we rely on other people to recognize our contribution, it's too late. We have to do what the abolitionists did. They didn't wait for people. We have to empower ourselves.

When I was a child, I lived in all these different foster homes because the state told me that I had to. After the last straw, I had to do something on my own. It may not have been the right decision or the best decision, but it was my decision. I empowered myself, and if I did nothing more, I moved myself out of that situation.

I see what I'm doing now with the Underground Railroad as a continuum. For the most part in this country, we tend to deify individuals, and that's OK, but it's not consistent with telling the full story of people, because it tends to be elitist. Individuals who were the leaders, we cast up in the middle of parks and rotundas, but the common folk, in the case of the Underground Railroad, go unnoticed for all these years. Although we hear about people like Frederick Douglass or Harriet Tubman, they are not reflective of the true essence of what the Underground Railroad was all about.

The reason I connect with it so much is the fact that it represents an opportunity to elevate—without calling all the names—the little people and to show that they empowered themselves to create the strongest social and humanitarian movement in world history. It was a collection of all types of individuals who worked together, so the true essence of the legacy is this whole concept of empowerment. This quest for freedom, which has been with us since the beginning of time, continues. If we do nothing more, we have an obligation to recognize the legacy and

*Maggie Walker (1867–1934) founded the St. Luke Penny Savings Bank in Richmond in 1903, becoming the first female bank president in the country. Her bank absorbed other African American banks and became a major bank in 1929. Mary McLeod Bethune (1875–1955) was born in Mayesville, South Carolina. In 1904 she founded the Daytona Educational and Industrial School for Negro Girls (now Bethune-Cookman College). She founded the National Council of Negro Women and was a vice president of the National Association for the Advancement of Colored People.

the thousands of individuals and institutions that came together to symbolize this movement. There is no better expression we can leave to the next generation than the legacy of the Underground Railroad.

We have to be dreamers. The addiction you see out in the street today is a manifestation of people who maybe never had a dream. They never felt that they could. That's the new kind of slavery, so we have to create dreamers, and they come in many forms. Somebody has to talk about them. Somebody has to paint them. Somebody has to sing about them or write poetry about them.

All of us have been given different gifts. I know the power of spirit, and it can be spoken, it can be visual, it can be through hearing. We've been given the tools to resolve all the outstanding questions of this generation, or any generation. We just don't use them. That's why we need this idea of empowering ourselves with spirit, and that cannot be defined. It's the tool we've been given to accomplish supernatural things in our time. We have to believe that, in spite of every barrier we set up for ourselves. Once we start to put parameters on what we mean, then why dream?

For our survival, we are going to have to recognize that we are all one, that genius is manifested in all of us. ■■■

Caroline and Vincent deForest, with their granddaughter Kayla, in their St. Louis home, 1998

Caroline deForest grew up with her eight siblings in a strong Catholic home, the home where she now lives again in St. Louis. I was in awe at what she could grow in her large Takoma neighborhood garden. Many years ago we attended a master's gardening course together at the University of the District of Columbia. She is now a consultant with a local nursery on garden planning and design. Hers and Vince's bright and engaging granddaughter, Kayla, lives with them. She was eight years old when I met her.

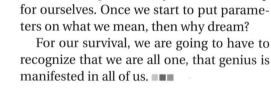

CAROLINE DEFOREST

I was born and raised here in University City, a suburb of St. Louis, one of nine kids in a basically Irish Catholic family. I did the Catholic thing all my life—Catholic schools, Catholic church, all those kinds of things. My father was a very strict Catholic in some ways. He changed as he got older because his children changed and forced him into major shifts in his attitudes about a lot of things.

When I was coming up, there was almost always a maid who was African American. The other contact I had as a young child with African Americans was the yard man who'd come around every two weeks and cut the grass. As a child, there are three things I remember in terms of myself, my family, and race: My father's mother taught him always to respect everybody. He was raised in Kansas City, Missouri. One time when he was nine years old they were getting on a bus and there was a "Negro" woman, as he said, who was waiting for the bus, and Dad started getting on the bus. His mother stopped him and made him back up. She said, "No, Joe, you always let a lady get on the bus first." He was obviously very impressed by that.

Caroline deForest (by the fireplace) with her eight brothers and sisters and parents

Second thing was when I was in high school I was on the bus with some friends and we saw a young Black guy who seemed to be our age walking down the street. I remember looking at him and saying to my friend, "Gee, he is really nice looking," and then saying, "It's too bad we can't really get to know him, because 'they' won't let us." He lived in his world, and we lived in ours, and they were separate. And third, when I was in elementary school—I went to a small Catholic school, very white and middle-class—there were two kids. One was white and very poor, and the nuns were so evil toward her. When I was in fifth grade, there was a Black girl in sixth grade who came to the school in 1952. (In 1949 the cardinal here declared that all the Catholic schools would be integrated—there would be no more separation.) This girl came to St. Joe's School, and again the nuns were evil. I don't remember specific things, just this constant carping. It struck me as something wrong. I didn't know what to do about it. I was taught that you support the nuns, that they're always right. But I knew this was wrong.

At Webster College—at that time a Catholic women's college in St. Louis—there were a few African Americans. In my freshman year I was in the registrar's office with ten to fifteen others crowded into this little space. There were a few chairs where some girls were sitting, and a Black girl came in and had to wait, so she sat on a chair, and the girl sitting next to her got up and moved away. It was something I had never seen before, and I knew what it was. At that time there was no way I would take any action or say anything. I was one of those scared people in so many ways. Life has brought a lot of changes, but that's where I was then.

Now I'm in a book club with a Black woman I went to Webster with, but I didn't know her that well then. This woman has a memory I didn't have. She came to Dad's funeral because she had read about his death. She said that when she was a student at Webster there were a lot of girls who were friendly with her, but when they had a parents' day, all of a sudden they didn't know her. She became invisible, and my dad was one of the few who made it a point to speak with her, and not just surface talk, but showing his interest. He had to be genuine, because he didn't know how not to be genuine.

After college I moved to D.C. and met Vincent. I lived with my great-aunt Josephine, who was a bitch. She did the best she could, but she was a mean-spirited person. She was also out front in a lot of ways. She divorced her husband in the mid-1930s when young Catholic women didn't do that. I knew I couldn't stay with her long, so I was looking for other places to live. I called the chancery to see if there were any places where young women could stay for a few months, and they said, "Yes, there's one at 14th and P Northwest, St. Augustin's Church." The building had been a convent and was now a community center and a residence on the second to fourth floors for women. I had to be interviewed and donate six hours a month, which wasn't much at all, either working with kids or answering the phones or whatever. So I went there to live. It was $40 a month for a room and kitchen privileges plus a built-in community.

Here I was, alone and the kind of person that doesn't go out to people and actually had this kind of depression which I didn't know until years later. I stayed there for two years, then met and married Vincent. He had come to D.C. in 1962 (two years before me). He was staying at the Y and walked past St. Augustin's, saw the doors open, turned around, and went back for some reason. He met this young priest named Geno Baroni. Vincent told him he was looking for a place to stay. Geno told him about two guys who had a place a couple blocks away who were looking for a third person, so Vincent moved in. The church was his second home, and he started volunteering there and helped build things for them. He also came to the center all the time because the women would feed him! He thinks they all loved him, and I guess some of them did. He was out of town when I got there, and he came back a couple of weeks later and "had to meet this new person," which was me. Actually, that was it. We started dating, and it was a casual kind of thing. We got to know each other through volunteer work at the church.

Our granddaughter Kayla is learning who she is as a young girl. The school she attends does a whole series on the body, the heart and the lungs, and how they all work together, and how different we are from each other. That leads into how alike we are, too. The school is not afraid to face the differences and bring them out as something really important and wonderful. They did this program with ten different colors of whites, off-whites, tans, and the same thing with yarn for hair, or the kids could draw themselves on white paper with different markers. All these kids tried to find their shade on their arm and draw it in.

In terms of diversity, the school focuses on all the different ways of learning and all the talents and skills different people bring. Kayla's talent—you see it in the way she loves to learn and the way she loves to do things—is to do them with other people. Everybody has their talents and ways of learning, and they are respected and encouraged. That is a big difference between this school and other schools where they may have the diversity, but they don't truly celebrate it. At this school it's a conscious thing.

You see these kids at free time—all the way through sixth grade—and there's none of this "one group's here and one group's there—these are the white kids and those are the Black kids." None of that. The director says that some of the white students who come back from college tell him that they are friends with every-body because they're not seeing race first. Their white friends don't under-stand how they can do it, and it's not that their white friends don't want to, it's that they're not comfortable.

When my grandfather came from Ireland, he had family here and was able to work and get money from his work. He was able to invest it (he was a lousy investor, but he had that op-portunity), and then he had the oppor-tunity to send his kids to school. It's the privilege that he had as a citizen

A family gathering at the memorial service for Caroline deForest's mother in St. Louis

of this country, but as a white citizen. Other white families who'd been here for five or six generations who came from eastern Europe, Italy, England, all had the option to work, the money was theirs—maybe they didn't have much money, but it was theirs, and they could use it to build themselves up and support their families. But those who were enslaved were brought over here (they were brought over, not because they wanted to), and they did that work one generation after another. They worked very hard, but they were never paid for that work, so while their work helped to build up the country, they were never able to build up that one generation to another to take what they had earned and invest it and educate their children. It simply was not permitted.

I'm still among those who are able to reap the benefit of being white, being among those who are first chosen for things. I don't face that daily challenge, that constant diminishing of talent or skill or abilities by the general society. It comes in lots of ways. It comes with being scared of young Black males walking down the street. They know it. They're not out there to scare people, they're out there to walk home from school, or buy a Coke, or hang out in the loop. They know that when they look for a job, people first see their Black skin. Most people are reacting to that at some level. They may say they're not, but I know in my life I'm reacting to that often on some level, and I've had years of experience in life, living with my husband and my kids and grand-daughter. ▪▪▪

M y son Hasani was born on May 29, 1975, at Georgetown University Hospital in Washington, D.C. His birth name was Jeffrey. With his godmother, he chose his African name on his nineteenth birthday. I will never know how it feels to be a Black person in our country, but from the day my son was born, I know how it feels to be the mother of a Black child, now a beautiful young Black man. I am blessed among women to be Hasani's mother. I wrote this letter to him when he was three months old:

September, 1975

Dear Jeffrey,
    It is now the middle of September and ever since you were born I've wanted to write some thoughts on your birth and how much you have meant to your father and me these first three months of your life.
    When I went to Cape Cod last fall, it was the first vacation I had taken without your father in seven years — and the first time I realized I was pregnant with you. I remember riding a bicycle alone on the dunes in Provincetown and thinking how good it felt to finally be grow-

ing a baby. I waited for eight years to be a mother, to create a new human being, and it was happening. When I returned to Washington, I went to my doctor who confirmed what I already knew—you were being formed.

At the time of your birth, I worked at the Department of Housing and Urban Development in their Federal Women's Program. I was also finishing my term as president of the HUD Women's Caucus and decided to work until the week before you were expected. We had scheduled a meeting with Carla Hills, the secretary of HUD. The meeting was held the day you were born.

The night of May 28th your father made some delicious brownies, which we enjoyed with ice cream before bed. About 2:00 A.M. I awoke with a vague feeling of abdominal cramps. About 4:00 A.M. I woke your father and he began timing the contractions—and indeed they were coming at intervals of 7–10 minutes. He called the doctor who suggested we go to the hospital. It was about 6:30 in the morning, and a beautiful morning it was. The sun was bright and the spring flowers blazed with color.

After we arrived at Georgetown Hospital, your father checked me in at the Admissions Office and we walked straight to the labor room where I was given a white robe. Your father was given a paper blue pair of pants and a pullover top which he wore throughout the day. After I got in the bed, the nurse examined me and was quite surprised to discover that I was already dilated 6–7 centimeters. As birth takes place when a woman is 10 centimeters, she assured us that you would be born no later than noon. (As it was, you arrived at 5:05 P.M.)

Your father was a constant source of strength, coaching me through the painful contractions and giving me continual encouragement. At 3:00 P.M. I was given an intravenous feeding of glucose to give me additional strength. Shortly before 5:00 P.M. the doctor was getting anxious to get the whole thing over with. He wheeled me into the delivery room down the hall which was filled with strange people (interns, I presume). The nurse asked your father to leave the room for a moment to drink a glass of orange juice, as he had not taken time to eat all day. Up to this point I had no medication at all.

On the delivery room table there were two handles which I held on to for my life—and recall vividly when the doctor inserted the forceps (although I did not see him do it). I screamed my lungs out. Your father told me to open my eyes so I could see your head, which had just come out, followed quickly and less painfully by your shoulder and the rest of your body. You did not need to be slapped. You were screaming loudly too! After the doctor cut the cord, the nurse put you in a weigh table next to me and informed us that you weighed 8 pounds 12 ounces. I was able to hold you for only a moment before you were taken away, labeled and cleaned. It was just enough time to see how beautiful you were. You had my long hands and feet, and many of your father's features, including his brown soft crinkly hair, brown eyes and brown skin.

One afternoon when I was holding you close to me in my hospital bed, I felt transported to another dimension for a brief moment. We were in another space. I can't explain it. It was like an epiphany, then it was gone.

The day we left the hospital was brilliantly sunny, just as the day we had come. I was anxious knowing we were on our own now, and your total care was in our hands.

Your sisters Leslie and Susan and your brother Victor spent the next two summer months with us in Washington. They took to you immediately, and I was elated.

It's hard to realize fall is already here. It seems like yesterday when your father, brother and I took you on your first bicycle ride along the C&O Canal. Your father carried you on his back in the Tote carrier we had bought at Toast and Strawberries.

It is now late September, and we've just had a terrible thunderstorm. The basement is flooded up to the fourth stair, and I'm not sure how we're going to get the water out. You are getting bigger and more special every day. Your father has begun to feed you apple juice and milk in a bottle and you're taking it quite well. You are constantly exploring the world around you, and we are thrilled you are now a very important and special part of our world.

With Love Always, Mom

Hasani with his grandfather at our home in Washington, D.C.

Hasani with his father Victor in West Virginia, 1975

Hasani and me in 1981

HASANI ISSA

I don't remember when I consciously became aware of race. I remember being in school in first and second grade being called "Zebra" and "Oreo cookie" because I was half Black and half white. I know it hurt my feelings, not because I had any awareness of its correlation to my color, but because I knew it wasn't supposed to be a nice thing to say.

In my early childhood I didn't feel I had too many problems with who I was—being mixed or whatever. There were many kids I grew up with, especially on 5th Street, who were the same way. Mark being one (although he wasn't really mixed) and Daniel being one. We were just a bunch of Black kids. None of them paid attention to it. You were just my mom and Dad was just my dad—not my white mother or Black father. So I was fortunate in that way.

After 5th Street, Dad bought the house on McKinley Place in a really white neighborhood. I've always been aware that we were the only Black people on that street. I think that growing up in America you become aware of race in strange and subtle ways. It's always in the back of your mind someplace that you're a certain color and everybody else is a certain color, and it's just the way it seems to be.

I never had any problems in my father's neighborhood, but I think he did. Our next-door neighbor took a while to get used to the fact that a Black guy was living next to him. I always wondered why my dad decided to move to that particular neighborhood. He always said it was because it was near schools, convenient to shopping, but there's lots of neighborhoods that are a lot more diverse than the one he lives in that have the same amenities. We're still the only Black family on the street, and he's been there over fifteen years. He's always the first to say that he's noticed all these new Black families that have moved into the neighborhood, but I'm more cynical about it. I think it was a mistake to move there.

I attended a predominantly white school, Waldorf, but had few problems about race there. As you know, I was very popular at Waldorf, and I don't know if it had to do with my race—that I was the "exotic" one, or just because of who I was. I never had any problems except for one kid in my class once called me a nigger, but he was ostracized by the other kids for doing it. So he suffered more than I did. Another time this kid, around Easter time, made a stupid joke and said that I didn't have to color my eggs because I was already colored.

We used to go off the school property—which was not allowed—

and once a group of friends and I saw this group of kids on bikes who began taunting us. There were nine of us, but they singled me out and began shouting "nigger nigger nigger," then rode off on their bikes. We chased them but we didn't catch them. That's the only time it really hurt because it made me painfully aware that I was different from everybody else there—and the bikers knew I was different and took the opportunity to make me aware of it. They were lucky we didn't catch them.

The rest of my childhood experiences about race didn't happen in Washington, but down South. I have a very low opinion of southerners based on the negative experiences I've had with them. When I was about nine years old I was in Pensacola, Florida, with my stepbrother Josh, when my dad was still married to Sally. We had just gotten these cork guns and were excited about them. We were at Josh's aunt and uncle's house, and we were shooting the guns on their porch. There was this white kid across the street—I'll never forget him. He had all these freckles on his face and bright red hair. He had a BB gun and began calling me all these names. At first I was confused and shocked and didn't know how to respond because I had never experienced that kind of blatant hatred before. He was shouting "nigger" and "chocolate monkey" and telling me to get the hell out of his neighborhood. Then he shot me in the chest with his BB gun. That was one of those overt cases of racism that you don't ever forget. Josh's aunt and uncle said something like, "We're sorry you had to deal with that, but it's just the way things are down here." It's not like they ever considered me part of the family, much like your family never considered me part of the family, with the exception of your brother. I was scared and angry because I was in a place I didn't know, had never been before, and had to deal with this kind of negativity coming at me in such an extreme way. When you're nine years old, you don't know how to process that kind of experience in any meaningful way.

Hasani with my brother Wayne and his granddaughter Eriana in California

When I was at Parkmont High School, we went down south to the Okefenokee Swamp and me and my friend Traveun were approached by a Boy Scout leader, a white guy. We were teenagers and were being loud and obnoxious. He came up because we had been cursing and started yelling, "All you niggers are the same, cursing and carrying on, blah blah blah. You should go back where you came from." So Traveun and I got in his face, then our principal came and broke it up, apologized to the guy, and got mad at us for confronting him.

On that same trip we went to a convenience shop and I bought a package of donuts and chocolate milk. It cost about a buck fifty, and I gave the man my money and went out and sat in the van. We were about to leave after we filled the tank, and this man comes running out the door and pointing at me furiously and says to the principal, "He just stole something from my store!" and I said, "What the hell are you talking about?" He looks at me with his brows furrowed, "You just stole those donuts and milk!" I said, "You're a goddamned liar! I paid you for this," but he was swearing up and down that I stole the items. The principal again gets mad at me and pays the guy a buck fifty. I told him, "Don't give him any money. I just paid him." I guess he was doing it to simplify the situation. It disgusted me that this stupid ignorant southerner would just out of the pure hatred of his heart come out with this blatant lie. He knew it was a lie, and I knew it was a lie.

You always get "the look" from southerners. They always have this air about them. The South is the only place in America where they talk about the Civil War as if it was yesterday. They still feel bad that they lost. It's the only place in the country you can get into a fistfight about bad-mouthing Robert E. Lee. It's sad, but it also speaks to the very different mentality that exists down there.

Whenever I go down South—and I think a lot of Black people think this way—you have to bring on a whole new mentality. Your whole sense of reality changes. When a Black person goes South, it's like you're in a war zone, like I imagine some people in Vietnam must have thought when they were walking in the woods. You're just walking in the woods, but you don't know if there's somebody up in a tree waiting to shoot you. It's the same way down South. You're constantly on your guard, and every white person you meet, you eye with a sense of suspicion and fear. That's what racism really is—fear. You don't trust anybody. It might be different for southern Blacks, because if you grow up around it, you might acculturate it differently. I have very little regard for southerners, even though I think the South is beautiful.

One of the first experiences I had about Black history was when you and I were going to Harpers Ferry. I was asking you about someone named Malcolm X, and you told me about his book. I went out and bought it and read it. It was a real eye-opener for me. It was the first time in my life that I consciously thought of myself as Black, not just as a skin color, but also culturally.

In terms of Howard University, I didn't choose a Black university, it chose me. I applied to several places, but Howard was the only one that accepted me. In retrospect, it was the hand of God that made that choice, because I couldn't imagine myself anyplace else. It has been the best place for me, even though, as you know, I have many problems with my department and the school in general. The benefits I've received far outweigh the negatives. It's a completely artificial environment, but it's an important environment for Black people. In very rare instances in the United States are you going to be in a collegiate environment that's almost 100 percent Black. It's important, I think, because it gives Black people, in four short years, the opportunity to interact with one another without feeling ashamed or intimidated because white people are around. You can just be who you are. You can be Black.

Hasani (with bow tie), his sisters Susan, Leslie, and Diane, and his brother Victor at his high school graduation in Washington, D.C.

One of the negatives of the experience is that it lulls some people into a false sense of reality, and when they get out of school they don't know how to deal with people unlike themselves. That's dangerous, because this is an Anglo-Saxon society in which we live for the most part. At least it's controlled by that ethnic group, so you do need to know how to relate to them. Since I've been around white people most of my life, I am more comfortable than some in that world.

Racism is an immense topic, and it's consumed a large part of my life. When I finally got through high school, I went through a very angry period of basically hating white people. A lot of the poems I wrote came out of that period. It's frustrating, especially for someone who's young —eighteen or nineteen—to think about all the hatred and all the lies and evil that white people have perpetrated on Black people and other people of color. I just wanted to pick up a gun and shoot every last one of them. It's hard not to want to do that. I know a lot of white people today say, "I didn't do that. My grandfather did that!" That may be true, but white people are reaping the benefits of what their grandfathers did. It is also erroneous to think that just because your grandfather "did that," you are not in some way responsible. If your grandfather did not apologize, that does not mean you are absolved. One of the biggest problems I have with this country today is that it does not feel it needs to make an apology for all the stuff they've done to Black people over the centuries. Even Germany apologized for what they did to the Jews, and that was just over fifty years ago.

White people need to take responsibility for the actions of white people who came before them, because they are reaping the benefits of what those actions were, just like Black people are reaping the detrimental effects of what slavery has done to people. Slaves are no longer here, but most of the violence we see in our communities today can be directly traced to those activities that happened over 100 years ago. You cannot separate one from the other. No event in history happens in a vacuum. If you oppress and keep people down for hundreds of years and you take away their culture and you take away their language and you take away everything they hold dear, and everything they associate with being a human being, then you say, "OK, we fought a war. We won and the other side lost, so you're free now," you can't just erase what happened before. Even after the Civil War Black people were not free. We're still not free. It's just been forty years since we gained basic civil rights that white Americans have taken for granted for over 200 years. All these things are still in their infancy in my mind.

When I got to Howard and got a little older, I realized that race is relatively new in the long scheme of history. It's unimportant. It's false, it's not real. To commit all my energy into thinking and being consumed about race is destructive and counterproductive to what I want to do with my life. So I've slowly begun to grow out of that, and for the most part, I think I've succeeded. I don't hate anybody anymore. At the same time I will always feel that people should take responsibility for their actions. Not because someone makes you take responsibility, but because you willingly choose to, and it's the right thing to do.

Not much has changed here in Washington, D.C. The kind of change that needs to take place in the Black community happens at a much more important and fundamental level. Those two things are education and family. I put education before family only because poor Black families now are so dysfunctional they need to be reeducated as to how to be families. If those two things can really be worked on and made to be world class, then we will be headed in the right direction of restoring Black communities. Even the Black middle class is a second-class middle class compared to the white middle class. There was a time when the Black middle class lived in the same community as poor Black people. When that happens, you have a better community for lots of reasons— financial, educational, moral reasons. Unfortunately, a lot has happened during the 1980s where you have this American concept of looking after "number one," the whole "me" generation. When that happens, people look around and say, "Hmmm, that Black guy down the street didn't graduate from high school. My kids are going to school with a lot of rowdy kids," so they all pack up and move to the suburbs. I'm not saying that the destruction of Black neighborhoods happened only because the middle class left, but I think it had a part in it. The Black middle class is not the same world as the white middle class, and it seems to exist in a world outside the rest of America to me. We're not plugged in to the rest of America because we've been segregated for so long.

There isn't the same social awareness—or even care—in my generation. (I hope to be proven wrong on this point.) There are many who are cynical, apathetic, and desensitized. My generation is definitely the television, MTV generation. Our attention spans aren't nearly as long as prior generations'. We quickly forget and quickly don't care anymore. That's not a blanket statement. There's lots of examples where that hasn't proven true, but I think for a lot of people it is true, and it disturbs me. But I also think that my generation is more sophisticated than your generation when you were our age. I don't think we're as idealistic, we're more practical and realistic in our goals and what we can accomplish. We're not so quick about picking up picket signs and marching around and wearing buttons. We're more apt to do it from the inside, in a quieter way, and maybe more effective way.

There are students at Howard trying to make positive change, like a couple of years ago when we tried to keep our autonomy as the College of Fine Arts. I worked with some people on that campaign who were very intelligent, very passionate, very determined, not self-serving—trying to do something for the greater good of the university community, which is really the Black community in a microcosm.

A lot of things that change the world are from people you never hear about. One of them is my friend Chad. I generally don't look up to many of my peers, but Chad is someone who I truly look up to. Most of the people I've found as mentors are a good deal older than me. I don't consider Chad a mentor, but I do consider him with great respect. He's an amazing person. He fights for justice. He has a strong sense of right and wrong. He doesn't care a rat's ass if anybody cares who he is or what he does or what he says. He doesn't do what he does for himself—he does it because he generally wants to change things. He's articulate, talented, and works hard. He also has an extreme sensitivity about his own Blackness and about his responsibility to other Black people as an artist and as a person.

My friend Imiri is another one. We call each other brother, like I'm his brother and he's mine. He's an amazing person in my life. I love him a great deal. He's also someone who's trying to make changes in the Black community, not for himself but for the betterment of the community. He wants to open a performing arts school for Black kids, and I have no doubt that he'll do it.

I had the good fortune to attend the Million Man March. The challenge of the twenty-first century for Black people has to do with the principles mentioned in the speeches that day. The whole concept was that we are now in a place where we can no longer expect white people to help us or give us anything, nor should we want them to. Black people have to take responsibility for themselves and support themselves and lift themselves up, just like Jews, Koreans, and many other ethnic groups have done. It's much more difficult for us because Jews and Koreans didn't have to endure the things that African Americans have endured. Nobody has. The only people who've had it anywhere near as close is Native Americans—who may have had it worse in a lot of ways. It's also water under the bridge. It can't be changed, so we have to take the cards in our hands, and instead of showing them to a white man and saying, "Give me new cards," let's make it work with the cards we have. We can win with the cards we have if we take responsibility for them, accept them, acknowledge them.

That's where I am now. In my own little way, I want to help Black people to the best of my ability without thinking about what the government's going to do for us or what rich white folks are going to do for us. It's easy to dwell on the chaos, poverty, and destruction that's around us and say, "It's hopeless." Pyramids were not built in a day, and you have to take one step at a time.

One day we will be able to be a strong and powerful portion of American society. We already are. There is no American society without Black people—there just isn't. We know that. I think the rest of America is loath to admit that. Just like they're loath to admit anything Black people have done throughout history. That's why white historians have attributed the great structures and achievements of Egypt to everyone from white folks to aliens, because they will do anything to deny the accomplishments of Black people. Because they're scared of us. I've never understood why. There's the old cliché of the darkness of Black people when they first came from Africa, and the "sexual prowess" of Black men. That's why so many were lynched in the South, because white men feared they would sleep with their wives.

Early European explorers thought of Africans as savage or not worthy

Hasani at his Howard
University graduation
party, 1999

of respect because they did things differently, which is ridiculous. If there were no Africa, there'd be no Europe. More anthropological facts are pointing to Africa as the origin of man. I think in the end Black people will be vindicated. It's not a question of Black people saying, "Aha! We *are* better than you." That's not what Black people want. Only white people are obsessed with that concept. They're the only people in history who've wanted to say they're better than everyone else. All Black people are saying is, "Look, we have made some fundamental contributions to the civilization of the world. You need to acknowledge that and look at the evidence." Until white people are willing to accept that, the fallacy of Western superiority is going to continue to perpetuate itself, which most of the world knows is erroneous and a patent lie. ■■■

When Hasani was two years old, his father and I amicably separated, and I returned to work at HUD in its Women's Policy and Program Office. I also became active in the National Organization for Women's D.C. chapter. Betty King was a key leader in the National Women's Political Caucus, and for many years she held an influential job in the District of Columbia's Office of Boards and Commissions. Betty is now retired and divides her time between Washington and Florida.

As you will see, she grew up in a very wealthy family in Cleveland at the same time my friend Vince was growing up in its urban core. Betty chose a different life from that wished for her by her privileged parents, creating enormous conflicts over the years, then reconciliation.

BETTY KING

I was born in 1932 and grew up in the country outside of Cleveland, Ohio. We lived in a very wealthy community. I didn't know what "restricted" meant, but it certainly was that. No one lived there except rich WASPs and their servants. Our socioeconomic group was never threatened; we were kings of the hill. Until I was in my twenties, the only people of any other group I knew were servants. All of my friends' families had servants in their houses and on their estates. Some of them were Black, they were all treated with respect, and some I truly loved.

When the war came in 1941, our life became even more isolated because we lived twenty miles out in the country, and gas rationing cut down our mobility. My friends and I spent our time at our expensive private schools and exclusive (and restricted) country clubs and in each other's lavish homes. We had a few (very few) Catholic friends, and in junior high there were a couple of Jewish girls whose parents were both doctors. When I went away to boarding school, the same isolation from diversity continued. Somehow through all this I bought into the "American Dream" that all people are created equal because there was no one in my life who wasn't equal, except perhaps economically.

Betty King as a young girl in Cleveland, Ohio, early 1940s

I was quite grown up before I became aware that racial, religious, and ethnic bias existed. By the time I was in my twenties, I felt there were good people and bad people, but it never occurred to me that goodness had any relationship to color, religion, or ethnicity. The restricted life I led, unthreatened with no intergroup tensions, made it easy for me to develop friendships with people from all backgrounds.

In the early 1950s I moved to New York City to work in the professional theater and became personal friends for the first time with Black people and Jews. My first job was in a talent agency owned by a Jewish couple. Later, I worked for a young producer who was trying to raise money to put on a new musical by Duke Ellington, based on a novel by South African author Peter Abrams. Brock Peters and Thelma Carpenter—great talents—were to star in it, and over the months of trying unsuccessfully to raise money, we became very close. Later, I worked on the Broadway production of *The Cool World*, a play about gangs in Harlem, which marked the Broadway debuts for Billy Dee Williams, Cicely Tyson, James Earl Jones, and Calvin Lockhart. Throughout my professional theatrical career, which lasted almost ten years, I developed many diverse friendships. But the religious or racial background of my new friends was immaterial to me; they were talented, and they were a whole lot more loving and open than most of the people I'd known until that time.

I was the rebel in my family. I was the youngest of four children, and somehow I was always out of step, breaking rules and making a life for myself. For starters, I went to work in the theater, which for my father, with his Victorian outlook, was just about the same as going on the street! He expected me to teach after I finished my education; that would have been acceptable. In fact, for several years after I moved to New York, he and I barely spoke. Then in the mid-1950s, a Jewish partner and I opened the first new theater to be built in New York since the late 1920s. There was a lot of publicity about it, including a small article in *Time* magazine with a photograph of me painting the lobby. Mother and Father's friends kept saying to them, "You must be so proud of Betty." I guess they decided they were because they came to New York City to see the theater, and we "made up." Ironically, when I later decided to leave the theater, after working for almost three years on two Broadway flops, my parents said, "Why do that? You've been so successful."

In the early 1960s I went to work for the African American Institute (AAI), administering scholarships for African students in the United States. For the first time I had African friends. Then in 1963 I went to live in Dar es Salaam, Tanganyika (later Tanzania). My great-uncle had traveled widely in East Africa in the 1920s and 1930s to collect specimens for the Cleveland Natural History Museum. Although I remembered his black-and-white films, until I went to AAI, I knew very little about modern Africa.

At the institute, I met Dr. Eduardo Mondiane, the American-educated first president of the Mozambique Liberation Front (FRELIMO). He was applying to the Ford Foundation for a grant to establish a school in Dar for refugee students. I helped him put together the grant proposal, and when the money came through, he and his (white American) wife hired me to be executive director. I was to be gone for about eighteen months. I came back almost nine years later. I wasn't at the Mozambique Institute the whole time. After four years, we recruited a Mozambican to replace me, and I became the managing director of an affiliate of an American multinational mining and trading company. We mined rubies and other gemstones and sold fertilizers and tractors—all of which I knew squat about when we started, but I knew the country, knew the ministers and other government folks, and was a good administrator.

In the fall of 1964, after months of correspondence, my parents were planning to visit me in Dar and then go on a photographic safari. At the last moment, Father canceled and Mother came alone. She was initially evasive about why he didn't come, but eventually said, "He just didn't want to see you working with those Black communists." (I don't know if it was their race or their socialistic tendencies that disturbed him the most.)

Later that year I returned to the States for an operation. The night I arrived in Cleveland, the whole family came to dinner, and in the four to five hours we were together, not one soul said, "Well, you've been in Africa for eighteen months now, what's it like?" The next night I went to visit my sister and remarked on this curious behavior. My brother-in-law told me that Father was so upset at what I was doing with my life that he refused to discuss it. I noticed, however, that when we went out together socially and others asked me about Africa, he would often be nearby where he could hear what I said. On the eve of my departure to return to Dar, Father and I had a colossal, hurtful row, and I didn't communicate with my parents for more than a year. I just cut them off.

Toward the end of that estrangement, my sister was visiting her daughter in Paris. Apparently my parents said to Kate, "Why don't you go to Dar and check up on Betty?" She had no firm grasp of the distance she would travel (thousands of miles instead of a few miles). But she came and had a wonderful time. She enjoyed my friends, and since I wasn't an "official" American, I had a wide variety of chums—a huge number of Mozambicans, Tanzanians, Israelis, English, French, and Americans. Most of my time in Dar I had a house on the beach where I held open houses on Sundays. People would come with their children, dogs, overseas visitors, and a dish for the buffet table. I never knew if I'd have ten or fifty people. We'd swim, eat, play bridge, and talk endlessly about politics and social change in Africa, Vietnam, the USA, and the world. Kate had a great time, and a few months later my parents decided to come for a visit, both of them, and loved it.

In Tanzania, I was closely associated with all the African liberation movements and the many African refugees for whom Dar was a mecca. I continued to help FRELIMO after I left the Mozambique Institute and also had many friends from the liberation movements of South Africa, Rhodesia, Angola, etc. My open houses were a meeting place for an incredibly diverse cross section of Dar residents and visitors. All of us were interested in politics and government. The Mozambique Institute, originally an academic program, branched out into training for paramedics and elementary public administration after the Mozambican war for independence began in 1964–65. Those skills were badly needed in the liberated areas. I had a lot of friends, both Black and white, who were in the Tanzanian parliament and government, but as an expatriate, politics was perforce a spectator sport. I hungered to be more directly involved as a voter.

In 1971–72, I had to make a decision about what to do with the rest of my life. I had lived in Tanzania long enough so I could have become a citizen and stayed there, but I learned my sister was dying of cancer and decided to repatriate myself. When they learned I was returning to the States, my parents said, "Why are you leaving? You had such a wonderful life there." So after all these traumas, and in spite of my associating with Black people, they could ask that question, much as they did when I left the theater.

In May 1972 I moved to Washington, D.C., to work for George McGovern's presidential campaign and start my career in politics. That caused the last big fight I had with my father, who was not only a rock-ribbed Republican, but thought McGovern (and me) to be idiotically liberal. The animosity didn't last as long as our previous fights. I guess my parents gave up the thought I would ever lead the kind of WASP socialite life they wanted for me and came to eventually accept my individuality. After my sister's death in 1975 and through the remaining years of their lives, we became much more sensitive to each other's feelings and eventually even got to be friends. I managed (sometimes with tact, sometimes not) to wean them from making casually insensitive racist remarks, at least in my presence.

Father was born in 1894 and Mother in 1897. They grew up in an era when Jews, Catholics, Blacks, etc. were simply not one's friends. There was no particular malice in their biased attitudes, since they were never threatened by other groups. It was a reflex for them to believe that people who weren't white, preferably WASPs, were not as smart or as worthy as they were. Eventually, as they began to visit me in D.C. and meet my diverse circle of friends, their attitude changed. It was their first social contact with nonwhites. One year when they visited me over Father's birthday, I arranged for them to meet Mayor Marion Barry for the first time. I had worked for him for a number of years. Unbeknownst to me, my staff had arranged for a proclamation in honor of Father's birthday. When we went into the mayor's office, he gave Father a document (complete with red ribbon and seal) proclaiming "W. Griffin King Day" in the District of Columbia. I had it framed for him, together with the photograph of the four of us taken by the mayor's photographer. Father boasted about it for the rest of his life.

Since 1963 I have always been part of a white minority in any city I've lived in, but my friendships and associations have long ceased to be homogeneous. One of my fondest memories is a day in the early 1980s in my office. Several women were discussing the formation of an organization to be called the Committee of 100 Black Women, which was to undertake advocacy for women in public and political life. Since I had a history of involvement in the women's movement, someone turned to me and suggested that I should join. With some amusement, I pointed out that I might be genetically unqualified.

It would not have been easy for me to live the privileged, white, country-club life my parents envisaged for me. I would have been unhappy, possibly alcoholic, and maybe suicidal. I wanted a completely different existence, which has been infinitely more fulfilling. ■■■

Valerie Joan and Betty were codirectors of the District of Columbia's Office of Boards and Commissions for many years. They were responsible for a significant increase in the representation of women and people of color addressing critical issues facing District residents. Valerie and I were also cochairs of the D.C. Coalition for Women. Her story addresses the painful issues of internalized oppression, of "Black people wanting to be like white people," and "light brown skin is better than dark brown skin." She is now learning to love herself for who she is.

Betty King at Valerie Joan's, 1996

VALERIE JOAN

I always want to go back. I want to go back to "why." Why did things happen to me the way they did? Was my perception about my early growing years reality then?

I grew up never understanding why I was the person I was. In my adult life I wondered why I was named "Valerie" when my sisters—one who came before me and one after—were named after my mother, my father, my grandmother, and my aunt. "Valerie Joan" has no connection with anyone in my family. I used to think I was adopted, especially since I felt my mother treated me differently than my sisters. Having a name that didn't match anyone else in the family seemed to confirm that for me.

I'm the black sheep of the family in many ways. My mother is a very proud woman, but she had a way of excluding me because I didn't fit the mold she tried to develop in her children, and later her grandchildren and great-grandchildren. Both my sisters are very fair skinned and have long hair, and I don't have either.

Growing up, I was so much in conflict with myself and my thoughts about who I am and my worth to myself, my family, my race. This confusion contributed to my growing up very insecure and with a very low self-esteem that I fought every day of my life. My internal struggle with myself included how my mother wanted me to perceive myself versus how I wanted to see the way I really am. Isn't the struggle usually against how others perceive us, not the demand that we perceive ourselves or make ourselves different than what we know we are?

My grandmother—my daddy's mother—was the daughter of a white slave master, a landholder down on the eastern shore of Virginia. She was very fair skinned, and I sensed she knew my heart and my struggle within my family. She always came to my rescue when I felt neglected by my mother. She was my idol of a "Black woman," not because she was light and could pass for white, but because she was sensitive and very giving of herself.

My mother's mother died the year I was born. I have heard she was of Indian descent. She had long hair and was fairer than my mother. My mother is the darkest person in my family. Yet she was the one who couldn't come to grips with the "color" issue within our race.

To this day, my mother dotes on people with long hair and fair skin. She still thinks there is some redeeming grace for them. I have to correct her whenever she remarks about how long my grandchild's hair is, telling her to focus on her being smart and how well she excels in school.

Mother was always making a fuss over my sisters, and I wanted to be in the center of attention too. I had that middle-child syndrome playing against me as well, so I had to work harder to be noticed. They were trying to get attention, too. Today, my sisters understand and acknowledge what I went through growing up. But back then, they didn't show me that they understood how I felt. It was as if we were forced into competition within the family to see who would get the most attention. I always seemed to come up short.

I was different than my sisters. I accomplished more academically and was talented too. I even won second place in the annual Shriner's Beauty/Talent Contest at sixteen years of age. This contest had the same format as the Miss America Contest. I struggled with my mother not to enroll me as a contestant, but I lost the battle. My talent, playing the piano, is what really stood out, because there were some beautiful contestants participating with long hair and very fair-skinned bodies. I remember being truly intimidated, but I played Chopin's Polonaise and put everything into it—the way I positioned myself on the piano stool, the way I dramatically placed my handkerchief on the piano, pausing to hear a hush over the audience and the right moment to let the emotion and passion pour from my fingers onto the keys. I was saying to myself that my mother just wanted to embarrass me when she forced me to enter this contest. But I was a winner. It seems my mother knew better than I that I could compete and be recognized for my "real" abilities.

My mother grew up in Georgetown on Dumbarton Street. Her family was very active in the church around the corner, the oldest Black Methodist church in Washington. It was part of the Underground Railroad for freeing Blacks and harboring them as they moved from the South to the North. My mother said they would come through the house next to the church and were kept down in the basement until the passageway was ready. So in terms of history, we go back, and we were there. But from that experience I think Mother got the wrong messages about the struggle of Blacks and passed them along to the point where they confused me.

Teenage Valerie Joan at a beauty/talent contest in Washington, D.C.

We were raised to act like white people. Mother took us to plays and concerts and we all had to play the piano, which was fine for any race. But we always had to emulate white people so we could be accepted and not be embarrassing, she would say. When she took us to these plays and concerts we had to sit in the balcony, but she never told us why. She didn't state any information about racism. She wanted us to act like white people. We weren't taught to act like our folk.

Why couldn't I be like Black people? Our folk were educated, cultured, and knew how to act in public. My family was not embarrassing but well-accomplished people. How come my mother didn't recognize that? Why did she see the negatives in our race? Oh! She gave us so many wrong messages. Why? A lot probably had to do with the way she was raised. She often went to work as a child with her mother, who acted as a "secretary" to a well-known, well-to-do white doctor who lived in Georgetown where my mother grew up. When he took his family south for the winter, my grandmother took charge of daily work and matters at his Georgetown home. My mother used to pretend a lot about being a part of that family, I suspect. She probably fantasized as a child of being just like them. Today, she still talks about their lovely homes and how well her mother was treated by them.

My daddy was not often home, largely because of his relationship with his wife. My mother was a nagger, and my daddy was stressed out about it. He developed diabetes, and now I have it too. I'm a spitting image of my father. When you look at his picture, you see me. Both my parents were professional people. We were a family who worked as servants to the government. D.C. being a servant town to diplomats and statesmen, we grew up thinking the best thing we could do was to get a good government job, and that's what we all did. Both Daddy and Mother retired as middle managers in the late 1960s. That was quite a feat for Blacks back in those days.

Today I'm back in the neighborhood I grew up in. The urban city has taken its toll. Communities like ours were pretty much middle-class back then. We bought our home in 1944 and were the second Black family in the neighborhood. We watched the neighborhood go through its changes. Blacks continued to move in as the whites continued to leave. We had to walk to Monroe Elementary School about twenty blocks away until Parkview Elementary School was turned over to Black folks. My neighborhood didn't change too fast, because until we graduated, my oldest sister and I had to walk past the white elementary school that was about fifty yards from my home and cross two major intersections to get to Parkview, more than seven blocks away. I was in third grade when I first went to Parkview. That next year, my sister was crowned the first Black May Queen of the school.

I went to Bannecker Junior High, and I did well there. I didn't have any problems with racism because the student body was 99 percent Black. It wasn't until I went to the mostly white Theodore Roosevelt High School that I really got a sense of the outward racism that was so blatant. I went to high school in 1955, a year after the *Brown* decision. The principal was extremely racist, and outwardly so. She called us names like "animals" and "monkeys" and said we were ignorant. Somehow we got the courage to rebel openly and publicly, and she was gone within a year after a long tenure at that school.

Roosevelt was 75 percent white to our 25 percent Black, and that was a real eye-opener for me. I was a B+ student in junior high, and it wasn't until I went to Roosevelt that I discovered I could get a grade below a C. I got a D in biology my first year, and it hurt me to my heart. That teacher also was a racist. These ugly attitudes and pressures were rampant throughout the school. We, as a Black race, were going into their school after the *Brown* decision, so they had to let us filter in, but it was definitely their school. They wouldn't let us have a cheerleading team because they didn't want us to commingle at all. When we graduated, we had to have our own separate prom. It was in the same building downtown—Presidential Arms—but the whites were on one floor and we on another on the same night. Some of us visited the other prom and commingled anyway.

I was number 43 out of a graduating class of 240, so I didn't do badly. With the white flight, by the time I graduated the school was 60 percent Black and 40 percent white. I grew up thinking we couldn't get along, there was no way we could have white friends. In my neighborhood I remember a little white girl up the street named Karen. She was my

friend when we were very young. She could come to my house, and Mother welcomed her in, but her family wouldn't let me go inside her house. We played in the dirt and made mud pies for our little dishes. We grew up and apart without any explanation or closure to our childhood closeness.

I went right out of high school to work. My government jobs helped me understand white people more. When the riots came after King's death in 1968, I was working for the federal cochairman of the Appalachian Regional Commission. He was from Fayetteville, Arkansas, and he and his wife included my family in their lives, including dinner parties. They had me bring my children to

Valerie Joan, in the middle, with her two sisters

their house during the riots because the neighborhood where my babysitter lived was burning. His wife baby-sat my daughter and son so I could go to work.

I had good experiences with white people over time, to the extent that I realize today that despite what I experienced growing up, I'm comfortable with "perception being reality" because I gained my awareness from insight.

Today, I've gone back to my natural hairstyle. This is my "I don't give a damn about being someone else" hairstyle, because I'm really exploring who I am without all my past inhibitions. It's back to the basics and what is real.

I love my mother, then and now, and I couldn't have accomplished all I have without her love and direction. I survived my childhood thoughts and fears, but it was very hard, and I'm working hard to love myself as I am. As they say, nothing good comes without hard work, sweat, and tears. And it feels good!

There's so many multiracial people coming into this country that whites will soon be the minority, and that's got to have an impact on racism. Sociologically, we are becoming a multiracial society, but economically, we still have a big rift. People with the money aren't African Americans. There's a lot of African Americans who have money, but on average, we haven't come to the economic center. We just aren't there with the money. ■■■

M ary Zepernick is a self-described late bloomer when it comes to consciousness about racism, sexism, and classism. I met Mary when we were both active in the National Organization for Women in Washington, D.C. In 1976 we cochaired the Equal Rights Amendment march and rally down Pennsylvania Avenue, a large and joyous event.

Mary has generously contributed her knowledge, skills, and spirit to peace, justice, and democracy issues for many years through the Women's International League for Peace and Freedom and the Program on Corporations, Law, and Democracy. For the past seventeen years she has made Cape Cod her home.

MARY ZEPERNICK

I was unaware of class issues growing up, but I came from a working-class family on both sides: railroading, farming, and millwork. My father was an insurance manager, my mother was a nurse, and I was the first in my family to go to college.

Mary Zepernick
as a little girl
in Ohio

When asked how I came to hold the beliefs and do the work I do, I've realized that despite a conventional adolescence, I picked up a sense of fundamental decency and fairness from my parents. My father was outraged by the treatment of American Indians and was an inveterate letter-writer to Congress. When I finished reading *Gone with the Wind* in high school and announced that I would name my first daughter Melanie, he held forth on the evils of slavery. Dad and I loved to argue, and despite my unformed worldview and limited information, his taking me seriously provided an important foundation for my eventual independence.

I grew up in white neighborhoods near Cincinnati, not because of a conscious family choice but simply because that was the way it was. It didn't cross my horizon that anything was wrong or missing. When I was around six I had my first experience with democracy. My friends Sally, Sandra, and I formed the Oak Club on our block, later voting two to one to hold meetings on Tuesday afternoons, when Sandra had Brownies. Let's exclude her "legally"! The Oak Club was philanthropic. Sally and I raised nickels selling lemonade in order to buy candy for George Rodney. Sally's mom, the only single mother I knew, worked and had a housekeeper named Louise. She and her grandson George Rodney were the first people of color I have any memory of meeting.

To my everlasting chagrin, I missed the historic march and "I Have a Dream" speech in 1963, even though the gathering took place only a few miles from where I lived. Five years later, as the war in Vietnam heated up, I still thought my country's intentions were good, even if a given policy was mistaken. A respected friend and colleague was appalled by my lack of knowledge and critical thinking, a turning point in my paying attention.

In 1969 friends came from New York for the first large anti-Vietnam mobilization in Washington, and I went along. What an eye-opener! Signs and slogans and a sense of being in it together, my first taste of a people's movement on the march.

My real awakening was in the women's movement. One day in the fall of 1971 I saw a notice in my neighborhood newspaper that the Washington, D.C. chapter of the National Organization for Women was holding its monthly meeting that Saturday at the local library. Something clicked: I need to go. I became active in NOW, willing to work but avoiding leadership roles for quite a while. As a white feminist focused on women's equality, I believed that everyone would be better off if society seriously addressed gender roles.

Another major turning point was living in the Philippines in 1980–81 and seeing firsthand the colonizing role the United States continued to play. I was there with my third husband, Fred, who worked with trade unions in Asia, while I helped found a counseling agency, primarily for expatriate women.

One of my critical experiences there was in the fall of 1980 when I returned to Manila from a rural province. I opened a newspaper and read that Ann Kusmuk had become the first U.S. citizen to be killed by a bomb. Ann and her husband were newly arrived in Manila, and I was conducting a women's group in their apartment. She just walked into a department store and died, and I spent that evening alone and enraged, experiencing myself as wanting to kill. Shocked by my reaction as well as by Ann's death, I had to look at my own capacity for violence. The personal is indeed political, and I wrote a column that appeared in the *Manila Bulletin*. Writing, including an opinion column I've written in the *Cape Cod Times* since 1988, has been a major way I have both clarified and expressed my political beliefs.

A few months after Ann's death, a friend sent me the Unity Statement of the first Women's Pentagon Action. I opened the mail and read what I had come to believe without realizing it. Arrived at by consensus, those words are as fresh and alive today as they were in 1980: speaking of our connectedness; addressing racism, militarism, and human needs; opposing the links between the Pentagon and the multinational corporations it serves. "Those connections are made of gold and oil. We are made of blood and bone, we are made of the sweet and finite resource, water." I've come to realize the enormous power of words to awaken and mobilize me.

When Fred and I returned to the United States, I looked for a job combining women's and peace issues, finding a staff position with the

Women's International League for Peace and Freedom members with Mary Zepernick, lower left, at her home on Cape Cod, 1998

Women's International League for Peace and Freedom in Philadelphia. WILPF was founded in 1915, when some 1,400 women suffragists from warring and neutral nations gathered at The Hague to address the war and get on with their work. Lo and behold, "identifying and eliminating the economic, political, social, and psychological causes of war and violence" became WILPF's work. From its beginnings among primarily white, middle-class European and North American women, the organization has struggled with racism ever since, both the world's and its own.

Working with the Program on Corporations, Law, and Democracy since 1995, I've learned more about how our minds are colonized and our common good hijacked. In 1886 the Supreme Court declared corporations "natural persons" under the law, entitled to the equal treatment and due process protections of the Fourteenth Amendment to the Constitution, passed for newly freed slaves after the Civil War. Ten years later, the Court put the judicial seal of approval on segregation in *Plessy v. Ferguson*, effectively removing African American personhood while the corporate form continued to accumulate the rights and privileges of human beings. Between 1890 and 1910, 307 Fourteenth Amendment cases came before the Supreme Court, only 19 of them dealing with African Americans and the rest with corporations. Every time there have been civil rights gains under the Fourteenth Amendment, corporate "persons" have gained illegitimate rights and privileges.

Throughout this century, the struggle for personhood has continued as the corporate usurpation of the power to govern threatens to reduce citizen sovereignty to the level of my early childhood Oak Club— excluding "legally" but not legitimately.

Over the years, my feminist perspective has expanded to encompass how patriarchal societies, for at least five millennia, have given unequal value to basic human differences, assigning these differences dominant or subordinate status and doling out rewards and oppression accordingly. When someone pointed out to me that this is not only unjust, it's unnatural, I was reminded of a colleague who delivered a report from WILPF's lesbian and bisexual caucus at a national conference in 1993. Jean said it's not enough to appreciate diversity or celebrate it or even work toward it; we must actively crave it. Crave diversity —this phrase has come to represent for me our task of creating the world we have a right to live in, the only kind of world in which I believe human beings can ultimately survive our own violent divisions.

When I get discouraged, I think of my late husband Fred. I asked him one day whether he expected to see that world in his lifetime, and he said no. When I then asked how he kept going, Fred replied, "It's my work."

WILPF women in the U.S. section were very involved in the civil rights movement, marching in Selma and elsewhere and organizing in their own communities. In 1987 the national board decided to take our struggle against racism to another level and contracted with the People's Institute for Survival and Beyond to do a series of "Undoing Racism" trainings for the U.S. section board, staff, and branches. By that time, I was a member of the board, and the training opened new windows into myself and onto the world. Since then, I've often heard and used the definition of racism as "prejudice plus power." This was my introduction to this institutional description and to myself as a racist, infected as a beneficiary of unearned white-skin privilege with the societal disease of racism. Somehow I heard this as liberatory rather than accusatory, as an impetus to stronger antiracism work rather than a cause for guilt.

As a result, I've learned that the core of my privilege as a white woman is being able to walk out my door in the morning and spend the entire day without giving a thought to racism. Understanding that has helped me become more aware and intentional, to more often interrupt racist language, jokes, or behavior. However, despite the civil rights gains of the past half a century, issues like economic disparity, racist drug policies, the death penalty, police harassment and brutality present a grim picture. We can hardly call ourselves a democracy when we can't or won't hold a serious national dialogue about race, much less acknowledge and eliminate the racist patterns rooted in the first European landing and the ensuing genocide against indigenous people and the enslavement of Africans.

In the face of such daunting realities, I'm blessed to be part of a strong WILPF branch and others on Cape Cod who support one another in the struggle. ▪▪▪

I also met Sharon Parker at a National Organization for Women meeting in Washington, D.C. The year was 1977, and we had our small, rambunctious sons in tow. Sharon's strong roots are in both the African American and the Native American traditions, and she credits the richness of her life to those historical and spiritual foundations.

Sharon and her husband Alan now live in Olympia, Washington, where she continues her work on critical racial and gender diversity issues, as well as serving on the national board of the Diversity Leadership Forum. She and Alan are the parents of three activist and creative adult children: Christina, James, and Jimena.

SHARON PARKER

I grew up in a wonderful place called Washington, D.C. It's my home, and I love it. I never thought I'd say that, because as soon as I was old enough to get away, I did.

As a child, you only see what your parents show you, and I was also aware that D.C. was a very segregated city. My parents always taught us that anybody who discriminated against you or acted hatefully because of your background was "prejudiced," which means they are simply ignorant and should be pitied. I had two values come together: the importance of education to our well-being and enlightenment; and the negative stigma of being prejudiced against in relation to our culture, race, and ethnic background.

Both my parents were low-level federal government employees. Since I was rebellious, I never wanted to be a government bureaucrat.

My mother was not career oriented. She wanted a job to bring money home to the family. When she retired after twenty-nine years with the Army Corps of Engineers, she was only a grade three.

My dad worked as a D.C. policeman. He was one of the early Black members of the Metropolitan Police Department in the 1940s. He was very proud of that. He was only on the force about five years before he was severely injured and had to

Sharon Parker's parents in the early 1940s

retire on disability. That's what turned his life around. It took away his reason for being, and he turned into a different person for many years. The father I grew up with was a man of bitter disappointment in his life and the constant pain he endured. By the time I was in high school, medical technology had improved, and he underwent several operations that restored the full use of his leg and relieved him of pain.

My family is very interesting to me because we're so racially mixed. My dad is primarily African American and came from a small town called Middleburg, Virginia. In recent years I've been doing research on my family. Apparently, Middleburg had a thriving Black community where Blacks had their own shops and businesses. Although racial and ethnic discrimination was quite present, the environment seemed not as racially oppressive as other places. There was a lot of intermarriage, even though it wasn't legal in Virginia. There were a lot of Blacks and whites who intermarried, and it was also the home of a lot of Native Americans who were separated from wherever they originally lived.

My grandmother's mother was an Indian from the Susquehanna River Band. When my uncles and cousins talked about Indians they always talked about "white" Indians and "Black" Indians, because if a Black person and Indian married, their offspring would be Black Indians. White Indians were offspring of whites and Indians.

My mom spent part of her childhood in Manassas, Virginia, and part in Washington, D.C. Her parents also have Native American roots. Her father was Irish American and worked for the Government Printing Office for many years. He met my grandmother at a boarding house where she worked near the GPO. Twenty years ago, I met a number of relatives who lived in Bolivar, West Virginia. There was a group of Cherokees who were not rounded up and sent on the Trail of Tears. They managed to stay in the hills and survive, escaping the forced relocation. They formed very furtive communities and often traveled from place to place. It was dangerous to announce who they were, so only certain people could be trusted to know their origins.

My mother's maternal lineage is Tslagi. We went to Bolivar and interviewed some aunts and uncles. I even met a man who was a Blackfoot, a woman who was a Pawnee! You wouldn't think that in the hills of West Virginia there's a Native and Black community living together, mingling and marrying. I'm one of five children, and in my childhood we were made aware of our heritage. I learned about Native history and traditions as much as my mother and other relatives could tell us.

By the time my father was ready for high school, his parents sent him to Baltimore to live with an uncle in order to get the education that wasn't available in Virginia. Being career minded, my dad left Baltimore for the big city of Washington, D.C., as soon as he could. In 1935 he met my mom, a beautiful, accomplished woman who knew both city and rural life and had grown up in a very interracial environment in Virginia. They married in 1937 and raised five kids in Washington, D.C., with this whole outlook of openness and a mind-set against prejudice. Even though D.C. was segregated then, communities were strong in themselves. I was very grounded in my family history, brave deeds and tremendous accomplishments of ordinary people. Events like slave revolts and Indian uprisings made you realize people didn't lie there and take the oppressions of slavery and bigotry.

Even though our family has a strong Indian identity and consciousness, the outside world only viewed us as Blacks. We understood this view dated from slavery: "one drop of Negro blood classifies a person as Negro." We understood that the perpetuation of this notion past slavery is a psychological control mechanism to keep people in their places. So while the outside world labeled us one thing, and therefore our options were limited, our sense of ourselves was quite different.

That understanding is such a part of me that whenever I give a talk I include some historical event or story of the lives and struggles of Native and African American peoples and relate it to the present, seeing the historical connection. If you go back and see who we were, then we can understand more of why we have the divisions, the hate, the uncomfortableness with each other, whatever it is that keeps people from coming together as human beings and appreciating each other's cultures.

Due to segregation, there were places we couldn't go or see in D.C., but it didn't bother me as a child because I had a strong community and friends. As a little kid, my mother took me and my little sister to the White House to roll Easter eggs. Before that was allowed, Blacks would go to the National Zoo and roll eggs down the long hill there. I also remember Glen Echo. We'd say, "We want to go swimming!" and if my parents answered directly, they would say, "You can't go to any of the pools. They don't let our kind in there. They are prejudiced." That was a code term for the fact that whites didn't let Blacks or other people of color in the pools or other places. We didn't whine and say, "Oh, we want to go!" It was a sober reality that this was what the world was. These white people were so ignorant, they didn't understand that nothing was going to happen if we went to their pool or house.

There are still two Washingtons. There's the historical parts for whites and the historical parts for Blacks, like the church we attended because my mom was a devout Episcopalian. St. Mary's was established in 1866 for free Blacks. It continues today as an active parish. The things we did I never appreciated as a child, but now I know it was the church where Black Episcopalians could worship when you couldn't go to other churches. The people who went there were dedicated to the education and "uplift of the Negro race," as they used to say. They were people who had suffered greatly due to segregation.

I went to Bancroft Elementary School, which is now a multicultural magnet school. Bancroft was predominantly white then. There was a very strict and proper principal with snow-white hair who looked like she stepped out of an 1890 catalogue. Her name was Miss Andrews. She was very imposing and hated Black children. You could see the hatred in her eyes and face. I went there in the second grade, and she picked on me all the time. If I walked down the hall and my step was too sprightly, she'd call me to her office. If we kids were standing in line in the hallway and talking, it was me she'd pick on. I wasn't the only kid of color there and not the only one she picked on. I just seemed to get more than my share.

Sharon Parker on the right, with her sisters Martha and Natasha in their Washington, D.C., backyard in the mid-1960s

When I was twelve we moved to 13th and Decatur Streets. That was the pinnacle of my parents' achievement. They both had the same notion of the home in the country with the wide porch around it, and at last, they had it in the city. It was a big, rambling house that could handle five kids, all their friends, and lots of relatives and visitors. It had a big yard for playing and gardening. I have many memories of our times in that home. Unfortunately, in 1994 I had to sell it to support my dad, who had to go into a nursing home.

I went to Antioch College in Yellow Springs, Ohio, in 1966. This was the "hotbed of radicalism," but I had no idea of that when I applied. I had been attracted there by two things: their freedom of intellectual pursuit—students were allowed to study in depth whatever academic subject motivated them—and their Cooperative Program. Students didn't just absorb intellectual material, but learning was linked to work and life. So I entered an institution that none of my family had heard of, and I demonstrated the independence that had saved my ancestors from extinction.

In 1967 I met Alan, the man I married thirty years ago. I met him because of Antioch. I had always been a language student, and my co-op adviser asked if I'd like to go someplace to use my language. He encouraged me to go to Mexico, where I had a wonderful time living

Sharon and Alan
Parker's wedding
day, 1969

and working in Guadalajara and speaking Spanish. When I came back, I stopped in Killeen, Texas, to visit my older sister, who was married to a man in the army. They had a beautiful toddler baby, and I wanted to see my nephew, as well as my sister and her husband. They set up some blind dates for me with some of my brother-in-law's army buddies. One of the guys was Alan. He knew my sister because he was from a western tribe and was very lonesome for other Native people. He met my sister through her husband, so he had the comfort of talking with someone who understood about Indian people.

This was during the Vietnam era, and my brother-in-law and Alan were about to be shipped out to Vietnam. Nevertheless, for Alan and me, it was love at first sight. After my Texas visit was over, I went back to college in Yellow Springs, Ohio, and Alan drove there from Texas to see me before he shipped out. Imagine a young, tough, skinny, shorn army guy coming on my radical campus of long-haired, revolutionary, antiwar students to see me before leaving for Vietnam! When he came back, we were married in the chapel at Antioch.

Alan was very dedicated to his tribe and Native people, so we had a basis for talking about cultures, discrimination, and how people are treated. I was interested in languages because of my interest in cultures and communities. I went into language education, got a master's degree in bilingual education, and became a language teacher.

I loved teaching, but I didn't stay long in the profession. Due to a job opportunity for Alan, we moved to Albuquerque, New Mexico. Because it takes time to be recertified for teaching, I got involved with the local chapter of the National Organization for Women (NOW). I found the group by reading about their interesting events in the newspaper. I was in a new part of the country, I had two babies, and Alan was in a new job. I needed intellectual stimulation and an outlet for my activism.

Through NOW I learned of the National Women's Political Caucus Regional Conference in Phoenix. The speaker was Audrey Rowe. This was in 1975, and here was a Black woman going around the country talking with women about being involved in political office. I knew I had to go hear her speak. It was as though the waters parted and the skies opened. It was an epiphany for me. Everything that happened there was for me. Here I was, a young mother, in love with my husband, in love with my life, and this woman spoke to me about the responsibilities and challenges of women. She spoke about turning barriers into positives by speaking up and bringing to the public arena things we needed in our lives, like child-care centers. It wasn't about ripping off your bra and castrating men. It was more like: Get involved to make women's lives better. It was just that basic.

When I returned to my NOW group, I must have sparkled all over them, and they tapped right into me. That led me to advocacy work to promote displaced homemaker legislation. Displaced homemakers are older women of all economic and ethnic backgrounds, left by their husbands due to death, divorce, or desertion without any means to survive. I developed a network of these women in New Mexico, and it was the first time many of them shared their stories with anyone else. Lobbying the state legislature was easy (I grew up in Washington!), but it was the women's stories that really touched me. As we became more successful, we ran up against "the establishment." They wanted to take over. They didn't want these "NOW radicals" getting credit for this important work.

I then put into action a political principle I've come to practice ever since, and that is that credit is not important. What's important is that legislation be enacted because lives will be impacted. We laid out the program and got the state to commission a study. When it started, they said, "There is no such thing as 'displaced homemakers.'" But when I brought the women to testify, they saw that across the state there were thousands of women who were left destitute and would never be able to get on their feet again unless there was some means to help them. This included job programs, life counseling, and support centers. That program ran for many years—and might still be operating today.

In 1977 we moved back to D.C. because Alan had gotten a job there. I became the assistant director of the National Commission for Working Women and was able to combine my interest in women's affairs with my interest in communities of color. I was very dedicated to making sure that whatever the commission did included women of color. That became one of its major achievements and a national model in a time when the focus was on white women.

Although I stayed involved with NOW, it became clear that I was being drawn more strongly to support efforts for women of color. I could see that we were always an adjunct and not integrated into things. I brought together a special group of women of color—Black, Native, Asian, Latin, even at later points Arab and Jewish—and we formed the National Institute for Women of Color. That organization gave us our own voice, a means of advocating for our needs, to express our perspective fully, and not as a footnote to something else. The group grew and lived for ten years, headquartered in Washington, D.C.

Eventually I headed up the institute full-time because people wanted to know how to build multiracial coalitions and networks in workplaces and communities. Many times I had to overcome the issue of their inherent racism. They wanted multiracial groups, but were they willing to go beyond "show" to really integrate people into their organization? Were women of color an adjunct to their primary work, or were they an integral part? That led me to do a lot of antiracism work with various organizations. I used the institute to sponsor workshops on antiracism, which led me to the YWCA, whose total mission is the elimination of racism, for which it has received little recognition. One of the labels that was hung on me during this time was "change agent."

In early 1990 I learned through a friend that Stanford University was looking for someone to head up an office on multiracial, multiethnic, multicultural affairs. The first line of the job description said, "We are seeking a change agent." I looked at the description and said, "They're talking about me. I can do this job." Alan was very encouraging, as were my friends. In July of 1990, the president of Stanford University called me at my home and said, "We want you to come and do this job." Then I had to face the reality of, "Oh my God, I have to go to California!" I did go, and Alan and the kids stayed here, and it was extremely hard. My mother was alive and living with us then, and she was a big source of comfort to me because she was here with the family.

I worked there until the president left and the politics changed, then returned to D.C. By coincidence—meaning there is some divine pattern in what I am to do—I came to be where I am now, which is the president of the American Institute for Managing Diversity in Atlanta, Georgia. AIMD is a nonprofit organization that developed the framework for approaches to diversity and how we look at diversity. The first approach we, as a nation, used to actively deal with it in recent history is through the political legislative system, i.e., the civil rights movement, equal employment laws, affirmative action, the whole legal apparatus. "Legal" has had tremendous meaning to people of color in this country. It's only in recent years that people of color have gone into the law profession in larger numbers to effect some changes on our own behalf. This approach says: If we are going to change society, we have to do it on its legal terms.

The second approach that's now prevalent is what the institute calls "understanding our differences," or "understanding diversity." It's sensitivity courses, antiracism seminars, how you attract and retain women and people of color, etc. People need to reach out and overcome their fears and phobias, their uncomfortableness—it goes all the way to acts of conflict.

The founder of the institute brought the third approach into being, which is now prevalent in U.S. business and becoming more so in educational institutions. That's called "managing diversity." The goal is to integrate people into organizations so that they're fully utilized, not just a token or adjunct. How do you do that? You don't do it through sensitivity courses or conflict resolution, and you don't do it by legal mandate. You do it by teaching decision makers that the diversity in their organizations is directly related to their mission. If they are going to achieve their mission, they need to deal with their diversity.

Demographics have changed, and that's what's driving businesses and educational institutions to pay more attention to this issue. They have new kinds of workers, new kinds of students and consumers, so it's imperative for those who lead organizations to know how to manage the diversity within their organizations.

When Judith Winston was appointed executive director of the President's Initiative on Race and Race Relations, I invited her to Atlanta to talk with some of our folks. Barbara Arnwine from the Lawyer's Committee on Civil Rights also came. They said that President Clinton's race initiative would be helped by the involvement of businesses because the Lawyer's Committee would not have the huge backlog of discrimination cases it now has. Most of the cases were about poor management and not so much about discrimination. If you grew up in Iowa City, for instance, and had a very limited perspective on life, then became head of a manufacturing plant, you probably would have to deal with people and issues you had no experience with. Your initial reaction is likely one of fear and prejudice. All you know are stereotypes, and you react to the workforce in a stereotypical way, instead of managing it so that everybody gets to contribute to the success of the organization. If people had better managerial skills, we wouldn't have half the legal cases we have.

Businesses are in the forefront of this third approach, and they're doing it mainly because it impacts their bottom line. If they're going to be competitive, they've got to figure out how to deal with diversity. I was contacted by a woman in Barcelona, Spain, who heads up a major consulting firm in managing diversity for companies there. We've been visited by a woman from Ireland who has written a book called *Managing the Mosaic,* who is looking at the diversity of Ireland and England. It's worldwide. Interestingly enough, it's women who are doing this work, more and more. Maybe it's because, as women of whatever racial or ethnic background, we are already bicultural. We operate in both the male-dominated world of business and the female-dominated world of homemaking.

For a long time I've been fascinated by the cultural origins of knowledge. Whose civilization? Where do we get knowledge from? How do we generate new sources of knowledge? If we were open to the ancient cultures of Mali or China, for example, we would increase the pool of knowledge and well-being for all people. That goes back to who I am and my origins. I have been able to live my life combining Western knowledge and technology with Native knowledge and wisdom, and ancient African and African American knowledge. It has kept me healthy, sane, and helped me produce a healthy, sane family. I see myself as an inseparable part of my family and the generations to come. That makes me a little different than the average U.S. citizen, or the average white male citizen, because I'm drawing on other fountains of knowledge and traditions to give me a wholeness. ■■■

Alan Parker is Native American and grew up in his strong and respected family on the Rocky Boy Reservation, a "colonial outpost," as Alan called it, but not recognized as such by the American government. A mountain on the reservation is named after Alan's grandfather. I've had the privilege of visiting his boyhood home twice — once with Sharon, and once with my son Hasani.

After years of working on Capitol Hill and with tribes across the country on numerous legal and economic development issues, Alan is now director of the Northwest Indian Applied Research Institute at Evergreen College in Olympia, Washington.

ALAN PARKER

I grew up on the Rocky Boy Indian Reservation in northern Montana, which was my father's home where he grew up as a member of the Chippewa-Cree Tribe. He moved our family there when he returned from World War II, where he served in the navy. I was born in 1942 when my mother was living with her family on the Standing Rock Reservation, which is the home of the Hunkpapa Sioux in North Dakota.

My earliest memories are as a little kid on a farm on the southern end of the Rocky Boy Reservation. My father, like many World War II veterans, wanted to settle back and have a family. So he moved us onto a small farm that he leased from the tribe. I remember crossing creeks in the wintertime, falling in and coming home a frozen chunk, and my mother giving my older brother hell. I remember my grandfather (my father's father). He used to cart me around on his shoulders. He and my grandmother took me on a trip to Big Sandy, a nearby town about twenty-five miles away where they'd go for shopping. We made this trip in a wagon drawn by horses.

Living on the reservation, we took it for granted that everybody lived the same way. There was no electricity, no running water, so we had to chop wood every morning

Alan Parker's maternal grandmother and grandfather with their children

and learn the etiquette of outhouses. Social life was mainly getting together with family. My father came from a big family of thirteen children, and there were more cousins than I could keep track of. It seemed we were always at some relative's home. We knew we were all part of the same community.

On the reservation, the government agent for the Bureau of Indian Affairs (BIA) was clearly in charge. There was always a succession of white government officials, and the agent was the primary authority figure. All the BIA families, about twenty of them, lived at "the Agency," a government compound consisting of a square block of white sideboard houses, all looking inward at the neatly kept lawn and flagpole. This was probably the only green lawn on the whole reservation. Nobody else I knew had a lawn.

Although the United States never acknowledged they had a colonial system of government on the Indian reservations, the system I knew had all the trappings. Rocky Boy and other reservations we visited were just like any other colonial outpost in Africa, India, or South America.

In our family we were very much aware that the non-Indians (and there were only white people and Indians) looked at us as second-class citizens and rarely invited us into their homes or community. There was intermarriage between tribes, but I rarely saw any other intermarriages, except for my uncle marrying my aunt. He was a schoolteacher from

Alan Parker at age
seven

Pennsylvania, and his father was an immigrant from Norway. Generally, the non-Indians didn't mix with the tribe, either the teachers or government officials. I don't remember instances of them being disdainful or unfriendly, but they just kept to themselves and only socialized with the non-Indians in the nearby towns. It must have been a lonely life for them.

We lived at Rocky Boy for ten years, then moved to Billings, Montana, for a couple of years. It was in the fifth grade there that race first impacted me. This was in the early 1950s. Before that I attended school with everybody who were members of the same tribe. It was all little Indian kids and no consciousness that anybody was any different except for our white teachers. For the first time in Billings I was the only Indian in a school of white children. I can remember one little girl who came up to me and said, "What kind of person are you really? I saw your skin and thought you just had a good suntan, and somebody said you were Indian—what's that?" They were just unaware of who we were, even though their families had lived in Montana for several generations.

When we were moved by the federal government to East Los Angeles, race again became an issue. This was when I was in the seventh and eighth grades. The government had a program where they would send Indian people off the reservations into large cities to give them training. My father volunteered for the program, and the whole idea was to resettle Indian people. The government's way of solving the "Indian problem" was to move most of the people off the reservations, then there wouldn't be an Indian problem anymore. They could then terminate all the special government services—health and education primarily, but also management of land resources on reservations. This was very much a part of the so-called termination policy of the Eisenhower administration.

As a kid, all I knew was that when I moved to East L.A. we were very much discriminated against by the Mexicans, because we were these little brown-skinned kids who didn't speak Spanish. My father worked at a nearby refinery. He'd learned to be a welder in the navy. For a lot of people who volunteered for this program, it was a permanent move. They'd come back for tribal get-togethers or family reunions, but they stayed in the cities. This "Indian relocation program" lasted for about eight years, and many who stayed in the cities years later felt a sense of disconnection from their tribal community. On the other hand, since poverty and lack of job opportunities were always very high on reservations, it was a trade-off. If you acquired a good marketable job skill, in the city you at least had a job.

Nominally we were Catholics. On the reservation, you were either Catholic or Lutheran, because years before the government had outlawed Native religions. They made it against the law to practice, in our case, the Sun Dance, so most people, if they went to church at all (and they were encouraged to do so by the government), went to either the Catholic or Lutheran mission. We used to be jealous of the Lutheran kids because at Christmastime these packages would be sent to the mission from these probably wealthy parishes, and they always had better toys than the Catholics!

When we lived in East L.A., my mother wanted to protect us from the violence in the schools in those days. This was the Pachuco era, so this was the first generation of gang activity. She sent my sister and me off to Our Lady Queen of the Angels, and we did great there academically and also learned to be good Catholics. We came back to the reservation —my dad just couldn't abide the congestion and was also concerned that my older sister was getting into trouble. There were six kids in my family at the time.

I got straight As at Our Lady, and when I got back to the reservation, my mother mentioned that to the local priest. He made arrangements to send me to a Catholic boarding school in North Dakota. It was preparatory to going into the seminary when I got out of high school.

I remember traveling all night on the train and getting off on this windswept prairie with this tiny little town wondering, "What am I doing here?" I couldn't go home, except for Christmas and the summer. I was one of three Indians in this Benedictine monastery in North Dakota. Most of the students weren't there because they had an interest in religious life; they were there because it was the only good school in the state. A lot of the German Catholic families who were farmers could afford to send their kids to this school. I found it very alien and was very unhappy. Socially I made a few friends, but I never felt welcome there. Most of the kids just ignored me. During my first quarter, however, this priest discovered me, and what a find I was—can you imagine finding a smart little Indian kid that you could send off to seminary?

I was happy when my family moved again to Billings so I could finish high school there and live with them again. I was the only Indian student, but there was another brown-skinned person in the school, and that was Ben Sanchez, so he and I had to be friends! He's Mexican. His family came up to work on the railroad and were part of the small Mexican American community in Billings.

After graduation from high school in 1960, Ben and I and three others from our school went off to the Catholic seminary outside of Seattle. I think it was a sense of idealism—dedicate your life to a higher cause—that drew me to the seminary. The Catholic Church in those days was like a family. Strict family, but you belonged. There was no race or color limitation to being accepted. I stayed for five years and left in 1965. That was the beginning of the Vatican Council in Rome that turned the church upside down. The changes that swept through society in the 1960s also influenced young people of that generation in so many ways. I concluded it would be a mistake to spend my life as a Catholic priest. There must have been a 90 percent dropout rate in the seminary back in the 1960s. When we started in the early 1960s we didn't question anything. The attitude was: "Here are the rules, here's what's expected of you, your job is to do it." Our textbooks were written in Latin. Can you imagine what a mind-bender that was? By the time I left, things were being questioned and people just weren't accepting everything like that. I don't think the church has ever recovered from that as far as the number of people willing to sacrifice their life for the ministry. A tremendous number of women also left the convent, partly because the rigid doctrine the church taught and expected everybody to accept was just not logical. Nor do I think it's humane or just to treat women as perpetual second-class citizens in the Catholic Church.

Two weeks after I left the seminary and went back to Billings,

Montana, I got my draft notice. I was off to the army, where they decided to train me to be a radio operator. After I got through that training, I got orders to go to Vietnam. This was in 1966, at the height of the draft. I decided to apply for officer candidate school. (I didn't want to be an officer, but I didn't want to go to Vietnam as a radio operator. The radio operator is the guy who carries the target on his back in the infantry platoons. The enemy knows that if he can knock out the radio, you're not going to call in jets or artillery. That logic didn't escape me.) Officer training was very rigorous and inspired self-confidence if you could be one of the 20 percent who survived and got a commission as a second lieutenant.

That's when Sharon and I met. I was stationed in Texas after officer candidate school, and she was coming back from an Antioch College co-op assignment. Her sister, Martha, was the only Indian person I knew in Fort Hood, Texas. We used to enjoy each other's company, and her husband and I were best buddies and shipped out to Vietnam together. We were put on a ship and sailed out under the Golden Gate Bridge. After twenty-eight days across the Pacific Ocean, we landed in Vietnam.

They sent a platoon down to the Mekong Delta, and I was in charge of deploying my troops to different isolated special forces camps. We were radio people and set up radio connections to headquarters. My platoon then set up a station on top of a mountain overlooking Cambodia, and we supported the 101st Infantry Division, which was engaged in a big campaign during the Tet Offensive. For most radio people, you didn't see much action because you were back behind the lines. We were the exception because we were out there by ourselves on this mountain. We were attacked many times, but we were dug in.

By the time I came back from Vietnam, I was very disillusioned. It was clear that it was just a terrible waste, a waste of people, a waste of money, inflicting terrible things on the people there. The experience I had that was the most difficult was coming down into a village that had been napalmed and seeing women and children's corpses that were burnt to a crisp. It was very traumatic.

I was glad to get home. I was mustered out in Oakland at the same time Sharon was there working for the California Legal Services in Modesto in 1968. They were in the forefront of the poverty law movement. It was inspiring to see what people were doing. I didn't have a clue about what I would do next, and she suggested law school. "That's a good idea!" I said. I graduated from UCLA's School of Law in 1972.

A lot of young Indian people in my generation—and it continues to happen—became very angry when they learned about the generations of Indian people who had been terribly oppressed by the United States over hundreds of years, about the lies the government engaged in and the violence that was inflicted upon tribe after tribe all the way from Rhode Island to California and Alaska. Then you look and see poverty-stricken people on isolated reservations in conditions of powerlessness, and it makes you very angry. Our generation set about trying to do something about that, and we found common cause with the militant Chicano movement and the Black movement.

Probably the most significant law reform on behalf of Indian rights has been carried out by the Native American Rights Fund, which was patterned after the NAACP Legal Defense Fund. Thurgood Marshall was the hero of that movement, so those were very exciting times, the late 1970s and early 1980s, waging an all-out struggle to change society.

I was involved with organizing among Indian lawyers and went to work with the U.S. Senate shortly after I graduated from UCLA. I was offered the job as chief counsel to the Committee of Indian Affairs in 1977, so five years out of law school, I had the opportunity to serve in this very challenging position. My boss looked to us, the Indian people who were on the staff of the committee, to set the tone. We had spent the two previous years working on a congressional study commission, and we had an agenda. We had a comprehensive look at Indian policy, so I came to D.C. with ideas of what we were going to change, and we've been working on that agenda ever since.

A lot of it revolves around asserting tribal sovereignty. Basically, we recognize that to change the situation from being powerless minority people (under the thumb of the government), we're trying to seize control back of our own destiny, our community. There are a variety of legal fronts that we've fought this battle on: The 1975 Indian Self-Determination Act was a big move forward. For the first time, the tribes had a right to administer their own local government services. Sovereignty played itself out in the fields of education, health care, child care, and the rights to protect children.

One of the biggest battles we fought in Congress was the 1978 Indian Child Welfare Act. This law was necessary because there was a history of Indian children being adopted out to white families. We had social workers who served all across the West who were using non-Indian standards in terms of what was a fit home or fit parents. They would make a home visitation and find a poverty-stricken family on a reservation and say, "You're not fit parents because these kids are running around in filthy diapers, you're gone to ceremonies or some party and you left them in charge of the grandmother." The Mormon Church deliberately engaged in this campaign. It was part of their religious belief to save Indian people, so they adopted out their children. Catholics, Lutherans, Methodists—well-meaning liberal white people had also waged this campaign. It took a major effort to pass a law that required that before any Indian child was placed, the tribe had to be notified. The first preference for placement was with a tribal member of the extended family.

With all these movements—asserting treaty rights to fish, to hunt, to protect the land from being further eroded, buying land back and putting it in trust—these were all fronts to make tribes into entities that could protect their people. You had to find ways to regain power in jurisdictional fights with states and counties, with surrounding municipalities, with the federal government. There's nothing comparable to it that was experienced by other people of color in this country. The battles other people of color were fighting—probably if they could, they would have tried to protect their community, if there was such a thing as sovereignty. The law didn't provide that, but it did for us. That's how we've been waging our struggle.

We passed the Self-Governance Act, which was stage two of self-determination. Under self-governance, a tribe could enter into a self-government agreement with all the government agencies that had responsibility to provide services. You eliminate the need for the Bureau of Indian Affairs because you're doing all those services yourself. That's what we have at Rocky Boy, and I've pushed them to do that.

The next stage of what we have to do is to heal ourselves. My generation has been engaged in a struggle to build up the tribes so they can protect the members of the tribes and their interests. We've discovered that the scars of colonialism and oppression have gone much deeper than we thought. The way in which our tribal societies govern themselves is still using the same methods as the colonial administrators used. This continues to mean deeply divid-

Alan Parker with his daughters Christina and Jimena and my son Hasani at the Rocky Boy Pow Wow, 1994

ed, fractionated communities, so we must rediscover the ways of self-governance that are traditional to the people. It's part of relearning and reintroducing the Native languages in schools. It's revitalizing the culture. It's a vision that's being more and more embraced by leaders around the country. It isn't enough to just protect yourself; you have to recognize that four to five generations of being the subject of forced assimilation have inflicted very deep wounds on the society. Plus, if we look around and say, "We don't want to be like Americans, we don't want to live by the values that American society lives by. Those are anti-human values." You just have to look at what's wrong with society, and you can see this is not a society that we like.

I'm not concerned about the image other people have about us Native Americans. I'm only concerned about what we do about ourselves. That's their problem if they have a stereotype about Native Americans. I know the reality is that you have children who grew up in alcoholic homes; they saw that behavior and repeat that behavior. That's happened now for three generations. You have people who grow up, and when they begin to understand the situation, they're filled with rage and frustration, and that's just one form of escape.

On a broader level, the healing happens by supporting alcohol-free communities, the revitalization of culture, looking for values to live by, spirituality in terms of the teachings of our ancestors. It's not a perception that you're better than anybody else. All we can do is take care of our own and try to be strong.

It's necessary to identify the lie that has been out there, call it what it is. If you step back and ask, What would it take? it would be overwhelming. Global capitalism now is such a powerful force and such a destructive force. I don't know how you can take away the power of the handful of multinational corporations that control the world. All you can say is that with those around you that you work with, you try to do the right thing. There's nothing more powerful than an idea, like the idea in the Northwest of saving the salmon is catching on. It's a powerful force. That's enough to feel hopeful about. Some of the people I respect the most talk in terms of hope. ■■■

n 1985 I was forty-five years old, and Hasani was ten. I had already left my job with the Department of Housing and Urban Development and decided it was time to return to San Francisco.

PART 3

SAN FRANCISCO

1985-2000

JUDY HEUMANN

BILL SORRO

GIULIANA MILANESE

GIULIO SORRO

JOAQUIN SORRO

MAURICIO VELA

LYNETTE LEE

BARAKA SELE

KAREN KAHO

JOHN KAHO

SHILOH KAHO

GABRIELLE KAHO

JOSEPH SMOOKE

SHARON LI

NANCY BLACK

DIANA BLACK

ROBERTO CHENÉ

FRED PERDOMO

CHRIS PERDOMO

It had been thirty years since my family moved from San Francisco to Long Beach and twenty-three years since I flew east to Philadelphia from Oakland for a summer job. Hasani was looking forward to his new life in the West. He thought he'd like the city, but he hated it. Tearing him away from his close friends at Waldorf School was too much for him to bear. Five months after we arrived, his father and I agreed that he should return to Washington and continue his schooling there. Letting him go was like losing my heart, my breath. For him, it was the right thing to do.

Returning to San Francisco after living in cities with large Black populations, I confronted a new cultural shock. There were substantially fewer African Americans compared to where I'd lived back east. In 1990 San Francisco was 35 percent Asian, 14 percent Latino, 41 percent Caucasian, and only 10 percent Black. I never adjusted to that imbalance. According to the 2000 census, the city's Black population has decreased to 8 percent.

After flying 3,000 miles and with no job prospects, I was blessed to find the Women's Economic Agenda Project. Based in an old semiabandoned building in the heart of Oakland's downtown, WEAP was — and continues to be — a strong voice for California women, particularly poor women of color. Ethel Long-Scott, its Black executive director, is a fighter like few women I've ever met. In 1987 we published a major report, *A Call to Action by and for California Women*, which covered issues of economic justice for women at home, in families, and in the larger society. It provided a clear action agenda that is still relevant today.

Through WEAP I met one of my heroines, who was a board member at the time. Judy Heumann lived in Berkeley in a wheelchair-accessible home, having contracted polio when she was only eighteen months old. In 1986 she was the executive director of the World Institute on Disability. She later moved to Washington to be assistant secretary for the Office of Rehabilitative Services at the Department of Education during the Clinton administration. Judy met her husband, Jorge, in Mexico, and they continue to live and work in Washington while advocating for the rights of the disabled throughout the country.

221

JUDY HEUMANN

I was always aware of my ethnicity because my parents both lost their parents—mothers and fathers, a grandparent, and other relatives—in the Holocaust. For me, the issue of being Jewish is linked to oppression; there's never really a time I don't think about it.

I grew up in Brooklyn and had my disability when I was eighteen months old. My parents got thrown into a whole other world of trying to deal with discrimination based on disability. One of the complexities of the situation was that when they came to the United States, they wanted nothing more to do with Germany. They came here and threw themselves into the ethic of work, which was very much a Jewish ethic —you work, go to school, take responsibility for the family—but disability was something that was very different. There were no other people in our family who had a disability, and they had the same reactions to my disability as other people, which was "this is a tragedy, this is a terrible thing." There wasn't a lot of support my family could get from anybody around them, although I don't recall any feelings of rejection from the immediate family.

My path was different, because when it was time for me to go to school, I wasn't allowed to go. The principal said that because I was in a wheelchair I couldn't attend. So I had a teacher who came to the house, sent by the board of education, from first grade to half of the fourth grade. During that time I was in Brownies after school and went to religious school a couple times a week. Everyone around me was basically white, except that I was the only disabled person. Disability isn't race, but at a certain level it was a significant difference. At a very early age I didn't understand why I wasn't going to school, and it made me different from everybody else.

When I finally did go to school I went to a health conservation class. In New York City they had all these different kinds of special-education classes. They were totally segregated, but not in segregated schools. You had to be screened to get into these schools. We got a call one day saying, "Could you come to this school for a week," where they would evaluate me. You didn't have a right to go to school. The following week they had a screening meeting, and my mother and I were invited in for part of the meeting. They did accept me at the school. It was kind of a joke that I integrated the special-education classes, because they had been mainly for children with cerebral palsy, and I was the first kid with polio. But these classes were racially integrated. It was a white school, except for the special-education classes, which were in the back of the basement. I never thought anything about the fact that these classes were racially integrated. I didn't know anything different. I didn't go to the same camp as my two younger brothers because it didn't accept disabled kids. My camp was racially integrated, so in the disabled community, I was always racially integrated!

My first boyfriend was from Puerto Rico. It's kind of ironic that in the end I married a Mexican, because there were a number of incidents in my early life where I had Puerto Ricans come up to me and say in Spanish (and I didn't speak Spanish), "You're denying your heritage." When I finally went to high school, I enrolled in a Spanish class. (I went from a segregated set of classes in elementary school, with no more than eight to ten kids per class, to a high school with over thirty-two kids per class.) There were no other disabled kids in the Spanish class. Two of my disabled friends were taking French, so I dropped out of Spanish in one day because I was afraid to be in a class by myself as the only disabled person.

My family told me at that time, "You have a lot of strikes against you because you have a disability. You don't need to set yourself up in more adverse situations, and if you are looking to get involved with someone with another minority background, it would probably make your life more difficult." But that was all they said, and there was never anything against any of the people I was seeing.

Many of the minority kids in my elementary school, high school, and camps came from poorer backgrounds, so they clearly had fewer advantages than I had. My father was a butcher, working class, and I'm sure we had different opportunities. But when we went to school, I didn't feel a sense of difference. There was one African American teacher who we felt was the best teacher in the program, Mrs. Edwards.

When I went to Long Island University in Brooklyn in the mid-1960s, I was thrown into an environment where I was significantly the only disabled person. I joined a sorority, which was a good thing, because I was living away from home, although I went home on the weekends. At that time I didn't have a motorized wheelchair and was very dependent on people pushing me. The campus I went to had two steps into the dorm and a step into the bathroom, so I needed assistance every which way.

Judy Heumann, center, in a high school play in New York

Racial issues were becoming much more prevalent at college and in the society overall. What was important to me then was looking at the parallels between racism and handicappism. I was looking at Martin Luther King, SNCC (Student Nonviolent Coordinating Committee), and the other civil rights organizations. The first director of the Disabled Students Program at Long Island University was an African American man who was very much my mentor, Dr. Childs.

I had an Italian friend, Tony Malley, and we were both interested in education. Our college was located in a section called Fort Green, "the Harlem of Brooklyn." There had been a lot of criticism by some of the students that we weren't really doing anything in the community, so Tony and I and a couple of other people set up an after-school program at one of the community centers. The people we worked with were 100 percent minority, primarily African American.

Dr. Childs was very helpful to me when I graduated and applied for my teaching credentials. We had to take a written exam, an oral exam, and a medical exam, and they were all given in completely inaccessible buildings. I had friends who had to carry me up one or two flights of stairs. The medical exam had a really bad doctor who was very rude and insulting and said I had to come back for another medical exam and wear my braces and show her how I could walk. (This was so bizarre.) Dr. Childs came with me the second time (they wouldn't let him in the room, though). For me, it was great to have him there. He had been a founding member of an NAACP chapter, and he was very supportive of the work we were doing on campus for disabled students. There was an incident one day when a student had gone to a class where the instructor told him he didn't want this student in his class because of his disability. Dr. Childs was really angry and said to the teacher, "You have no choice because this student has been accepted into the school and he's going to go to your class. If you don't want this student in your class, then you should leave the university." Dr. Childs was very reinforcing around issues of discrimination and how things needed to be dealt with.

As I became involved in setting up disability organizations, those groups tended to be more white because it was people who knew each other from colleges and universities, people who had advantages. That's not to say these organizations didn't have some minority individuals in them, but the issue of double or triple discrimination based on race and disability wasn't something we were focusing on specifically. Always for me, race and disability have been a stronger linkage than disability and nondisability. I found for myself (and through discussions with friends) that as disabled people, regardless of color, we feel more of an affinity toward each other than our respective group, whether it be white, Jewish, women, Latino, Asian, African American, or Native American. For each one of us there is a level of disconnect when we go back to our majority group, because it really isn't our majority group. The majority group for us is really disabled people.

Over the years, what I've tried to do in my work at the Center for Independent Living (CIL), the World Institute on Disability (WID), and even more in this job is to focus on issues from a race and disability perspective. It's very clear that discrepancies exist for the two communities. Since poverty is a link to disability, you'll find higher rates of disability in some of the minority communities than the white communities—disability based on low birth weight, lack of access to medical care, and other problems based on poverty and race.

I met my husband, and he is Mexican. It's been a very powerful and sometimes rocky experience because we both have disabilities. That's definitely what drew us to each other (certainly our personalities and our interests, also), but the disability was an equalizing factor between the two of us. Experiencing his discrimination—I can't really experience his discrimination, but I am involved in it.

When Jorge came to the United States, his English was very limited. He came to this country because of me. Seeing him learning another language and how people treated him, in some cases my friends who can't deal with a second language, was very difficult. He's now been here eight years, so his language is much better, but it isn't perfect. It takes a while for people in their thirties and forties to learn another language. What I really learned— and am still learning—is in Mexico (you wouldn't say there isn't racism, but primarily everyone is from the same race), there's

Judy Heumann and her husband Jorge Piñeda in Washington, D.C.

classism big time. My husband clearly has Indian blood in him, and according to him, there aren't many Mexicans who don't. But I didn't feel a sense of racism there.

But he's learned a level of hatred, you could say, because of the discrimination he has experienced here. We had some amazing experiences when he first came. He moved to Berkeley because that's where I lived. There are a lot of Latino organizations in the Bay Area. He wanted to work but couldn't work until we got married five months later. He is an accountant, and in Mexico he was a CPA and supervised twenty-two people.

I was on the board of the Over 60 Health Clinic. There are a lot of health clinics in the Bay Area, including the Clinica de la Raza. I thought, "Maybe he could get some volunteer experience over there," because they were a pretty big organization. Someone called me from their accounting office and said they were doing a big audit and could really use some volunteer help, but she had to speak to her supervisor. We did say Jorge had a disability, but the ironic thing was that in Mexico he didn't use a wheelchair. He used crutches and braces, worked and drove his car, and walked up and down steps. The woman said that the accounting office was on the second floor and there was no elevator. I said, "That's no problem because he can walk with his crutches and braces." I then linked this woman up with Jorge. We didn't hear anything. Jorge called, and she didn't know yet. He called again and was finally told that the supervisor said no, their insurance didn't cover them for liability if something happens, and this is a health clinic!

Then one day I'm listening to the radio (I was kind of relentlessly stupid), and there was a man on NPR who was the head of the Bay Area Latino Accountants. I said, "Jorge, you gotta talk with this guy." What Jorge needed was somebody who could help him get some work experience and also look at his résumé. Nice guy that Jorge is, he calls this guy up. He said, "I don't think this is going to be good. This guy isn't Mexican." (So I'm learning all these new things. It's not just Latin, there's all these subcultures.) He goes to see this guy, and he hadn't told him that he had a disability. The guy takes one look at him, and (from Jorge) he has no use for Jorge any further. They talked for no more than ten minutes, he never looked at his résumé, told him he needed to learn English, which of course we knew.

A number of weeks later we went to a Center for Independent Living party, and a friend of mine (a disabled woman who was an accountant) talked with Jorge and hired him in twenty minutes. So his work experiences, even here in D.C., have only been with disability agencies.

What I see going on with him and his friends is that the disabled Latinos are organizing. They don't feel a part of the African American community, so I see all these subdivisions. There is a national organization that was set up for minorities that is controlled primarily by nondisabled African Americans who are in the field of disability. They put Jorge on the board because he was an accountant and the only Latino. He went to a meeting one day and said, "I think we should change the bylaws to say that 51 percent have to be disabled individuals who are racial minorities," and they said, "That would mean that most of us couldn't be in our positions!"

As assistant secretary for the Office of Special Education and Rehabilitative Services, I have a budget of about $8 billion and a staff of 360. This job has been a great opportunity because I've been able to advance an agenda within the Department of Education and try to get this office operating more effectively. It's a job that won't be done in a year and a half, but I think we've been successful in getting some of these issues addressed in a way they haven't been before. For me, this work is a way of life. As I look at my next job (which I'm completely unsure about what I want to do), disability is integral to who I am, my work and my life. It's who I am.

What I've learned so far in my life is that there are amazing disparities, and left to your own, you could easily go off to your separate communities. The ability to try to develop connections, where people can learn from each other, is so important. We have a strong race initiative going on which the president has started, but my office has taken it on stronger than most of the other offices in the department. I have two special assistants who are Latinos and very strong bilingual people who are challenging me on how we do our work, how we look at issues like hiring and promotion and helping people move along their career pathways.

There's so much more that needs to be done. For disabled individuals who come from racial minority backgrounds, particularly from poor communities, our office is fighting hard to get policies established that would help poor kids whose families are not involved to the degree that middle-class families are—time, money, and language. We're trying to level—or at least make the step toward—the ways we look at issues like service delivery and results.

Society itself is still so divided—the lack of knowledge of what racism is, how to accept that racism is a reality and how to move forward in addressing it. For me, discrimination against disabled people is a reality. People need to understand it and be willing to own it and figure out ways of dealing with it. It's the same thing in the area of race, and it's multiplied when dealing with race and disability, and certain disabilities carry more negative perceptions than others. If you look at the data on employment, you have a larger number of racial minorities who are unemployed than whites. When you compare white disabled men to African American disabled, Latino disabled, Asian, Native American, they all earn less than white nondisabled men. But the disparities are bigger as you go down the racial ladder. The same is true for women. ■■■

Shortly after I returned to San Francisco, I found and bought a small one-story house on a steep street in Bernal Heights, just south of the Mission District, where most of the city's Latinos live. Bernal was a mixed salad of people, with pockets of Blacks, Filipinos, Latinos, and an ethnic mix of white folks, including old Italian and Irish families. It also included a healthy combination of gay and lesbian families, as well as very low-income families who lived in the neighborhood's two public housing projects. There were two large and active Catholic churches in the community, as well as a small, well-attended mosque.

In July of 1988 my next-door neighbor and friend, in her late sixties at the time, came running up our steep street with a flyer in her hand, shouting, "Helen, this is the job for you!" I glanced at the description and agreed. After two intense interviews, I was hired as the Bernal Heights Neighborhood Center's executive director, a position I held for the next ten years.

Also in 1988 my father died of throat cancer. I wrote this "letter" to him in my journal shortly after his death:

You grew up an only child in the small rural town of Republic, Kansas.

Your aunt was the first resident to have indoor plumbing in the 1940s. I remember our visit to her home and bathroom on our way to Grandpa's in 1951.

You never talked much about your past, but you wrote to me once that you had to ride your horse seven miles to get to high school, and "in the winter, it was really rough." You also said the first paved road in Republic's 600 member community was built in the 1930s. I gave your cousin Cleo an old photograph of some of the town's people, including a large group of Native Americans. He couldn't remember what tribe they were.

A week before Mother died in 1982, a long lost cousin of yours, Ruth Nicholes, visited with you and Mom. She was putting together a family history of Jesse Helfer, your great-grandfather, and his large family. A letter dated August 5, 1952 from the Department of the Army states: "The records show that Jesse Helfer was enrolled and mustered into service 20 August 1862 at Waterloo, Iowa; as a private, Company C, 32nd Regiment Iowa Infantry and was honorably discharged as a private, 24 August 1865 at Clinton, Iowa.

My dad as a young man in Republic, Kansas

At the time of enrollment he stated that he was born in North Carolina and was 42 years of age. . . . He is shown present with the company until 9 April 1864 when he was detailed as a nurse for wounded at Pleasant Hill; was absent as a prisoner of war in parole camp, St. Louis, Missouri, from about July 1864 to December 1864 and was detailed in supply train from January through April 1865."

I learned that Jesse Helfer's first wife, Rurie Ann, died during the Civil War and he was given leave to go home for her funeral. She gave birth to eight children, one of whom, Daniel Bradley, married Jane Smith in 1876 in Republic, Kansas. She gave birth to William Henry in 1877, your father. The long list of children goes on, ending with your son Wayne and his wife Bev's children, but no mention of my son Hasani's birth two years before Ruth Nicholes printed her booklet.

You joined the Merchant Marines in the 1920s, traveling to the South Seas and New Zealand, bringing back treasures of three beautifully carved Maori busts and brightly woven cloth. I still have the embroidered picture of the two lions you gave us. You were later stationed at the Presidio in San Francisco for three years, where you met your future wife, Wayne's and my mother.

I never knew your mother. Her sudden death occurred three months before I was born. Etta Helfer seemed a strong willed woman, a devout and active Christian Scientist who wrote regularly for the *Christian Science Monitor.* She had at least one of her songs published, as well as several small cheaply made paperback novels. The one I found after your death is called *Loose Stones: A Romance and a Stray Sermon.*

Her first child died at birth, and she doted on you throughout her life. Close to your death, you told your daughter-in-law, "My mother is the only woman I ever loved."

I enter the hospital's double doors and up the elevator to your stark room — number 356. You are alone, as you have been since Mom died six years ago. Your operation is over — the cancerous growth taken from your throat. You are lying in a narrow bed — a frail morose old man with tubes coming out of your mouth — tubes going into your arm — tubes out of your rectum.

You recognize me and nod. There can be no conversation anymore — there never really was. I sit near your bed and tell you that Annie is fine and I'm taking her with me back to San Francisco. I have her dog dish and food in the truck, plus the file you made for her with all her shots and medical history. You nod. I tell you that I need to leave soon because I don't like to drive in the dark anymore.

You are distracted by the TV and try to form a word while pointing to it with your untubed skinny arm. I don't understand. You form the word again, more forcefully. "Four" you hoarsely shout again, "four." I look back at the TV and realize you want me to change the channel to four. I reach up and comply. You nod and begin looking at the program. I kiss you lightly on your forehead and say good-bye.

I drive slowly to your now empty home, pick up Annie and begin the long drive north. You die two days later. I do not attend your funeral.

During your long life you kept up with your Radiomarine men by short wave radio. You knew Morse Code as well as English. I remember as a child hearing the "tap tap tap tap tap" sometimes late at night on your short wave radio. Whenever one of your friends died you'd write in your address book "Silent Key" and draw a line diagonally across their name.

I did the same for you.

The Neighborhood Center greatly reminded me of the Philadelphia settlement houses where I worked in the early 1960s. It was a multiservice organization that served seniors and at-risk youth and provided affordable housing for low-income families. It was the housing program that would take all my strength to make it survive and succeed.

Market Heights, my most controversial housing development, stands proudly behind the best farmers' market in San Francisco, forty-six units of family housing and the most integrated in our community: 46 percent Hispanic, 30 percent African American, 11 percent Asian Pacific Islander, 2 percent American Indian, 9 percent Caucasian, and 2 percent other.

Market Heights shortly after completion
(Courtesy of *Architectural Record* magazine, July 1997)

It took me seven years to get this project built. A small group led by neighbors hiding behind a screen of racism initially objected to the project because, to quote from one of their flyers, "it would bring in drugs and crime and lower property values." They later changed their tune and simply said, "It will destroy the farmers' market."

After we greatly reduced the number of homes and shrank the project to just the hillside behind the market, this group still took us to the ballot to stop us. My staff, board members, volunteers, and I traveled all over the city with our housing model, dialoguing about the desperate need for affordable housing and dispelling the rumors that "unsavory" people would be living there.

"Being poor in this county is not a crime, and with good management, Market Heights will succeed," we told folks. They listened, and we won at the ballot box 69 percent to 31 percent. The project got built and is thriving.

While my brother Wayne and I were growing up on the white west side of San Francisco, Bill Sorro was growing up in his large Filipino family across town in the Fillmore, one of the city's two predominantly Black neighborhoods. I often wished I had known him back then. I finally had the privilege to meet and work with him when he was on the Neighborhood Center's board of directors and later its president. He's worked for many social justice causes ever since he was a young man, first through the Communist Party and now through low-income tenant organizing in the largely Latino Mission District. His nonpaid job is with the Manilatown Heritage Foundation, assuring that Filipino history and culture in San Francisco are remembered and respected. Bill's story is one of extraordinary survival and giving back to his community throughout his life.

BILL SORRO

San Francisco is a beautiful place because of the people who've made it what it is. Today we think of San Francisco as being this multicultural community. In that context, my family is a part of the city's fabric.

My father was born in the Philippine Islands before the turn of the century, immigrated to the United States around 1907 with the first wave of Filipino immigrants who came to California. They were originally enticed to work the agricultural fields of the San Joaquin and Salinas Valleys of California.

My mother was a native San Franciscan. She was born in 1900 on Hill Street. Today it's an uppity neighborhood, but when she lived there it was a working-class community of mainly Irish and Scandinavian people. Her father was a Scotsman from Liberty, Missouri, who came out to California before the turn of the century and settled in Castroville in the Salinas Valley. He met my grandmother, whose family came from Spain. Unfortunately, they've always maintained they were

Spaniards and not Californios or Mexicans. Therein lies this whole chauvinism or racism—and a class thing too. I frame it like this because around 1920 my father came as a farmworker in the Salinas Valley to help develop the salad bowl industry.

This is a wonderful story: As my mother tells it, my father would pass by the house every day on his way to the fields across the road. He'd flirt with my mother when she'd be outside the house doing things with her relatives. One Sunday she went to church and looked around and saw my father at the back of the church. On the ensuing Sundays he'd continue to go to church, and their courtship began. One day my father and mother started talking with each other, and frankly began to fall in love. The aunts, who were Spaniard, had total disdain for any relationship with the Filipino farmworkers. When they got wind of my mother and father seeing each other, they sent her off to another aunt who lived in Vallejo, California. In those days, although Vallejo was only 100 miles away, it was like 1,000 miles away. It took my father seven months to find her, then he followed her there.

They eventually eloped in the early 1920s to Oakland, California. At that time there were antimiscegenation laws in California that said a man of color could not marry a white woman. A justice of the peace married them. They then caught the ferry back to San Francisco, and the sheriff arrested him and threw him in jail for white slavery. He

The Sorro family today—
Giuliana, Joaquin, Giulio,
and Bill—on their back porch

stayed in jail for a week—now this was on their honeymoon. My mother's family told her that if she annulled the marriage, they would drop all charges against my father, and if she didn't, they would disown her as a daughter. In so many words, my mother said, "I'm not going to do it, and go to hell." She was only sixteen at the time, which was not an uncommon age for women to get married in those days. She made that move, and her family disowned her. What's pivotal about the decision she made, as a Spanish woman, as a white woman—and I didn't understand it until years later—was that the decision imbued in her a whole fight for civil rights and equality. She never used those words; she just did things to make that happen. What it brought to us as children in a mixed marriage was the strength of a woman who made that decision.

The major influences of my family came from my father's side. There were no immediate blood relatives in the United States, but he had a whole grouping of Filipino families who came from the province where he grew up. I always understood I was Filipino. In my house we always referred to white people as "Americans." Whenever I'd see a white person out in front of my house, I'd say, "Oh Mama, look at that American lady!" And we were Americans, too—but Filipinos first. It wasn't that I was especially proud of being Filipino, it was just that that's who I was.

The clearest memory I have of racism was when I was about four years old. It was the first time I got on a San Francisco municipal bus (we never had a car in my family). My mother and father paid for themselves (my sister and I were too little), and we walked by a white lady who was sitting toward the front. She was able to talk right into my ear, "Oh, the poor children," and I went back to sit with my sister and I didn't understand what the lady was saying. It was a recurring situation whenever I was with my mother and father; people would say, "Oh, the poor children." One day it finally came to me that they were saying something about my mother and father, a mixed couple. As a kid, I didn't understand it, but I remember it as clearly as I'm looking at the watch on my hand. I'll never, never forget it. From that period on I'd always get ready for it whenever my mother and father were out together, because it was always there. Somehow, white people felt they had a right to have the final say on what people were supposed to look like. These experiences stayed with me and left an imprint on my heart that I'll always remember. What I learned is that people are beautiful—and never to get into a situation of looking at someone by the color of their skin.

Bill Sorro's family in the early 1940s (Bill is the shortest boy in the front row)

I grew up in the Fillmore all through the war years, from 1939 to 1949, until I was ten years old, and later moved to the Mission District. In the Fillmore, most of our neighbors were Black, with a few Filipino families. We were also part of a group that was Russian, Japanese, Jewish, and Chinese. The Fillmore in the 1930s and 1940s was a very diverse community. It was the heart of the Black community, and I am forever indebted for growing up in the Black culture, because being a minority within a minority has helped me shape a lot of things I understand about equality and civil rights.

My little friends were Black, white, brown. There was never any discussion about who we were. The consciousness was there on many levels, but amongst ourselves we were just friends. Children are not affected by all of this stuff that separates them. They're only affected by the stuff in their home and the other things that help shape their experience.

My father wasn't the point person on issues of civil rights. He was an immigrant to this country, and he really felt like one. He was here as a guest, even though he was a citizen and worked here. He wouldn't allow white people to harm us, but he wasn't the one who talked about the inequities or his own experience as a brown man from another country.

Some of his jobs were working in rich hotels like the St. Francis Yacht Club. When you're in that kind of situation, they let you know your place, a goddamn peasant. Since I was nine years old I've always worked, first hustling papers (I've always been a "newsy"). When I was fourteen years old I started working with my father at a motel near the old Hamilton Air Force Base in Marin County. In 1954 it was really the country, and this place, Rancho Raphael, was very exclusive. It had a swimming pool and cute private rooms. A lot of the would-be rich would come up for the weekends, and I'd help my father wash dishes.

When I was fifteen and when we'd get busy at a banquet, my father would help out for two to three hours cleaning up in the kitchen for extra pay. The manager's name was Nieberg. One night we were busy as hell, and I heard the chef (he was Filipino) talking with Nieberg about needing some help, and Nieberg said, "Go get Sal after he gets off of his other job." Mario said to Nieberg, "Should we start paying him when he gets here at 6:00?" and Nieberg said, "No, let's just pay him for the last hour. He can help his son." So I'm washing these dishes, man, and I'm furious. This man is going to take advantage of my father, so my father comes over and I said to him, "Daddy, don't work here, they're only going to pay you for the last hour you work." He looked at me, then at Mario, and didn't say anything. What hit me was this white man taking advantage of my father. I knew he was exploiting my old man, and I started crying. I said, "Please Daddy, don't do it." He turned to me and said, "Shut your goddamn mouth. You don't know the shit I've had to eat, " and he was furious when he said it to me. He continued to work, and when I went to the bunkhouse where the workers slept, I cried again. I was so hurt and devastated I could hardly look at my father the next day. I'll never forget it, just like riding the bus, the shit my father had to put up with because of racism. My mother later told me of the times he'd have to pass as Chinese to get a job. They knew what a Chinese houseboy was.

That was a time I had a lot of bad feelings about white people. There was always a playing around with "gray people, fey people, paddy people," which all meant white in my language. It was never with vehemence—I never considered my mother white. Mama was Mama. She was more Filipino than anything else. When she would talk about white people, she called them "American people" too!

I remember going to a Scout meeting in Glen Park, the only meeting I ever attended. I was the only nonwhite kid sitting there, and the scoutmasters made me feel like the only nonwhite kid sitting there. I was poor and didn't have a uniform, except for a small tie. When you experience racism it always leaves you with a button in your soul, and when the alarm goes off, you know what's going on. You just know it. The worst part about it is that you always learn to put up the defenses so that you can get through a situation. It's almost instinctive. It's part of survival, and you just learn it. Some people learn how to turn it off. Some people put on a veneer, psychologically mask it, but no matter how you do it, it's not healthy for a human being to prepare for a situation that they have no control over—and shouldn't have.

I was married when I was eighteen years old to a young woman I knew from high school, and she had two children when I married her. They're my two oldest kids today. Daphne is forty-two and Gjango is forty years old. By the time I was twenty-one I had four kids. Let me tell you, having four kids at age 21 was one of the major influences in my life. It shaped my life, and I don't recommend it to young people. Growing up in San Francisco in those days, there was a lot of work for young people. I wanted to be a merchant seaman, so after high school I went to the Sailors Union of the Pacific. I started sailing before I got married and two years after. I then had a job delivering baby formulas, lost my job, got evicted, then moved to Hunter's Point. This was about 1962, and we lived there for three years.

Hunter's Point was a major shaper of my life in terms of poverty. I had my suit from my high school graduation in 1957, and I used to pawn it every week just before we'd get my welfare or unemployment check. It was always $5, and it'd be enough money to buy groceries.

We were one of the few non-Black families who lived in Hunter's Point, and it had a real impact on my kids. They caught the brunt of other people's frustrations because they weren't Black. In some ways it jarred them, but it never jaded their affinity with Black people. It was an eye-opening experience—being a minority amongst minorities and feeling the wrath other people were feeling, but we being the brunt of it because we weren't Black.

Some people like to "glamorize" the ghetto or the barrio. It's bullshit, because people who live there don't glamorize it. There's an affinity because it *is* a community. But when you live in a poor community and you know it's a poor-ass community, you understand there is something better, particularly living in the United States.

It was through dance that I became more politically aware about peace issues in 1964–65, when the Vietnam War was really happening. I was part of a dance program that was federally funded in San Francisco, and the teacher was a real progressive. Her name was Gloria Unte, a beautiful sister. Her husband was a Communist, and he was one of the principals in the movie *Salt of the Earth*. He played the boss of the mine company in New Mexico. Gloria had great politics, and she brought the issues of the day—the Vietnam War and of course the issue of racism—into our dance workshop and theater groups. "The Village" was one dance I remember commemorating the heroism of the Vietnamese Liberation Front fighting for their freedom and independence. I didn't know the specifics of what was happening in Vietnam back then. I knew it wasn't good.

There was a lot going on in 1967–68, such as the Third World Strike at SF State that laid the precedent for ethnic studies there. As a result of the victory in that strike, ethnic studies found their rightful place in universities around the country. I didn't have a sense of politics at that time but knew intuitively that I needed to be there and add my strength to that cause—whether it be the strike at SF State or a march against the war in Vietnam—and I began moving in that direction. It was a very subtle process, not that one day I woke up and saw the light that U.S. imperialism and capitalism were the enemy of the world.

In late 1969 a friend of mine talked with me about going to Cuba. The timing was right. I had just gotten laid off from my warehouse job. I was collecting unemployment, and this was a chance to go to Cuba for two months. One of the reasons I went was to study dance. So in March of 1970 I and 700 other Americans left for the second Venceremos Brigade. We cut sugarcane, were introduced to the Cuban people and the revolution, were exposed to many different kinds of ideas and the difference between capitalism and socialism. In Cuba there were all these countries of the world that were blackballed from coming to the U.S., such as North Korea, China, the Soviet Union, Albania, etc. Cuba had opened its doors and its hospitals to the war victims of Vietnam. Cuba was sending doctors to Vietnam for their need for medical supplies and care. It really struck me to see this poor little country with the ability to do that—to send to another poor little country doctors and help. That kind of solidarity I had never seen before.

While we were there we had the opportunity to meet with some of the Vietnamese soldiers who were in Cuba receiving medical care. They said to us as young wanna-be revolutionaries, "If you want to help in our revolution, you need to go home and build the peace movement in the United States." For many young people, building the peace movement was for old white ladies to do, and we didn't want to hear that! We wanted to be urban guerrillas and fire automatic weapons because it was romantic to do that stuff. But the Vietnamese were telling us this was what they needed from us more than anything. At the time, it went over our heads. We weren't prepared for something so profound from these people we respected so much.

It's been over twenty-five years since I've been to Cuba. The Cuban revolution and that experience is one of the single most important crossroads of my life. It was there that my life took a 180-degree turn. I understood there the relationship of the family I came from and the problems we had in so many ways being victims of a system that didn't respect us, no matter how we struggled.

I never understood that—we got in trouble, we went to jail, we were poor. One of the things I learned in Cuba for myself and my family was that we were not fuck-ups. We had been victimized like so many people of color who were poor in the United States, and racism was at the core of it. We never copped out but tried to fight it the best way we could.

It put into my heart an anger that I'll never, never not feel—the anger about why people are poor and what's the major cause. Straight up, it's greed to accumulate wealth at the expense of the majority of the people. A few people exploit and use the majority of the earth's resources for their own benefit, and that means the masses of people on all the continents don't have adequate living, housing, etc.

The anger I feel keeps me going. It's healthy. Part of the problem is that people don't feel angry enough about what's going on. There's not enough anger or resistance to the cutbacks that we see, the escalation of poverty in this country, and the return of sweatshops in the United States.

Cuba said something else to me. That the system of capitalism sucks. The division of wealth and the way it's laid out has to be buried. In my time, we said that socialism was the answer, that the means of production were in the hands of the majority of people and there was no private ownership. All of that stuff is more ambiguous than it was years ago, and that's OK as long as people realize that capitalism ain't the answer. There are some pieces of it that work, but the bottom line is profit—profit at the expense of the majority of people. We can't sustain it. Look around at the natural resources being cut up, the seas being poisoned, and for who? Just a few individuals. ■■■

Giuliana Milanese, or "Hule," as she's known to family and friends, met Bill during the Venceremos Brigade in Cuba and was also very involved in the Communist Party and related social justice issues. She and Bill were married at the International Hotel in San Francisco's Manilatown. Hule is currently an organizer with the California Nurses Association and a tenacious and respected leader in campaigns ranging from a decent living wage to continuing the fight for affirmative action programs in California. She is also the best Italian cook in the city and a gatherer of extraordinary people in her and Bill's Bernal Heights home.

A recent Sorro holiday celebration in their Bernal Heights home

GIULIANA MILANESE

I was born in Oakland, California. I have one brother, Don, who is three years older than me. My parents were from Italy, and we moved into an Italian neighborhood. In those days, you were either an Italian or an American, and it wasn't until I began Catholic school that I met people outside of Italians.

My dad owned the grocery store in a community where all my family had little businesses. My mother, father, and relatives who came from Italy worked in the grocery store, and I started working there when I was

Giuliana Milanese
as a little girl in
Oakland, California

twelve. Among the non-Italians who'd come to the store were a group of Black women, mostly cleaning women I'd presume. They picked out what they'd want and I'd deliver the groceries to them. I remember my father and anti-Semitism when I grew up, but never anything about Black people. My mother and I used to deliver the groceries, but my mother hurt her back, so my father went to the middle school across the street and asked the principal for a kid. The principal said they were only Black, and my father said he didn't care what color they were, so he hired this young man called Donzel. I saw Donzel twenty years later (he had become a Communist, as I had). He reminded me that my father asked him what his name was, and he said "Donzel." My father said, "What kind of a name is that? I'll call you Dano after my son. You work, you get paid; you don't work, you don't get paid." Donzel and I delivered the groceries, and a couple of days later an Italian woman entered the store and began yelling at my father for allowing me to ride with this young Black man. My father kicked her out of the store. It wasn't that he was antiracist, it was that nobody told my father what to do. But he died early in life, so I always wanted to pretend that. There were some Black kids in our school, and they would come over. We didn't socialize, and we never had dinner, but I never remember anything racist. My father died in 1965 before I became consciously involved in the Black community.

My mother was an Italian who couldn't wait to become an American, and I never remember her thoughts on anything, nor anything negative. She worked hard so I could move to the suburbs and become a suburban wife. She did make a statement later in life to me, "How come all your girlfriends are Black?" I called her on it, and she became very self-conscious about it. It wasn't true anyway. My two closest friends were Black, but I had many other friends. That was in the 1970s.

When I grew up and attended a Catholic school, the nuns would make fun of me because I didn't speak English good or Italian good. I also felt this anti-Italian thing from the Irish kids. My brother also experienced a few anti-Italian things.

I hate to make a big thing about this, but it sensitized me. I was always embarrassed about my parents speaking Italian, and I didn't like being Italian. My father never became an American. He was very much into Italy Italy Italy. When I was fourteen years old we were going to live in Italy, and I didn't want to go. But I fell in love with Italy and my culture. We only stayed six months, but when I came home I was a different person. I developed a sense of confidence. I knew who I was after that, and I think it sensitized me to other people's suffering.

My first consciousness in understanding racism was in seeing Black women from the flatlands of Oakland get on the bus and go up to the hills to clean rich people's houses. I compared that experience with my mother and dad, who had been in this country a short time. They had come over when they were eighteen and had done very well with their grocery store. It was something in my instincts that said: How come these Black women who've been here for generations were so poor, and my parents and our Italian friends had come here and made it? These Black women—one who worked in our house—worked for so little and were given hand-me-downs. My gut said there is something wrong with this country.

When I was twenty I went to live in Italy for a year. It was then that I really began to understand more about this country. I fell in love with this crazy Italian who was a lefty and he would raise questions about this country I couldn't answer. I was never a student activist, but when I had to return home because my father died suddenly, I had developed a consciousness about my country I didn't have before.

I began to work in the Black community in East Oakland with a bunch of kids. The year was 1966. At that time, there were a lot of white students working there. I didn't know a lot. It wasn't intellectual; it was mostly from my heart. I'll never forget, there was a Black minister who'd take me into his office and talk with me about Black people. He'd spend hours with me to educate me. I then became the director of this community center. I remember getting upset with some of the students from Cal Berkeley because they were there mainly to get grades or do alternative service during the Vietnam War.

For the next long period I worked there and hated white people for what they did to Black people. That didn't make me always feel good about myself, but I moved on. I left the center because some of the Black people were putting inside of me the idea that I needed to work with white people to educate them about racism. I remember going to a church in Piedmont (an upscale white community) with a young Black fourteen-year-old named Timmy. He was a strong kid, but after we parked the car and started toward the church, he was shaking.

We began going to churches, and I worked with the Unitarian Church and other churches with more white people. The problem was I didn't have a framework then, and in the beginning I made white people feel bad about being white rather than helping them move forward. In time I did learn, and I brought in some of my cousins to help. It was the kind of work I wanted to do my whole life. Later when I became a lefty, I began to understand a lot more of our history, and how our country functions in terms of capital and labor—one class of workers against another race of workers. I became more grounded and educated.

It was during that time that my brother was a witness in an important trial for a young Black activist, Wade Green. There was a bombing at UC Berkeley, and my brother went to the police department and told them they had the wrong person, it was a white kid. He was a key witness, and it was a hung jury. My brother was devastated that they didn't believe him. Finally, after the second trial, Wade Green was released.

My family wasn't really political. My parents didn't understand racism because they were so new to this country. They were so involved in just making it that it didn't affect them. Had my father lived, as much as I loved him, I don't think he would have been supportive. I'm sure that if I had a Black boyfriend it would have been really rough. When I married Bill, who is Filipino, I had to convince my mother that he wasn't like a Sicilian, that he was a person of color and needed to be respected for that. But my mother was upset with everything I was doing during that period.

Until I met Bill I was basically involved in the Black community. I then went to Cuba in 1970 and was beginning to be more rebellious, but wasn't a lefty at that time. I went to Cuba, as Bill had done, and met him there. He was a divorced man with four children. That was a more difficult issue than his race. It was rough because my mother had all these dreams for her daughter, and I was breaking all those dreams. Here was a divorced man with four kids and we were moving into the International Hotel together. (The International Hotel was in Manilatown in Chinatown. It was a hotel of Filipino immigrants who'd come here to work without their wives, and would then go up to Alaska to work in the fisheries or work in the canneries. After a long struggle, the hotel was torn down and the land lay dormant for over twenty-five years.)

My mother had trouble with all my visions, and we went through a rough time in the 1970s. In terms of Bill's family, we accepted each other and it was very beautiful. Of course, I didn't know anything about the Filipino community, and it was a new education for me. We lived in the International Hotel, and it was an incredible experience, along with working in the Black community. Manilatown was very small, but it was the heart of the Filipino community—the barbershop, the pool hall, the restaurants. The "I" Hotel had Black people, white people, but was predominantly based in the Filipino community. People would call me "Mrs. Bill," and they accepted me. I never played a leadership role in the hotel. Bill was the organizer, and I helped.

Bill's children would come and visit on the weekends. When I met Bill I fell in love with his four children, and they've always been an important part of our relationship. We were going to break up once, but I couldn't because I didn't want to live without his children. Bill's first wife was also white, and when he first lived at the "I" Hotel he realized he had never been with an Asian woman. We weren't living together then. I was living in Oakland with two Black women who had become my community (still are), and Bill wanted to go with this Asian woman. I was beginning to feel profoundly insecure. The white guilt came out, and my Black sisters were very supportive of me. They wanted to go and bust his ass. But eventually I sat down with the Asian woman. Her name was Judy, and she was incredible. "First of all," she said, "I'm not really interested in Bill, and second of all, I would never do that to another sister." I did feel the baggage of being a white woman for a while after that, but then it worked out.

I'm glad I didn't take it for granted. There was a period in the 1960s and 1970s where a lot of white women were going with Black men, and there was this whole thing in Berkeley about having Black children. Within that were some beautiful relationships that have continued.

My mother has slowed down a bit, but she's still active. She's now in her seventies. Our extended family includes my Black friends of twenty-eight years, Cassie and Matenah, and their children, and my mother wonders why we don't invite her when we have them over. I think she's realizing that she pushed herself out of much of my life and she wants to come back in.

Bill's son Django lives in Modesto. He's a firefighter. He's fighting on affirmative action and comes up here a lot to talk with Bill and me. I don't want to invade another place, but I want to try and figure out how we can be helpful in other areas and do some education on racism.

Now I have two beautiful sons. Giulio is twenty-two and Joaquin nineteen. One of the issues of race within my family is that my son Giulio is visibly a person of color, and the world responds to him that way. When Joaquin was born, my aunt said, "Filipino my ass, he doesn't even look Italian!" The world responds to him as if he's white. It's been a very interesting dynamic. My godson recently lived with us for a year, and he's Black. The dynamic of these three kids was even more powerful and has had a positive impact on our family.

I've continued to go to Italy throughout my life, and when I took Joaquin when he was twelve, he really began to identify with it. He's always had a lot of friends who are people of color, but I remember when he was little he'd take his arm that was exposed to the sun and he'd say, "That's Giulio," and the side that wasn't exposed, he'd say, "That's Joaquin." I remember Giulio once called Joaquin "a white boy," and I said, "Call him an asshole, but let's not do that."

A lot of us white progressives have backstepped on the issue of racism. It's no longer the strong message about white progressive people needing to take some initiative. How you do it is a very difficult discussion, but we don't even have those discussions anymore. A lot of our politics is only about who we elect, or fighting right-wing initiatives.

I think there are questions in San Francisco that need addressing—a lot of subtle racism comes out around the public schools, particularly among white parents. When you get into the struggle of public schools, it really divides people. A lot of the education needs to come from people of color, but also from white parents. There's a lot of education that's not in the academic world about understanding other people—their lives, their problems. To me, that is education, and I don't think that happens enough. Along with fighting for Black, Latino, Asian, Native American studies, we also need to fight for the history of the "good" whites like John Brown who fought against racism. ■■■

G iulio Sorro is Bill and Hule's older son. He graduated from San Francisco State University in 1999. Before and after graduation he has worked as a passionate and outspoken advocate for young, poor people of color in San Francisco's unequal and divisive education, affordable housing, and employment arenas. Giulio has a large and eclectic group of friends and loves all his family, including his "white trash" relatives.

GIULIO SORRO

I was born July 22, 1975, in Oakland but lived my whole life here in San Francisco. My parents met in Cuba in 1970, and they've been together ever since. My dad is Filipino American and grew up here in a big Filipino family, eight brothers and a sister. My mom is Italian American and she really is Italian—she speaks Italian fluently. I've been to Italy five times, and we have a lot of connections there. We still practice a lot of the traditions that many Italians have lost in terms of family dinners and everything family orientated.

I'm from the city. I went to Junipero Serra Elementary School right down the block, Horace Mann Middle School in the Mission, then Philip Burton in the Bayview. I'm presently at San Francisco State trying to graduate—a history major. My plans are to work for a while and save some money. I want to apply for a community job in the trenches, particularly in low-income housing. I have a deep, heartfelt interest in that. I then want to learn Spanish, come back to school and get my teaching credentials, and be a high school history teacher.

In my household growing up I was exposed to everybody you could think of. My first baby-sitter was Chicana. Throughout my life I've been exposed to so many people of different backgrounds, particularly Black people. My mom's best friends (whose son became my best friend) are

Black. On the Filipino side, because my grandfather was an orphan, we didn't have any blood kinfolks. I've had to learn over time my Filipino family. People look at me and say they don't think I'm Filipino. With the young Filipinos that are doing things in the Bay Area around the World War II veterans and the International Hotel, they're just like my family.

I have a white family—an Italian family from the suburbs and Mt. Shasta—and we have a real sense of identity. I also have cousins from Stanford and cousins locked up in prison. I got family from the hills of Oakland to family in the flatlands. I got family in the South—Tennessee, Alabama—"white trash" family who I completely love. I love white trash, I don't care what people say, because it's a deeper connection than just working-class values. I define "white trash" as working-class white people. The white skin privilege—they didn't necessarily get that, and they're working side by side. Race is a big question with them, because people in power have preyed on their fears and used racism as a way to keep separation. My sister married this guy from Alabama, Randy—white trash—and I completely love him and his daughter.

Given I come from a household of ex-Communists and progressives and have seen all nationalities in my house—white people, Asians, gays—my identity was never a question, I really didn't know what it meant. My best friend was Black, and I was like, "I must be that, too," and my baby-sitter speaks Spanish, and I really didn't trip on that. I took pride in who I was. But my first experience questioning race and what I was all about happened when I was a freshman in high school. Every Thanksgiving my dad would go to L.A. to see my sister, and my mom would go up to Mt. Shasta to visit her relatives. For four or five years I would go to Kendra and Franklin Alexander's house for Thanksgiving. Their son Jordan is my best friend. They're African American. Kendra was my godmother. There was no one closer to me other than my mother and grandmother.

This one year we went up to Lake Tahoe, and at the time Franklin worked at Esprit. They had this big cabin at Lake Tahoe, and we got to go up there for a week. (At the time there were these two other white girls staying there, twenty-six or twenty-seven years old.) Our tradition was to have a night out on the town at a casino, but before that, we had a nice big dinner with steaks and potatoes, and everyone was digesting and sipping some champagne. After dinner, Jordan and I were playing Monopoly, and these two white girls walk in, and they were immediately shocked to find a whole house full of Black people. They didn't know how to handle the situation. Kendra was in the kitchen finishing cleaning up, and they came in and said something like, "Oh, we're so happy you cleaned up after yourselves," and Kendra completely flipped out. "What do you mean, because we're Black? That we're supposed to be cleaning up after you because you're white? That we don't have the privilege of being here?" She went on and on, and these white girls were scared. They went up to their rooms for at least two hours! All of this heated emotion went on, and I had never really seen this kind of racial thing go down. These white girls looked like my blood cousins. I started thinking about things, and I went to the mirror. At the time I had my varsity baseball, my Wilson jersey, and I had my hair long, so I kind of looked like Jose Canseco. "I really don't look like these Black people—my hair ain't kinky," and I was looking at my skin. Something's going on here. I came back downstairs, and the white girls had come down, too. They were talking, and Kendra apologized but also explained to them what went down, how it hurt and the history behind their statement.

We left Tahoe Saturday night, and after thinking about all this—race and what I am and white people and Black people and Filipino—and knowing who my family is, knowing who my loved ones are, knowing who hugged me and gave our family coats when we were on welfare—I know who they were. So we returned to Jordan's house Saturday night. He lived in Berkeley, right on the edge of Oakland. Jordan's friend Asani lived right up the block in a big old house with three stories, and there was like five birthdays, two graduation parties, celebrations—just like that Marvin Gaye record—and the house was completely packed with people. His mom and grandmom asked, "Are you hungry? Get your food, and if you don't want none, you'd better say somethin'!" and people are dancing, playing dominoes, smoking, drinking, talking loud. I've been to his house many times, and I was comfortable. I remember sitting at the bottom of the stairs in the middle of everything and looking around. I probably would have never thought this because I never questioned what I was, or my relationship between me and Black people, and I thought, "Man, there's a lot of Black people here. I'm like the only one that's not," in terms of kinky hair and dark skin and slavery and all that. But I felt this is where I feel more comfortable than any other place. I discovered something about me.

The next day my mom picked me up, and I went to a meeting with her in the East Bay. At the meeting I was looking around and I thought, something's not right about this meeting, somebody's not here. What I realized was there were no Black people there, and at that point in my life I came to an understanding that I've always felt connected with Black people, and I've always known that something ain't right if Black people ain't there. Not that they have to be there, but in terms of looking at the presidents, looking at the teachers, looking at all the things we see, something's not right.

Black is beautiful. You see all these young Asians, Latinos, sisters and brothers, white kids, they're Black culture if you want to get down to it in terms of the music, the dialogue, the slang, the hip-hop, the walk—all that stuff. I know I'm not African American, but I know that in terms of my history and culture, and with my dad growing up in the Fillmore —I grew up with him coming home from work, cracking open a beer, and listening to Marvin Gaye.

I know I have a very unique upbringing in terms of my home. In terms of race, I know that sometimes white people can trigger things in my heart that no other people could, just like an anger in there—certain words. How I explain 1998 racism, particularly with white people, is that they don't understand their own racism. We all want to live together in a multicultural society, but they don't understand how they've been brought up to believe that what they think is right, and what others might say may not be as valid. They've been taught that they're right and others should be copying their way of living.

My first day on the job, it's not accidental that the first people I talk to and make friends with are Black people, just because I have a comfortability like no other people. There's nothing patronizing about it—it just came from family. At Christmas we have a huge Sorro family thing, and we'd always have a Kwanza celebration. I'm not African American, but there's something Black—and I know what it is for me.

Race is so confusing. One of my friends, Gus, is Greek. His parents hardly speak any English. They work in a produce market. He's European Greek—he ain't white, OK? He's like a third-world European, like some of the Russians here. Two of my best friends, Ivan (whose father is a city attorney) and Adam, are both white. A lot of things about race is your experiences with people of color—your experiences with other white people and being able to see other things and not be isolated in life. Ivan went to private school, grew up with middle-upper-middle-class kids. We have deep discussions about race. He's like, "Why can't people just look at people for who they are," and sometimes a lot of fears come out because when he's around people of color, particularly working-class who may talk loud and get down and dirty, he's kind of insecure. He thinks everyone is looking at him as a white boy, an oppressor, someone who's trying to bite off people's culture, but nobody is looking at him like that. He's told me that if he had to redo it, he would have gone to public schools because he's felt segregated away from other kids. But he's different from a lot of kids because he wants to learn. He knows that this race thing isn't right. You can feel it. People with good hearts is basically what it all comes down to, and Ivan's one of them.

Adam, on the other hand, grew up here in Bernal Heights and was the only white kid in all the schools. There never was an incident about Adam being the white boy because he never perpetrated. Adam was just Adam, and all his girlfriends and friends have been people of color. That's how he grew up. So those are two very different experiences.

I'm a firm believer in public schools. A big thing happened with my nephew who lives in Modesto. My brother is a fireman; he's Filipino and grew up in the ghetto. They tried to get away from everything the ghetto was. He married this nice woman who's Portuguese and Italian and comes from a real good working-class background. But like white people over time, they've been striving for that middle-class lifestyle. The whole thing came down to my nephew.

Modesto is a completely segregated place. You got the Chicanos, the Blacks, the Southeast Asians on one side, and you've got the middle-class whites on the other side, and it came down to where my nephew was going to go to high school. Modesto High is where the Blacks, Latinos, Asians, and working-class whites go. That's the school that's stigmatized, like you're not going to get as good an education, there might be a little bit of a problem with crime. The white high school has drugs and problems there, but those aren't talked about, because "white" can't be looked upon as something that's failing. I firmly believed he should go to Modesto High because that's his people. He's Filipino. His father was born in the projects. His father knows what that meant. That's where my nephew wants to go. His mom wanted him to go to the white school and get the best education, but he's going to Modesto High. Like my friend Ivan said, "I'd rather have gone to a public school, and maybe I didn't read 400 books and my academic standard and vocabulary might not be at this level, but I would learn people experience, and that's important."

You could read all you want about racism, but unless you make an attempt to try to talk with some Black people—talk to them—you're not going to know. And this is the future of America on the left. And these white kids are going to be looking to them—young Cambodians and Latinos and Chicanos—and they already are, as a source of guidance. And I say guidance because white culture is offering nothing. My ideal is to take 50 percent of the white kids and put them here and there because we all need to go to school together, so we can learn to grow together.

Another example of racism that angers me so much: I'm working at the E.R. Teller School in Bayview–Hunter's Point in an after-school program. It's designed to help the elementary school kids with the lowest test scores improve them. Eighty percent of the kids are Black, with some Latino kids, and they're some of the most intelligent kids you could meet in the world. It's not that these kids can't do the work, it's behavior problems there. Home stuff. There is not a white kid at that school. (One Russian kid, and he's tough.) We're in this meeting of all the teachers and counselors, and there was one Black woman and one Latino who's the secretary, and twenty white teachers. I can understand why some of the older white teachers were there, who had been there for fifteen years—good people, tremendous—but it hurts my heart to see the new people they're hiring. We need people of color teaching in our schools. And these teachers, fresh from Northwestern, Cal Berkeley, Temple University, they're still not hiring people of color.

The shit came down about this one student whose daddy is locked up and his mama went to jail a week before. This boy was completely out of control, and I sat there and listened to these white people say, "What is wrong with this kid's family? Don't they want him to learn? Why don't they bring him to school?" I heard this and it burnt my heart so fuckin' bad to hear white people talking about "Black people don't even understand how important education is for the children," when Black people were hung from trees to put their children to school. They know better than anybody on this planet how important education is. I yelled, "You know, you don't fuckin' understand as a white person coming into this community, there's not a white kid in this school. You don't fuckin' know what's going on here. You don't know our culture, our history, what we go through, that these children need help because their mama's gotta wake up and work twelve-hour shifts, that maybe like Jeffrey's mama, are locked up. You don't know all the family stuff that's taking place here." It is inexcusable to have a school of 1,000 Black children and have 90 percent of the teachers white.

There's a Black woman at Philip Burton High School who, if she was not Black, would be convicted of all the racist theories you could ever possess. But she's a Black woman heading up this academic high school for kids of color, and it's the farthest thing from academics. All it is is a behavior school. If you can shut up and keep your mouth closed, then you'll graduate, but if you have problems behaviorally, you're gone.

She wanted to create this school with a higher academic standard— it was supposed to be a Lowell for the other side of town. They strove to be like Lowell, but the kids did not have the same background. When I started out at Burton, 30 percent of my freshman class was Black. When I graduated, seven Black students crossed that stage. Is that a successful school for Bayview–Hunter's Point? That's our 1999 racism. It's how we value education, how we value what's a solid citizen, a well-balanced human being. Kids at Burton don't feel valued there, if you cannot stay with the pace. I graduated there not knowing how to read or spell, I swear to God. It was not an academic school. It's such a political tool for this city that's saying, "Look, we have this great academic school, children are taking more and more units and college prep classes." But we were all graduating dumb, without confidence and a love for reading, or finding the beauty in writing or the imagination of science. They were setting standards but not encouraging and developing minds. No thinking. I wouldn't have gotten into State if it weren't for the program called Step to College.

When we talk about race it gets confusing, because there are class issues involved. And that's a big one, but in my view, I use "White" as a metaphor, or an image that goes beyond skin color. "White" to me, over the last 400 years, represents individualism over community—more competition—it represents a false sense of power. "White" has become an image of intellect, an image of something that's clean and neat and proper. "White" has become something that others should strive toward —and if you want to be accepted, you have to be articulate and you can't have the "street" in you—so what I'm talking about is this image. That's what gentrification is to me—whiteness.

Things eat at my heart when I see racism, like some of these white people who come into Bernal Heights and the Neighborhood Center. Maybe they're good-hearted and don't want to see children suffer, but to ask the question as someone recently did: "What is the gang prevention program there for? What is this doing for my kid?" Unbelievable.

In order to deal with racism, they must recognize where they stand as white persons. They need to recognize what they can do to deal with their own shit, they got to. But white people don't, because for so long, no one's told them they're wrong. No one's told them to rethink that, or that their opinion is biased, because they've been taught their whole life that they are right. ■■■

Joaquin Sorro is the younger son of Bill and Hule. Although he looks white, he proudly identifies racially and culturally as an Italian Filipino. Joaquin was very active in Filipino issues at San Francisco City College, where he was a student. He strongly believes that the direction we're going is a "mestizo-type people. You're not even going to be able to call them a racial word."

Giulio and Joaquin Sorro
as little boys

Giulio and Joaquin
Sorro today

JOAQUIN SORRO

I come from a strong Italian family and Filipino family. Because my father's white mother was disowned by her family for marrying a man of color, there's no history between our family and my grandmother's Spanish side. So I just say that I'm Italian and Filipino. My father has taken on the Filipino culture, but we still don't have a big Filipino family in the Philippines. My Italian family here has been very strong because I have an Italian grandmother and Italian family. I've always believed that my Italian side is superior to my Filipino side because I was never exposed to strong Filipino things. My favorite actors are Italian; I love biking, which is one of the biggest events in Italian history; my favorite food is Italian. I think I've been "Italianized!" I eat lumpia and adobo, but I don't know much about Filipino culture. My dad fixes soul food, Chinese and Filipino. He grew up in the Fillmore, and he's more a San Franciscan Filipino American.

With my skin being the color it is, Filipino doesn't show up in me physically. Italian shows up in me physically in my hair and nose, so I've always stayed with that. My father and I were having this conversation the other day about why I'm still so attached to Italy. The many times I visited and worked there in the past I really saw the "Italianness" in me. When I was there I felt such comfort.

I've lived in Italy, but I've yet to go to the Philippines. I'm in a PEACE Club (Philippinos for Education, Art, Culture, and Empowerment) at City College. We don't have an Italian Club there. I've been working with the Filipino veterans who fought in World War II. In the last couple of years of my life I've seen myself as more Filipino Italian because through lectures and books, I've been able to learn more about the Filipino culture than ever before.

I've had a hard time identifying with being Filipino because I've seen a lack of energy there. The Filipinos I work with at City College are more interested in clothes and Nike shoes than helping out elders in the Tenderloin. There's a large percentage of Filipinos at City College, and only six in our group who are working with Filipinos. They're so caught up in hip-hop and rap they don't even want to help and learn about their own. These are people who have been colonized. Eighty percent of the Filipinos are Catholic. I see the Catholic religion as one of the most useful psychological methods of brainwashing. I still don't understand why so many Filipinos are loyal to a religion that colonized them. It's so complex, but I don't see myself as part of the Filipino culture.

I don't know who to identify with. I see Robert DeNiro out there and Georgio Armani and Michaelangelo and Pacino. In the Filipino culture you don't have anybody doing anything, except for the Bill Sorros, Al Robles, and Emil deGuzmans here in San Francisco. I see Filipino Americans—and this is going to sound blunt—as dumb, deaf, and blind. I'm just a quarter Filipino, but I'm mad at what Spain has done, and I try to talk with some Filipinos about it, and they don't care. We've got these World War II Filipino veterans who fought hard for this country, and we ask for help to document these men, and the students ask, "Is there going to be food at the meeting?" I'm still involved because I'm doing it for the people and trying to understand Filipinos in our country, but on one level I'm extremely disappointed in them.

When a girl that I like asks me what nationality I am, I can't wait to say "Filipino Italian." It's not like your normal American. When I ask people what they are, they say, "I'm American," like they don't know who they are or where they come from. I definitely don't feel like your "normal American." Here in San Francisco, just knowing some of the history of the Filipinos who first came here—they came without wives for many years —it's no surprise that you see a lot of people who are Mexican Filipino, for example. My grandfather met my grandmother here. In California you have a lot of Filipinos who are mixed. It's not a new race, but you're going to meet a lot of mixed-race people, especially in San Francisco.

I've always wanted to go to other parts of the country where there's a strong American culture and let them know where I'm coming from. I have a buddy who is going to school in North Carolina. Because he has long hair, he's already looked upon as "not normal." I have other friends going to school around the country, and they're saying, "It's so boring out here. Everybody's the same bread and butter." Maybe because I'm between lumpia and pizza I'm not that kid named "Joe Thomas." I'm Joaquin Sorro, Italian Filipino, and it just rings.

When you look at my father, he doesn't look like a normal Filipino. He looks like he has a mixed influence as well. He's a mestizo man. He always used to tell me that we're mestizo—blood mixed with Spanish blood.

It's always a trip when we have family gatherings. My folks always talk about opening a restaurant called FBI: Filipino, Black, and Italian. We have food from all over the world, and people too. My parents are two open and intelligent people coming together, and just imagine what the by-product of that is going to be. That's how I see myself and my brother. We're not simple people. I'm always curious where people come from. So many look like they could be many races, like us. I consider myself an extraordinary person, so when I look at people I often wonder where their parents came from to make the person in front of me.

I went to Wallenberg High School, which was made up of a lot of Asians—Chinese, Vietnamese, Japanese, Cambodian, Filipino, Eastern Pacific Islanders. There may have been 2 percent Black, 3 percent Latino, 10 percent white. Because it was such a small school, everybody hung out with each other. My best friend was Black and Japanese. Two other friends were Nicaraguan and Italian, one was Jewish and Greek, and one Vietnamese. That was our clique, and we looked like a damn rainbow. We separated ourselves from everybody (that's because we thought we were better than everybody!). We had everything covered, and we were cool with everybody. In our minds, we were the hottest shit in the school.

I want to be lots of things, but ten dimensional—a teacher, psychologist, a chef, an actor—not just one thing. I'm not just one race. I'm a Communist "red diaper" baby, and that is a huge part of my history. Being exposed to a lot of stuff here and abroad has made me who I am, and I'd like to do that for my son or daughter in the future.

I want to marry and have kids with an Italian Filipino woman. I want to raise my kids in Italy until they're twelve-fourteen years old, then move back here. It's a strong culture there. Living in Italy for a year opened my mind and way of thinking. I also want to go to the Philippines and see what's going on there. I don't even like Filipino food, but I can't really make that judgment until I taste real Filipino food. The Italian food here in the city is terrible. In Italy, now that's real Italian food!

Here's how I see the race issue: If an Israeli marries a Palestinian, these are two hot backgrounds. I'm not saying it makes stronger love, but their child will go into this world and be part of this big change. There's a power in multiracial relationships that I was trying to tell my father. The world is getting closer and closer to each other.

When Africans were enslaved here, nobody thought they'd become African Americans and someday participate in our government, and now we have Black Filipinos and Black Italians. You go to Latin America and you'll have everything from the lightest complexion to the darkest, and now these people are called Nicaraguans or El Salvadorans or whatever.

Throughout history, people have really fucked up with negative intention (like slavery, manifest destiny, and imperialism), but people are coming together on different color levels, and you're not going to have this one race where Chinese are just Chinese and Italians Italian. The direction we're heading is mestizo-type people. You're not even going to be able to call them a racial word. ▪▪▪

My mother's parents were immigrants from Piedmont, Italy. They arrived in 1906 with my aunt Angelina, who was only two years old. My grandparents, whom I never knew, came from a mining community in northern Italy and moved to another one named Dawson, in northeastern New Mexico. My mother was born in 1908 and was christened Secondina Perdomo in the town's only Catholic church. Her brother, Frederick, was born four years later.

After my mother died in 1982, I kept her Dawson High School scrapbook, a collection of memories she carried with her from Dawson to Marshall, Tomales, San Francisco, and lastly Long Beach, California. A typical example is the yellowed newspaper article in the *Dawson, New Mexico, News,* Thursday, May 26, 1927: "One of the largest audiences ever assembled in the Dawson opera house was present Friday night to see the senior class play,

Angelina, Secondina (my mother), and Frederick Perdomo in Dawson, New Mexico, circa 1918

'Miss Molly,' which was presented by the class of '27 under the direction of Miss Naomi Underwood. The personnel in the chorus included Josephine McDermott, Sentina Albani, and Secondina Perdomo."

I delighted in her classmate portrayals : "Sentina Albani, the chatterbox of DHS whose vocabulary has no finis; whose velocity is unmentionable. We have gone through the same torture together. Rudi Brozovich, or Brick Top is a rather good fellow — bashful, and O-h-h-h my — you should see the freckles. Genevieve Hotchkiss, our DHS basketball star — not stuck up. Amelia

Lopez, a very sweet Spanish girl, a good singer and piano player. Erminio Maruzzi, known as Joe in our play. Sat across from me in English Lit and read modern literature instead of the English novels we read. Clever indeed."

My favorite handwritten note was from one of her Dawson High School teachers: "In the future may you be as successful as you have been in DHS. My memory of you will always be filled with your jolly laugh and your remark 'I'm here' when you came into class nearly $\frac{1}{2}$ minute late sometimes. Edith Calhoun"

In 1994, twelve years after my mother died, I finally visited her hometown of Dawson, New Mexico, for the first time. I had learned from my cousin Doris about a biannual picnic that has taken place there ever since the mining company shut down and dismantled the town for scrap in 1950.

I decided it was time to see the place of her birth and growth to womanhood. It was also a longing to reconnect with her in a way we never could in life, and to find out why her father disappeared so many years ago. I made plans to join my cousins Joe and Ray at that year's picnic on Labor Day weekend.

After a night in Taos, I headed northeast toward Dawson on Route 64, a two-hour drive through Angel Fire, the Vietnam Veterans Chapel, around the mountainous road in Carson Forest, and down to the small village of Cimarron in the flat sagebrush desert.

Joe said to look for a small road off to the left about eleven miles north of Cimarron. "The only sign is for the Dawson Cemetery, so look closely or you'll miss it," he told me. I watched my odometer and found the turnoff easily. I drove onto a two-mile dirt road that passed the historic cemetery and a

Mom in front of the Catholic church in Dawson, New Mexico

large metal gate, open wide for the picnic traffic. I was greeted by a tall friendly man handing out key chains that read, "DAWSON PICNIC 1994." There were dozens of cars, trucks, and RVs parked all along what looked to be the town's old main street. I parked toward the end and found Joe and Ray sitting under a large shade tree near the road. We greeted each other warmly. Ray is heavier now but still has his jocular walk and broad smile. Joe is also aging well, tall and handsome as ever, still the artist and lover of life.

There is nothing left of the once flourishing town of 8,000 except for the historic cemetery, a couple of small buildings, and remnants of the coke ovens and smokestacks. Gone are Dawson High School, where my mother, Aunt Angelina, and Uncle Freddy graduated; St. John the Baptist Catholic Church, where they were all baptized; and the simple wooden home in the Italian "suburb" of Loreta where they grew up. At one time, Dawson boasted an opera house, a large community swimming pool, and a department store where you could buy everything from a fur coat to screwdrivers. Toby Smith wrote in his book called *Coaltown*:

> If Dawson is anything, it is a town of neighborhoods. Though Dawson is known as the place where people get along, segregation typically exists in those neighborhoods. Simply, people in Dawson want to live among their own nationality. The Italians and Slavs and Greeks set-
>
> tled most of Number Seven Camp, established to serve Mines Seven, Eight, and Nine. Italians and Hispanics make up Capitan, both Old Capitan and New. More Hispanics dominate Five Hill. For the most part, Anglos are downtown, in the houses that edge Main Street. . . . If you go way up past Mine Number Six, you'll probably meet the most pleasant Black man, Charley Burrell. He'll be hauling water with his half-dozen or so Black neighbors, in a nice place with a terrible name: Coontown. Save for an abbreviated Ku Klux Klan incident, racial problems in Dawson are nonexistent, because Phelps Dodge will not tolerate discrimination.

My cousin Ray Laval (Angelina's son) and me on the steps of what remains of Dawson High School, 1994

I've been told that my mother was the spitting image of her mother, who died before I was born. Unlike Aunt Angie and Uncle Fred, whose Italian hair and eyes were dark brown, her hair was blonde and eyes light blue. I looked so much like her that one of the women I met at the picnic, at age eighty-seven, mistook me for her and began calling me "Secondina."

My favorite Dawsonite that day was an elderly, thin, spirited man who actually knew my grandfather. "I used to deliver groceries out to Loreta when I was a young man. I remember your grandfather well!" he boasted. "He was a rogue, and could he drink! I pulled a trick on him once, I'll never forget. One night when he really had one tied on, I snuck a few grams of dynamite in his pipe to give him a little kick. Boy did it ever! He thought his wife was the culprit, and was he mad!" The old man howled with laughter as if the trick had happened yesterday, not over seventy years ago. I asked him if he knew whatever happened to my grandfather, and he didn't. I lingered past our conversation. This old man was the only human being I'd ever met who gave me a glimpse of my grandfather's character and his presence in this distant place.

Even at the time of her death in 1982, my mother had never told me of her father's leaving Dawson, nor did I ever think to ask. She'd only say, "My father was the town cobbler and repaired all the miners' boots, and boy, were there a lot of them!" Did Grandma tire of his drinking and throw him out? Did he return to Italy? How did Grandma and the family survive after he left? "I'm so glad I left Dawson when I did," Mother would quickly continue. "I lived through two funerals of over 100 men each. It was dreadful. The first one was in 1913. I was only five years old — too young to know that the black box I sat on was a casket. 'No, no, Dina!' my mother scolded, and abruptly pulled me off. After the second large blast ten years later, I told myself I'd never marry a miner. Never."

After a simple picnic lunch, my cousin Ray and I decided to hike up to the site of the old high school where our mothers had graduated over sixty-five years ago. It was built on the highest hill in town, and with the help of some native Dawsonites, we made our way up a steep path to a large plateau, seeing ahead what was left of the huge stone foundation and the wide granite stairs leading up to where the large front doors of our mothers' high school had once stood. We sat quietly on the steps, looking out to the magnificent view of the rudbekia-laden hills and the valley below that used to be the town of Dawson.

Walking around the ruined building, I could imagine hearing some of those voices from a time long past and felt a closeness to my mother I hadn't felt in years. Here in Dawson she was her own person with her own dreams. But she would leave this mining town three years after graduating from Dawson High School. With her mother Henrietta, her sister Angelina and brother-in-law Raymond, and their young son Joseph, she moved to San Francisco to begin a new life.

Mauricio Vela followed me as executive director of the Bernal Heights Neighborhood Center in 1998. We worked together for over nine years. Both his sons, Carlos and Eddie, attend public schools, and Mauricio continues to be a dedicated advocate in the educational, Latino, and youth communities of San Francisco. His life's epiphany came during the year he spent in jail.

MAURICIO VELA

I was born on December 18, 1959, at Mary's Help Hospital, which no longer exists. My mother was a nurse who worked there, then she moved on to St. Luke's and retired from there.

I'm the youngest son of eight children, the youngest son of my mother's five and my dad's eight children. I consider all three of my father's first children my brothers and sister. We first lived by the Levi-Strauss Factory on Valencia Street on Clinton Park Alley, then moved to the house on 30th Street and Noe right before I was born. My parents have been there for forty years. Both of them are immigrants from El Salvador, from San Salvador. My mother came over as a nurse and first lived in Philadelphia. I remember her telling me she didn't like the snow. It was too cold! My dad was a journalist in El Salvador and wanted to be a lawyer, but he didn't speak English, so he got involved in other activities. He was a successful businessman in terms of being a notary public, someone who did taxes for people, and helped people immigrate to the United States. He was always located on Mission Street, serving the Latin community. There's a term called "Algun que sabe," which is "someone who knows," so people would say, "Go see Mr. Vela, because he knows." He then spoke English and Spanish, so people who would need an intermediary would see my dad.

Mauricio Vela as a little boy in San Francisco

My dad was always out working seven days a week and still does to this day. He's eighty years old now, born in 1918. My mother worked as a nurse three days a week, so she was the primary caregiver in rearing the children—getting us into activities and out of trouble. Noe Valley at that time was mainly Irish, Italian, and Latino. There were very few African Americans at St. Paul's where I went to school, but those of us there got along with everybody. I remember John F. Kennedy getting killed, and Martin Luther King because of all the media and the significance of it. That was the first "race" thing that stuck with me. I remember when Shirley Chisholm ran for president in 1972—this woman is running, and she's Black.

I started Sacred Heart High School in 1973, and that's when race became a factor. Immediately I hung out with my friends from St. Paul's. It was a segregated school, in that the white kids sat together, the Black kids sat together, the Filipinos sat together, the nerds sat together, and Latins from the Mission sat together. It was self-segregation and there was some name-calling because I had an Afro, and we wore polyester shirts with wide collars, and platforms. Just like the zoot suits in the 1940s, we liked flash. My friend Michael Lopez wore a long coat with a fur collar, and they'd ask, "Is that your sister's coat?" Kids would make fun of my kinky hair. I wanted straight hair, so I slept with a nylon on my head to try and make it go back. People would even call me "nigger," but I had naturally curly hair, so in my junior and senior years I let it grow into an Afro.

Mauricio Vela, on the right, with his friend Ron at San Francisco City College

As I moved through high school, I hung with the Latinos out of natural interests, mutual support, and a need to identify—plus just the boredom of the Noe Valley playground, where mostly the white guys just wanted to hang, get drunk, and freeze at night. I wanted to go to the Mission and cruise and chase girls. Also, the Sacred Heart spirit was great. The teams were all integrated, and I got to know a lot of white guys because my best friend Tom Sandoval, a Latino, was a star on the team. We went to a lot of the parties in other communities, like the Marina Greens, the Sunset, and Ocean Beach.

The other thing is the girls liked us because we were brown. When we went to all these places, we were new to them. We had brown skin tone and it was an asset, because there were all these pale faces! They would like us, and that was another plus. They liked to dance and weren't so stiff. I don't mean to stereotype, but the girls liked Latin guys because we were different for them. They were experiencing something new, reaching out and testing.

The counselor at Sacred Heart, Mr. Teppes, assigned me and my friend Ray Torres to take the military test, because in his view, that's where our potential was. (Ray now has a doctorate in geology and grew up in the Bayview with African Americans.) I clearly remember both of us sitting at the table and saying, "Screw this, we're not going into the military. Why would we want to go into the military? We're going to college or have some fun," so we tore up our sheets and left. We weren't invited to the college presentations either. They always came to Sacred Heart, but we weren't invited.

After high school I was working at Safeway here in the neighborhood at 30th and Mission, got into low riding, put on more of a Latin persona, got more into the problems, into the drugs and violence. I started going to City College trying to figure out what I wanted to do. I wanted to be a cop. Race played a part in that decision, too. I always thought as a kid the white guys in white hats, like John Wayne, were the good guys. The bad guys were always darker. Also in high school we were always pulled over. My friend Tom had a lime green '63 Impala with two Black *Playboy* bunnies on the side. When the cops saw us, they'd be behind in thirty seconds! If they couldn't get us for something, they could harass us. They'd say, "All right, Vela, get out of the car." I'd ask, "What for, man? I'm not doin' nothing, just driving around." "Get out of the car or we're taking you to Ingleside Station," so I'd run home and tell Tom to meet me at the park. The good thing is that we went to Sacred Heart, and they'd treat us OK because we were Catholic school

Bell-bottomed Mauricio Vela with his mother and sisters

guys, but shitheads because we were Latinos. There were a lot of cops who came out of Sacred Heart. The joke was that St. Ignatius produces the lawyers and Sacred Heart produces the cops and firefighters. My girlfriend's father was a cop, so it was a power thing. I was attracted to power and still am.

In February of 1980 I got arrested and was incarcerated for a year with three years' probation. I got to jail and immediately connected with the Latinos. You had to hang, so you said, "What's up?" to the Latin guys first. I also connected with the white guys from the Excelsior who took care of me because they knew my girlfriend Sue's family. They helped me be a painter at the jail at night. I also became a trustee because I knew how to read, write, and speak Spanish. The guys from the Excelsior had the plush jobs because the guards tended to be white and took care of their own.

There was commerce in the jail. You'd trade cigarettes for pressed clothes. You'd get nice stuff if you paid for it, you'd get drugs if you paid for it. There were guards who'd get you drugs and bring them in. You'd just have your outside person go to the guard's house and give him money and he'd bring the drugs in. You'd pay double, but you'd get what you needed, and he'd get what he'd needed. It was just commerce.

The jail was very race defined. The whites stuck with the whites, the Blacks with the Blacks, and the Latins with the Latins. If you were alone, you'd get jacked up and your stuff taken away from you, or beat up because you were alone. I was able to get a work furlough for my job at Safeway, but I had a drug problem and screwed up. I needed to dry out, and that's the way God works. He put me in there to think about what I was doing. The second time I got rolled up was around the Fourth of July and I was crying, feeling like an animal locked in a cage. We were throwing around toilet rolls as part of our Fourth of July celebration and I was asking myself, "Why am I here in this tiny cell throwing these rolls?" It was a traumatic evening in my life. No more work furloughs. No more freedom. "You're here for eight more months."

In 1981 I got out of jail, married Sue, and returned to City College. I got involved with La Raza Unida, a Latin group on campus which really turned me on to Central American politics and made me feel proud of my heritage and background. There was a Filipino group and an African American group, and again you could see the race divide, but we also worked together on different events. I had leadership skills, even as a kid, and would take charge. I also became more aware of the politics of the United States and how they were exploiting third-world countries, brought war to other countries, or supported regimes that were unfair to their people. I was beginning to wake up and say, "This is really screwed," and started to get a broader perspective about the world and not just my own life. I ran for student government, became a senator, then a vice president, and we fought City College around the issue of tuition. They wanted to raise tuition. It was free when I first got there, and I said, "If you raise tuition now it's going to open Pandora's box and keep going up and up and exclude people." And sure enough it did—and still does.

A white counselor at City College told me not to apply for Cal Berkeley because I wasn't going to get in. I applied anyway and got in because of affirmative action. No doubt. I wasn't a highly skilled student. I had like a 3.0. I was a Latino, and that's how I got in.

Cal was a very rewarding and eye-opening experience. I was a Chicano studies major and learned about the American minorities and their disenfranchisement by white people, the loss of the Southwest by Mexico, the Filipino farmworkers in Washington, the Native American struggles—I got to see other injustice throughout the United States. I was part of MECHA, the student movement of Chicanos and Aztlan (a mythical land, mostly in the southwest). There were very few Latinos on campus then, and probably less now because of the elimination of affirmative action. We hung together and worked with other students around the issue of apartheid.

Desmond Tutu came to the campus, and we worked hard to force the school to stop doing business with corporations doing business with South Africa. There was also a big fight because a white fraternity had Cinco de Mayo parties where they'd put up barbed wire and you had to have a green card to get in. They beat up a lot of Chicanos one night who went to protest the insult. The fraternity ended up being closed for a year. Race was very clear. These guys were from privileged families and didn't understand a thing about how we got there and thought we didn't deserve to be there because of affirmative action. We'd have discussions about affirmative action, and they'd say, "Well, maybe my grandparents screwed you, but I shouldn't have to pay." We'd say, "We don't have the same background or resources you have. We're trying to level the playing field so we can all produce."

In my Chicano studies class, Larry Trujillo was a criminal justice professor and was showing photos. Sure enough, one of the slides was of me and all the Latino guys in jail with our blue jeans, goatee, and mustache, our hair longer than our ears. It was funny when my classmates were sitting there (I didn't tell anyone I was in jail), and saw me on the screen. They'd look at me and back at the screen. "Mauricio! That's you!" And the professor didn't know it at the time either. It was good because I was able to use that experience to teach my fellow students about the criminal justice system and issues around being incarcerated. They got a better sense because I'd tell them, "Look, I was in there, but now I'm next to you."

My experiences at Cal really made me want to work in my community. So after I graduated I came back to work at Jamestown in the West Mission. It's a community center that's part of the Catholic Youth Organization. It had an animal room, a library, tutoring, a boxing ring, and weights. We also went on field trips and summer outings. It was primarily serving Latino clients, trying to be a role model and give back to the community. We gave many kids their first jobs, and I'd work with them to make sure they had a successful experience. We taught them life skills and had substance abuse and family planning workshops—getting them to think before they act.

In 1989 I moved on to the Bernal Heights Neighborhood Center and got involved with other efforts citywide—Youth Employment Coalition and Coleman Advocates for Youth. I had my second child in 1987 and bought a house in 1989. We couldn't afford private school for Carlos, our oldest son, so we got him into a good public school.

In Bernal back then there were a lot of problems on the streets, drugs and unemployment, people living in commercial spaces, problems with public housing. We worked hard on those issues and built pride in the community. More recently, though, a lot of people from higher economic brackets are moving in and pushing out the poor families.

Everything we've done at the Neighborhood Center has been to try and build community, and we're losing that sense—becoming more isolated and individualized. We have a lot of work to do if we're going to keep Bernal mixed and work with the Black families, the Filipino families, the Latin families. It's important that we become more conscious of the changing neighborhood, the class and economics of the neighborhood.

I've been involved with the Latino Democratic Club because we need representation—and all the disenfranchisement has been as a result of the lack of representation and power. Consciously I've been trying to build a Latin movement. Although we've not been successful, we keep trying. I'm now working with District 9, a new Democratic Club that contains the Mission District and Bernal Heights. It was cut to elect a Latino supervisor. We won't be able to do that in the year 2000, but hopefully in the future we'll be organized enough to do it.

I've run for the school board, and the race factor is always there. This last time we tried to cut it more as a parent and youth advocate than my just being a Latino. We tried to get the campaign away from the race base, but people still pigeonhole seats.

I continue to appreciate San Francisco. Its diversity has taught me a lot, and I believe I'm the person I am because I've lived here and worked with different groups. But it's becoming very difficult to live here. I was disappointed last week when I read about Lowell High School—ninety-eight Latinos were admitted in the 1998–99 class, and this year it's down to forty-four Latinos. That's very depressing because I worry about Eddie, my younger son, getting in. We're not getting equal access to the quality education that one needs to succeed. It's hard for me not to be angry at the Chinese because they filed a suit, but both the Black and Latino student populations have been reduced by half in this year's freshman class. It worries me that we're pitting ourselves against each other when there are other high schools we should be fixing.

The issue of race is scary. I was thinking of the urban military exercise the army wanted to do here and ended up doing in Oakland recently. It's like the government is getting prepared for when the masses revolt so they can suppress us. These guys are getting ready for urban war. It may not be true, and I might be paranoid, but I think we're going to get fed up between the haves and have-nots. It's getting worse, and we're going to revolt because you can only push someone so far.

We're going to have a lot more people of color in California, and that's a good thing. But unless we figure out how to economically bring people to a survival level, we're going to have a lot of problems because we'll be fighting over the crumbs. If we don't establish policies to keep people of color here, San Francisco will become an upper-class all-white city in ten or twenty years. I don't have a solution, only that more people need to struggle with it and more policies put in place to safeguard against pushing more poor people out. ■■■

I met Lynette Lee through my affordable housing work at the Bernal Heights Neighborhood Center. She is the soft-spoken but very persuasive executive director of a multiracial community development agency in the heart of Oakland. Even though its name is the East Bay Asian Local Development Corporation (EBALDC), Lynette has built strong bridges not only within Oakland's diverse Asian community but also with the city's many other ethnic communities. Her story clearly shows that by working together toward common goals, we can overcome fears of one another based on race, even with "bumps" along the way.

LYNETTE LEE

I was born and raised in Honolulu. My parents had a small pharmacy and worked twelve hours a day, so essentially my sisters and I were raised by my grandmother. We lived at my grandmother's house for many years. My maternal grandmother lived a block away, so living with my grandmother and grandfather we always had relatives coming over and visiting and lots of cousins around.

I'm Chinese. Both my parents are Chinese. Hawaii has a very large Asian population. I went from kindergarten through twelfth grade to an all-girls Episcopalian school that was run by nuns. When I was little, all my teachers were white. Somehow I had this image that white people were different. They never had to go to the bathroom, so they were set apart!

Lynette Lee (with the big ribbon in her hair) with her siblings and cousins in Hawaii

My parents had a few white friends who lived on the mainland, but most of the people in our circle were Asian.

When I was young, some of my older cousins came from the mainland to visit. They introduced me to a little girl who lived down the street who could become a playmate. My grandmother discouraged me from playing with her because she was Portuguese, and also discouraged me from sharing food with her. That really sticks in my mind.

My schoolmates were more mixed—Asian, Caucasian, other kids who were part Hawaiian. Many of the friends I grew up with were more Asian, especially Japanese and Chinese. Race wasn't a clear issue in school. As I entered high school we had one teacher who was Asian, so there was some change going on, but it was slow. It was significant for many of us to have that one Asian teacher.

The bigger issue for me was how I was dealing with boys! As I grew older and approached the dating age, I didn't actually date much in high school. I remember clearly my mother telling me who it was OK to date, and what her list of preferences were. Top of the list was someone Chinese, then maybe other people who were Asian, then further down was Caucasian and Filipino, and at the bottom of the list was African American. Actually there weren't very many Blacks in Hawaii. They were mainly connected with the military.

My grandmother, then my mother (although it was a much milder thing), stick clearly in my head regarding race, so I try to encourage my kids to be open to all races.

I went to the University of Hawaii and met a number of students who were from African countries like Ghana or Zambia and talked with them and occasionally got together with them as friends, but didn't really go out with any of them on a "date." My family was prejudiced. I studied English literature in college but also took courses in Asian and Russian. One of the reasons I left Hawaii was because I wanted to learn about different cultures, so I came to the West Coast to get a teaching credential at San Francisco State. While there I also took a course in African American literature.

After I got my teaching credential, I moved to Oakland to take a job with a youth group. I was one of two credentialed teachers in a community program in Chinatown teaching high school kids, primarily immigrant kids. They'd spend half a day in our program, and we taught ESL (English as a second language) and American government. One of the key people setting up the program was Karen Jones, who was Asian. Her husband was African American. She was working to make sure immigrant kids didn't get bypassed in the whole school system.

I also taught as a substitute teacher in the Oakland public schools. As I look back at that period, being young and naive, I didn't have a lot of experience in life. I was sent to almost every school in the district, and as you know, substitute teachers aren't treated well by students or by the administration. I was sent to a lot of schools that were primarily African American and walked into classrooms where I would be greeted with racial slurs like "ching chong Chinaman." One of the ways I tried to deal with it was to say, "Well, how do you know I'm Chinese? How do you know I'm not Japanese or something else? Can you tell by my face?" So I got engaged in a discussion with them and would say, "You calling me 'ching chong Chinaman' is how you would feel if somebody called you 'nigger,' so it's not a good thing." One of the students told her parents that we had this "discussion," and one of the parents called the vice principal and she came down on me. "Why were you calling the kids nigger?" I said, "I wasn't. Where did you hear that from?" She said that one of the parents had called. I said, "No, this is what happened," and I explained we had been involved in a discussion. She backed down, but I was offended by how she automatically assumed I was wrong when she approached me.

I've worked primarily in the Asian community, but I've always tried to be flexible and open. Within EBALDC I've seen that it's always comfortable to stay within your own circle. I also saw how important it was for us to bridge out to other communities, especially as we saw the difficulty of just staying in Chinatown to do housing development. Property was too expensive to acquire, so we followed the Asian community, which was moving outside of Chinatown because there wasn't available housing. They moved into East Oakland and West Oakland, especially the immigrant and refugee communities.

Many of us who were more forward-looking saw that it was important to be a bridge between the newer Asian community and the longer-established primarily African American community. One of our strategies was to partner with a local-based nonprofit group if we were going into another neighborhood. Through that partnership we'd share some of the development fee, and if they didn't have development experience or limited experience and wanted to learn more, we'd share our expertise and experiences with them. Over the years, we've been involved in a lot of partnerships, not only in real estate projects but also in some of the economic development and welfare-to-work programs we're doing now.

We helped facilitate a comprehensive neighborhood plan in the lower San Antonio neighborhood, the most ethnically diverse neighborhood in all of Oakland. Oakland itself is considered one of the most ethnically diverse cities on a block-by-block basis throughout the whole United States, with people from all parts of Southeast Asia, Chinese immigrants, longer-term Filipinos, Native Americans, Hispanics (a lot from Mexico, but also other parts of Central and South America), Bosnian refugees, refugees from Ethiopia, and Russia, and longtime Caucasian residents. It's also a neighborhood that has the highest birth rate, the most overcrowded schools, and a lot of substandard housing.

Lynette Lee, on the left, with an affordable housing colleague in Oakland

The multicultural synergy is happening there. Groups are coming together and sharing resources. What it comes down to is forming relationships and building trust. That environment invited the attention of funders. We started out with a plan that had no money but was a very careful long-term process. We built in little successes along the way so people could see things were happening. What really gave it momentum was when the neighborhood got the Koshland Award from the San Francisco Foundation. Twelve neighborhood leaders got $5,000 each that they could contribute to their favorite organization or project for the first year. During the next four years, as a group they needed to decide how that money would get spent, $60,000 a year for five years. The plan is now completed, and what's really exciting is that different organizations were willing to step up to the plate and take a lead role to make it happen.

Our organization has gone through some ups and downs and bumps to become broader, because we've had some board members who have felt we should serve primarily the Asian community. Fortunately, we've had others who have been more broad-minded about who we serve, who believe that it is important we serve low-income folks in general, which includes the Asian community. Our staff has become much more diverse over time as well. We advertise our property management jobs to our tenants first, so we've hired a lot of them.

The Madrona Hotel, for example, has a real mixture of elderly immigrants, immigrants who are working or on welfare, people who are on general assistance, people who have come from drug rehab programs. One of our tenants was originally homeless. He's African American, and we tried him out doing janitorial work in the building and he did very well. Eventually we made him resident manager. There was an issue about how he would communicate with some of our elderly Asian tenants, a lot by sign language! Some of our elderly Asian tenants were initially afraid of him, just out of the stereotype they have about African Americans. As he helped them change lightbulbs or fix their sinks, they got more comfortable with him to the point where they were making breakfast for him every morning. We just have to give people the opportunity, hopefully in a comfortable environment, for them to get used to each other. We must also recognize that not all of it will be rosy, that there will be problems along the way and we have to be willing to deal with them.

It's important to acknowledge our differences and problems in race and culture. There are also class issues that we really have to recognize which are interwoven through all of this. Nothing comes easy—getting people comfortable with each other takes time and work. Once they feel more comfortable, they can start to appreciate the differences. I've actually told my daughter it would be more interesting if she married somebody else! And she might, but then it's her choice. ∎∎∎

met Baraka Sele in 1993 through my son. She helped him choose his African name, Hasani Olushola Issa, when he was nineteen and has been his godmother ever since. Baraka has held key positions in arts organizations throughout the country, bringing a wide array of gifted performing artists from around the world to our shores. Baraka dedicates her story to her parents, who are no longer living, and to her brother, Michael Emmanuel Cobb.

BARAKA SELE

was born in 1950 in Detroit. My mother, Claudia Mae Harrell, was born in Selma, Alabama, and my father was born in a small town outside of Chicago called Rockford, Illinois. Both his parents were ministers, so he was named Sabbath Emmanuel Cobb. After I was born, my parents moved from Detroit to a small farming community in Belleville, Michigan.

Belleville was predominantly a white community, but there were several old Black men who lived down at the end of our road. Newton Road was a quarter mile long and not even considered a county road. (If snow came, we had to shovel and scrape it ourselves. The school bus would not come down this road, and so we'd have to walk a quarter of a mile just to catch the bus every day—rain, sleet, snow, cold.) There was also a Black family on Beck Road called the Cummings, and they were my first godparents. We were all farmers. The fact that everyone else in

our community was white didn't mean much to me because we were pretty insular, and everybody got along. "Old Man" Padgett was our white next-door neighbor and actually sold us our land, which was twenty-eight acres. Everybody shared tractors, plows, chicken feed, grain, whatever you needed. This was back in the 1950s and it was the kind of community where you could leave your doors open and your kids with somebody else.

Even as a child, I had a sense that I was living this very special life. I would spend most of my days wandering up and down roads and forests and woods, climbing trees and fishing down at the creek. My father had briefly been in World War II, and his hobby was guns. In those days, it wasn't like it is now. He was very respectful of guns and taught us how to be respectful of them. We had to learn how to clean them, assemble them, and carry them properly. We did a lot of hunting, and I can remember times when we were very poor. My father would sometimes go to the city and work three jobs because there was not sufficient income from the farm. We grew up on venison, quail, pheasant, rabbit, raccoon. If it was in our fields, we shot it, my mother cleaned it, and we ate it.

Baraka Sele with her brother Michael in Belleville, Michigan

In 1954 my brother Michael started school. My brother learned how to read, and I was very jealous. My mother used to read to us all the time. When I discovered that school was where you learned how to read, I thought, "Oh my God, I want to go!" One night I said to my brother, "I want you to teach me how to read," and he said, "No!" I went to my mother and said, "Mommy, you have to teach me how to read! Michael won't teach me," and she said, "Yes he will." So between the two of them I started learning how to read, and by four years of age, I could read, write, count, and color inside the lines. I wasn't just reading Dick, Jane, and Sally, I was reading stories about the Pancake Man! Reading on my own opened up a whole new world to me.

I had an extraordinary mother. By the time I entered school, I knew most of what they were trying to teach me. On my first day in September 1955, I was put in the corner because I had spent so little time with other children my age that I couldn't stop my little mouth from running. I was such a chatterbox that Mrs. Gleason had to put me in the corner to get me to stop talking!

Up until the seventh grade, my brother and I were the only two Black children in Denton Elementary School, which included grades K through six. It wasn't until I was in third grade, about age eight, that Dickey Palmer called me a nigger. That was my first encounter with racism, because nobody had ever said anything insulting to my face, which was quite surprising. My parents are part of the PTA, my brother's in the Cub Scouts. I'm in the Brownies. Race is not an issue until we grow older. I told my brother Michael and said he should beat Dickey up, and he did! Dickey Palmer left me alone after that. I also remember two little white girls with natural platinum blonde hair who were sisters. They got on the school bus and sat behind me. They asked me, "Wouldn't you really want to be white and pretty like us?" I had the wherewithal and intelligence to say, "No, I don't." Even at an early age, my parents had obviously given me enough confidence and self-esteem to know that I really wanted to be myself.

At our secondary school, Belleville Junior High, there were five other Black students. They came from Sumpter Township, where most of the Black families in our area lived. As I entered seventh grade, something strange happened. For seven years at Denton Elementary, I attended classes with the same children. However, at BJHS, they are all put in one class, and I'm put in another class with mostly people I don't know, including the other Black children. Here I am in a new school, a new environment. The children I grew up with was the only comfort-support group I had known, even though they also had their challenges. I just know I want to be with my friends. I asked myself, "What's going on here?" I went to my homeroom teacher, Mrs. Helen Nass, and I say, "I don't understand. What's happened? I'm sure there's some mistake. I really think I should be in the class with my friends." She said, "Well, if you could prove to me that you will do well, you can get into the other class." Not until high school did I find out my white friends had been automatically put into a college prep class and all the Black students and slow-learning students had been put together in another class. I always had excellent grades, mostly As in elementary school. My class placement, I learned later, was strictly based on race. I was shocked, because Belleville seemed to be a fairly enlightened community, especially considering how I was treated by my previous teachers. Both my brother and I were perceived as "model little colored children," to be quite honest. For my seventh-grade teacher to say that I had to "prove myself" became very offensive to me in later years.

It was during this time that my mother and father got divorced, and my whole life was feeling disrupted. My mother, brother, and I moved to another rural community into a three-bedroom wood frame house with two and a half acres. This was in a white community also. The white neighbors threatened our family, saying if we moved in they were going to burn down our house. My mother declared, "Nobody can tell me where to live." She hired an attorney, who made the sale of the house and land possible.

Belleville High School is big, awesome, and exciting. I encounter, firsthand, the phenomenon of busing. There used to be a Sumpter High School where the Black children attended. The school is torn down and the students are bused to BHS. This occurrence not only impacts my life in a major way, but begins to change the relationship between me and my brother. I'm so excited that there are Black youth in my everyday life, because primarily my experiences with children of my own race had been either going to Detroit and hanging out with my older cousins or going to our church in Ypsilanti, Michigan, where I was baptized at Brown Chapel AME. This was a life transformation, because in addition to my cousins and the Black children at church, now there is a whole new community of Black folks with whom I come into daily contact.

Baraka Sele, back row right, with her high school band in Belleville, Michigan

It seems to me that the Black students aren't particularly happy about being in this sea of white students. When we go to the lunchroom, they all sit together at one table. I started sitting with them, and not really thinking anything of it. I recall my brother going home to tell my mother that I'm segregating myself from the other students and losing all my friends (which meant white friends). I thought, "Now this is really interesting." I recall saying, "I think I have a right to choose to sit wherever I want to sit, and to choose the friends I want to have."

This was our first rift in consciousness, because my brother and I are symbiotic. We have always been very close. But his attitude starts to rub me the wrong way. In his senior year at Belleville High School, he decides he wants to date a young white girl. Her parents live on Belleville Lake and seem to be financially well-to-do. They get wind of this relationship and, of course, they don't want their daughter dating this young Black man. One day Michael sits down at the lunch table with his white friends on the football team, basketball team, and track team —he did everything—and they get up and walk away. Everybody. My first thought was, "Well, it serves you right for thinking these are really your friends," but I instinctively knew the rejection truly hurt him. I thought, "You cowards, it's OK to slap each other on the back on the football field, it's OK to play games, but when it comes to really being a friend, you can't do that just because he's dating what you perceive to be as one of your own." All these unsettling thoughts start to accumulate in my mind. I begin to think, "There's something not right in the state of Denmark."

I graduated in a class of about 400 students. Out of that number, maybe 8 to 10 percent were Black—about forty students. I was in the band, the orchestra, the French club, the girls' athletic club, biology club, all of that. I was a joiner, but very few of the other Black students were in those associations and clubs. I'm still living a somewhat isolated life within this school scenario. After my graduation in 1968, something happened.

At age eighteen I could feel myself becoming disenchanted about something, but I couldn't put my finger on what it was. I became very serious. I used to have this big smile and happy-go-lucky, Pollyanna kind of personality, and it left me. I started reading the poetry of Allen Ginsberg (I didn't know a lot of Black writers) and began to take a completely different look at the world. I also started seriously writing poetry. Perhaps my feelings were predicated on an accumulation of incidents and experiences: an eighth-grade student teacher accuses me of plagiarism because I turned in an essay that was, in her opinion, "too well written"; a tenth-grade speech teacher gives me a C on a report card, even though I have been given As and Bs on all my speeches; a biology teacher tells me that Black people do not have scientific minds.

When it's time for me to graduate from high school in 1968, I auditioned and was accepted into a program called Musical Youth International. The organization toured a group of young people from the state of Michigan, both symphony band and choir, throughout Mexico and the Southwest United States. I began to realize that not only is "something not right in the state of Denmark," but something's wrong with the world. In Mexico there is literally a revolution going on around us. At night we would hear gunshots and people screaming and running. Young students in Mexico City converse with me and ask me to tell people in the United States about their cause. I am not sure what they mean. Also, 1968 was the year of the summer Olympics in Mexico. I will never forget those brothers standing with raised fists when the U.S.

national anthem was played during the medal award ceremony. I think my political awakening happened there.

Our musical tour started at the Yucatan Peninsula, and we traveled up to Villahermosa, Guadalajara, Pueblo City, and Monterrey. In addition to the Mayan ruins, we visited the marketplace in Merida, and all of a sudden (even though there are a lot of people who are dark in southern Mexico) I am rushed by people who obviously have not seen a Black person. People want to get a look at me and touch me. Someone tells me, "Mexico is not like America where you come from. Either our people are very rich, like the home where you are staying, or people are very poor." One person takes me by the hand and says, "See this little old woman? She lives right across the street from the wealthy home where you are staying, but she lives in a hovel," and my eyes get awakened to a world that is very different from Belleville, Michigan.

When we visit Guadalajara, I am introduced to a family who approaches me with an elderly lady, helping her to walk. They're saying something about a blessing. They want her to meet me, so I think she's going to bless me. "No," they say, "we want you to bless her. Do you see your skin? We are one and the same people." These are concepts, at eighteen years of age, that I do not understand: What does that mean? So I bless this woman, wondering who am I to be blessing this woman. If anything, I need her blessing!

I return home from Mexico and the tour to find out that my brother has been drafted for the Vietnam War. Vietnam had not really entered my consciousness, although I saw it on television and read the newspaper reports. Now it is real. I'm angry and terrified that my brother is going to have to do this thing. It really politicizes me.

Also during the summer of 1968, Detroit erupts into rioting. I am about to learn another lesson. My mother and I are sitting in the back of our house in the den, watching television. We're now the only two people living in the house. The front door is open and unlocked. I remember making a flippant comment because on every channel there was nothing but buildings burning up, and I said, "I'm tired of this— can't they put the regular programs back on television?" My mother said to me, "You should really be a little more sensitive and concerned about what's happening." She no sooner gets the words out of her mouth and we hear this noise outside, which we think is rain. She had asked me several times to put the car in the garage, and I hadn't, and it was sitting out front. Thank God it was sitting outside rather than in the garage, which is connected to the house, because this noise which we thought was rain is our house going up in smoke. I run back to the den to scream to my mother, "Our house is on fire!" She replied, "I'm going to call the fire department. Run across the road and get our neighbor to help." Now people come running. We find out later that our next-door neighbor has been standing down at the end of the road with another white man, laughing and talking about how he is the person responsible for setting the fire. The police come, the fire department comes. We all know who has done this, but will anybody make a statement? No. Nobody will say that this man did it. Besides setting fire to our house, he poisons our dog. This was the last straw for me and white folks. My mother was always trying to teach me to love everybody; there are good people and bad people; you try to get along. But I cannot accept her "turn the other cheek" philosophy any longer.

I begin college at Eastern Michigan University in Ypsilanti in 1969. I felt overwhelmed and intimidated. But in my sophomore year I have an English teacher who is radical and young. I want to mention his name because I credit him for changing my life and helping me transform into a conscious adult. His name was Tom Heisler. Also, I take a course in African American literature with professor, poet, and publisher Naomi Long Madgett. Naomi publishes my first collection of poetry, *Inside the Devil's Mouth*, when I am twenty-five years old. Subsequently I ask her to become my godmother. We remain loving and close to this day. She has been a blessing in my life. Both Naomi and Tom told me, "You need to read more." They started giving me books by Amiri Baraka (Leroi Jones) and others. I was always an avid reader, but now I am devouring everything—politics, religion, history, metaphysics, African American literature. I can't get enough. I met students who were members of the Black Panthers. Between reading Amiri Baraka, Mao Tse-tung, Che Guevara, Huey P. Newton, Malcolm X, etc., I start protesting the Vietnam War, the university, and the lack of Black studies. I'm in army fatigues twenty-four hours a day. I feel inspired and revolutionary.

One day, I'm walking through campus and on a bulletin board a leaflet says, "Come to a revolutionary Black church service." This is June 1973. I went to Ann Arbor and checked it out. I know no one. The service is hosted by a student group that is part of the Shrine of the Black Madonna, the Black Christian Nationalist Church. I join the same day. What made me join was the preacher, who said: "We believe that Jesus was a revolutionary, that he did not intend for Black people to accept themselves as slaves, whether it's slaves in chains or slaves in our minds, which is what we are now. We believe that Black people should have power. We believe in the liberation struggle of African people." The minister is pushing all my right buttons, but then I am thinking,

"Oh my God, if I join this organization, what is my mother going to say?" No sooner had the thought entered my head, and he said, "Now don't sit there and think about what your mother is going to say," and I said, "That's the sign," so I get up and join. The Shrine of the Black Madonna becomes my life.

The church was founded in Detroit, and every two weeks they'd send a *mwalimu* (which is Swahili for "teacher") to our campus. They taught and trained us in revolutionary struggle and strategy. In the fall of 1973 I'm given my African name during an African naming ceremony at the home Shrine in Detroit.

I became deeply involved in the Shrine. I pledged to be totally committed to the liberation struggles of Black people throughout the world. Detroit is where the Shrines of the Black Madonna were founded. What really impressed me was not only the seriousness and dedication of these Black folks, but the founder of the Black Christian Nationalist (BCN) Church, Reverend Albert Cleage, whose African name is Jaramogi Abebe Agyeman, who is author of *Black Messiah* and *Black Christian Nationalism*.

After I completed my master's degree, I committed the next five years of my life helping the Shrine to establish BCN centers in Atlanta and Houston. When we were out on corners collecting money, there were all kinds of people who were nasty and negative, but I knew in my heart that the Shrine was doing positive work. For example, in Atlanta, we purchase an apartment complex; we buy a former theater that is renovated and made into a church; we buy an entire block which becomes a cultural center, a day care and nursery, dining hall, and other facilities. These are Black people, not just the ministers, but everybody, building institutions for Black people. They are teaching and training Black people. We had to study everything from yoga, meditation, revolutionary philosophy, history, politics, religion, martial arts, science—this for me was my real college education. Even today, people ask me, "How do you know so much information?" And I say, "I don't turn a television on when I go home at night. I read." The Shrine reinforced for me the love of reading and learning my mother had instilled in me as a child. Eventually I became an advanced training group leader. I also taught classes in African history, the Bible, and tutoring for children who had difficulty learning to read.

In 1979 the Shrine creates a competition that offers the three top fund-raisers from each region—Houston, Atlanta, and Detroit—a trip to Africa. I've never won anything in my life, so I'm just doing my usual collecting with no expectation that I would win. The next thing I know,

I get a call from our home office in Detroit and they ask, "Do you have a passport?" This was in 1980, I'm thirty years old, and I'm on my way to Africa for the first time. This is another life-transforming experience. We went to Senegal in West Africa. (When I first went to college, French was my major. My friends, especially those from Detroit, would say, "What is wrong with you? Black people don't speak French.") When we get to Senegal, I learn that the official language is French. I think to myself, "This is why I have been studying French." Even though most of the people of Senegal speak Wolof, their indigenous language, they were taught French in the schools and by the missionaries. When we were out in the bush, there was a young man who said in French, "We cannot speak your language, but I am the one person in the village who can speak French. Can anyone speak French?" I raise my hand, and this young man says to me, "All my life the missionaries have told me that Black people in the United States care nothing about us, that you are not our brothers and sisters. I just want you to tell me if it's true." And tears start welling up in my eyes and I say to him in French, "No, it is not true. All of the Black people you see here with me, we belong to a church and a group of people who believe that nothing is more sacred than the liberation of our African brothers and sisters. You are indeed my brother, and I am so happy to come home." Now we're both in each other's arms crying.

After my mother's death in 1982, I learned that she left both my brother and me a sum of money that allows me to temporarily quit work and travel. Again, a transforming experience. I have read so much history about the ancient Egyptians being Black. However, if you say that to people, they respond, "Oh, that's Black Power propaganda, and you are trying to make the world Black now." I decide I will no longer discuss politics, history, or religion with anybody except members of the Shrine of the Black Madonna, because people want to argue with little or no information.

Baraka Sele today

I go to Egypt with a legendary Egyptologist whose books I'd been reading for years. He lives in Harlem and his name is Dr. Joseph ben Jochannan. Doc Ben, as he is fondly known, is originally from Ethiopia and an incredible scholar. Each night after we've had our tour of historic sites, he'd give a lecture and answer questions— it was remarkable. In Luxor, I am in the tomb of

Tutankhamen. The guards search your bags because you can't take a camera or recording devices, nothing. I am in King Tut's tomb and I start hollering and screaming because the people on the walls are not just light-skinned Black people, they are BLACK. I hold up my hand, and their skin color is my skin color, if not darker. I shout, "They're Black, they're Black! It's not a lie. We didn't make it up. This is not just about propaganda. These are Black people!"

Finally, we get to Cairo in the north. (By the way, every country I've visited, the further north you go, the lighter the people are.) We have a tour guide at the Cairo Museum who looks like a white Arab woman with dark hair. We come upon a statue of King Tut that is actually painted Black. Some of us, including myself, ask the guide, "Would you please explain the Blackness of this statue?" And she responds, "The king was in a very dark mood that day." This ridiculous statement caused us Black folks from Detroit, Harlem, Houston, who have done research and had Dr. Ben with us, to jump all over her, unfortunately to the point that she's crying. But she does admit, "I am just a tour guide! I don't know this history. This is not my history! I say what they pay me to say!" That's all she needed to say. We only made one more request, and that was to show us the hair. Everybody kept telling me to see Egyptian hair in the museum. The tour guide claims, "That part of the museum is closed, and I can't take you there." So we waited until the woman was out of sight, and about five of us went exploring. You often see pictures of Egyptians with their heads shaved. They used to cut off their own hair, style it, and make wigs, and this hair is still in glass cases centuries later. The long hair wigs that I saw for Egyptian women were styled in cornrows, and the male hair was styled in dreadlocks, and I was screaming again, "They are Black! This is kinky, cornrowed, and nappy dreadlocks!" I felt affirmed and overjoyed.

A friend who recently visited Cairo came back and said to me, "I didn't see any Black people. You must have made this up," and I said, "You know what? That's like you saying to me, 'Indians never lived here. I'm looking around and I don't see any Native Americans. They must have never been here. You made it up.' You can't just go to Egypt and look at the people who are there now. Most of the people in Egypt are not the indigenous people, just like the people here in the United States aren't the people who originally inhabited this land.

For the past nineteen years I've worked professionally with arts organizations throughout the United States. Frequently I encounter people who believe that the arts are the panacea for social problems and political issues. I often hear, "Art is a universal language, and everybody can relate." I've done a lot of research regarding how racism exists in the arts, and how people use the arts to manifest subtle and overt racist tendencies. A lot of that is manifested in how the arts are funded. Historically, the lion's share of monies has gone to major mainstream institutions that are run by white males.

There's also the whole issue of "standards and quality." For many years, the only standard for artistic excellence was the European standard. So many cultures—African, Asian, South American, Australian—were labeled as "folk" or "traditional" cultures. However, these cultures have their own aesthetics, classics, and standards. The rest of the world has begun to realize that Europe is not the only measuring stick.

It's frustrating to me when you confront people in the arts about their own racism. They comment, "I work in the arts, I could not possibly be racist." You can even give them an example of something they've said or done, but there is a presumption that working in the arts is a liberal and enlightened profession.

In my opinion, racism is always going to exist in our lifetime. I don't think it's going to change until the next generation—but how long have we been saying that? Our ancestors who were slaves, when they were taking the shackles off, said, "At least our children won't have to deal with oppression and racism, or our grandchildren." But we're still dealing with it, and unfortunately, I believe we always will.

My challenge, beyond bringing artists from all over the world to perform in this country, is fighting racism in the arts. That's my other job, the one they don't pay me for. What will be the hope of the future is people like Hasani Olushola Issa, and when Black people have our own major arts institutions. The lesson the Shrine constantly taught me was: The reason we are powerless is because we don't have and control our own institutions. My hope is that years down the road, Black people will have our own institutions and facilities. Then we'll be able to say, "This is what we're doing over here. Other folks can continue to do what they have always been doing, but we control what's happening here." ∎∎∎

met Karen Kaho through our mutual friend, Judy Goddess, when they were neighbors in the Parkmerced neighborhood of San Francisco. Karen is the mother of three grown biracial children and is now the California ombudsman for foster children throughout the state. She was also the very proactive vice chair of the Women's Democratic Forum in San Francisco. Karen currently lives in Sacramento, sharing her home with her son Trevor. She is keenly aware of the racism in our country and understands the need for the Holocaust Museum in Washington, but wonders, "Why don't we have a Holocaust Museum for African Americans and Native Americans?"

KAREN KAHO

My father was in the air force, so we moved around. From kindergarten to third grade, we lived in a small farm town in Southern California. Potatoes were the main crop back then, and now it's a tract home suburban community. There were always African American and Hispanic kids in my class.

As a kid, the whole issue of race was not conscious. I have pictures of kids together in our school who are Black and white. But then we moved to Altus, Oklahoma, and there were no children of color at all. I remember coming home and asking my mother, "What have they done to all those other kids?" She didn't know exactly how to explain but said, "Well, they go to different schools on the other side of town."

So I was first raised in a farm town which is very isolated and insular and you can know someone from kindergarten all the way through. Then we moved to places like Oklahoma and Okinawa, and I experienced totally different geography, lifestyles, and culture in each place. In high school we moved back to our small farm town, and there were still Hispanic and African American kids in our high school, but I didn't have much contact with them. It wasn't a conscious thing that they were excluded. It was just the way it was. They all lived in a certain area, and we lived in a certain area, and I didn't know why. We lived where we did because our parents lived there.

Karen Kaho at San Diego State College in the mid-1960s

I remember hearing gossip about a guy who came from one of the town's "good" white families who married a woman who was Hispanic and moved into our neighborhood. There was an African American girl who was really smart, and she was on the Student Council. I remember hearing comments like, "She's an exception." There was a really good friend of mine who was Hispanic, but people would say, "Well, she's more Spanish," like she's not Mexican. There were lots of these subtle racist messages.

Race was never discussed in school, in history, in social sciences. I'm sure for the kids of color they were much more conscious of this. That's one thing that's important to remember in terms of any kind of oppression. When you're enjoying the privilege, it's not a conscious thing. It's like oxygen. You breathe it. It's just taken for granted. It's the way things are, but if you're deprived of something, like if you can't breathe, you feel the deprivation of it. A lot of the things I've learned about racism I would never have been aware of if I hadn't married a man of color.

I went away to college in San Diego in 1963. At that time, it was a very white conservative environment. Then around 1964 I became aware of the issues of Vietnam and the civil rights movement. The messages I received from being raised in a farm town were basically that we're the nation of the free and the brave, and in America you can accomplish anything if you work hard. I had this illusion that the people who were our leaders were people who were honest and capable. My awareness started to change when I took a course in international relations. I researched the conflict in Vietnam and its history, which brought a new perspective on the colonization of countries and what that does. Through this project I started examining the foreign press and saw the difference in how the American press was reporting the skirmishes in Vietnam and how the French press was reporting it. I realized that we were not getting the total picture. That was one of my most upsetting moments, to comprehend that our government was not giving the public the whole truth. I believed all those myths that had been perpetrated and realized how naive I had been.

That was the beginning of an awareness that things are not always as they appear, that you can't always believe people and our government. The whole issue of race also became an issue with me because I realized that people are really discriminated against. It was something I had not been sensitive about, but was now aware of because of the civil rights movement. I ran for student body president as a Students for a Democratic Society candidate on an anti–Vietnam War and civil rights platform. Giving speeches to various groups also expanded my awareness of people's attitudes on race and the war.

I became more politically active and met a lot of interesting people from different backgrounds. They were honestly able to share their lives and experiences, and it humanized a lot of the political and philosophical ideas I was exploring. You're raised on these myths that things should be fair and just and people should be able to achieve based on their ability; then you meet people who say that's genuinely not the case if you are a certain color. That was another eye-opener to me.

I moved from Berkeley to San Francisco and took a job with a treatment facility for adolescents. There were kids of color in the program, and that's when I met John. He was directing a program for boys, and we were trained in psychodrama together. The African Americans I had previously known were pretty radical politically. When I met John I thought he was really old because he wore a suit! Nobody I knew in the 1960s and 1970s wore a suit. He claims it was a sports coat, but to me it looked like a suit! He was Black and had an Afro, but with a suit it didn't quite jell in my stereotyped view of things.

John and I got to know each other on a more personal level. We started dating, and to be honest, the racial thing never was an overt issue. The problem I had with him was that he seemed so straight and older. Two years later we decided to live together in Noe Valley. He was an administrator at this point for mental health. The group of people we hung out with were from all over the United States. There was a mixture of people from Jewish backgrounds, African American, Hispanic and Puerto Rican backgrounds. We all had a place where we came from and everybody just shared where that was. It wasn't a big deal for any of us.

With my parents it wasn't a big issue either. My father was a very eccentric person and a very deep-thinking person. He wrote and played music. When I was in college he'd write me letters that brought tears to my eyes. He had to make a living to support his children, so he stayed in the air force. He was the kind of guy who didn't have much use for most people, whether you're white, Black, whatever. He wasn't racist, but one time when he stayed with John and me we picked him up at the airport. He saw Mayor Alioto, and he made a comment about "that wop walking around the airport thinking he really was something." I said to dad, "You know, you don't need to make those kind of racist comments," and he said, "God damn it Karen, you know what's wrong with your generation? You people don't know who the hell you are. When we were coming up, we knew who we were. I was a mick and I knew I was a mick, and if you're a kike you're a kike, if you're a wop you're a wop," and he went through the whole litany of every group. It was like, we are who we are and that's OK. John and I were going, "Oh my God, this man is so funny."

We lived in Montara (a very white suburb) when Shiloh was a baby. That's when race hit me personally. I remember I'd go to the market with Shiloh, and because she was darker skinned, people would find it necessary to ask about the father, which I thought was very intrusive. At first it upset me, then I started thinking that I'd better get used to it and get on top of it. John and I had some interesting conversations. He told me,

"Just because someone asks you a question doesn't mean you have to answer it," so I got into a state of mind where I would answer truthfully, but really make them get down to what the issue was, which was color.

When we moved back to the city Gabrielle was born, and she was very pale. I had one brown-skinned and one light-skinned daughter, and this confused people even more! What I found fascinating is that strangers who didn't know me would ask really intrusive questions. One incident that I'll always remember was at Kaiser Clinic when I was waiting with the two children. There was this older white woman sitting next to me. She said, "Oh, what cute little children." "Thank you." "Gee! Are they both yours?" "Yeah, they both are." She was puzzled then, so she asked, "Oh, do they have the same father?" That, to me, is a very intrusive question. If the children were both white, nobody would have asked that question. So when I said, "Yes, they both have the same father," that shut her up for a few moments, then she was really curious and asked, "What nationality is the father?" (No one ever asked this question to my white friends who married white men. Color is the issue. People want to know, where did this color come from?) So I answered, "Well, he's a walking United Nations," which is true, because John's grandfather on his father's side was German, blonde and blue-eyed. His grandfather on his mother's side was full Irish. His grandmother on his father's side was African American (probably mixed with the slave owner), and the grandmother on the other side was French and African. That answer didn't stop her. She wanted to know where the color came from. She wasn't a hostile woman. She was a sweet little old white woman. Why did she have a need to know?

That kind of intrusion came up a lot through the years. The thing it made me aware of, which I wasn't before, was America's preoccupation with color. You could be married to the biggest creep who is white, and who cares? But if someone has a little color, that becomes the issue. And it's not just in the United States. I've done a lot of traveling, and in most of the countries where there's been a colonial experience, that ends up getting translated somehow. Whoever the victor was—usually Europeans—became imbued as the superior. The sad thing is that a lot of the indigenous cultures in many ways had things the Europeans could have learned from in terms of how you relate to each other and to the earth.

We bought a little house in an integrated neighborhood in San Francisco. I was home with the kids, and John was working. Trevor was born, and he used to tell me that people would ask him, "Are you Black or white?" and he used to say, "Well, I'm a brown boy!"

In San Francisco, the main issue is economics, not race. If you can pay your rent and afford to live here, that speaks much more than race. The unfortunate thing is that racism impacts a lot of people's economic ability to do that. What's ending up happening here is that the whole Western Addition used to be an African American community and culture, and that's not the case anymore. There's Marcus Bookstore and John Lee Hooker's place, but that's about all I can identify. The rest of it is pretty yuppie. A lot of people have had to move across the bay because they can't afford to live here. The Housing Authority has also torn down a lot of public housing, and they haven't replaced it with the same number of units.

I've always been curious about the South because of the American writers who've come from there. I wanted to take a trip and see where John's grandparents lived in Louisiana and Mississippi because I thought his family's history was fascinating. John wouldn't go there with me. He said, "Are you crazy? A Black man and a white woman traveling together?" He wouldn't do it.

When I visited Atlanta, the hotel where I stayed had some Black debutante balls. You could see there was money in the Black community there. When I went to the jazz clubs there were Blacks and whites in the club, but they weren't sitting at the same tables with each other. It wasn't like San Francisco, where people would actually have friends

Little Shiloh, Trevor, and Gabrielle Kaho in San Francisco

from different backgrounds. I didn't see that in Atlanta. We have a good friend who is African American who got a good job there. He hated it because you were expected, as a professional Black, to associate with the Black bourgeois, which he found stifling. He ended up leaving.

One year I took the train from Orlando to Boca Raton in Florida on the "back side" of reality. I saw a lot of shacks with Black families sitting on the porch. They had that look in their eye saying, "I have no place to go and I'm sitting here until I die, and I have nothing." Then I get to Boca and all this affluence. My friend drove me back to catch my plane —through West Palm Beach, the Trump mansion, and the Kennedy compound. How is it that in this country we're not even embarrassed about this discrepancy? And people don't think there's a class structure in this country? You have on one side all these mansions facing the ocean, and on the other side you have people crammed into little quarters. I just don't get it. I think people should be rewarded for their successes in life, but you have to realize that our successes are built on other people's knowledge that came before us. Nobody's been able to achieve anything totally on their own. Why do you need more than you can use in this life?

I remember when John's niece was graduating from San Francisco State, and there was an African American graduation, so we went. I looked around and felt like I was the only white person in that audience. I had to go to the bathroom really bad, and I told John. He said, "Well, get up and go," and I said, "Are you crazy?" I felt so visible, and it made me sensitive as to how Blacks or somebody of color feels in an all-white situation, because you feel they will notice you much more. I wasn't going to walk out and have everybody make comments like, "Did you see that white woman? Isn't she rude?" The other thing I found interesting in the graduation was that all the African American kids either thanked God or Jesus and their parents. I was thinking to myself, if this was a graduation with a bunch of white kids, nobody would have thanked God or Jesus, and a lot of them would not have thanked their parents. Culturally, when you're an oppressed group, you turn to, in many ways, the only dimension you have to turn to, a spiritual dimension. It gave me an insight into why the church has become such an important part of the African American experience.

Slavery is such an abhorrent concept—that you actually own people —and part of the way to justify it is to put them at the level of an animal. That has done long-term psychological damage to both Black and white Americans. We all need to look back at slavery and see what that experience has done. It's affected our whole culture. That's why white and Black racism is so much more of an overt problem than racism among the other groups, although it is still a problem.

White Americans are not aware of the trauma of slavery. I never studied it in school. In terms of white Americans, we are unaware of the privilege of just being white. The stereotype is that everyone who is Black lives in a high-rise public housing project, is a single Black mother on welfare. I was working with an African American woman who was third-generation college educated. Her parents both have Ph.Ds. I am the first generation of college educated in my family. Now if you sit in front of a group of people and ask, "Which of us is third-generation college educated?" you'd probably pick me.

As whites, because of the cultural shame, we refuse to look at this with any level of objectivity. Anybody who has power has the ability to say what we'll look at and what we won't look at, so this is obviously an issue in our culture that we don't want to look at. We won't even look at what we did to the Native Americans. The way they were perceived in history and the movies was primarily, "the nerve of these savages to get in the way of these white settlers."

I went to the Holocaust Museum in D.C., and a lot of that is federal money, and the people who work there are federal employees. This is our tax money, and I think the museum is a great thing and am in full agreement that it should exist. But why have we funded something like this— a holocaust that happened in Germany, a foreign country—and we have no acknowledgment of the holocaust in this country with the African slaves and the Native Americans? I think we should create side by side the American Holocaust Museum and talk about the horror of slavery.

I can't for the life of me imagine what that must have been like for those Africans to be kidnapped, put in holding pens, shoved into boats to cross the ocean, chained and lying in feces. They arrive in this country and don't know anything about it, they don't know the language or anything. Then they're separated from their families. Just the fact that anybody could have survived says something about the human spirit. Our forefathers of European descent also felt perfectly justified in slaughtering the Native Americans. Those who didn't die from diseases that the white man brought over died from bullets.

I think it was good that we apologized to the Japanese and gave them a little bit of money to repay them, but why hasn't that happened to people of African descent or Native Americans? What is the answer? ∎∎∎

John was Karen's husband and is Shiloh, Gabrielle, and Trevor's father. He is Creole, and his family includes several members who passed for white. John and two of his siblings could never visit his aunt because they were "too dark." Today John is optimistic about the growth and acceptance of interracial relationships but very pessimistic about the huge and growing economic and racial schism between the haves and have-nots.

JOHN KAHO

I was born in a unique neighborhood around the University of Chicago, the Dorchester–Hyde Park area. Chicago still is, in my consciousness, a very segregated, very racist city, although my experiences as a kid were very different than a lot of people. Our neighborhood was international and intellectual, mixed with all kinds of people from every race you could think of, and people got along. I was born around the time of the Second World War, and the neighborhood filled up with even more people from other areas. We didn't know then that it was the center of operation for the Manhattan Project.

I had three brothers who all went away to war in each branch of service. As a result of that, my parents took in boarders. One of them was a woman who identified herself as a secretary who worked at the University of Chicago. Later on we found out she was a physicist on the Manhattan Project.

My family is Creole, and most of our block were Creoles from Louisiana, all Catholic, and the kids went to the same Catholic school. We were a very tight-knit group, but I didn't feel any consciousness of racial disharmony until after the war. When people could move, all the white people moved out to the suburbs, where they were building new homes. The neighborhood became primarily minority at that time.

My mother was married prior to marrying my father. She was widowed during the depression and had four children. He married her with the four children, they had two more children, myself and my sister, and they adopted two children. We always had tons of people in the house, and sometimes in the same bed! We never complained, because we always had enough to eat. When my father left the plantation, he worked wherever he could find a job. He was a longshoreman, a deck hand on a Mississippi riverboat, a lumberjack.

There was no regular work in Chicago back then, but there was work for anybody who would go out and stand in line every morning and have people pick you. He was such a good worker that very soon he was being picked every day. Eventually, he worked for the University of Chicago and the stockyards. I remember as a little boy (I told this story in his eulogy) the many

John Kaho's mother's social club in Chicago during the 1940s

times my dad came home with his clothes torn and him bloodied. He was out there on the line fighting for the union to come into the stockyards. They finally won, and the pay became equivalent to that of a longshoreman in San Francisco.

My mother and father had very similar backgrounds in two ways. Both of their fathers were white plantation owners. My grandfather on my mother's side was Irish, my grandfather on my father's side was German, and they married women of color of mixed origin. Both men were landed gentlemen who had not just "taken" these women, as men in the South did, but actually married them. One was on the Mississippi side of the river and one on the Louisiana side. They knew each other and had respect for each other.

My mother's father was a very gregarious man. I never knew him because he died before I was born. He was always taking a chance. He'd sell land, buy land, lose land. He lost a lot of what he owned, so he went down to Cuba, where his brother had plantations. He was overseeing his brother's plantations and got sick with malaria. He came back in bad health. My mother's mother—she did everything she could to raise their six children in New Orleans. I was absolutely frightened by this woman all my life. Her children loved her, but I just saw her on visits and she seemed the meanest woman on the face of the earth!

An interesting aspect of my family is that different members, because of how they looked, would pass for white. They went over entirely to the white community, and some of them, like my Uncle Seeb, lived his whole life as a white man. A number of family members chose to do that. My Aunt Iris, my mother's sister, did that. For professional reasons, my youngest sister also did that. She's still in her job in Chicago, perceived as white. She never joined that environment, though, and always lived in the community she was part of.

There were many reasons for this, especially because you could get better jobs. My aunt Iris lived close to us in Joliet, Illinois. My sister Margaret, my brother Eugene, and myself could never visit her, but the rest of the family could. We were too dark and too perceptively minorities. Interestingly enough, even though there were members of my father's family who were not perceptively minority, none of them chose to cross over. My father's family chose to seek their success through higher education—a number of doctors, lawyers, and entrepreneurs.

I was always conscious of other neighborhoods in Chicago where I could and could not go, where the boundaries were and what the consequences were. As kids, we didn't experience people relating to us in any unkind way in the city, but until the early 1960s, Chicago's major newspapers still had the separate "colored" and "white" employment sections, and the city still had different places for "colored" and "white" only. If you went shopping in major department stores downtown, you could buy anything you wanted to, but you couldn't try anything on.

The first really bad incident I had in Chicago in terms of racism was when I was in the Boy Scouts. We were this nice little Catholic troop, mostly minority, that was going to a weekend camp. You had to take the city bus all the way to the limits of Chicago, then walk through the town of Trumble Park to the Boy Scout camp. (This town later became very famous for racist-type activities and was a significant part of the civil rights movement in terms of demonstrations.) We were walking through this two-block area in the town. I was just twelve years old and had never experienced hate like this before. The people in the town—women, children, men—stoned us, and some of us got hurt. I got hit by some rocks and wasn't really hurt, but emotionally I never experienced any-

John Kaho as a little boy in Chicago

thing like it. The racial epithets they hollered at us—"Nigger" this and that—it was one of the most hurtful things that I've ever experienced in my life. I wondered, "Why would these people hate us? We haven't done anything, and we're Boy Scouts. We're the good guys." Our troop leader called our parents, who got us back from there. We went to our church, and the priests worked with us about this hatred. We were crying because nobody had every done this to us before.

After I graduated from high school I joined the Marine Corps. The year was 1961. I ended up as a lieutenant with my body intact. There was definitely racism there, but not toward me. I was very lucky and had a commanding officer who thought I was the best thing since sliced bread. I was promoted at every opportunity, but around me was an awful lot of racial prejudice. In one incident, because I was so squared away, the word had gotten out in another outfit that I was an Uncle Tom, and these guys were planning to kill me. In the Marine Corps they'll do that. They're a very violent group of men. My friends had to get to these guys and say, "You got him all wrong. This is not who this guy is. He's not sucking up to anybody, he's just doing his job the way he needs to do it." They then called the whole thing off.

Another time I was talking with an officer who asked me, "Why do you guys separate yourselves when you go into the mess hall? All the Blacks eat at the same table." I told him, "You take a look at it. We are just perceptible when you look at the tables. All the Polish guys are eating at the same table, all the Irish guys are eating at the same table, all the Italian guys are eating at the same table. People do get together with their own culture."

I think the military, even back then, was ahead of the general society in terms of opportunities. The military today, if you compare generals with corporate executives, there's a much higher percentage of minorities who are in the general ranks than in the corporate ranks.

After the military, I went back to Chicago, got in my car, packed everything, and left! Eventually I got into the area of work I wanted to be in, the nonprofit area. I continued to move up to bigger and more challenging positions. I've primarily worked as a counselor, social worker, and most of my years as an administrator in mental health, child abuse, developmentally disabled programs, and disturbed adolescents.

John Kaho in the army

I was very aware that San Francisco would be the place I wanted to live, not only because it's beautiful and I was familiar with it, but on a racial basis. It was better for people racially, particularly if you come from the Midwest. I certainly wasn't much of a radical or that different, but I wanted the right to think my own thoughts without anybody bothering me.

Even today when I go back to Chicago, as open as a number of neighborhoods are, and things have changed legally, Chicago is 80 percent as segregated and narrow-minded as it was in pre–civil rights days. You still can't move into the Back of the Yards unless you're Irish, let alone if you're Black. There are many neighborhoods in Chicago still like that. Nothing has really changed, except that the people who live there now come to work and work shoulder to shoulder with you on the job because they have to. We've gained a lot of legal rights, but the social and community rights are very lacking.

I have a friend who's a psychiatrist in the East Bay, and she graduated from Mehara in Memphis, a Black college. About ten years ago, she said that someday she would return to Mehara and be head of the department. The opportunity came along, and she got the job. I told her, "Annette, you can't go back to the South. You've been in the Bay Area too long." She said, "What are you talking about? I can go back to the South. I'm from the South." So sure enough, she was back there for about a year and she called me and said, "John, start looking for a house for me. I'm no southerner." Her perception was that somehow, through progress, more things had changed than really had. She decided that the really substantive things really hadn't changed—the attitudes hadn't changed. Even Blacks there wouldn't go into really nice restaurants with their white friends. You just didn't do that, you don't mix socially. She found that unacceptable because people here related to each other as colleagues and peers, and not on the basis of color.

My children all went to the same Catholic grammar school. My older daughter didn't have much of a problem there, and for all practical purposes, it was an all-white school. This was a parish that was predominantly Irish middle class. My younger daughter is not perceptively minority. She's a blue-eyed blonde and had tons of friends there, very popular. My son, who is light brown, played all the sports and was on all the teams. He was voted most valuable player in basketball twice. The teams were made up of primarily the same kids and he knew them very well, and they knew him well. He never got invited to any of these kids' birthday parties. All the time he was in school, I think he got invited to one birthday party. We would always invite everybody that our kids knew. But they never invited him. The girls did OK in this regard, but he had an entirely different experience. When the girls graduated, his life at that school was miserable. He didn't reveal it to me beforehand, but some of the kids referred to him as "nigger," and various epithets, and he was treated very differently than the girls. I pulled him out of there, and he went to another smaller school with a greater ethnic mix and did very well. Even in San Francisco there are underlying issues that you don't even know.

Where I am encouraged is that interracial marriages and relationships are ahead of the people who would like to put them behind. The younger generation—you look at magazines and see models, many times you can't tell what ethnic group they belong to anymore. The people in the industry are picking people who look like Shiloh, my older daughter. It speaks of progress that people are becoming more comfortable with people who are not someone you can classify. At least the media, the advertising world, has jumped on that, and they think it's really cool. Evidently the people who buy their products think it's pretty cool, too. Humans are humans, and we're getting used to seeing these differences, so that's encouraging.

What's not encouraging is that since the civil rights movement, educated Black and Latino bourgeois, as a class of people, have made tremendous progress, but that group is so small in comparison to the larger group of minorities. The larger group is in worse shape today than they were in 1962. I see them losing ground, and particularly minority youth. They're getting to the point where, even if you decide to spend money for training, they're so far behind it wouldn't be as easy to bring them up to par as it would have been back in the 1960s. Technologically they're very far behind. They're not prepared for what's going on today.

One of the by-products of the civil rights movement was that we used to have some entrepreneurs and industry and positive people in our neighborhoods, segregated as they were. We had different levels of people kids could look up to. When we had the right to move out to other places, all of those positive and motivated people, including storekeepers, teachers, and ministers, moved out because they could. They left this void. Here in San Francisco, except for a couple of them, most of the Black ministers are buffoons, like Amos Brown. They're not there in the community, and there's no support systems anymore.

Working with kids ten to fifteen years ago, I had a lot more resources. People like Ronald Reagan and other mean-spirited people, and laws like Proposition 13, started cutting all the support. Today we don't have any resources. I tell the kids, "You need to do the right thing because it's the right thing." "Go to hell," they say, if they have any sense. I have nothing to offer them.

I see a population that's developing into the haves and the have-nots, and that's wrong. You don't have a great middle class anymore that was the backbone of this country. You have people not making enough money, working too many hours—and people making more money than they need—and the minorities are the ones being hit the worst by the whole thing. ▪▪▪

Karen Kaho and her children today — Trevor, Shiloh, left front, and Gabrielle

Shiloh Kaho is Karen and John's older daughter. She with her partner Jason are the parents of Nathaniel, now four years old. She is often mistaken for a Latina, and has personally identified with their discrimination, particularly when she lived in Orange County in Southern California. Her interpersonal experiences there made her appreciate her life in San Francisco, where "we're all humans and everyone has their own culture."

SHILOH KAHO

The first time I was conscious of any kind of difference between people was at school. As a little girl, people always thought I was Latin. There were no Black students in our school. It was primarily Irish Catholic, some Asians, and three Latinos. I remember one girl,

Eclaya Lopez, because we looked almost exactly alike. We both had brown hair, brown skin, brown eyes, long brown hair. Everybody thought we were sisters. People just assumed I was Latin, and it never bothered me until someone tried to speak Spanish to me!

Even at the beginning of high school, race wasn't an issue. I had a whole group of friends—white, Black, Latin, Filipino, Chinese. Mercy High was pretty diverse. We had this class where we had to talk about our culture. It was interesting, because when I talked about my dad being Black (French Creole) and my mom white, the girls who were African American became interested in having me around more than before. I've seen that as an adult too. I was working with United Airlines in L.A., where there were Black women who found out through my job application that I was Black, and they would say, "Oh, come sit and talk with us." In San Francisco I had friends at the office who were Black, but they apparently liked me for myself, not knowing what my cultural background was. It made me see that San Francisco is really different than the rest of the state and country.

When I was in high school, I'd have teachers come up to me and say, "I've never seen a student who has such a diverse group of friends." One day I'd sit with one group of friends, then the next day another group. It got to a point where I started introducing my friends to other friends, and we just started to all sit together. These stereotypical ways that people would talk, like racist kinds of remarks, totally went away as people got to know each other as individuals. They became more open to getting to know other people, and that was really nice.

Because I went to an all-girls high school, I didn't have a lot of racist things happen with men. I dated a lot of guys who were Black, and I also dated guys who were white. I started to hear and feel in the body language of the Black guys that I was like a token because in the Black community it was a big deal if you had light skin and hair that's not kinky or nappy. I started to feel like a status symbol, and I had to step back and say, "OK, does this person like me for me, or am I someone who looks nice in a picture?" and that was a little odd.

I've never perceived myself as one thing. When I applied for a job at United Airlines, the application had me down as Black. I didn't put it down—my cousin on my dad's side had filled it out for me. They make sure they can take advantage of that for jobs or funding for schools, etc. I usually put "other" or "decline to state." Now there's a "multiracial" category too. When my son Nathaniel was born, Jason and I lived in Southern California. On my birth certificate I don't have anything, and I thought it was neat that my parents decided not to put anything. But when Nathaniel was born the hospital insisted that we put something down, or they couldn't process the birth certificate. We put "Caucasian, Black, and Hispanic," and the woman asked, "Can't you narrow it down?" and we said, "No, if you need something, that's what you get."

In Southern California, especially in Orange County, it's really "undiverse" and I believe very racist against Latin Americans. Because I'm usually perceived as being that, I feel more racism there than I feel here. Southern California is such a conservative area. They put signs up: "Don't let this be the illegal immigrant state." They had to take those signs down because Hispanic organizations were going to boycott groups that had signs near them. There's a whole movement to keep immigrants from Latin America out of the county. The racism is clearly against people with brown skin. That was one of my concerns living there. We have this child, and does he have to deal with this schizophrenic discrimination thing because they want people who are bilingual for jobs, but they don't want to allow bilingual education in schools? They want these people to take care of their children—it's almost like the South, with the Blacks being the nannies and raising the kids, and the kids learn to be racist from their parents, but they also learn to love these people because they're taking care of them.

Orange County is primarily white. There are a lot of Mexican Americans who work in people's homes, but a lot of them don't live in the county. They're the ones taking the buses to L.A., Long Beach, or San Diego. Most of the Mexican Americans in Orange County live in Santa Ana, which is the ghetto of the county. It's really scary down there. It's not even a culture I belong to by blood, but it's a culture that people have identified me with, so at some point I have to say, "If you're going to identify me with these people, then you really can't treat them this way." It's sad that I would have to defend someone on the basis that I'm being perceived. But I'm sensitive to a lot of different minorities and the discrimination they face, like I'm not homophobic. I don't think people should be discriminated against because of their sexuality either.

The thing about race is that you were born into this mother-father and you can't help it, even as an adult. You can't help the color of your skin. You can help the way that you talk and the way that you dress and other social aspects, but you can't change your skin color. Jason and other men who are minorities have said to me, "This organization discriminated against me, or this person." Even when I've been with them, I'm completely oblivious to it. I say, "Really? I didn't see it." I think a lot of minority men, when they can't get a job or the apartment they want, they blame racism. It's not to say there isn't racism out there. I know there is, because I've felt it. But someone really needs to be obvious about it for me to notice it. I don't feel I need to blame racism for failures of different kinds. But I feel a lot of men do. I also know they're perceived as more of a threat. Maybe I'm not being discriminated against because I'm a woman and it's more like a pity: "We won't discriminate against you because you're just a woman, you can't do anything to us." I think a lot of white men are afraid of Black men. I don't think they're as afraid of Latin men because they're smaller.

I do think that discrimination definitely exists and that San Francisco is an island to the rest of the country. Growing up here, my mindset is that everyone is the same and we're all humans and everyone has their own culture. In L.A. where I worked, this woman told me how she hated Indians (from India), and I looked at her and asked, "Why did you say that, and second of all, what if I'm Indian? You've no idea what my ethnicity is." She was like, "I'm sorry." And I said, "Good, because that's ridiculous," and I got up and moved. Nobody in L.A. says anything when people make racist comments. People just stay silent. It's really weird.

One time I joined Jason on a business trip to Oroville in Northern California, past Sacramento. Even there we saw people who had Confederate flags draped over their cars and on their license plates. Forget the stereotype that Northern California is more liberal. These people are completely crazy. You find it everywhere. Jason, this tall dark guy, and I are in this car, and I'm thinking, "We're going to die." And there were no phones on these country roads. "They're just going to kill us and dump our bodies." Because whenever I see a Confederate flag, I can't believe that people even have them. ■■■

G abrielle Kaho is Karen and John's second daughter. She looks white but identifies strongly as biracial. She was a junior at the University of California at Berkeley when I talked with her. Gabrielle's experience in her racial relations class spoke volumes about how we judge people by their physical appearance, regardless of their racial self-identification, family history, and life experience.

GABRIELLE KAHO

I didn't really think about race until I went to college. I didn't have a defined image of myself or the world. When I was seven, my mom sent us to camp, and all the kids there were Black. I went with my younger brother, who looks Black—somewhat ambiguous. None of the kids played with me or talked to me. I was alone the entire day. So I came home and never went back again. I really felt hurt that no one was talking to me, and felt very different.

I always knew that I was mixed-race, but I didn't know what that meant. It got confusing, because "if you're mixed-race, you're Black," and that was a major thing and how I grew up thinking. Lately, because it's become popular to be a person of mixed-race or because of affirmative action, they find that it's a privilege to be a minority. Because of that I have a lot to prove to people that I'm Black, because I don't look like it. When I was younger, people would say I was Black because my dad was Black. Now people want me to give them the percentages to make sure it's real.

My mom is Irish and English and Protestant, and my dad is Creole (French and Black), Irish, and Catholic, so I was raised Catholic. When I was at St. Cecilia's Elementary School, all the parents were around, and all the kids knew who your parents were. I didn't go to the same high school as my brother and sister, but everyone's coming from the same place and knows everyone else. But as soon as you get to college, you're this person who has no connection anywhere, and you have to prove where you came from. That's when it became really hard, because I've always been very in touch with my African American side. Both my roommates my first year at Cal Berkeley were Black Muslims, and I felt like I could totally relate to that. We had a really good relationship. They had all their Black friends, and I have a tendency to have a more diverse group of friends, not just one race.

The first year at Cal I took an African American studies class, and nobody in the class would talk to me. There was one Asian girl in the class, and one white girl who looked like a punk. She was a women's studies major and was writing her thesis on the Black feminist movement. Every time I'd raise my hand in this class, nobody cared about what I had to say. Cal Berkeley has a tiny Black population and it's diminishing quickly. One girl who is half Creole, half Swedish joined our sorority the next year, and it was the first time I got to know her. She said how she felt really out of place in that class, too.

The next year I took a racial relations class, and there were people from all different races there. A friend had taken the class the previous semester, and she's half Guatemalan and half white, but she was raised in Marin County and has gone to private school her whole life. She has never had any connection with her Guatemalan side. She looks really white, so you'd never know.

The way the class works is that if you're mixed-race, there's a mixed-race presentation at the end, but you do both of your races' presentations early on. There were two teachers in the class; one is a gay man, the other a Black woman. When the Black presentation came around, she called all the Black people's names in the class and didn't call mine, so I just left the room. I then went back and said, "I don't know what's going on, but I was wondering why my name wasn't called," and she said, "Well, do you feel you have enough to say?" She was questioning me over and over. "Do you feel you've had enough of an experience? The presentation we're planning on doing was more like how it feels to be a Black person every single day of your life." I said, "Well, I can't obviously relate to that because when I walk down the street that's not how people see me." She questioned me again and again. I started crying and I didn't know what to say, so I sat down and she said she was sorry. But after thirty seconds they weren't talking to me anymore. They were planning their presentation. I felt completely rejected, like my identity had been entirely denied. I left the room.

The time comes the next week for the presentation, and they talk about how it feels to be a Black person and not know where your ancestors come from because they're slaves. So why was I disqualified? I could totally relate to that. I have no clue where any of my family came from on my dad's side. All I know is that they ended up in Louisiana and Mississippi. That's as far back as I go. I was so angry.

Then the white students did a presentation, and I refused to participate. I said, "If somebody's going to say that I can't represent one half of myself, then why should I participate in the other half's presentation? That would show favoritism."

We then had meetings with the professors about how the class was going. I went to talk with the gay teacher and I told him what happened. He said, "I think you're defensive about your race, and I think you expect other people to make you feel Black, and you blame Black people for not including you." And I was like, I don't even want to talk with you about this. You do not understand. This guy is so white, comes from a totally different world than I do. He was raised in a small farm town in Southern California. He thinks that because he's worked in racial relations his whole life he has some understanding of what it's like to be a person like me, and he doesn't. Then he tried to give me a hug, and I told him, "I don't really want to hug you."

Then the mixed-race presentation came. (I got really excited, because that semester I had been taking another class that focused on people of mixed descent, which was phenomenal. I loved that class, so I had all this material and was ready to make this presentation.) There were only two of us in the racial relations class who were mixed-race. The other girl was half Latino and half Irish, and she was all about being Latina and into salsa and the Puerto Rican liberation movement. I was trying to relate to her and would say, "I've been to Puerto Rico twice, I lived there for a summer, and I speak Spanish," and she barely speaks Spanish. She did her Latino presentation but not her white presentation.

The way we did our presentation was to give people cards. One said how they looked, like this was their new identity, and we asked them to go and find people like themselves. Then we gave them another card that was who they really were—like maybe one person looked Black but they were really half Asian and half Black. Then we gave them another card about where they came from, like if they were rich or poor, or had been raised with contact with only one side of their family or both sides. They tried to group themselves, and by the end, there were some groups that had nobody in them, and some had four people. And everybody got it.

Then we went back to our discussion and we talked about interracial dating. The girl who was doing the presentation with me said how she was in a club, and "this girl went up to talk with my classmate's boyfriend, and I looked over and wondered who was this white bitch talking with him." Then she realized the girl was Latina and she was like, "Oh, it's cool, I bet she's just hanging out." I got so angry with her. We were giving a presentation on people of mixed-races and she's talking about a "white bitch." I was like, would you call your mother a white bitch? (Her mother's Irish.) The last day of class I confronted her. "The reason no one argues with you personally is because you always put yourself on the 'right' side, like 'you can't talk to me because I'm always down with every minority,' but the minute somebody could attack you for having a white part of yourself you totally deny it." She couldn't say anything about it because she knew I was right. It was so frustrating, because it would be like me calling someone a "nigger ho."

We had to do a final project in the racial relations class. The project was to do something that makes you uncomfortable, so the professor decided he wanted me to start attending these Black retention and recruitment meetings. It was a Black organization on campus that goes to public schools and encourages people to go to Berkeley, and once they're there, they offer tutoring to keep them on the right track. I went to a meeting and quickly realized it was something I didn't want to do because it was a totally hostile group. Even the guy who was the president of the group was in my racial relations class, and he said, "We totally discourage any other races joining our group."

So after taking the class I went through a major identity crisis. I basically came out of the experience identifying as a person of mixed-race. I can't identify as a Black person because that requires me looking somewhat Black. But as a mixed-race person, I can say that I'm multicultural and I have experienced Black culture in my own way and it's a part of me, but it's not the only part of me.

Having to identify yourself is totally annoying because society is not structured in such a way that's healthy. In my mixed-race class we talked about the census and how controversial it is to allow a multiracial category. Now Republicans and all these conservatives have jumped on it because "it's so great because we are this diverse society," but others think that if you identify as mixed-race you're taking away from the power of individual racial groups. I feel like whites have enough power in this society, I feel like I should be supporting African Americans, but at the same time I don't feel it's fair. I feel embarrassed to turn something in with that box checked because the person looking at me is going to think I'm lying. It's just a total struggle every day to figure out what you want to be.

My class on people of mixed races was taught by Steven Small, and he's from Liverpool, England, which has the highest mixed-race population in the entire world. It was a port and there were all these prostitutes, poor whites, and slaves, and they mixed together to create this huge mixed-race population. He's hilarious and a great guy. His dad is Jamaican and his mom is white. When he first walked into the classroom, no one could figure out where he was from. I thought he might be Maori from New Zealand because he's light skinned and has freckles and a beard. He talks about how he gets stopped on planes because people think he's Arab. We learned so much in that class on how America is so into denial about mixed-race. Hawaii is 75 percent mixed-race. Maria Root wrote this great anthology on people of mixed-race. She's Filipino and Native American. She came up with a bill of rights for mixed-race people. One day I'm going to frame it in my room. Every annoyance I've had about being mixed-race she totally addresses.

Right now, diversity is such a big issue. I think people are going to let go after a while and realize that people are just people. In the real world you're not talking about this all the time.

My boyfriend's grandfather is Italian—this big, powerful, wealthy man—but he's totally racist, as is his wife. My boyfriend has told his family that I'm half Black, but somehow I don't offend him. His cousin is married to this Black guy who was a professional basketball player, a real nice and responsible person. Every year the family has Christmas gatherings, and last year the grandfather didn't come because he didn't want to be in the same room as this Black guy. The children of these two people are very Black little kids, but somehow they don't offend him. It's just the guy. ■■■

I hired Joseph Smooke as housing director for the Bernal Heights Neighborhood Center over seven years ago. He recently completed building Bernal Gateway, a fifty-five-unit housing development for very low-income and working-class families, a project I began before leaving San Francisco. Our unique service provider, The Family School, is located on the ground floor. For over sixteen years TFS has helped hundreds of women —primarily mothers of color—make the transition from welfare dependence to economic independence, as well as helping the fathers who are seeking better parenting skills and job security.

Bernal Gateway recently won the prestigious Maxwell Award from the Fannie Mae Foundation. Joseph invited me to participate in the ceremony, held in Washington, D.C. It was a grand reunion with staff I'd hired over the years, and an opportunity to learn from other groups that provide desperately needed affordable housing across our land.

Joseph is Jewish, and his wife Sharon is Chinese. I talked with them before their millennium wedding, with a rabbi and priest equally performing the unique ceremony. They asked friends to participate by reading special quotes they had gathered for the occasion. I felt honored to be included in that group.

JOSEPH SMOOKE

I was born in L.A., and my family has always been very close. I have a sister and a brother, and we're still close. There is a very strong Jewish population there, not only in the Fairfax area, but all over L.A.

I had many generations of family there—I even had great-grandparents for a lot of my childhood and was very attached to them. They and their children (my grandparents) were the generation who moved to this country, except for my mother's father's family, which has been in this country, in the South, since before the Civil War. All of my family is European Jewish heritage, with three-quarters very new to this country, and the other being steeped in the southern tradition.

Joseph Smooke, right, with his sister in Los Angeles

My father's family came from Poland and Hungary in the era during the pogroms, when people were going around the countryside rounding up Jews and killing them. The pogroms started in Russia and spread to eastern Europe. There was a large immigration of Jews to this country at that time—the late nineteenth and early twentieth century. In eastern Europe, if you were Jewish you were generally bilingual in Yiddish and the native language of the country you lived in. My father's grandparents spoke Hungarian and Yiddish on his father's side and Polish and Yiddish on his mother's side.

I'm still struggling with the question: Where is Judaism a religion, and where is it a race or a culture? Where do Jews define themselves as a race? It's still something I'm trying to understand. The whole practice of Judaism blurs those lines because a lot of Judaism is rooted in family tradition and ritual rather than the synagogue. Going to synagogue is not like going to church on Sunday. A lot of Jews observe the Sabbath by going to temple, but that's not necessarily what Judaism is all about. A lot of what you do spiritually as a Jew manifests as ritual you perform at home and with your family.

My parents didn't regularly practice the Jewish tradition besides going to temple every year for the major holy days. When we were kids, we went to school at the temple on Sundays and Jewish camp in the summers. I liked going to Jewish camp. This is where I made most of my childhood friends. It also served to ground me in my Jewish traditions.

My community was white and mainly Christian. We were in the geographic center of L.A. on the San Fernando Valley side of the hills that separate the city from the valley. I attended a big neighborhood elementary school that was mostly white. In seventh grade I went to a private all-boys school that was more diverse, because they were making a concentrated effort to give scholarships to minorities. I had some courses there which introduced me to African and Asian cultures and mandatory language study in Latin, French, Spanish, and Russian.

I went to Cal Berkeley in 1984, which was diverse, but not as diverse as it is now. My roommate tried to bring attention to the university that the student body and faculty should be a lot more diverse. They weren't paying as much attention to diversity as they should have. But having grown up in a Jewish environment, it was interesting to come into contact with Arabs and Palestinians and hear their viewpoint on events I had studied growing up. It was very eye-opening.

A few years after graduation I became engaged to a Jewish woman. There are so many ways to be Jewish, and there have always been divisions between different kinds of Jews throughout history. Her family is Conservative and her grandfather had been a rabbi in Russia, so the family was very concerned about assimilation. I was raised as a Reform Jew. The issue of assimilation has been difficult for Jews throughout history. One cause of anti-Semitism in Europe is that Jews developed their own Yiddish language and lived in ghettos. The kosher laws are an important factor as well, because Jews must prepare their own food to ensure it adheres to the kosher laws. For centuries, Jews felt a strong desire to be a part of the country in which they lived, but they had to live somewhat apart to preserve their purity of ritual. The dichotomy of the Jews' success and separateness led to hostility. Despite this separateness, Jews have contributed to mainstream culture through science, philosophy, and other major arenas.

Retaining some of your own culture and transferring culture from generation to generation grounds us and enriches our experience. In this country there are more Jews than anywhere else in the world. Because the country is so large and diverse, there are many ways to be Jewish. My family is associated with the Reform movement of Judaism, which started in Israel. Reform Judaism attempts to adapt the teachings of the Bible to relate to modern day. Despite my Reform upbringing, I was attracted to some of the Conservative traditions as well. In fact, I just recently switched affiliation from a Reform congregation to a Conservative one where the rabbi is also a Buddhist with strong leadership in areas of social justice.

My family never pushed me to be with someone Jewish. If you go back another generation, they might say that the grandkids should be with Jewish people, but maybe not. They have always been pretty open-minded.

Sharon and I have been together four and a half years now, and the first time she met my grandmothers it was amazing. They didn't really respond to the fact that she wasn't Jewish. They acknowledged the fact that she was Chinese in a positive way. My dad's parents loved to travel, and their house was filled with beautiful relics from everywhere they had been. China was a particular favorite of my grandmother. The first time Sharon visited her, Sharon was incredibly nervous until my grandmother started showing her the jade and porcelain she had collected and told Sharon stories about each one. This helped the nervousness fade, and a wonderful bond emerged which developed for years.

I think people retaining their cultural identity is very important, and it's incumbent on everybody, if there's going to be a dent in addressing the issues of racism, to learn as much as they can about different cultures. You can't legislate an end to racism. You can educate an end, but obviously people have to be willing to learn before you can really make a dent in it. The more you learn about another culture, the more tolerant you are, because you understand why a culture is that way. There are so many things that may look stupid, weird, or funny, but when you understand them, you realize that what you're looking at is a slight deviation on a very similar human response. Most things people deal with are very common to everybody. ■■■

SHARON LI

I grew up in San Francisco in the Richmond area, where I live now. It's largely a Russian community today, but when I was growing up it was mainly Chinese. I have two nice parents and an older sister and brother (also nice). My parents immigrated from China, initially living in Chinatown, then they were helped by my father's parents to move out to the Richmond district. When my father came over here, he lived with his oldest brother—there's a twenty-year age difference—and worked in his corner variety store on Fillmore Street. When my mother came over later, she also worked in my uncle's store.

I went to a Catholic school, St. Monica's on 25th Avenue, a couple of blocks from where I grew up. I had to wear a uniform in grammar school and high school. The population was mixed between Caucasian and Asian, with very few African Americans and Latinos. I went on to St. Rose Academy, an all-girls Catholic high school, then to the University of San Francisco, a private Catholic Jesuit university. I was always a minority in my schools. Now the population of Asians in my grammar school and USF has increased.

Sharon Li, middle, with her brother and sister in San Francisco

My family, especially my mother, hung on very tightly to all the Chinese traditions. My father was able to become more acculturated to American society because he came over when he was younger and went to Galileo High School (a racially mixed public school). Through his work as a butcher at Cala Foods, he interacts with all sorts of people all the time, and his English is very good. My mother was sheltered for a long time and didn't know very many people outside of the neighborhood and church. She was a homemaker and never had an outside job. When she did make friends, they were always Asian. She didn't trust American society. Growing up, she would encourage me to have Chinese friends, speak more Chinese, and be more Chinese. It was really difficult. My father had a sense of race, of different people and American culture. She did not let go of the hope that her daughters would marry "good" Chinese men.

The biggest step in my life was moving out of the house during college. No one else in my immediate or extended family had done such a thing, because you're supposed to stay home until you get married.

After college I met Joe. At first I didn't tell my parents about him, because I didn't see my parents much. Our relationship was strained because I was living on my own. At a certain point I felt confident and happy enough after dating Joe for a year that I wanted to let my parents know about him. Telling them about Joe was one of the first steps in rebuilding my relationship with them. It just happened that my mother wanted to have dim sum with me. It was an unusual move on her part, since we never had lunch together, just the two of us. She "just wanted to see if everything was OK and was I getting enough to eat." Then she ventured out and asked, "Are you going out with anyone?" And I said, "Actually, I am." She asked, "Is he Chinese?" and I said, "No." She said, "Well, OK, invite him over for Chinese New Year's dinner." I thought,

"Wow, that's huge. Chinese New Year's dinner! If he comes and it's bad luck, it's for a whole year!" Once they met him, they didn't make a huge issue out of anything, except for his being a vegetarian. The more they saw of Joe, all their preconceptions were proven untrue.

Joe and I now go over to my folks' home for dinner often, and they've gotten to know him—and me at the same time. It's really strengthened my relationship with my parents, and they trust me.

Regarding racism, I think it will always be around. We make great leaps and bounds, then we fall back. You probably saw in the newspaper about the leaflet in the Sunset district (a racist piece aimed at the Chinese community, basically saying, "Get out"). Then there were the swastikas two years ago. It's just going to keep going back and forth.

Sometimes I think too much attention is paid to race. When you bring up race, it almost creates racism. You have Ward Connerly* saying, "We don't need this special treatment," and other people saying, "We need this special treatment," then suddenly everybody is against each other. "You get this privilege? Maybe you shouldn't get this privilege." If you don't bring up race (I guess you can't help bring it up), there probably wouldn't be as many issues or problems. I wish it were that simple, that we could just be who we are without saying, "I'm Chinese, you're Jewish, you're Latino." It brings up all those stereotypes you were taught or read about, and they don't go away.

Sharon Li and Joseph Smooke on their wedding day, 2000

Time magazine did a cover where they morphed a whole bunch of races and what people will look like in the year "whatever" when the whole world becomes a melting pot. Technology moves quicker than sociology. People are interested in making things work, but they don't pay much attention to human and social issues as much as they should.

I think one main reason Joe gets along with my parents so well is that they show so much respect for their traditions and culture. I've gone to temple and participated in Seder with Joe's family because I have respect for that too, and they are welcoming to me in their traditions.

Joe and I are getting married next year, and we're planning an interfaith and intercultural wedding. We look forward to combining both

*Ward Connerly is a University of California trustee who authored a statewide initiative to ban affirmative action. It passed.

Jewish and Catholic faiths and representing both religions, as well as taking into account people's culture. Joe found a rabbi in Menlo Park who supports interfaith marriages and gladly agreed to do the ceremony. He said, "Rejecting interfaith marriages because they foster assimilation will have the opposite effect." I'm also lucky to have a priest who was willing and open to perform the ceremony with the rabbi. ■■■

The Southwest has always been a very special place to me, not only because my mother's roots were there, but also because of its haunting beauty and enduring peacefulness. In 1999 my English friend Edwina and I traveled over 3,000 miles throughout that breathtaking region of our country, from the Grand Canyon to Canyon de Chelly, Monument Valley to Acoma, Santa Fe, Taos, Mesa Verde, Bryce, and Zion.

We caught up with our friend Nancy Black when we were in Albuquerque, New Mexico, where she's lived for many years. We first met Nancy in Findhorn, Scotland, when Edwina took me there several years ago for a week of meditation, gardening, dance, and smooth scotch at the local pub.

NANCY BLACK

I grew up in very white suburbs and knew absolutely nothing about Black people for quite a while. I remember a gal who helped take care of me, and she was white and had red hair. I think she was from Ireland. So even the "servant class" was white. That was in Woodmere, Long Island, where I was a child just before World War II.

I had no awareness of race. I remember things like Shirley Temple and Bill "Bojangles" Robinson, and that's a movie—not real life. I wasn't aware of racial differences until we moved to Winnetka, Illinois, which is a white suburb of Chicago. There was still not an issue except for going into Chicago. Seeing people through a bus window, I was aware that people come in different colors. That was my only sense of it.

I went to Northshore, a white country day school, for my middle school years, and we had field hockey teams that competed with other schools. Francis Parker was a very good school in Chicago, and their team came out to play us. There were three Black kids who were part of their team, and their parents were part of the audience. I didn't feel negative, but I was curious. "Oh, they have kids who go to school," like I didn't know anything.

My next memory is my family flying to Florida from Chicago through Atlanta. I remember very clearly walking through the Atlanta airport and seeing water fountains marked "White Only" and "Colored Only," and it shocked me. My next thought was, "That will hurt their feelings," and it just struck me as uncomfortably rude. I guess my heart was in the right place, for as little as I knew, that offended me.

We moved into Chicago, and I went to that Francis Parker school and for the first time had contacts with Black kids. There were four in a class of forty-two, and one Asian kid whose father was a wealthy Chinese businessman. One of the Black kids was a very beautiful girl whose father was a successful attorney. She was being raised to be "a credit to her race." There was a lot of pressure on her to do well. She just died last year of cancer, and I thought, "Shit, man, you pushed her too hard." I had written her a card when I found out she was sick, but she died before she could read it.

I wasn't close to any of those kids because I wasn't socially adept. I didn't have any really good friends, but the Black kids were just as involved and integrated into Francis Parker as anybody else. It was a very sophisticated school with very bright kids. We had a sense of shared superiority over the public schools. I remember arrogant

Nancy Black and her daughter Diana in Memphis, Tennessee

comments like, "The difficult we do immediately, the impossible takes a little longer." The "we" included everybody at the school. Parker wasn't a rich kids' snob school—it was intellectually snobbish, and that's different. I'm sure the Black kids would have felt some social isolation, but I felt it too, so I didn't know the difference. I wasn't in the "in" group, and I was white. We all volunteered on Saturdays at a settlement house in a poor Black neighborhood. We got involved from the point of view of the responsibility of privilege.

I started having a split between my parents and my peers and teachers that I respected. My father was bigoted, rigid, and a jerk, but I am fourteen years old, and it's OK if you don't agree with your father. You just go with people you respect and to hell with the fact that he was a jerk. It didn't affect me except in terms of resentment. I knew he was wrong, and I don't think he would have commented on the colored water fountains in the Atlanta airport. He didn't go out of his way to do racist things, mostly because he could ignore the whole issue. That was the generation that could pretend it didn't matter—who could say Lena Horne's a good singer and think they were being liberal.

By the time I went to college, I felt like I knew what I was doing. I became a liberal Democrat and active in the integration movement. I was at the University of Miami by then—a lily-white private school in the middle of Florida. I was taking a human relations course in 1954. It was a good class. We read the hate literature of Gerald L. K. Smith and others: analyzed, interpreted, and understood it. I had never read hate literature before or seen anything so nasty. I think the hate stuff was aimed against the dispossessed, the poor whites, to give them someone to resent. "It's got to be somebody's fault, it must be them!" I learned about leadership and mob psychology. A lot of things came together so when *Brown v. the Board of Education* came out in 1954, our teacher went over the meaning of the decision and all the justices involved. It was very good opportunistic teaching.

I and half a dozen others decided we were going to start pressuring the University of Miami to admit Black students, even though the court didn't say they had to because they were a private school. We started raising hell, and we had more fun. It was my first social action, and then it got a little scary because after you leave campus there are some bad neighborhoods, some working-class white neighborhoods, and those were the people troubled by all this. We had a demonstration going and attracted some white hate. People screamed at us from their cars that we were "a bunch of stupid fuckin' nigger lovers," and I was proud of that. We must be doing something right!

Forward to living in Albuquerque, being divorced, and having two small kids. I became active in politics and got to know all the current politicians. I had a friendly acquaintance with a guy named Lenton Mallory, who was the only Black Commissioner we had. (There aren't many Black people in New Mexico.) He stopped in to give me some papers, and I offered him coffee and a plate of cookies. My little boy, who was then four years old, was trying to be charming and asks me, "Can I have a cookie?" I had a bunch of assorted cookies, and I said, "Yes, you can have a cookie, but don't touch it until you're sure which one you want." He starts saying, "Eeny meeny miney mo," and I hear Len take a deep breath and hold it, and then "Catch a tiger by the toe," and Len exhales in relief. I said to Len, "You gotta be taught." And we didn't say anymore about it. He knew what I meant and I knew what he meant. "You gotta be taught."

In 1965 I met the senator from Los Alamos and northern Santa Fe, whose name was Sterling Black. He's the son of Supreme Court Justice Hugo Black. He was the darling of the liberals and was the smartest, sweetest, handsomest man. The interesting thing was that I really knew about his father, and I had a lot of strong positive feelings about him. I knew his father had written the *Brown v. the Board of Education* decision, although Earl Warren was the chief justice of the Court. Hugo Black put pressure on Felix Frankfurter to make the decision unanimous. He had to negotiate with Felix. They were strong standing adversaries, not enemies. It was essentially Felix's fault that they had to put in the phrase "with all deliberate speed." That's the one thing Hugo Black regretted. He was not a warm family man at all. He was awesome and distant, but that made it more interesting to talk with him. He's known as the First Amendment scholar: freedom of religion and protected free speech. Legal historians consider him one of the top five justices in our history.

There were a lot of reasons why I fell in love with Sterling, not the least of which was his civil rights background and his connection with a tradition for which I had enormous respect. It was an issue of character, and that was a good reason to marry him. I would have slept with him anyway, but marrying takes more than just being hot for someone! I wanted his child, too—in a couple of years. We were then involved in the civil rights movement and anti–Vietnam War. Then we got me pregnant after that was over.

In 1968 we were in the middle of Gene McCarthy's campaign for president. Lyndon Johnson was not going to run, at which point we felt we had won, because that's what we wanted. We wanted to take down the president, who kept insisting that an anti-Vietnam movement was treason against his terrible, illegal, and immoral war. We didn't expect Gene McCarthy to be elected president, least of all Gene himself, who really didn't want to be president at that point. It was about a much larger issue. It was also very interwoven with the civil rights movement, and I had been active in that but wasn't on the front line or in the bus.

The day that Martin Luther King was assassinated, Sterling and I were driving down from Los Alamos, where we lived, to a meeting of county coordinators in Albuquerque. It was an in-group of the McCarthy campaign in New Mexico, and Sterling was chairman. We heard of King's assassination in the car on the way down. We got to the meeting, and a few people were there already. They heard the news and were shocked, and we talked about canceling, but there were some people coming in from a long way. We decided to have another kind of meeting. One of the people coming in was from Farmington, near Shiprock. He had just expressed interest in helping with the campaign. He was a newcomer to us, and he sounded like a "good ole boy." He came in mouthing obscenities about "Well, he was just a troublemaker. We're just as well rid of him," and Bob Harris, who was hosting the meeting, said, "You will leave my house," and this guy couldn't believe it. He didn't know how violently we disagreed with him.

We then made phone calls to our political allies who were Black, and we all went together down to the federal courthouse at 5th and Gold. We collected a whole bunch of people, about ten white people and several dozen Black people, and we start doing a ritual for King. That night we stood there and did a close circle, where it's hand over hand and you're with a hundred people, but it's a really tight circle. We sang together for a couple of hours, and I do believe that was why there was no rioting in Albuquerque when Martin Luther King was killed. We had blended with, mourned with all the Black leaders in our community. We were where we belonged.

After the Vietnam movement was over I had twins, and we also have other older kids. My favorite story is when the twins were fifteen years old and it's the centenary of Hugo Black's birth. (He died when the twins were a year and a half old.) The post office comes out with a new stamp, and they decide to have the party of all parties. Everybody connected with Hugo Black was invited. We get on our good clothes and go back to Washington. All living members of the present and former Supreme Court were there: Sandra Day O'Connor, the first woman; all of Justice Black's former law clerks (a lot of them now famous people in their own right); and it's an awe-inspiring event. My kids did very well, and I was very proud of them. They met and talked with everybody.

We're back in the hotel room after this big bash, and my son Stevie is saying to Diana something about Marshall. "Which one was Marshall?" Diana asked. And Stevie answered, "The fat one who sounded funny when he breathed." Stevie did not identify Thurgood Marshall as Black —he identified him as to what was important to him, and Justice Marshall did have a breathing problem and a tummy. That was much more important to my son, even though Thurgood Marshall was the first and only Black Supreme court justice at that time. Sterling and I looked at each other and grinned. Our son hadn't been raised to focus on skin color, and I thought, "Well, we did something right."

As a psychotherapist I have learned how to connect with and be useful to patients of all different backgrounds and ethnicities. It always takes effort to enter another person's worldview, use their vocabulary, catch the subtleties of their communication. But basic emotions and primary experiences are universal. We are all much more alike than different by virtue of being human. ▪■▪

D iana Black is Nancy's exceptional daughter, who recently received her graduate degree in education from the University of California at Berkeley. Diana's rich and poignant experiences with the Teach for America program in the Mississippi Delta provide powerful insights into how we can connect with one another across racial lines if we try, as well as the ongoing institutional and personal racism that continues to stain the South and the rest of our nation.

DIANA BLACK

I was born and raised in Albuquerque, New Mexico. I lived there until I was eighteen, then I went away to college. During that time I went to two schools—both small and private that were independent and pretty homogeneous, especially in regard to money, but also in regard to race. There was one Black person, a couple of East Indians, one or two Native Americans, and one or two Hispanics. Everybody else was white. Although it was a very liberal school and everybody was very well intentioned when it came to race, there was very little actual experience with different races. I had a couple of friends who were Hispanic and went to public schools, and I dated one of them. He was also very educated and came from a mixed-race background—a Jewish mother and Hispanic father—so there weren't very many cultural barriers for us to overcome. He was the first one to tell me stories about day-to-day racism. For example, he and I had very different experiences driving through Oklahoma.

I got stopped for speeding, and the police officer became very fatherly to me and decided that I was going to make something out of my life (maybe because I had college stickers on the back of my car). He wasn't going to give me a ticket, and by the way, "Don't stop for strangers, and make sure you don't pick up anyone on the side of the road," and all of this very paternal thing, which was nice. My boyfriend, on the other hand, was going to the University of Oklahoma in Tulsa with a couple of friends, and they got stopped for speeding. They were asked to step out of the car and go ten feet away and turn their backs on the car while the police officer searched the car.

The family I was raised in was very involved in civil rights, and historically was involved. I was highly aware growing up that that was part of my heritage. I knew that my grandfather had written the decision for *Brown v. the Board of Education.* I knew that my father and mother had been involved in politics and that race was a big issue. On the other hand, as my brother pointed out to me once when we were about seventeen, "Do you realize we've never had a Black person walk through our doorway?" It was true—partially because we're from New Mexico. There's the theoretical in not being racist, and the actual dealing with other races and understanding them.

The first Black person I ever met was at Northwestern. I remember being excited that I knew him because we were very comfortable with each other and spent a lot of time talking. I remember things like looking at his hand. I had never known before that Black people's palms were lighter than the backs of their hands. I never knew the veins in their palms were darker. I had never touched Black hair before, and he and I had a very comfortable relationship, so he didn't mind me looking at his palms or touching his hair. Northwestern was a small, private, expensive white school. There weren't that many people of color—of any color.

The whole thing repeated again at Indiana for my master's degree, a very white place. Here I was, a white woman who's as white as you get, culturally speaking, but well intentioned and well meaning! I applied and got into Teach for America and was placed in the Mississippi Delta. (Teach for America is an organization that works for educational equity through a national corps of dedicated teachers who work in areas of chronic teacher shortage.)

I had never heard of the Mississippi Delta before. I didn't know where it was. I started reading up on the place, and it turns out that the Delta is to Mississippi what Mississippi is to the rest of the country. It's the place of the biggest gaps between rich and poor, the biggest gaps between whites and Blacks. It's the poorest place in the state, which is the poorest state in the nation. It's got the worst education in the state, which is the worst education in the nation. It's a place that's completely suffering from its history as a plantation area, which is what it was. It's the best cotton-growing area anywhere, other than Egypt. It was controlled completely by rich white landowners, and its history is completely shaped by that.

The area itself is 40 percent Black. The public school system is 97 percent Black. As soon as desegregation was pushed through around the mid-1960s, the whites left immediately and built their own schools. Some of them are good, and some are terrible. They're just white. In my two years of teaching, out of over 300 children I had three white students, one of whom dropped out halfway through.

The area is incredibly isolated and poor. Most of my children had never been out of that local area. I took a field trip once to Memphis with some of the kids, and one of the most exciting new and challenging things for them to do was to ride an escalator, because most of them had never ridden escalators.

The school was in a place called Ruleville, where Fannie Lou Hamer* is from. It always struck me as a metaphor of what's going on in that community, because here is the spirit of Fannie Lou Hamer, the biggest hell-raising spirit that Mississippi ever turned out, and what happened to that spirit of productive rebellion? It doesn't exist anymore.

The school itself had 380 students in it from ninth through twelfth grade. It fed from Ruleville itself, which is a town of 2,500, and Sunflower, a neighboring town of 500.

The school is called Ruleville Central High School, because before desegregation it was the Ruleville Colored High School, and they didn't want to have to change the sign that said "RCHS." So despite the fact that it's the only high school in Ruleville, it's called Ruleville Central High School.

Diana Black, back row left center, with her class in Ruleville, Mississippi

The system itself has over a 50 percent dropout rate, starting in fifth grade, so we had 180 freshmen and 60 seniors. There were at least six of my students who had children during the time that I taught. There were many more who had children from before.

I was the only Teach for America person there. Out of twenty teachers, I think five were non-Black, one of whom was Chinese, and the rest were white. There was hostility toward me from almost everybody, white or Black. I think it had less to do with the fact that I was white and

*Fannie Lou Hamer (1917–1977) was born into a family of impoverished Mississippi sharecroppers. She became a national symbol for disenfranchised Blacks in her state, and a key founding member of the Mississippi Freedom Democratic Party.

more with the fact that I was there for two years. A lot of the teachers felt stuck. They had never been anywhere either. Most of them had graduated from Ruleville and went to the college down the road. I was dropping in for two years then leaving, and there was a lot of hostility toward that.

There were two wonderful father figures who took me under their wing. The janitor was one who gave me the best advice the entire two years, looked out for me, protected me when I needed it, told me how to handle students, and gave me culturally specific advice. One other teacher had been in the army in Korea and was older. He came out of retirement, although they weren't paying him. Go figure. He was an excellent teacher and was very nice to me. He saw me at one point when I walked outside crying, and he just talked me down. He'd say, "Yeah, I understand, sometimes it's too much, this happens to me," and just calmed me down.

My first day or two on the job I was a little intimidated. I had never had any experience with Black people. I had to walk through a whole gauntlet of students who were waiting out in the hallways, and it was pretty intimidating. After the first two days I realized I had nothing to fear, and for the rest of the two years I was never scared by any of my students. That's a big difference between urban schools and rural schools.

The closest thing to intimidation that was ever tried on me was by one of my students named Anthony. He was in my ninth-grade English class, and I told my students that at the end of nine weeks if they got an A on the final they would have an A for the course, and he was flunking. He decided he wanted an A, so he cheated on his test. I walked up to him after I heard his paper rustling and picked up the sheet that had all the vocabulary written on it. I looked at it, took his test, ripped it up, and threw it away. He wasn't happy. He's got to be six foot three, and his brother (another student of mine) is probably six foot four. At lunch they walked into my classroom with another boy I didn't know, equally as tall. They surrounded my desk as I was sitting at it, and I looked up and said to myself, "OK, they're trying to intimidate me about the test." I looked up at Anthony's brother Floyd, who is one of my very favorite students and I have a pretty special relationship with. I said, "Are you still thinking of dropping out of school, like you were saying this morning?" and he said, "No, ma'am." I said, "I'd miss you so much if you did that. I'm glad you changed your mind," and he said, "Yes ma'am," and he walked away! So I turned to Anthony and said, "Why did you do that this morning? That killed me to have to tear up your paper. You would have been so much better off if you'd just studied and done what you could. We're going to work this semester to get you to where you need to be, and to make sure you're OK. Just don't do that again," and he said, "No ma'am," then he walked away! The third guy said to me, "You tore up Anthony's paper today, " and I said, "Yeah, I had to. He was cheating," and he said, "You're not going to give him the chance to retake the test?" I said, "No, I can't, that would be unfair to the other students," and he said, "Yes, ma'am," and he walked away! This is intimidation, Mississippi style.

Respect is thought of very differently down there. There's a heavy focus on fear and physical intimidation. Respect for most of the students is not something you earn by knowing things or having a skill. It's what you earn by intimidation, by kicking butt. The teachers who got respected were the ones who would yell at the kids or hit them in a fair way. A lot of the students interpreted my style of teaching as being scared—the idea that I would negotiate with my students, that I would allow them to do certain things that they weren't allowed to do in other classes. The first year I especially had problems with this, that I wouldn't send them to the office to "get whupped" if they did something.

I did a lot of African American literature and history with my students, and one of them said, "How do you know so much about us?" And I said, "Well, it's important to study, and this was one of my focuses in graduate school." The idea that white people would know about Black people was remarkable to them. I tried to use the fact that I was white and they were Black as often as possible to normalize racial differences. They've never met white people before. I let them touch my hair. That was a big deal. They'd never touched white people's hair before.

My first year I gave a lecture on slavery, and I had them write a response on how they felt being lectured about race by a white woman. All of them said, "As long as we're getting the information, as long as you're not racist, we'd rather be told by somebody than not know it. What you've told us is stuff we didn't know." I think that was true for most of them. In fact, most of them stopped considering me white, because in their minds, if you're white you're racist; therefore, if you're not racist you're not white. They sort of glommed on to the fact that I was Jewish as the reason I wasn't white.

Most of the kids' families were on welfare. Ninety-five percent of the students were on free or reduced lunch. One of my students showed me a food stamp at one point and I said, "Oh, what's that?" He was shocked and called everybody over and said, "Come on over, Miss Black doesn't know what a food stamp is!" The stores around there didn't take credit cards, but they did take food stamps.

A lot of the students had very unrealistic dreams about getting out of there, the ones who wanted the football and basketball scholarships. A lot of the students actually went on to college, although they're all local colleges, and they aren't better than most high schools. Most of the students wouldn't go to the best college around, which is primarily white. They wouldn't even conceive of it. I had one student who went to Ole Miss in Oxford, which is by far the best school in Mississippi. He was incredibly smart, and his whole family put all their energy into getting him out of there, and he knew this. He wrote different times about his ambivalence about it, and how he knew that's what he needed to do, but he was scared to do it. He drew a picture at one point representing "here" and "there" (a guided imagery practice that my mother had taken the students on), and "here" was drawn with flowers and colors, and "there" was a big city all in black and white, very looming and scary. The thing that was supposed to connect the two sides was a bridge, but his didn't touch either side.

I talked with other students about Ole Miss, and they said, "Oh, that's a white school. You don't understand, Miss Black, they don't want us there." One or two of them told me the KKK was still strong there. I don't know if it is or not, but it would not surprise me.

One time I was walking with some kids and they were telling me who lived where, and one of them said, "And a white woman lives there— Oh, I'm sorry Miss Black!" I said, "It's OK to say that people are white." We tried to dialogue about this. They told me how they did their hair for prom, how they got it all shellacked, and they let me touch it. I tried as much as possible to let that kind of thing happen. One morning I came in and had scratched my neck, so it was red. They were like, "Oh, you have a hickey." And I explained that I had scratched my neck. "Your skin doesn't turn red if you scratch your neck!" I went around and scratched my arm, showing them it was turning red. They had never seen this before.

I never tried to be cool in front of my kids and talk their language, but if I needed to, I could. At one point one of my kids was leaving and said, "Peace out, Miss Black," and I raised my fingers up and said, "Peace," and he said, "Oh! Miss Black, you're catching on!" A kid behind him said, "No, man, she's just doing that because that's one of them '60s hippie things!" He knew it meant two different things in two different cultures.

I knew on a theoretical level that race was a huge problem, but I didn't know how deeply embedded it was. I didn't know how much internalized oppression there was. I hadn't realized how tightly locked the system was. All the checks and balances that go from poor education, lack of economic opportunity, to family rearing habits that keep kids docile and poor performers, all of that kind of thing feeds back in itself to maintain the status quo. I hadn't realized that, so part of me has become much more dark about the possibility of change. Anyone who seriously looks at the issues of race in our society has to feel pessimistic to some extent.

One hundred thirty years after slavery ended and thirty years after the civil rights movement ended, I teach my students, "Then came desegregation," and I look around the classroom and ask, "So, do you guys think we're desegregated?" "No." "You're right." I ask my students, "Do you think it's still the same? Have there been improvements?" I think some of them understand that there have been some improvements. I always want to make it clear that "you guys are better off than slavery time, nobody owns you," but at the same time, on so many other levels, the whole system of the United States is built to keep them from winning these battles.

I feel like I'm this prophet trying to talk with my friends who are upper middle class, mostly white, or some way privileged, who really don't understand how far down the bottom of our society is. I have one friend who's a Republican and Libertarian. When you talk to him about economics, he says, "I understand poverty, I was poor when I grew up. I was the only person in my high school who had to work to go to Europe over the summer." One of my students once asked me, "Miss Black, do you always have food in your cabinets at the end of the month?" That is a whole different range. That is so far removed from having to work to go to Europe. I think it's really dangerous for people to be that ignorant about how far down the bottom is, because they think that everybody can solve their problems the way they do. The "pull yourselves up by your own bootstraps" mentality only works if everybody is, at worst, lower middle class. They don't understand that these kids are not going to be able to make it no matter how hard they work. Furthermore they probably won't work that hard, not because they're lazy, but because there's absolutely no reason to. ▪▪▪

I met Roberto Chené through Dr. Beth Roy, my next-door neighbor and friend in San Francisco. He is a respected consultant on intercultural leadership training and conflict resolution in Albuquerque, New Mexico. Roberto and Beth served together on the board of the National Conference on Peacemaking and Conflict Resolution, which provides resources on cultural competency, race, racism, and diversity for mediators across the country.

When I began talking with Roberto in Albuquerque, I was astounded when he told me that he was from Dawson, the town where my mother had been born thirty-seven years before him. Roberto's analysis of our major societal problem as one of white dominance and subordination of people of color presents a clear path out of the labyrinth of racism and classism in our country. White people just need to decide personally and institutionally to walk our way through it.

ROBERTO CHENÉ

I was born in 1945 in a small mining camp in northern New Mexico called Dawson, my mother's hometown. My father, who died six years ago, is from Las Vegas, New Mexico. When my folks got married in 1944, they stopped by Dawson on their way to California to say good-bye, and somebody said, "Hey, we have jobs here," so they stayed. My dad got a job in the tipple, which was part of the processing plant outside the mines.

Roberto Chené as a young boy in Santa Fe, New Mexico

When the town closed down in 1950 we moved to Santa Fe, following jobs and other family members. I started school there. When you're a child, you don't think about "this is who I am," but in retrospect, you begin to see how race or ethnicity is a factor in your life.

I went to Catholic school—had a lovely nun in the first grade and a mean nun in the second grade, and I began to feel that school was becoming unsafe for me. I'd come home crying and finally convinced my parents to send me to public school. The nuns would punish us and slap us if we spoke Spanish in class or on the playground. Even if you didn't directly get hit, you'd know that you could be, or your friends would get hit. This was all part of how the education system was used to "Americanize" the Mexican Southwest—New Mexico in particular.

We didn't speak much Spanish at home and were quickly socialized to speak English. My grandmother spoke Spanish, which allowed me to preserve Spanish fluency. The assumption was that if you want to make it in the world, you'd better speak English. One consequence of this is that it was not uncommon in Spanish class in middle and high school that Anglos would get better grades than us native speakers. What the

Anglos didn't have was the language oppression we dealt with. When you oppress someone because of their language, you instill a set of feelings that make it difficult or uncomfortable for them to speak their own language. The same people who oppressed the language out of you also wondered, "How come you don't speak your own language?" It's a contradiction you grow up with. Anglos are not taught that they are members of the dominant culture, so they are often very naive about the consequences of cultural dominance. They view themselves as innocent. It is a form of institutional ignorance.

To their credit, my parents took me out of Catholic school and sent me to public school. We were racially and ethnically mixed, but when I'd encounter other young Latinos or Chicanos, I wanted to avoid them. I'd get picked on a lot by bullies who were Chicano. Even when we moved to Albuquerque in 1955, anytime I got in a fight it was with another Chicano. I began to have this sense that there was this threat among my own, and I didn't have that threat with Anglos.

Looking back, I had three strikes against me: my name was Chené, which did not identify me as Hispanic; I was light skinned; and I got good grades—all of which, in young minds, identified me as being on the Anglo side. This is another common internalized consequence of white cultural dominance.

I went back to Catholic school in the sixth grade, hoping it would be safer, and it was. It was predominantly Hispanic, but ethnicity wasn't a big factor then. When I got to high school, it became more of a factor. There were also some Anglo friends who socialized in our direction. There were some Native American people who were part of this mix, and once in a great while African American. We were all being pressured to socialize in the Anglo direction to varying degrees, which becomes an issue in modern-day New Mexico and the United States: To what degree is anyone socialized in the white direction? Who's more assimilated than who? I was very much aware, for example, that my name, Chené, was a French Canadian name originally. (French Canadians moved into northern New Mexico—fur trapping, lumber work, etc.) Chené, LeDoux, LeFebre—those names are thought of as Hispanic or Chicano names today, but they were originally French Canadian.

My father was French Canadian and Mexican, so that part of the family tended to be fair skinned. He was Chené through his father and Lopez through his mother. Nobody was quite sure what kind of a name Chené was. We were also predominantly English speaking, although bilingual, so it was not quite clear who we were. If you're light skinned and your name is Chené, you're not Chavez or Sanchez. All those factors contributed toward my feeling of being marginalized from my own Hispanic community. My mother is Trujillo through her father and Roybal through her mother. Her heritage is Mexican and Pueblo Indian.

After high school I got an academic scholarship to the University of New Mexico. By then, I had developed a love for Spanish and everything Spanish—from Spain to Mexico. I also got involved with the Catholic Newman Center on campus, and through that connection I went to work in a barrio project in Chicago's South Side—my first time away from New Mexico. That experience, leaving home and going to a big city, more than anything cemented my self-identity. I joined the Dominican order to become a priest, and I did that for seven years. I lived in Chicago, Minnesota, and Iowa. Outside of New Mexico I was related to as Mexican, which forced me to confront my sense of identity. I claimed my identity as alternately Chicano and Mexican American.

A few months prior to being ordained, I decided to leave and get married. My wife had been a nun for eight years. We met in Cuernavaca, Mexico, where she was studying Spanish and liberation theology.

Roberto Chené and his family in Albuquerque, New Mexico

I gave my first sermon in Dubuque, Iowa, on December 12, 1970. I had become aware of the Mexican migrant population because of the farming in that area. My sermon was on Cesar Chavez and social justice issues. It was a significant thing for me to speak before a church full of people talking about these issues and publicly claiming who I am. It's a process of putting yourself out there and saying, "This is who I am." It forces one to think, "Am I really that?" You become clearer in terms of which parts you're in touch with and which parts are hurt because of your experiences. Being a Chené, for example, left me feeling that I'm not quite Hispanic enough compared to others. That becomes an issue. I'm sure you've had the experience of meeting people, regardless of how they look or how they talk, who don't appear to be who they are. We all know what that looks and feels like. These issues aren't exclusive to any particular race or people of color. Any human being oppressed enough can lose who they are. That's life. But in a society that values whiteness primarily, the dominant culture, it becomes an issue, just like male dominance becomes an issue.

If you're not white in America and you're aware at all, you know you're going to struggle to some degree, no matter how successful you are. Most people of color understand that, and it seems very few white people do. That gap of understanding needs to be bridged, because by and large, people of color understand more about bridging and have the skills to do it better than white society. That's the twenty-first-century challenge. Very few people are teaching white society that it needs to do some bridging in our direction. The weight of the historical melting pot has been on people of color and cultural minorities to do the melting. We need to equalize the "melting" for the twenty-first century.

One thing I say in my workshops is that people of color are more qualified for the type of interracial and intercultural competence we need in the twenty-first century. New Mexico, for example, suffers from what I call "bureaucratic colonization," where people will say, "This agency needs to become more culturally competent. We want more access, more availability to Indian and Hispanic populations, etc.," but it's a strange issue, because 80 percent of the people who work in these agencies are of those populations they claim they want access to. When they say they need intercultural competency, why do they need it if the people in those agencies are of those cultures? Between our 500-year legacy and the current form of bureaucratic colonization, it's not uncommon that agencies are culturally white and supervised by whites who may have come from out of state but credentially can move into a position of power.

It's a form of injustice that you're going to spend time, money, and resources either training these white people directly, or having the people of color in the agencies train them to serve the populations they came here unqualified to serve. It's institutional injustice. It's odious. It's extremely common, and people get offended when you point it out. I've said, "You don't need training. What you need to do is share power and let the people who are already competent do what they need to do, and you get out of their way. Your job is to facilitate their skill and collaborate to share power. Better yet, they should be running the show and you should be working for them." Not that that doesn't happen, because there are many white people who have bridged, who go out of their way to develop the competency and are sensitive enough to let themselves be transformed by what New Mexico is all about. They have become intercultural people who are allies you can count on. Fortunately, we also have many Hispanic and African American leaders at all levels in the state who model intercultural competence.

There are a lot of cross-cultural coalitions working together, but it's never enough. The other model is more predominating—the person who doesn't "get it" is the one with the authority, or the newcomer either comes with the naiveté of typical uneducated America about our issues, or they come at another level with millions of dollars and buy up whatever they please. Santa Fe is an example of a city where gentrification is destroying the local community, and it's painful to watch. I have friends who have either left town or moved to trailers.

A lot of the conflict resolution work I do now I structure around "cultural dominance" or "coercive assimilation" frameworks. The big conflict now between people of color and white liberals is about that. White liberals try to eliminate racism while practicing within the framework of assimilation to white culture. It's still their world that they're trying to be liberal in. What we need in the twenty-first century is intercultural reciprocal skills whereby you begin to work together to eliminate cultural dominance. The premise is that a social structure where some people are coerced into being like others is dysfunctional and can never be repaired by its nature. No matter how many affirmative action programs you have and how many scholarships you give, it's fundamentally flawed.

I think affirmative action is necessary because we need to keep the pressure on. The purpose of affirmative action has gotten lost in the debate. You don't provide opportunities for women and minorities because they are somehow deficient. You provide opportunity because you're deficient. The institution is deficient. It goes the extra step because *it is* dysfunctional. That's what affirmative action should be. An institution that understands this practice is what I call "recruit and nourish." They'll say, "We want women and minorities here, and after they come, we'll do whatever it takes to move in their direction and restructure ourselves so they're safe and welcome here." Most institutions practice what I call "recruit and abandon." We want these quotas, you come, but it's another form of assimilation. "Now that you're here, you carry the burden of fitting in to us, and we'll go out of our way to make it hard for you anyway, then we'll blame you when you drop out." This scenario happens a lot in our schools.

Historically, what the world has done is to try and resolve differences through dominance. No matter where you look—the U.S., Serbia, Northern Ireland—it's all the same thing in varying degrees. Resolving difference through dominance eventually unravels, because it's fundamentally antithetical to the relationship of healthy human beings. Ultimately, you need a framework that says, "Why don't we deal with the basic flaw—that dominance doesn't work." And what our society does, whether it's in terms of gender, sexual preference, race, etc., it transforms all these beautiful, diverse relationships into relationships of dominance and subordination. We are in conflict, but it is not about the differences ultimately. The conflict is about the dominance. There's a lot of work going on about white awareness, defining whiteness as a privileged reality that needs restructuring. Much more of that needs to happen, because the bulk of the work has been on the people of color side.

In terms of leadership, I find that people of color either don't need to be trained, or they just need to be validated for the leadership skills they already have. If you turn the experience on its head, the dynamics of exclusion from the mainstream becomes an incredible training ground for becoming functionally intercultural, an opportunity most white people do not have access to.

We need to frame leadership training so it's not a further exploitation of people of color. They basically possess the body of knowledge that's necessary to create an inclusive society. But their knowledge isn't taken seriously. We need to reframe our roles so that people of color can take their power in a nonvictim sense by creating an integrated world coated in their knowledge base. White people help create this world by learning how to listen and learn, and by being nonexploitative in how they learn. Right now, what often happens is that when white people become aware of how bad it is, they do another step in the oppression. White privilege causes them to say, "Oh man, this is awful. Can you now teach me how to make it better?" The burden of articulating the change still falls on people of color.

On the other hand, the way people of color step out of their victimization is to take their power and set the conditions of the learning. They reframe that privileged status and say, "Look, I'll work with you, but I'm not going to work with you until you're ready. If you were ready, you wouldn't have asked me to train you. So go and work with Helen for a while, who is our ally, then come back to me, and we'll try it again." We all need each other, but we need to eliminate the exploitative part of the transfer of knowledge.

So many of us Latinos and Latinas are bilingual or bicultural. We can live in our own culture and in the dominant culture. The dominant culture in the twenty-first century is at a major deficit. There is no institutionalized way for the dominant culture to become intercultural. Even when they want to, you can send them to a training program, but that's different than being forced to be interculturally competent by the social context. It's like you can help a man become feminist in a sense, but that's different than being a woman living in the context of male dominance. If it doesn't get you, it's an incredible training ground for incredible leadership skills. Us guys have to go and beat on drums, rip off Native culture, and we still don't get it! I asked these guys, "So what did you do? You beat on drums, and then what? How come you don't have a policy to eliminate male dominance in the work site?" And they say, "We're too busy drumming and feeling good."

My role as a person of color is to take my power and become a wise teacher, hopefully. Somebody else, say a white person, their role is to become a wise listener and learner and let themselves be transformed by my wisdom. This flawed relationship has within it the solution, but we have to be willing to take on a new role within that oppressive context. Ultimately, it has to be in terms of self-motivation. When you talk with people who have crossed these barriers, it's not about race ultimately, it's about human beings being human. ■■■

My uncle Fred Perdomo in San Francisco, 1939

My aunt Edna Perdomo on the left, and friend in her Mission District neighborhood, San Francisco

Fred Perdomo is my youngest cousin and has lived in Carson City, Nevada, for over twenty years. His father was my mother's younger brother, and he had a busy corner grocery store in San Francisco's Mission District, an amalgam of Italian, Irish, German, and Latino subcultures at that time. Uncle Fred, Aunt Edna, her German parents, and my cousin Fred lived above the store in a large, sunny flat. On the rare occasions we'd visit for dinner, Uncle Fred would take me downstairs to the closed store, turn on a light, and let me pick out my favorite candy bar, which was always a Peppermint Tree.

Fred and his wife Chris have taught and worked in the Carson City school district ever since they moved to Nevada. Fred is the vice principal at Carson City High School, the city's only high school. He took me on a tour of the large building the last time I visited. Their children, Rick and Kate, both attended the public schools in their community.

Fred is a very open and fair-minded man, and although we have different opinions and experiences about race, I greatly appreciated the opportunity to talk freely with him and hear about his experiences. He also has a great sense of humor. When I told him the book was finally being published, he quipped: "It's about time. Otherwise, you'd have to call it *Footprints in the Sand!*"

FRED PERDOMO

I was born in 1946 and went to our neighborhood elementary school, Bryant, where my mother went. When I look back at my first-grade pictures, it reminds me of the Bowery Boys. I never thought we were such a motley looking working-class—or below—group of kids! I didn't know the difference. I always had a good childhood. Even though we were working-class, I got everything I needed.

My group of friends in the neighborhood were white. Michael Kolvert was Irish, Mike LaFrankey was Italian Swiss, Vic Marolla was Italian Jewish, Victor Polley was Italian. The neighborhood was becoming a real melting pot, and by the time I went to high school, there were many gangs in the neighborhood that you had to be careful of. The Black Barts was a gang that reportedly had 200 members. You could tell the Black Barts because they wore those black Big Ben work pants, and they had bell bottoms. They were mainly Hispanic, but there were others in there, too.

Baby Fred Perdomo in 1946 with his cousin Ray and Aunt Pauline

Back in those days, we were just looking for a place to play street football or street baseball. That's all that mattered. Lilliana, the Italian war bride, her house happened to be on the fifty-yard line, so she'd always come out if the ball bounced against her house. There was no lawn in our neighborhood, it was all concrete. She would shout, "I'll hitta you in the face, I'll kicka you in the ass!"

For about four blocks around our store it stayed German and Italian because the people who lived there never moved. Their kids did, but there was always that nucleus. Then it became Hispanic all the way up to Mission Street. We were like this little island, but we were also a business. We not only provided French bread but also tortillas. My father spoke some Spanish, too.

My parents decided, in order to keep me safe and give me religion (which they were not willing to do!), to send me to a parochial junior high school on the other side of town—St. Paulus Lutheran School on Turk and Eddy. I spent my life on the Municipal Railway.

Our store was on 20th and Hampshire, and we had a car barn four blocks away at 17th and Bryant where most of the Muni buses were. A lot of the drivers would come to our store and buy a fifth of Johnny Walker scotch and sit out in their cars. My dad would always provide free Dixie cups for them. I got to know a lot of the bus drivers. In those days, in order for me to get over to St. Paulus, I'd go down to the stores on 24th Street and buy a car ticket. For fifty cents you'd get ten rides. Every time I'd get on and see Lucky or Slim—they were all Black drivers —they'd say, "Hey, let me see that," and they'd double-punch everything.

St. Paulus was a very sheltered white school—ninety students only. Then I ended up at Lowell High School. Lowell was very white also, and very Jewish. When Yom Kippur or any of the Jewish holidays came, you might as well have closed the school. I'd show up and there'd be empty hallways. Even half the teachers weren't there. In the group I hung with at home, about three-quarters of them went to Lowell. I met my good friends Julian Munoz and Birchman Rivera there. All the Mission District kids hung out together. There was no way we could fit into Lowell's wealthy Jewish society. I won't say we were segregated against, because, for example, Mike Geddings was able to cross over the line through athletics. Today you see Black basketball players able to cross over the line. Mike, a white Protestant, was trying to be accepted in a rich Jewish school!

When Chris and I moved to Carson City, my parents would take a gambler's shuttle up to Reno and visit us. My mother would say, "I've never seen so many blond-haired, blue-eyed kids in my life!" which was pretty typical of this town. Carson City had 17,000 people back then. This is a very close-knit community. It took Chris and me fifteen years to be accepted into the "in crowd" here. We were not Nevadans. We didn't go to the University of Nevada.

Up until ten years ago, the biggest minority here was the Native Americans, and if there were any racial problems, it was with them. We also had a children's home here that was like an orphanage, but they would also take wards of the court. Most of them were Black kids from Las Vegas. It was almost like, if you saw a Black kid, you knew where he lived.

In the last nine years, because of the low-paying hotel and restaurant business in the state of Nevada, the Hispanics have been coming in—a lot trying to escape the gang problems in Los Angeles—but many didn't realize their children were already infected. The kids would come up here and not be very successful, because Carson High was a relatively lily-white, midwestern, middle-class type of school at the time. Now it is a reflection of the community because we're a one–high school town, and the minority population is 20 to 25 percent, mostly Hispanic (about 300), a few Black students (maybe ten), and Native Americans who come from the Indian colony or reservation at the south end of town (Washo and Paiute tribes).

The racial tension occurs more between the Native Americans and the Hispanics than between the Hispanics and the whites. The Hispanics come up here to seek a better life and don't have the federal support system the Native Americans have, and therefore have to work hard to survive and take any job that's available. The Native Americans don't have to work at all. At eighteen they get an $18,000 to $20,000 check from Uncle Sam, they get free housing, $600 a month, and there's not a whole lot of incentive to be out in the community competing with everybody else. They've gone from the largest minority here to the smallest—and that change has created a tension.

At the beginning of this school year we had a murder a couple of blocks away at a motel, and it was a Hispanic former gang member. The gang here is called the Eastwood Tokers. This former Toker had a party, and a Native American girl who was friends with them was slapped by a Hispanic. She went back to the colony, told her cousins about it, and a whole group of them went back to the motel to find the guy who slapped her. The party had dispersed by that time, and there were only three Hispanic guys still there. One was in the bathroom, one was on the bed, and one was passed out on the floor. The one on the bed was beaten so severely he died.

So we started this school year with potential racial tension between the Native Americans and the Hispanics. We thought it was going to tear the school apart, but it actually helped us, as far as everybody getting along. Twelve Native Americans were arrested for the murder, which was two-thirds of that group at Carson High. We've had the best year we've had because the tension was pretty much diffused right after the murder. The boys were arrested and thrown in jail. We don't have the "stare-downs" we used to have. That's a real cultural issue: Native Americans stare, and for Hispanics, that's an insult, a challenge, so you have a natural friction. The Native Americans would always congregate on the balcony and stare down at the Hispanic gang members who would congregate right below on the opposite side. The rest of the Hispanics not affiliated with the gang members were dispersed throughout the school.

The white students are into sports as much as they can be—the middle-class whites who are established or who have moved here. The lower-class whites are into skateboarding, and as soon as they get a break they go smoke in the park or leave as fast as they can. At Carson High, a school of 2,500, neighborhoods develop, just like any large city. When the "neighborhoods" start moving, that's when I start worrying. If I see a "neighborhood" of gang members start moving down through the school in a direction they've never taken before, I usually follow them, because I know that something is up. Everybody has a comfort zone, and if they move out of that zone, it's either because they're being chased or because they're going out to challenge somebody.

I'll tell you the funniest thing: We have a twice-a-month housekeeper who is from Nicaragua. One day her daughter got up in the middle of a home economics class (there were several Mexicans in there) and called them all a bunch of beaners, and here she was from Nicaragua! So I had to go around and explain the pecking order of Latin America to the local teachers. "There's Costa Rica and there's Mexico." We had complaints once when one of the Spanish teachers was celebrating Cinco de Mayo and the Costa Ricans and Nicaraguans said, "Hey, this isn't anything for us!"

For a predominantly white high school, we all have a sense of fair play. Our principal recently gave me a survey from the Office of Civil Rights. They wanted to know our "out-of-school suspensions" last year by race and gender. It was almost to the number representative of the cross section of kids. It was like twenty Hispanics and 120 white kids that were suspended. There were two Black kids—one boy and one girl —and two Asians. I went through twice to make sure I had all the statistics right. We treat everybody equal. As long as you're behaving, you're going to be treated equal. The only thing I'm prejudiced against is jerks. You can be male or female, Black or white—I don't care what color you are—if you're a jerk, I don't like you. Maybe you can be good later on—you have that ability. White people can't be Black, and Black people can't be white, but a jerk can change. ■■■

My cousins Chris and Fred, me, and my aunt Edna in their Carson City, Nevada, home

Chris Perdomo clearly sees and understands the racial and economic line in Carson City—the east side versus the west side of town. She has taught in the elementary schools for many years and does not tolerate racism or bigotry in any of her classes. As she told me, "I teach the kids to celebrate our differences, but also to understand that we have something that's really unifying— we're all Americans."

CHRIS PERDOMO

was born in San Francisco, and I'm Italian and Yugoslavian. My grandmother's family immigrated from Italy to South America. My grandfather was a casket maker and had a very good business. My father was born in Buenos Aires, Argentina, and he came to the United States when he was thirteen years old with his mother and sister. My grandfather came later and didn't like it; he returned to Buenos Aires and died of pneumonia six months later.

My father met my mother in San Francisco, married her, and we lived in North Beach, a predominantly Italian neighborhood. I attended Garfield, a public school, which was predominantly Chinese. I don't remember the Chinese being the dominant race there, except that no one spoke English in my class but for seven other Caucasians and myself! The Chinese students spoke broken English in the classroom, but when they were out on the playground, they spoke Chinese, so there was a definite division of the races there.

A lot of my friends started going to Catholic school because their parents wanted them in private schools and away from the minority groups. My mom got me into St. Bridget's at Van Ness and Broadway, an Irish parish. It was all white (except for one Black student), and a higher economic group. I was working class, so I had two lives. I had my school life and Irish friends there, and I had my neighborhood Italian friends, and "never the twain shall meet."

I now teach fourth grade at Fritch School in Carson City. The school is located on the west side of town, which consists primarily of people who have lived here for many years, the more established Carsonites. Last year I did my internship at Empire School in the eastern part of Carson City, which is more the newly arrived Carsonites, or more the transient population. Empire School was almost 50 percent Hispanic, the rest Caucasian, and a few Oriental and East Indians. It's the only school in Carson with a large Hispanic population. About 60 percent of the kids are on free or reduced lunches, so socioeconomically, it's a lower strata. With that comes the other difficulties and challenges for the children: single parents, divorced parents, unemployment—and oftentimes with the Hispanic families, two jobs to make a living.

At Empire it's more like a San Francisco inner-city school. When I was talking with the teachers there, I said, "This is what it was like in San Francisco. No one ever thought if a child doesn't speak English they were different. It was accepted because we were a melting pot. You had

Chinese, Puerto Rican, etc., depending on where you were." This is wonderful, to bring the cultures into the schools so kids can see the diversity of the real society.

I couldn't believe how many Hispanic parents would come to school with their children—wanted to be part of their children's lives, wanted to make sure they were OK when they got to school, would sit with them when they got their free breakfast, then they'd go home. Whenever there were parent conferences, both the mom and dad would come. We have a very large ESL program at Empire. Also, what the principal has done is to try and organize all the agencies in Carson City into a fair at the school. Parents can come and learn about the library, adult education, high school–to–career programs—they had the public health nurse there—all the agencies and services that can help the families. They're really trying to draw the parents into the school to get them more involved in the education of their kids. The Empire School, because of the high population of Hispanics and the non-English-speaking Hispanics, their test scores are lower than the rest of the schools.

The city is rezoning the schools and trying to get the kids who live in each neighborhood to attend their neighborhood school. In the past, many white parents opted out and sent their kids to a year-round school that is more white. Now with the rezoning they're required to go back to their neighborhood school.

When the rezoning plan went before the school board, parents went and tried not to make race an issue. They said things like, "We really want our children to stay at Fremont School because our children have made a lot of friends there and it's such a good school." They went on talking about the education of the school and comparing it educationally to Empire, saying it was inferior because the majority of students are non–English speaking and Hispanic. One parent finally said, "I don't want my child going to that school because I don't want him socializing with those children." That's when it finally came out. It wasn't an issue of "this is my school and I really like it," it was "I don't like my kids socializing with Hispanic kids." The school board meeting was on public television, and it was dreadful. The teachers at Empire School felt like second-class citizens. They said, "We want you to know that every single teacher who teaches in this school district has been educated, many with master's degrees, and dedicated to the education of every single child in this district. We don't send inferior teachers to one school and superior teachers to another. There's no differentiation, but because you're saying that this school doesn't have the standards that other schools have, you're saying that we as teachers don't have the same capabilities as our peers. We find that very difficult to handle." The school board was very supportive of them and said, "This is going to stop. We're going to have six zones and kids will be required to go to their neighborhood school." The board passed the rezoning plan. They will allow some exchange of variances, only if there's reciprocity. If you want to go to this school, you have to find someone in that same grade level that is willing to go to the other school.

Everyone says, "No, we don't have a race issue in Carson," and yet we do. It's just that no one will acknowledge it. We're becoming an east-west town and more polarized—the haves and the have-nots. The playground at my school is beautiful. The PTA does a lot for my school. They raise about $20,000 a year for playground equipment, computers, or whatever. On the other side of town they have one set of swings, one monkey bar, no basketball courts, no grass. That PTA is only able to raise about $2,000 a year, if they're lucky.

The kids, particularly in the middle schools and high school, are becoming more conscious of race. They see the Hispanics and call them "the Mexicans." I've never heard that before. There's a change in the climate of the community. There's a division. At our daughter Katherine's middle school, Hispanics have their section and they hang out together. Everybody has their section, but the Hispanics are definitely separate.

As a teacher it's my responsibility to teach tolerance and respect for each other, to make sure that no matter what is being said at home, I'm teaching my students what should be done for the preservation of our society, for what we believe in—that we accept all diverse populations and cultures and integrate their beliefs and lives into our society, and we embrace them and support them. When I teach social studies to my class, we spend a whole chapter on our nationality and origins and where we came from.

I won't tolerate racism or bigotry, and I teach the kids to celebrate our differences, but also to understand that we have something that's really unifying—we're all Americans. ■■■

In December 1998, I celebrated with many friends, neighbors, staff, and board members the Bernal Heights Neighborhood Center's twentieth anniversary, my ten years there as its executive director, and my leaving to work on this book. It was an evening of great emotion and remembrance.

The clear highlight for me was a letter from my son that Mauricio Vela read to the large gathering:

> This is the fourth time I've tried to write this letter and quite frankly I don't know what to say. It's difficult to write a congratulatory letter for someone who has done so much for so many without it sounding too simple or too complicated, so I will do my best to land in the middle.
>
> You are an amazing woman. I've only been able to appreciate that fact in all its dimensions as I've gotten older. As I set off on my own for the first time in my life, filled with all the anxiety and uncertainty that living one's life entails, I take great comfort in knowing God chose me to be your son because it has been one of the greatest blessings of my life. I cannot say what you have given others who have had the good fortune of crossing paths with you, but the gifts that you have placed in my heart, mind and soul have left an indelible print that will forever guide me through the waters of life.
>
> You are now ending one phase of your life and beginning another. As you prepare to write your book know that I am completely in awe of your passion and persistence. I have watched you over the period of time open the door to your dream and begin to mold it into reality, a process that takes incredible courage, faith, and determination. All of us have dreams that we hold close to our hearts but only some have the courage to make them real. You definitely have that courage, and it is for that among many other things that I love you so completely. Congratulations for all your successes past, present, and future.
>
> Your Son, Hasani

PART 4

AMERICA'S UNFINISHED BUSINESS

The ordinary and extraordinary stories in this book are now done. As with most of the people you've met within these pages, I don't have a simple or profound answer to the racism that continues to taint our country and our lives, only a strong desire to squarely face it, talk honestly about it, and act to end it.

The noted author and columnist Anna Quindlen wrote in *Newsweek* magazine (March 13, 2000):

> In truth there are really no public discussions of race. There are discussions of affirmative action, and single parenthood, and, in the wake of tragedies like the [Amadou] Diallo killing, of police training and procedures. These are discussions designed to cause the least amount of discomfort to the smallest possible number of white people. . . . Poll after poll shows a great gap in understanding between a white America that believes things are ever so much better and a black America that thinks that is delusional. And that gap mirrors a gap more important than numbers, between what many of us believe we believe, and the subtle assumptions that creep into our consciousness, and which we are often unwilling to admit are there.

I have chosen four critical areas of America's unfinished racial business that have been woven within many of the life stories in this book, including mine. As we recite in the Pledge of Allegiance, we are one nation with "liberty and justice for all." If those words have any meaning in the twenty-first century, these areas must be consciously addressed within our families, the schools where we and our children learn, our diverse places of worship, the newspapers we read, the radio and television programs we hear and watch, the businesses we shop — in short, every place we are in this nation.

Teaching American History to Our Youth

When I hear my stepdaughter Diane tell me how little she was taught in high school about slavery and the Civil War, or Rudy Corpuz, a beautiful Filipino gang prevention worker in San Francisco, tell me that all he learned about his heritage in high school were two sentences about the War of 1898, I shudder. When, in the year 2000, I read a simple, poignant letter in the *Boston Globe* from Elizabeth, a freshman at Spelman College (a very old and respected Black women's college in Atlanta), I shudder. She tells her parents about a course called "African Diaspora and the World," a course she's very grateful to have, "but it is also something I should have had in high school. I have learned so much about the oppression of black women and minorities in general by so many different forces it's almost depressing."

I had hoped that since my graduation from high school in 1957, major improvements would be made in the honest and full teaching of our history, given the breadth of knowledge we now have about slavery and how our economic system was built on the backs of Black people, the atrocities committed against Native Americans, and the deep pain and triumphs of the civil rights movement. I was mistaken.

In Professor James Lowen's book *Lies My Teacher Told Me: Everything Your American History Textbook Got Wrong,* he states in his chapter "The Invisibility of Racism in American History Textbooks":

The struggle over racial slavery may be the predominant theme in American history. Until the end of the nineteenth century, cotton — planted, cultivated, harvested, and ginned by slaves — was by far our most important export. Our graceful antebellum homes, in the North as well as the South, were built largely by slaves or from profits derived from the slave and cotton trades. Black-white relations became the central issue in the Civil War, which killed almost as many Americans as died in all our other wars combined. Black-white relations was the principal focus of Reconstruction after the Civil War; America's failure to allow African Americans equal rights led eventually to the struggle for civil rights a century later....

While textbooks now show the horror of slavery and its impact on black America, they remain largely silent regarding the impact of slavery on white America, North or South. Textbooks have trouble acknowledging that anything might be wrong with white Americans, or with the United States as a whole. Perhaps telling realistically what slavery was like for slaves is the easy part. After all, slavery as an institution is dead. We have progressed beyond it, so we can acknowledge its evil. . . . Without explaining its relevance to the present, however, extensive coverage of slavery is like extensive coverage of the Hawley-Smoot Tariff — just more facts for hapless eleventh graders to memorize.

Slavery's twin legacies to the present are the social and economic inferiority it conferred upon blacks and the cultural racism it instilled in whites. Both continue to haunt our society. *Therefore, treating slavery's enduring legacy is necessarily controversial. Unlike slavery, racism is not over yet.* (Emphasis added)

As adults, as parents of children, we learn much from our museums and national monuments about who we are — and are not. Living in Washington, D.C. for thirteen years, I was fortunate to be near the extraordinary Smithsonian Institution's museums. There is now an African Museum, and a Native American Museum is being built on the Mall. But there is no Holocaust Museum for African or Native Americans. When my San Francisco friend Karen Kaho mentioned the need for such a museum, I quickly responded "Yes, it is long overdue." We can certainly honor and celebrate both Black and Indian cultures in the two museums mentioned, but there is a huge hole in our nation's history by not having our own Holocaust Museum, one that clearly shows to all Americans the underside of our history and how that history impacts Blacks, Native Americans, and whites to this day — economically, socially, and politically.

Jane Lazarre, in her beautiful and painful memoir, *Beyond the Whiteness of Whiteness*, writes about visiting the Museum of the Confederacy in Richmond, Virginia, when a traveling exhibit on slavery was there. She tells us:

> In the next large room of the museum, I am looking at a plain rag doll made of what looks like unbleached muslin, a tie near the top to fashion a head, two knots of thread for eyes, a line of thread for a mouth. The doll was left behind by an unidentified child on a plantation in Durham, North Carolina. Where was the mother of the child who left the doll behind? Had she been sold away? The catalog which I read off and on as I move through the silent awesome rooms says: "An Arkansas slave was brought to the auction block without knowing her master intended to sell her. . . . They had to get some men to throw her down and hold her to keep her from going back to the house. They sold her away from her baby boy."

Children were forcibly taken from their mothers frequently, of course. I write this sentence not because I think it represents some new knowledge, but because I know we must repeat it and repeat it in order to bring it to the surface of American consciousness. It tends to drown in a sea of repression, denial, and callousness; it tends to sink down. "They sold her away from her baby boy." I try to feel this mother, ripped away from her child, as I read the unadorned language, a simple declarative sentence: "Children were taken from their mothers with frequency."

By not learning the truth about our history, by not seeing that history in museums, textbooks, magazines, and newspapers, white people have the misperception that others need to be taught to "be like us," ignoring the old and enduring atrocities we committed to "them." In a powerful article in *Teaching Tolerance* magazine, Dr. Joyce King, associate provost of the City University of New York, states:

> As an African American educator, one of my main concerns is that we all need to be liberated from schooling that perpetuates America's myths. One such myth that constrains our freedom of thought and our ability to pursue social justice concerns our national identity. . . . Because most of [the white teachers] accepted the myth that America is a white nation that is becoming more diverse, they also believed that their mission as teachers was to help these diverse "others" to be like them. These relatively privileged white future teachers could scarcely imagine that there is anything wrong with America or that multicultural education has anything to do with them—with what is wrong with their education.

One notable example of someone who does understand the "wrongs" in his education and is doing something right for his students is Jeff Steinberg, a former history teacher at Capuchino High School in San Bruno, California. He has organized and led many large groups of ethnically diverse teenagers on a sojourn to Washington, D.C., then on to the South, "to see and touch the landmarks of the civil rights movement," as reported by Mark Simon of the *San Francisco Chronicle* on February 1, 2000:

> Along the way, the students sat on the steps of the Lincoln Memorial and listened to a recording of Dr. Martin Luther King Jr.'s "I Have a Dream" speech, crossed the bridge in Selma, Ala., where civil rights protesters were beaten in the single bloodiest day of the movement, visited the churches where King preached, and toured the Memphis motel where he was killed. . . .

They met people who had led demonstrations, who had been foot soldiers in the movement, who had prayed and marched and been beaten and jailed—from members of the Little Rock Nine who integrated an all-white high school in Little Rock, Ark., to Chris McNair, whose daughter was one of four girls killed in a church bombing in Birmingham, Alabama.

Jeff Steinberg has now founded Sojourn to the Past, a nonprofit organization that takes high school students from all over California, as well as the New York and Boston areas, on a ten-day academic sojourn to the South. In the year 2001, over 800 students had the opportunity to take part in this unique academic experience and have their lives changed because of their participation. The Sojourn project is one major model that can be replicated across our land so that today's youth can learn, see, and touch the racial wounds of the past and move forward as future antiracist adults.

White Privilege

When my brother and his wife wanted to move from their small home in Bellflower, California, many years ago, they were looking for a larger and newer place to continue raising their three young children. They found their dream home in Mission Viejo, a newly developed community in Southern California that was 99 percent white then and 99 percent white now.

Knowing my brother, I'm certain that race was not a conscious factor in his buying decision. It's just the way things were back then and continue to be. Wayne and Bev made a choice that millions of white Americans have made over the years. They moved to the lily-white suburbs, where they and their children had virtually no close social contact with people of other races or cultures. My brother and sister-in-law were privileged to move to a community where they wanted to live, without giving any thought to the color of their skin. Patricia Williams, a noted author and professor at Columbia, noted: "How can it be that so many well-meaning white people have never thought about race when so few blacks pass a single day without being reminded of it?" That's white privilege, and we who are white benefit from it on a daily basis.

I benefit from it. Whenever I speak up at a meeting, be it the local Women's International League for Peace and Freedom branch or my local Cotuit Civic Association, I am seen as speaking for myself, not representing a larger racial group, as people of color are often perceived. When I'm conversing with a small group of white friends on an urban or rural sidewalk, I am not seen as threatening, as a similar group of Black men are too often considered. When I drive on many of the state and local roads in our country, as I have over the past thirty-five years, I do not feel fear. But when I drive some of those same roads with my son, fear is a close companion. When my husband and I visited New Orleans years ago for an American Institute of Architects conference, we immensely enjoyed the French Quarter but dared not step outside the boundaries of the city. Were I with a white man, that internal restraint would not have been necessary. When I shop at a department store, I do not wonder if the clerk will closely watch me to ensure that my hands won't steal. When I call for a cab in New York, I am comfortably assured I'll be picked up, unlike a young Black female friend who recently wasn't. The driver saw her and her companion but chose to move slowly down the street to pick up a white woman instead.

White privilege is also not having to be labeled "white." When the white teenagers at Columbine High School wantonly and obscenely shot their fellow students, the press did not identify them as "white." Had they been Black, that identification would have immediately been slapped on them. We see color in our country, but "white" is not a color that is consciously recognized or identified, nor the privileges that go along with it.

Does this mean that white people, particularly those of us who are poor or have strong ethnic roots, never face prejudice or discrimination? Of course not. But in the political, economic, and social structure of our country, it is much easier to walk around wearing white skin than black or brown skin.

Professor Robert Jensen is a longtime and respected member of the Journalism Department at the University of Texas at Austin, a man of great and varied interests. A friend passed his 1999 article on to me, and I've sent it to dozens of people since then.

Last year I published an article about white privilege in the *Baltimore Sun* that then went out over a wire service to other newspapers. Electronic copies proliferated and were picked up on Internet discussion lists, and the article took on a life of its own. As a result, every week over the past year I have received at least a dozen letters from people who want to talk about race. I learned not only more about my own privilege, but more about why many white folks can't come to terms with the truism I offered in that article: *White people, whether overtly racist or not, benefit from living in a world mostly run by white people that has been built on the land and the backs of non-white people.* (Emphasis added)

The reactions varied from racist rantings, to deeply felt expressions of pain and anger, to declarations of solidarity. But probably the most important response I got was from nonwhite folks, predominantly African-Americans, who said something like this: "Of course there is white privilege. I've been pointing it out to my white friends and coworkers for years. Isn't it funny that almost no one listens to me, but everyone takes notice when a white guy says it."

Those comments forced me again to ponder the privilege I live with. Who really does know more about white privilege, me or the people on the other side of that privilege? Me, or a black inner-city teenager who is automatically labeled a gang member and feared by many white folks? Me, or an American Indian on the streets of a U.S. city who is invisible to many white folks? Whose voices should we be paying attention to?

My voice gets heard in large part because I am a white man with a Ph.D. who holds a professional job with status. In most settings, I speak with the assumption that people not only will listen, but will take me seriously.

Right now, I want to use that privilege to acknowledge the many nonwhite people who took the time to tell me about the enduring realities of racism in the United States. And, I want to talk to the white people who I think misread my essay and misunderstand what's at stake.

The responses of my white critics broke down into a few basic categories, around the following claims:

1. White privilege doesn't exist because affirmative action has made being white a disadvantage. The simple response: Extremely limited attempts to combat racism, such as affirmative action, do virtually nothing to erase the white privilege built over 500 years that pervades our society. As a friend of mine says, the only real disadvantage to being white is that it so often prevents people from understanding racial issues.

2. White privilege exists, but it can't be changed because it is natural for any group to favor its own, and besides, the worst manifestations of racism are over. Response: This approach makes human choices appear outside of human control, which is a dodge to avoid moral and political responsibility for the injustice we continue to live with.

3. White privilege exists, and that's generally been a good thing because white Europeans have civilized the world. Along the way some bad things may have happened, and we should take care to be nice to non-whites to make up for that. Response: These folks often argued the curiously contradictory position that (1) non-whites and

their cultures are not inferior, but (2) white/European culture is superior. As for the civilizing effect of Europe, we might consider five centuries of inhuman, brutal colonialism and World Wars I and II, and then ask what "civilized" means.

4. White privilege exists because whites are inherently superior, and I am a weakling and a traitor for suggesting otherwise. Response: The Klan isn't dead.

There is much to say beyond those short responses, but for now I am more interested in one common assumption that all these correspondents made, that my comments on race and affirmative action were motivated by "white liberal guilt." The problem is, they got two out of the three terms wrong. I am white, but I'm not a liberal. In political terms, I'm a radical; I don't think liberalism offers real solutions because it doesn't attack the systems of power and structures of illegitimate authority that are the root cause of oppression, be it based on race, gender, sexuality, or class. These systems of oppression, which are enmeshed and interlocking, require radical solutions.

And I don't feel guilty. Guilt is appropriate when one has wronged another, when one has something to feel guilty about. In my life I have felt guilty for racist or sexist things I have said or done, even when they were done unconsciously. But that is guilt I felt because of specific acts, not for the color of my skin. Also, focusing on individual guilt feelings is counterproductive when it leads us to ponder the issue from a psychological point of view instead of a moral and political one.

So, I cannot, and indeed should not, feel either guilty or proud about being white, because it is a state of being I have no control over. However, as a member of a society—and especially as a privileged member of society—I have an obligation not simply to enjoy that privilege that comes with being white but to study and understand it, and work toward a more just world in which such unearned privilege is eliminated.

Some of my critics said that such a goal is ridiculous; after all, people have unearned privileges of all kinds. Several people pointed out that, for example, tall people have unearned privilege in basketball, and we don't ask tall people to stop playing basketball nor do we eliminate their advantage.

The obvious difference is that racial categories are invented; they carry privilege or disadvantage only because people with power create and maintain the privilege for themselves at the expense of others. The privilege is rooted in violence and is maintained through that violence as well as more subtle means.

... The most creative piece of mail I received in response to the essay also was the most confused. In a padded envelope from Clement, Minnesota, came a brand-new can of Kiwi Shoe Polish, black. Because there was no note or letter, I have to guess at my correspondent's message, but I assume the person was suggesting that if I felt so bad about being white, I might want to make myself black.

But, of course, I don't feel bad about being white. The only motivation I might have to want to be black — to be something I am not — would be pathological guilt over my privilege. In these matters, guilt is a coward's way out, an attempt to avoid the moral and political questions....

What matters is what we decide to do with the privilege. For me, that means speaking, knowing that I speak with a certain unearned privilege that gives me advantages I cannot justify. It also means learning to listen before I speak, and realizing that I am probably not as smart as I sometimes like to think I am.

It means listening when an elderly black man who sees the original article tacked up on the bulletin board outside my office while on a campus tour stops to chat. This man, who has lived with more kinds of racism than I can imagine through more decades than I have been alive, says to me, "White privilege, yes, good to keep an eye on that, son. Keep yourself honest. But don't forget to pay attention to the folks who live without the privilege."

It doesn't take black shoe polish to pay attention. It takes only a bit of empathy to listen, and a bit of courage to act.

I've been privileged to recently work on racial issues with another white woman, Barb Steinau, eighty-two years young. As a result of her daughter marrying a Black man many years ago, Barb and her husband Mort became intimately aware of the discrimination, both subtle and overt, that Joan's family faced. But that awareness took time to take hold. Both Barb and Mort refused to attend their daughter's wedding. Unlike my father, they later opened their minds and hearts to their son-in-law becoming good friends with him for many years, and loving grandparents and great grandparents to their children.

Barb and I cofacilitate workshops on "Eliminating Racism and Understanding White Privilege," using as our basic text Dr. Beverly Tatum's book *Why Are All the Black Kids Sitting Together in the Cafeteria?* In a safe and supportive environment, our vision for the workshop is to broaden the discussion of racism, including its historical roots and ongoing impact on people of color—economically, socially, and politically. We also examine the visible and invisible benefits of white people's privilege and how our being oblivious to that advantage helps perpetuate racism. The discussions have been rich and informative.

In doing this work I'm often reminded of the Gandhi poster in the Coalition on Homelessness office in San Francisco, which reads: "Even if what you are doing seems insignificant, it is important to do it anyway."

Affirmative Action

I feel clear anger when the phrase "special preferences" is used with the phrase "affirmative action," as if our country never had a system based on special preferences. For over 300 years we've had an affirmative action program—a preferential system for white propertied men. We just never labeled it as such.

To those who complain about affirmative action being "unfair" and state that "two wrongs don't make a right," I say: Count the number of Black people who died coming here on slave ships compared with the number of white people who died coming to our shores. Count the number of Black men who've been hanged by white men in the early part of the last century, and how many white men have been hanged by Blacks. Count the thousands of indignities Black people have had to endure over the centuries to survive, beginning with slavery—don't speak your language (or we'll kill you), don't look at a white woman (or we'll kill you), bow your head when you pass a white person (or we'll kill you), answer to the name "boy" (or we'll kill you), don't sit in that bus seat even though it's empty and you're so very tired (or we'll kill you), don't register to vote (or we'll kill you), ad infinitum. I don't see "two wrongs." I see one wrong, and it is still very much with us.

A strong voice on this issue is the editorial page editor for the *Atlanta Constitution*, Cynthia Tucker. She wrote in her July 17, 1999, column:

Why are many Americans—white Americans mostly—so upset about college admissions programs that take race into account for a handful of students whose test scores are slightly below standards? Why are programs that boost the chances of black and brown students so controversial, while similar programs that benefit white students go without notice?

For example, the country's premier colleges and universities have long reserved places for the lesser-achieving children of their well-heeled graduates and donors. At the University of Georgia, family connections are one of the dozen or so factors—along with race—

used to assess about 20 percent of its applicants who don't quite meet academic standards. In other words, a kid whose test scores and grades are not quite good enough may get into Georgia anyway if his mom or dad is a graduate.

That practice allows weaker students — most of them white — to be admitted at the expense of better students. Yet no one bemoans it as an assault on the vaunted "meritocracy."

College admissions also grant athletic "preferences," a device that happens to benefit many kids — black, white and brown — who otherwise could not get near their chosen college. For some reason, a black kid with low SATs who can score touchdowns and generate a lot of money for the university is not nearly as offensive as a black kid with low scores who just wants an education.

. . . Much criticism of affirmative action in college admissions is based on myth, misunderstanding and — how shall I say this? — simple bigotry. Affirmative action programs exist only in 25 percent to 40 percent of the nation's institutions of higher learning; the other 60 percent to 75 percent accept all applicants. So the controversy centers around the nation's most prestigious institutions.

. . . William Bowen, former president of Princeton University, and Derek Bok, former president of Harvard University, recently conducted a landmark study of affirmative action at 28 elite institutions, including Atlanta's Emory University. They found that black graduates of those colleges go on to earn advanced degrees — medicine, law, MBAs — at slightly higher rates than their white counterparts, and also became more active in civic affairs.

Because America proffers advancement through education, programs to enhance educational opportunities for students of color remain critical — perhaps more important than any other form of affirmative action. Since my grandfathers would not have been admitted to white universities, it does not seem unreasonable to create a form of "legacy" for their descendants.

Nationwide, corporate and university leaders are sticking to their support of programs that give an edge to women and minorities who may otherwise be passed over. They see that the job of redressing historical discrimination is not yet complete.

. . . *Until white and black males and Latino and Asian males and white and black females and Latina and Asian females with similar education and skills earn salaries more in line with one another, the need for affirmative action programs will be with us.* [Emphasis added]

In the spring of 1995 I protested with hundreds of others at a meeting of the regents of the University of California at the San Francisco campus, where they passed a resolution to ban affirmative action on all UC campuses. Later that year—and buoyed by that act—the voters of California passed the California Civil Rights Initiative, banning affirmative action throughout the state. With thousands of others, I worked and rallied against the perniciously racist Proposition 209 and lost. *The San Francisco Chronicle*, usually conservative in its editorials, took a daring stand on the issue, stating:

> New figures from the US Census Bureau discredit arguments that the nation no longer needs affirmative action programs. According to numbers released this month, the median 1994 annual income of full-time workers with undergraduate college degrees was $48,600 for white males, $36,000 for black males, $33,700 for white females, and $31,890 for black women....
>
> While there were exceptions in the census findings—the census found that the overwhelming majority of educated African Americans is still woefully behind similarly educated whites in job remuneration.
>
> Supporters of the deviously named California Civil Rights Initiative want voters to believe special consideration for the historically discriminated against is no longer needed. But the Census Bureau figures, as well as a plethora of statistics on who runs companies and who holds the highest paying jobs belie that contention. Californians should be trying to figure out how to narrow that gap and declare unacceptable the prejudice that certainly contributes to such a discrepancy. Instead, the state is embroiled in a bitter initiative battle that widens the racial divide.

On May 17, 2001, I received the following e-mail from BAMN (By Any Means Necessary), a new, powerful civil rights group made up of college students and their allies, which stated in part:

> Today marks a historic proud day for the new civil rights movement for integration and equality. The University of California Regents VOTED UNANIMOUSLY TODAY TO REPEAL SP-1—we have reversed the ban on affirmative action in the UC System.... This day— one day before the anniversary of *Brown v. Board of Education* —marks a HISTORIC TURNING POINT for California and the nation.... The united stand of over 5,000 college and high school students and faculty and unions and supporters echoed in the meeting room. ALL SIDES, including Ward Connerly and others who had originally voted

for the ban, agreed to ending the UC Regents' association with the attack on affirmative action because of the power of our movement.

May their movement roll like a mighty river across our land.

Reparations for Slavery

Whenever I think about reparations, I remember the day over thirty years ago when People for Human Rights sat in on the Methodist headquarters in Philadelphia. We had just spent a week supporting the Black occupation of a small white church in the heart of a Black community. As we said in our press release: "We are opposed to racism and therefore support Black demands for reparations from white religious institutions. While we do not intend to prevent anyone from entering or leaving Methodist offices, we recognize that our presence will in some measure be disruptive. *By its very nature, opposition to the deeply ingrained racism of our society is disruptive.*"

The issue of reparations also makes me remember A. Philip Randolph, who was a descendant of slaves and the founder of the Brotherhood of Sleeping Car Porters, a man I greatly admire. As you now know, my father-in-law, Victor Wilburn Sr., was a Pullman porter in the 1920s and 1930s—a "very good job for a Negro," as they would say back then. The story he told many times over, which Victor and I talked about during our interview, was one I was first embarrassed to hear and one that still haunts me today as I grasp the racism and classism it roars through the years. John D. Rockefeller rode the trains frequently (he did own them, after all). He'd always ask for my father-in-law to wait on him because Mr. Wilburn knew how to fix his toast and bacon—almost burnt. John D. always gave him a silver dollar, a generous tip back then, and one that made Mr. Wilburn very proud, and rightfully so.

I am reminded that my grandfather William Helfer's grandfather, Jesse, was a soldier in the Union army. When I visited Grandpa Bill in 1951 I held his hand, the same hand that held his grandfather's hand when he was a little boy. Mr. Wilburn's grandfather was a slave. I'd like to believe he held his hand too. He certainly inherited his grandfather's drive to work hard, sometimes holding three jobs at a time to feed, house, and clothe his family. What he did not inherit from his grandfather was money, money to help him build a higher standard of living, a less stressful life, and the ability to hand down a larger financial inheritance to his three children.

As Derrick Jackson of the *Boston Globe* put it after the U.S. delegation fled the United Nations Conference Against Racism held in Durban, South Africa, in early September 2001:

America is not ready to admit that the $8 trillion being passed down from the World War II generation to its baby boomers was hauled on the bent backs of black people who were barred from full rights from 1776 until the 1960s. America is not ready to discuss how slavery was so critical to the nation that the South once had a larger economy than any European nation except England. America is not ready to discuss the government sanctioned housing and banking discrimination of the 20th century that will result in white baby boomers inheriting an average of $65,000 compared with $8,000 for black baby boomers, according to researchers for the Federal Reserve Board.

These daunting facts had their births at the beginning of our country and have been exacerbated by generations of national policy denial and ongoing obstruction of justice. When the slave ships began arriving on our shores, year after year we'd make excuses about why the trade needed to continue — over 300 years of excuses — and not one dime paid for all that work, and not one dime paid after the Civil War ended. The newly freed slaves had to build their futures covered with black skin and more than 250 years behind those of us covered with white skin.

The United Nations Conference Against Racism ended its seminal session by adopting a powerful platform that included the statement that slavery was, by consensus of the delegates, "a crime against humanity." Adjoa Aiyetoro, a key principal in drafting that statement and a leading advocate for reparations, recently addressed a group of 200 African Americans in a church in Chicago. According to an article in *Newsweek* (August 27, 2001), she asked:

"How many of you have heard of reparations?". . . About 10 hands go up. Undeterred, she explains the concept: in recent years, Holocaust victims, World War II era Japanese-Americans and Aboriginal groups in Australia and New Zealand have all been successful in extracting compensation from governments and corporations for the legal and moral wrongs committed against them. Are the descendants of America's slaves any less deserving of restitution? The crowd erupts with shouts of approval and applause. "In order to solve a problem, you've got to admit you've got a problem," says Aiyetoro, who for the past 14 years as cofounder and legal consultant for the National Coalition of Blacks for Reparations in America (N'COBRA), has been on a grass-roots campaign to make America do just that.

Webster's Dictionary defines *reparations* as: "(1) A repairing or keeping in repair; (2) The act of making amends, offering expiation, or giving satisfaction for a wrong or injury; (3) The payment of damages." This definition has no time limit. It does not state that reparations must be made within a specified number of years or decades in order to be given and received. It is never too late to make amends.

We cannot move on to an "equal playing field" until we've addressed those past injustices that continue to fester. We need to look squarely at what we, as a white power–dominated society, have wrought and how we can at long last fix it. Being engaged is essential — not with a sense of nonproductive guilt, but with a sense of responsibility and understanding about how our country was really built — on the backs of Black people on land stolen from the Indians.

EPILOGUE

I t was the week before Thanksgiving in the year 2000 when I wrote this brief chapter. In September of that year I moved from San Francisco to another place I've always loved, Cape Cod. Leaving my hometown again was as painful as when I left with my family forty-five years ago, but it was now solely my decision to move on to a quieter place where I could write, be closer to my son in New York City, and focus my energy on the issues of race, racism, and white privilege addressed in this book.

Before I gather with new friends in a cozy Barnstable home for Thanksgiving dinner, I will join a small group of Cape Codders and hundreds of others in Plymouth for a day of mourning with Native Americans and a protest to free Leonard Peltier. For the first time, I saw the statue of Massasoit, the Wampanoag Indian who welcomed the Pilgrims upon their arrival to the Native Americans' land. I also read the painful words of the plaque near him:

NATIONAL DAY OF MOURNING. Since 1970 Native Americans have gathered at noon on Cole's Hill in Plymouth to commemorate a National Day of Mourning on the U.S. Thanksgiving holiday. Many Native Americans do not celebrate the arrival of the Pilgrims and other European settlers. To them, Thanksgiving day is a reminder of the genocide of millions of their people, the theft of their lands, and the relentless assault on their culture. Participants in the National Day of Mourning honor Native ancestors and the struggles of Native peoples to survive today. It is a day of remembrance and spiritual connection as well as a protest of the racism and oppression which Native Americans continue to experience.

Erected by the Town of Plymouth on behalf of the United American Indians of New England.

You have met some of the remarkable people I've been privileged to know in all the special places I've lived and places I'd like to live if life would allow it. The journey continues with new extraordinary people who are working on the Cape for social justice and the end of racism as we know it. I joined the Women's International League for Peace and Freedom here, a local branch founded by my friend Mary Zepernick, whom you met during my Washington, D.C. years. We had our first Racism Task Force meeting yesterday in an old white wooden Unitarian church in the small town of Brewster. The day was blustery, and it rained hard. Only four of us were able to attend, but the discussion was rich, and the circle widened.

It is in these small and seemingly insignificant moments where I find hope in a sea of despair. I find hope in groups like WILPF, N'COBRA (National Coalition of Blacks for Reparations in America), the Southern Poverty Law Center's Teaching Tolerance Project, the Institute for Survival and Beyond in New Orleans and Oakland, Community Change in Boston, and hundreds of other groups coming together across our land to act, protest, heal, and learn about the most divisive issue in our nation. I find hope in the books you'll find listed at the end of this volume, and in the personal bookshelves of friends like Barb and Mort Steinau, Baraka Sele, Mare and Laurie Wallace, my son Hasani Issa, as well as thousands of others whose bookshelves I will never see and wish I could.

As I bask in the warmth of these moments, I must also face a deep hopelessness about our institutionally racist society. I despair when my friend, Dr. Beth Roy, a therapist and superb author, tells a large bookstore audience in San Francisco that in Little Rock's Central High School today, even though the student body is 50 percent Black and 50 percent white, every classroom but one is segregated—this after forty years of "integration." I despair when I read her interviews of white 1957–58 Central High graduates and see how most of them are as racist now as they were then, and worse, are passing their racism on to their children. I wonder, "When will this all end? Can we ever bridge the racial gap and be a nation of true "equality and justice for all?"

I despair when I see how many of us white people simply don't see the privileges afforded us by not having to think about the color of our skin when we leave our homes in the morning, walk down an unfamiliar street, go for a job interview, eat at a small café in a strange rural town, buy a house in a new community, or the thousands of other activities that make up our daily lives. But I am also reminded of what my old friend Harvey Finkle told me on his porch in Long Beach Island: "What keeps me going? It's what I do. Despair will come even when things are great at times. It won't stop me from what I'm doing."

I've learned over the years that, as a white woman, bridging the racial gap can be awkward and uncomfortable. But I have also learned that life is not always meant to be comfortable.

Over the last holiday of the twentieth century, I visited with my friend Margaret Welsh in Long Beach, California. We attended Woodrow Wilson High School together, graduating in 1957. After Margaret married and moved to Colorado, we lost touch, but we reconnected sixteen years ago at an Older Women's League Conference in Oakland, a blessed event. During our holiday visit, we read in one of the city guides that a Kwanza celebration was going to take place the next night in a small bar-restaurant in the heart of Long Beach. We decided to go and partake of this special event. It was sponsored by a Black-owned bookstore that Margaret had previously visited, located on the edge of Long Beach's newly renovated downtown district. On our visit to the store, I bought a book by Nikki Giovanni called *Racism 101*, and Margaret bought a book for her and one for me by Marian Wright Edelman called *Lanterns*.

We arrived at the Mbar/Restaurant early that evening and took a small table toward the back. It was a long and narrow place, painted in earth tones and decorated with large African masks and other colorful artifacts. Soon more guests arrived and began filling the space. By the time the entertainment began, there were close to 100 people laughing and talking together. I counted one other white person besides Margaret and me. It was a joyous evening, filled with the sound of African drums, dancing, delicious home-cooked food, and the reading of the seven Kwanza principles by a Black teenager. The principles are:

Umoja (unity): To strive for and maintain unity in the family, community, nation, and race.

Kujichagulia (self-determination): To define ourselves, name ourselves, create for ourselves, and speak for ourselves.

Ujima (collective work and responsibility): To build and maintain our community together and to make our brothers' and sisters' problems our problems and to solve them together.

Ujamaa (cooperative economics): To build and maintain our own stores, shops, and other businesses and to profit together from them.

Nia (purpose): To make as our collective vocation the building and developing of our community in order to restore our people to their traditional greatness.

Kuumba (creativity): To do always as much as we can, in the way that we can, in order to leave our community more beautiful and beneficial than when we inherited it.

Imani (faith): To believe with all our hearts in our parents, our teachers, our leaders, our people, and the righteousness and victory of our struggle.

Yes, great principles. It was another brief moment of hope.

BIBLIOGRAPHY

Books for Understanding Racism in the Past and Present

Almaguer, Tomas. *Racial Fault Lines: The Historical Origins of White Supremacy in California.* University of California Press, 1994.

Ball, Edward. *Slaves in the Family.* Ballantine Books, 1998.

Branch, Taylor. *Parting the Waters: America in the King Years.* Simon and Schuster, 1988.

Conot, Robert. *Rivers of Blood, Years of Darkness.* Bantam, 1967.

DuBois, W. E. B. *The Souls of Black Folk* (1903). Bantam Classic edition, 1989.

Gates, Henry Louis Jr., ed. *The Classic Slave Narratives.* New American Library, 1987.

Lowen, James W. *Lies My Teacher Told Me: Everything Your American History Textbook Got Wrong.* Simon and Schuster, 1995.

Norrell, Robert J. *Reaping the Whirlwind: The Civil Rights Movement in Tuskegee.* Vintage Books, 1985.

Robinson, Randall. *The Debt: What America Owes to Blacks.* Penguin Books, 2000.

Roediger, David R. *Colored White: Transcending the Racial Past.* University of California Press, 2002.

Stokes, Melvyn, and Rick Halpern. *Race and Class in the American South Since 1890.* Berg Publishers, 1994.

Takaki, Ronald. *A Different Mirror: A History of Multicultural America.* Little, Brown, and Company, 1993.

Weatherford, Jack. *Indian Givers: How the Indians of the Americas Transformed the World.* Ballantine Books, 1988.

Williams, Juan. *Eyes on the Prize: America's Civil Rights Years.* Penguin Books, 1987.

Woodson, Carter G. *The Mis-education of the Negro* (1933). First Africa World Press, 1990.

Informative Books for Unlearning Racism

Bullard, Sara. *Teaching Tolerance: Raising Open-Minded Empathetic Children.* Doubleday, 1996.

chideya, farai. *Don't Believe the Hype: Fighting Cultural Misinformation About African Americans.* Plume, 1995.

Dalton, Harlon L. *Racial Healing: Confronting the Fear Between Blacks and Whites.* Doubleday, 1995.

Katz, Judy H. *White Awareness: Handbook for Anti-Racism Training.* University of Oklahoma Press, 1978.

Kivel, Paul. *Uprooting Racism: How White People Can Work for Racial Justice.* New Society Publishers, 1996.

Stalvey, Lois Mark. *The Education of a WASP.* University of Wisconsin Press, 1970.

Steinau Lester, Joan. *The Future of White Men and Other Diversity Dilemmas.* Conari Press, 1994.

Tatum, Beverly. *Why Are All the Black Kids Sitting Together in the Cafeteria?* Basic Books, 1997.

Thompson, Becky. *A Promise and a Way of Life: White Anti-racist Activism.* University of Minnesota Press, 2001.

Memoirs, Biographies, Slices of Life

Braden, Anne. *The Wall Between.* University of Tennessee Press, 1999.

chideya, farai. *The Color of Our Future.* William Morrow, 1999.

Funderburg, Lise. *Black, White, Other.* William Morrow, Inc. 1994.

Gracie, David Mcl. *Other Sheep I Have: The Autobiography of Father Paul M. Washington.* Temple University Press, 1994.

Haley, Alex, and Malcolm X. *The Autobiography of Malcolm X.* Grove Press, 1964.

Howe, Irving. *World of Our Fathers: The Journey of the East European Jews to America and the Life They Found and Made.* Simon and Schuster, 1976.

Jones, LeAlan, and Lloyd Newman with David Isay. *Our America: Life and Death on the South Side of Chicago.* Washington Square Press, 1997.

Lazarre, Jane. *Beyond the Whiteness of Whiteness.* Duke University Press, 1998.

Lewis, David Levering. *W. E. B. DuBois: Biography of a Race.* Henry Holt, 1993.

McBride, James. *The Color of Water.* Riverhead Books, 1996.

Mills, Kay. *This Little Light of Mine: The Life of Fannie Lou Hamer.* Penguin Books USA, 1994.

Minerbrook, Scott. *Divided to the Vein.* Harcourt Brace, 1996.

Piro, Richard. *Black Fiddler.* William Morrow, 1971.

Raybon, Patricia. *My First White Friend.* Viking Penguin, 1996.

Reddy, Maureen. *Crossing the Color Line: Race, Parenting, and Culture.* Rutgers University Press, 1997.

Robeson, Paul. *Here I Stand.* Dobson Books Ltd., 1958.

Robinson, Randall. *Defending the Spirit: A Black Life in America.* Penguin Books, 1999.

Rothenberg, Paula. *Invisible Privilege: A Memoir About Race, Class and Gender.* University Press of Kansas, 2000.

San Francisco Writers Corps. *Same Difference: Young Writers on Race.* 1998.

Smith, Toby. *Coaltown: The Life and Times of Dawson, New Mexico.* Ancient City Press, 1993.

Terry, Wallace. *Bloods: An Oral History of the Vietnam War by Black Veterans.* Ballantine Books, 1984.

Turkel, Studs. *Race.* Anchor Books, Doubleday, 1992.

Academic and Sociological Books

Blauner, Bob. *Black Lives White Lives.* University of California Press, 1989.

Bowen, William G., and Derek Bok. *The Shape of the River.* Princeton University Press, 1998.

Davis, James F. *Who is Black? One Nation's Definition.* Pennsylvania State University Press, 1998.

Hacker, Andrew. *Two Nations, Black and White, Separate, Hostile, Unequal.* Charles Scribner's Sons, 1992.

Omi, Michael, and Howard Winant. *Racial Formation.* Routledge, 1994.

Record, Wilson, and Jane Cassels. *Little Rock, U.S.A.* Chandler Publishing Company, 1960.

Roy, Beth. *Bitters in the Honey: Tales of Hope and Disappointment Across Race and Time.* University of Arkansas Press, 1999.

Wilson, William Julius. *The Declining Significance of Race.* University of Chicago Press, 1980.

Collected Works and Anthologies

Bogin, Ruth, and Bert James Loewenberg, eds. *Black Women in Nineteenth-Century Life.* Pennsylvania State University Press, 1976.

Boyd, Herb, and Robert L. Allen, eds. *Brotherman: The Odyssey of Black Men in America.* Ballantine Books, 1995.

Hartman, Chester, ed. *Double Exposure: Poverty and Race in America.* M. E. Sharpe, 1997.

King, Adrien Katherine. *Critical Race Feminism: A Reader.* New York University Press, 1997.

Mullane, Deirdre. *Crossing the Danger Water: Three Hundred Years of African American Writing.* Doubleday, 1993.

Root, Maria P. P., ed. *Racially Mixed People in America.* Sage Publications, Inc. 1992.

Rothenberg, Paula. *Race, Class, and Gender in the United States.* Worth Publishers, 2001.

Schwartz, Barry N., and Robert Disch. *White Racism.* Dell, 1970.

ABOUT THE AUTHOR

Helen H. Helfer was a member of People for Human Rights in Philadelphia, Pennsylvania, and worked as a program analyst with the Department of Housing and Urban Development in Washington, D.C. She headed a multi-service neighborhood center in San Francisco, California, and currently lives on Cape Cod, Massachusetts, where she conducts workshops that address the ongoing issues of racism and white privilege.